STUDIES IN BAPTIST HIST
VOLUMI

More Than a Symbol

The British Baptist Recovery of Baptismal Sacramentalism

Studies in Baptist History and Thought

Series Editors

Dr Anthony R. Cross   Bath, England
Dr Curtis W. Freeman   Duke University, North Carolina, USA
Dr Stephen R. Holmes   King's College, London, England
Dr Elizabeth Newman   Saint Mary's College, Notre Dame, Indiana, USA
Dr Philip E. Thompson   North American Baptist Seminary, Sioux Falls, South Dakota, USA

Series Consultants

Prof. David Bebbington   University of Stirling, Stirling, Scotland
Dr Paul Fiddes   Regent's Park College, Oxford, England
Prof. Stanley E. Grenz   Carey Theological College and Regent College, Vancouver, Canada
Prof. Stanley E. Porter   McMaster Divinity College, McMaster University, Hamilton, Canada

A full listing of titles in this series
appears at the close of this book.

STUDIES IN BAPTIST HISTORY AND THOUGHT
VOLUME 2

More Than a Symbol

The British Baptist Recovery of Baptismal Sacramentalism

Stanley K. Fowler

Foreword by William H. Brackney

paternoster
press

Copyright © Stanley K Fowler 2002

First published 2002 by Paternoster Press

Paternoster Press is an imprint of Paternoster Publishing
P.O. Box 300, Carlisle, Cumbria, CA3 0QS, U.K.
and P.O. Box 1047, Waynesboro, GA 30830-2047, U.S.A.

08 07 06 05 04 03 02   7 6 5 4 3 2 1

The right of Stanley K Fowler to be identified as the Author of this Work
has been asserted by him in accordance with the Copyright, Designs
and Patents Act 1988

*All rights reserved. No part of this publication may be reproduced, stored in a retrieval system, or
transmitted in any form by any means, electronic, mechanical, photocopying, recording or otherwise,
without the prior permission of the publisher, or a license permitting restricted copying. In the UK such
licenses are issued by the Copyright Licensing Agency,
90 Tottenham Court Road, London W1P 9HE*

British Library Cataloguing in Publication Data
A catalogue record for this book is available from the British Library

ISBN 1-84227-052-4

Printed and bound in Great Britain
for Paternoster Publishing
by Nottingham Alpha Graphics

To Donna, who never gave up

CONTENTS

Series Preface xi
Foreword xiii
Acknowledgments xv

Introduction 1
The Limits of this Study 6

Chapter 1 The Historical Background: Baptist Views of Sacramentalism from 1600 to 1900 10
The Seventeenth Century 10
  Baptist Confessions of Faith 11
  Individual Baptist Authors 20
    ROBERT GARNER 20
    HENRY LAWRENCE 24
    THOMAS GRANTHAM 27
    BENJAMIN KEACH 29
    WILLIAM MITCHILL 30
    SUMMARY 31
The Eighteenth Century 32
  John Gill 33
  Abraham Booth 42
  Anne Dutton 46
  Andrew Fuller 48
  John Ryland, Jr 51
  Summary 53
  Analysis 53
The Nineteenth Century 57
  Robert Hall, Jr 59
  Alexander Carson 64
  Charles Stovel 65
  Baptist W. Noel 72
  John Howard Hinton 75
  Charles Haddon Spurgeon 79
  Richard Ingham 84
  Summary 86
Conclusion 86

Chapter 2 The Reformulation of Baptist Sacramentalism 89
H. Wheeler Robinson 89
Alfred Clair Underwood 98
Robert C. Walton 100
Henry Cook 105
Neville Clark 107
The Publication of *Christian Baptism* 113
   Criticisms of the book by Baptists 124
   Beasley-Murray's response 129
R. E. O. White, *The Biblical Doctrine of Initiation* 133
G. R. Beasley-Murray, *Baptism in the New Testament* 139
Alec Gilmore, *Baptism and Christian Unity* 145
Denominational Statements 150
Baptist Service Books 152
Summary 154

Chapter 3 An Analysis of the Biblical Foundations 156
Baptist Sacramental Exegesis 157
Baptist Exegetical Criticisms 164
   Matthew 28:19-20 165
   Acts 2:38 166
   Water versus Spirit 170
Baptist Hermeneutical Criticisms 174
Karl Barth's Critique of Sacramentalism .178
   Acts 22:16 181
   Hebrews 10:22 181
   Ephesians 5:25-26 182
   Titus 3:5 184
   Galatians 3:27 185
   Romans 6:3-4 186
   Colossians 2:12 188
   John 3:5 189
   Mark 16:16 190
   1 Peter 3:21 191
   Conclusion 193
Summary 195

Chapter 4 An Analysis of the Theological Formulation 196
Creation, Incarnation and Baptism 196
Baptism and Faith 199

Baptism and Grace 209
    Grace and paedobaptism 211
Baptism and the Holy Spirit 219
Baptism and the Church 223
The Necessity of Baptism 232
Baptists and Other Sacramental Traditions 234
    The Roman Catholic tradition 235
    The Lutheran tradition 237
    The Reformed/Calvinistic tradition 238
    The Disciples/Restorationist tradition 240
Summary 246

Chapter 5 The Significance of Baptist Sacramentalism 248

Bibliography 254

Index 273

Series Preface

Baptists form one of the largest Christian communities in the world, and while they hold the historic Christian faith in common with other mainstream Christian traditions, they nevertheless have important insights which they can offer to the worldwide church. Studies in Baptist History and Thought will be one means towards this end. It is an international series of academic studies which includes original monographs, revised dissertations, collections of essays and conference papers, and aims to cover any aspect of Baptist history and thought. While not all the authors are themselves Baptists, they nevertheless share an interest in relating Baptist history and thought to the other branches of the Christian church and to the wider life of the world.

The series includes studies in various aspects of Baptist history from the seventeenth century down to the present day, including biographical works, and Baptist thought is understood as covering the subject-matter of theology (including interdisciplinary studies embracing biblical studies, philosophy, sociology, practical theology, liturgy and women's studies). The diverse streams of Baptist life throughout the world are all within the scope of these volumes.

The series editors and consultants believe that the academic disciplines of history and theology are of vital importance to the spiritual vitality of the churches of the Baptist faith and order. The series sets out to discuss, examine and explore the many dimensions of their tradition and so to contribute to their on-going intellectual vigour.

A brief word of explanation is due for the series identifier on the front cover. The fountains, taken from heraldry, represent the Baptist distinctive of believer's baptism and, at the same time, the source of the water of life. There are three of them because they symbolize the Trinitarian basis of Baptist life and faith. Those who are redeemed by the Lamb, the book of Revelation reminds us, will be led to "living fountains of water" (Rev. 7.17).

FOREWORD

In their more or less four century history, Baptists have had more to say about baptism than any other subject. Most of what they have written about has to do with form and fitness of baptismal candidates, rather than engaging the Early Church or Reformation discussions about theological meanings. In fact, in order to avoid any seeming attachment to the establishment churches, Baptists early moved away from sacramental terminology to that of "ordinance." Here is where the present study makes a singular contribution.

Stanley Fowler examines a significant tradition among mainstream British Baptists who favor a more sacramental perspective on believer baptism. His thesis is that in the twentieth century leading British Baptist pastors and theologians recovered an understanding of baptism that connected experience with soteriology, and focused on the forgiveness of sins rather than a witness of a completed experience of union with Christ. It is Fowler's contention that twentieth century Baptists were merely recovering what many of their forebears had taught, though few of them acknowledged dependence upon earlier Baptist writers. Rather, they were more influenced by discussions in the ecumenical movement.

A primary value of this study is that the author surveys the entire scope of British Baptist literature from the seventeenth century pioneers in both the British General and Particular branches. He then covers those prolific polemicists of the next two centuries from John Gill and Robert Hall to Alexander Carson and C. H. Spurgeon. Fowler argues persuasively that during this period the British Baptist community retreated from the question of the effects of baptism to an emphasis upon discipleship and obedience. He attributes this transition to a belief that sacramentalism was for most Baptists simply "works righteousness." He is correct in his assessment and this has undoubtedly set the course for the vast majority of Baptist thinking about baptism.

Secondly, Fowler provides the next analytical and historiographical step in British Baptist baptismal studies. J. R. C. Perkin surveyed the problem through 1920 in his thesis, "Baptism in Nonconformist Theology, With Special Reference to the Baptists" (D.Phil., Oxford, 1955). Anthony R. Cross in this Series has taken a different tack in his *Baptism and the Baptists: Theology and Practice in Twentieth Century Britain* (2000), in which he provides a theological history of baptism in the context of influences of the ecumenical movement. Fowler now shows without doubt, that it was the revival of sacramentalism that was the vivid feature of the last century's discussions.

But this study is more than an historical survey. Fowler demonstrates his acumen as a biblical interpreter and theologian. He takes exception with major Baptist thinkers such as A. T. Robertson and joins the arguments connecting water-baptism and Spirit-baptism. He fully engages the critique of G. R. Beasley-Murray, one of the outstanding proponents of the sacramentalist school. Most intriguing, perhaps, is Fowler's response to Karl Barth's critique of sacramentalism, where Fowler contends that Barth avoided a natural interpretation of many baptismal texts.

Helpful to those in other traditions than the Baptists is Dr. Fowler's coverage of responses to British Baptist sacramental thought and his comparison of the Baptists to contemporary Protestant and Catholic thinkers. In so doing he has renewed the dialogue over baptism, the Holy Spirit and ecclesiology. The Christian community in general will profit from the contrasts he draws with other usages of sacramental terminology.

What is really important about this book is that it opens new possibilities of serious theological dialogue for a Christian community that values experience and symbol. It is to the credit of the British Baptist sacramentalist movement that they have carried forth an understanding of baptism as an act of powerful theological meaning. Along with a minority of North American Baptist thinkers, British Baptists have succeeded in providing an agenda to restore meaning to an ancient practice of the Church, and to engage a movement known for its theological obscurantism and radical individualism. Hopefully Fowler's work on the British community will inspire other such analyses, particularly in the North American context.

I commend this work among Baptists to awaken their thinking, and to non-Baptists as a piece of solid scholarship in the Baptist tradition.

William H. Brackney
Department of Religion
Baylor University
Waco, Texas, U.S.A.

ACKNOWLEDGMENTS

This book is a product of my studies for the Doctor of Theology degree at Wycliffe College, University of Toronto, and I wish to acknowledge various persons and institutions who facilitated those studies. Some of the material in the book arose out of papers which I wrote for Prof. John B. Webster at Wycliffe College, and I am grateful for his direction and insightful criticisms. When I first selected this topic for my doctoral thesis, Prof. Webster was to serve as my director, and I looked forward to that working relationship. Due to the demands of my work at Central Baptist Seminary, Toronto and later at Heritage Theological Seminary, Cambridge, Ontario, I was unable to pursue the thesis research for several years. When I was reinstated to the doctoral program to write the thesis in 1996, Prof. Webster was named the Lady Margaret Professor of Divinity at Oxford University, and I was forced to look for another director. I am profoundly grateful that Prof. William H. Brackney, then Principal of McMaster Divinity College, Hamilton, Ontario was willing to work with me on this project and now has graciously written the Foreword for this book. Few scholars in the world can match Prof. Brackney's knowledge of Baptist history and thought, and I am grateful for his scholarly insight and his friendship.

The reinstatement to write my doctoral thesis was possible only because the board of directors of Heritage Theological Seminary granted me a one-year study leave from September 1996 through August 1997, and I am grateful for their generosity. My colleagues at the seminary have been consistently encouraging throughout the time in which I wrote and defended the thesis, and also as I have revised it for publication, even when they had difficulty accepting my conclusions. Special thanks go to Prof. Michael A. G. Haykin, my colleague for 19 years, who shares my interest in the history of Baptist thought on the sacraments. I am also grateful for the students who have listened patiently and challenged thoughtfully.

Research for this project occurred at several libraries: our own library at Heritage Seminary; the libraries of McMaster University, Wilfrid Laurier University, University of Waterloo, Southern Baptist Theological Seminary, and Christian Theological Seminary; and especially the American Baptist Historical Society Library in Rochester, New York, where I was able to work with the early English Baptist literature without crossing the Atlantic Ocean.

I owe special thanks to Anthony Cross for many things. Just as I was finishing the first complete draft of my thesis in the summer of 1997, I discovered that Anthony had recently submitted his Ph.D. thesis at the University of Keele on a subject very much like mine. My initial panic turned to joy when we began to correspond and I discovered that his work was complementary to mine and in no way nullified my developing contribution to the field. I have been grateful for Anthony's comprehensive treatment of baptism in the life of modern British Baptists (an earlier book in this series), but more than that for our friendship which has grown out of our common interests. He encouraged Paternoster to consider my work for publication, and for that I will be forever grateful.

My thanks go to the editorial committee which accepted this book for publication, and especially to Jeremy Mudditt for his encouragement and help with all the details along the way.

Finally, I wish to express my appreciation to my wife, Donna, for all that she has done to make this book a reality. She encouraged me to pursue doctoral studies and an academic career after thirteen years of pastoral ministry; she went back to work full-time to make my full-time doctoral studies possible; she continued to believe that the project could be completed even when I was bogged down in seminary administration and unable to pursue research in any serious way; and she has endured to the end. I could never express my appreciation adequately for all that she has meant to me.

INTRODUCTION

One of the ironies of Christian history is that Baptists, in spite of their name, have been slow to develop a *theology* of baptism. That is not to say that Baptists have not spoken and written at great length about baptism, but it is to say that such literature has normally dealt with questions about the proper subjects and mode of baptism to the exclusion of a positive statement of what is presumed to happen in baptism, especially from the divine side. As William Brackney notes:

> From their intense preoccupation over textual details in the New Testament and a desire to re-create the primitive Church, Baptists have spent their energies on the techniques, styles, and fitness of candidates for participation in the sacraments, rather than the mystery of the divine-human relationships.[1]

In other words, Baptists have generally been much more certain about what *does not* happen in the sprinkling of infants than they are about what *does* happen in the immersion of confessing believers. J. M. Ross, a British Presbyterian lay scholar, has concluded that "the doctrine of baptism does not occupy a central place in Baptist theology," and that "this is a fact which always comes as a surprise to paedobaptists."[2] Although Ross's judgment would be false if "doctrine" were interpreted broadly as inclusive of all teaching about the *practice* of baptism, it is accurate if "doctrine" describes the interpretation of the divine-human encounter which occurs in baptism.

Ross is not the only observer to express surprise at this paradoxical state of affairs. Markus Barth, who is in many ways sympathetic to Baptist

---

[1] William H. Brackney, *The Baptists* (Westport, Conn: Greenwood Press, 1988), 69-70.
[2] J. M. Ross, "The Theology of Baptism in Baptist History," *The Baptist Quarterly* 15 (1953-54): 100.

concerns, has written:

> I have not only looked into the churches and the church history of the Baptists. I have also searched in Baptist theological literature, and have inquired from learned Baptist friends about a hidden mystery or revelation that might lie in or behind the Baptist position. I have perceived that most Baptist scholars have more or less convincing and valid reasons for rejecting infant baptism; that they are quite sure about the form of baptism (immersion), but that they are as vague or narrow, as contradictory or embarrassed as divines of other denominations when the nature and meaning of baptism is discussed.[3]

All this has caused G. R. Beasley-Murray, a Baptist scholar, to ask:

> Now what is the explanation of this paradoxical situation, that Baptists have been prepared to fight to the death about baptism, and they continue to be divided from most of Christendom because of baptism, and yet they have been and still are extraordinarily slow in committing themselves to a theology of baptism? And when they do take up the cudgels, why do they resist sacramental theology so fiercely and retreat to the defence of a symbolic ordinance that apparently effects nothing?[4]

His answer to the second question is that Baptists have wanted to avoid all appearance of superstition in their use of sacred rituals and to preserve the centrality of personal faith in religion, but as laudable as these concerns may be, they do not justify the neglect of valid questions.

One result of this lack of a theology of baptism is seen in the tendency to focus on narrative descriptions of baptism in the New Testament and to treat didactic baptismal texts only in a superficial manner. For example, although Romans 6:3-4 is often quoted by Baptists to justify immersion as the proper mode, it is used in some very surprising ways. This text is routinely interpreted as saying that baptism is a picture of burial and resurrection. However, while the text may well assume the practice of immersion (a whole host of non-Baptist commentators would agree), in point of fact the text does not *say* in so many words that baptism *pictures*

---

3   Markus Barth, "Weakness or Value of the Baptist Position," *Foundations* 1 (1958): 66.
4   George R. Beasley-Murray, *Baptism Today and Tomorrow* (London: Macmillan, 1966), 83. This source will be noted hereafter as *BTT*.

Introduction 3

anything. What it does seem to say is that baptism *effects* union with Christ and his vicarious suffering and resurrection. This is, of course, too strong for a purely symbolic view of baptism, so that many Baptists resort to interpreting this text as a reference to Spirit-baptism, while at the same time wanting to retain it as a proof-text for immersion in water. For example, a contemporary Baptist has written about this Romans text:

> It is almost always the case in the epistles that "baptism" means Spirit-baptism, with the word "baptism" being used pictorially. . . . So while the direct reference of this passage is to Spirit-baptism, the terms in which it is described make some reference to water-baptism. . . . Paul never speaks explicitly about baptism in his epistles and only once about the Lord's Supper. But this does not mean these ordinances are to be undervalued or neglected, for they are used as illustrations of salvation. Undoubtedly that is the case in the passage under review and, as long as the main subject is kept in view, we can learn a lot about the meaning of baptism.[5]

This situation has been modified somewhat in the 20th century by the work of some British Baptist scholars, who have shifted toward a sacramental understanding of baptism as an integral part of conversion and an instrument by which grace becomes operative in individual experience.[6] The purpose of this book is to analyse this recent Baptist development by describing the process of reformulation, evaluating its foundational New Testament exegesis, and assessing its theological meaning and coherence. Perhaps the most basic contribution of this book will be to demonstrate that traditional assumptions about the baptismal theology of Baptists are often inaccurate. These are not simply assumptions made by those outside the Baptist tradition, but are in fact the common assumptions of many Baptists themselves. For example, one contemporary English Baptist has made this sweeping statement about Baptists in general:

> For Baptists the ordinance of baptism is not a sacrament in which

---

5   Eric Lane, *I Want to Be Baptised* (London: Grace Publications, 1986), 93-96.
6   Alec Gilmore, ed., *Christian Baptism* (London: Lutterworth Press, 1959) brings together some of the developing thought of these Baptists. This book (hereafter noted as *CB*) represents both a statement of the results of this shift and a stimulus to further reflection. H. Wheeler Robinson and A. C. Underwood were influential pioneers in the early part of this century. The major thinkers in the later development included Gilmore, Beasley-Murray, Neville Clark, and R. E. O. White.

grace is infused into the believer in any way, but rather the ordinance is a testimony of what God has done in regeneration and is a testimony by the believer of repentance and faith. It is a testimony of one who can give a credible testimony of God's grace in bringing him into a union with Christ, a union symbolised in burial and rising again to newness of life, as well as a symbol of discipleship.[7]

In contrast to such assertions, this book will demonstrate that in fact a significant stream of recent Baptist thought moves along the lines of a sacramentalism which is firmly rooted in the New Testament language about baptism, which coherently relates baptismal theology to broader questions of soteriology, and which may rightly be seen as a recovery and elaboration of mainstream Baptist thought of the 17th century. Although this reformulation of Baptist thought has been British in origin, there is nothing uniquely British about its content, and it might well serve as a new paradigm for Baptist thought on a wider scale.

It is clear in the literature under analysis that these scholars believed they were breaking new ground and advancing ideas that had never been common among Baptists. Beasley-Murray, who represented in many ways the culmination of this sacramental shift, indicated that the major causative factors were involvement in ecumenical discussions and fresh study of the New Testament.[8] The evidence indicates that the contemporary Baptist sacramentalists have never suggested that their view is actually a recovery of a significant, and perhaps original, Baptist tradition. But given the intensity of Baptist commitment to the authority of Scripture over against tradition, if there is strong New Testament support for a sacramental view

---

7 Erroll Hulse, "The 1689 Confession–its history and role today," in *Our Baptist Heritage*, by Paul Clarke et al. (Leeds: Reformation Today Trust, 1993), 18. It should be noted that the same author, in an earlier book, affirmed his preference for the term "sacrament" over "ordinance" and asserted that one should expect a powerful work of the Holy Spirit in the recipients of baptism. However, in his explanation of appropriate baptismal practice, he argued that the candidate should give a testimony of the experience of regeneration before the whole congregation, to be followed by a congregational vote on the suitability of the candidate for baptism. Therefore, although he accepted the terminology of "sacrament," he clearly interpreted the grace of baptism as a grace of assurance related to a *prior* experience of union with Christ, thus disconnecting baptism from conversion in such a way that baptism is a reminder of the benefits which it signifies rather than a means to experience those benefits. See Erroll Hulse, "The Implications of Baptism," in *Local Church Practice*, by Baruch Maoz et al. (Haywards Heath, Sussex: Carey Publications, 1978), 47, 53, 55.
8 Beasley-Murray, *BTT*, 15.

of baptism, then it would be surprising to find Baptists taking over three centuries to discover it.

The first chapter of this book will survey British Baptist thought concerning baptism as a sacrament during the period from 1600 to 1900, and it will be demonstrated that when the earliest Baptists addressed the question of the efficacy of baptism, they spoke in sacramental terms. Specifically, this chapter will argue that the dominant strain of early Baptist thought conceptualized baptism as both a sign and a seal of saving union with Christ, a divinely-ordained ritual which mediates the conscious experience of entrance into a state of grace. For a variety of reasons, this baptismal theology was modified in a non-sacramental direction during the 18th and 19th centuries, so that by 1900 it was widely believed that Baptists had always interpreted baptism as a purely symbolic act of obedience, an *ordinance* as opposed to a *sacrament*.

Shifting patterns of Baptist thought about the meaning of baptism are related to similar shifts in Baptist usage of the terms *ordinance* and *sacrament*. In recent history the term *ordinance* has normally signified only baptism and the Lord's Supper, the sense being that ordinances are "those outward rites which Christ has appointed to be administered in his church as visible signs of the saving truth of the gospel," and as such an ordinance is "the external manifestation of a preceding union with Christ."[9] However, for Baptists of the 17th century the term had a broader signification, denoting (in addition to baptism and the Lord's Supper) at least the ministry of the Word and prayer (*The Baptist Catechism*, 1689),[10] and sometimes disciplinary censures (John Smyth)[11] or laying on of hands as a post-baptismal empowering by the Holy Spirit (*The Standard Confession*, 1660).[12] Imposition of hands was affirmed as an ordinance of Christ by much of the General Baptist tradition and by some in the Particular Baptist tradition, notably the *Philadelphia Confession of Faith* (1742). Although it is practised in some Baptist churches today, it is affirmed formally as an

---

9   Augustus Hopkins Strong, *Systematic Theology* (1907; Valley Forge: Judson Press, 1967), 930. See also James Leo Garrett, *Systematic Theology: Biblical, Historical, & Evangelical* (Grand Rapids: Eerdmans, 1990-1995), 2:503.

10 *The Baptist Catechism: Commonly Called Keach's Catechism* (Philadelphia: American Baptist Publication Society, 1851), 23.

11 John Smyth, *The Works of John Smyth*, ed. W. T. Whitley (2 vols.; Cambridge: University Press, 1915), 1:254.

12 William L. Lumpkin, *Baptist Confessions of Faith* (Philadelphia: Judson Press, 1959), 229.

ordinance by only a few.[13] General Baptists, sometimes under Mennonite influence, practised footwashing as an ordinance into the 19th century, but this continues only in a few scattered congregations.[14]

It will be shown below that the term *sacrament* was used widely by 17th-century Baptists to denote baptism and the Lord's Supper as two ordinances in a special category. For a variety of reasons, the term fell into disfavor among Baptists, but some continued to use the term (although not always with a clearly defined meaning). In early Baptist history, then, the *ordinances* were inclusive of the *sacraments*, but over time the denotation of both terms became identical (baptism and the Lord's Supper) while their connotations became distinct (pure symbol versus means of grace). For the purposes of this thesis, to say that baptism is "sacramental" is to say that it mediates the experience of salvific union with Christ, i.e., that one submits to baptism as a penitent sinner in order to experience the forgiveness of sins and the gift of the Holy Spirit, rather than as a confirmed disciple in order to bear witness to a past experience of union with Christ.

The Limits of this Study

This study does not treat in any substantial way British Baptist literature on baptism from the last third of the 20th century, and it is perhaps necessary to justify this choice. In brief the reason is that the literature from about 1967 to the present, although sometimes exploring the meaning of sacramentalism, does not manifest any felt need to argue at length that baptism is a sacrament as opposed to a mere symbol. Anthony Cross, who has written a comprehensive survey of British Baptist baptismal theology and practice in the past century, has said this:

> Mid-century witnessed the high point of Baptist writing on baptism, the great majority of which explored the sacramental dimension of baptism in some way. . . .Baptists have now generally accepted the word "sacrament," whereas, for over half a century, the word was regarded with suspicion and was frequently rejected. . . . Among Baptists, "sacrament" is now widely used, though the accompanying theology continues to be largely symbolic, and though a sacramental theology is increasingly common, chiefly among the theologically literate, ecumenically committed, and liturgically oriented. . . .

---

13   Brackney, *Baptists*, 67-69.
14   Ibid., 69.

Further, it should be noted that over the last thirty to forty years anti-sacramentalist writings have all but disappeared–though this is not to say that such convictions are not held.[15]

Cross interprets this mid-century stream of literature as the consolidation of Baptist sacramentalism, not in the sense that it represents a fixed and final form of British Baptist thought, but in the sense that it established a generally accepted framework for the ongoing reflection on the meaning of baptism. From that point on, whatever opinions may have been held privately or expressed orally, Baptist literature on baptism (at least that produced within the Baptist Union of Great Britain) has no longer debated the question of symbol versus sacrament to any significant degree. Cross locates the *terminus ad quem* of this consolidated sacramentalism in 1966, when Beasley-Murray published *Baptism Today and Tomorrow*, the second of his books on baptism, and it was also in that year that Alec Gilmore published his *Baptism and Christian Unity*.[16] Those books are the final pieces of literature surveyed in this study as well.

Much of the post-consolidation literature has been in the form of Baptist response to ecumenical issues, which is to say that the literature is not so much about baptismal theology *per se* as it is about baptism as one problem in ecumenical relations.[17] The official Baptist Union of Great Britain response to *Baptism, Eucharist and Ministry* was published in 1986.[18] Ten years later the Doctrine and Worship Committee of the Baptist Union produced a discussion document, *Believing and Being Baptized: Baptism, So-Called Re-Baptism, and Children in the Church* (Didcot: Baptist Union of Great Britain, 1996). In 1997 three Baptists were part of a nine-person task force which produced *Baptism and Church Membership, with particular reference to Local Ecumenical Partnerships*. The latter two documents assume a sacramental understanding of baptism but tend to see baptism as one moment in a process of the experience of salvation, which is a paradigm shift away from the focus on punctiliar conversion-baptism in much of the earlier sacramental literature. This focus on process as opposed to point supports the possibility of viewing credobaptism and paedobaptism

---

15   Anthony R. Cross, "Baptists and Baptism–A British Perspective," *Baptist History and Heritage* 35, no. 1 (Winter 2000): 107.
16   Anthony R. Cross, *Baptism and the Baptists* (Carlisle: Paternoster Press, 2000), 243.
17   Cross, "Baptists and Baptism," 108.
18   Max Thurian, ed., *Churches Respond to BEM: Official Responses to the "Baptism, Eucharist and Ministry" Text*, Vol. 1 (Geneva: World Council of Churches, 1986), 70-77.

as alternative approaches to Christian initiation, which in turn facilitates the participation of Baptists in union churches or other institutional forms of ecumenism at the local level. While this is a different way of speaking about the precise nature of sacramental action in baptism, it does not reopen the question of whether baptism is in fact sacramental.

In 1996 six Baptist scholars contributed chapters to *Reflections on the Water*, a book which views the baptism of believers from multiple angles, and two of the chapters are particularly relevant for the discussion of baptism as a sacrament. Christopher Ellis dealt with "Baptism and the Sacramental Freedom of God," and in doing so touched on the traditional Baptist reluctance to speak of baptism in sacramental terms. He suggested that this concern was rooted in various factors, not the least of which was the perception that sacramentalism overstated both the necessity and efficacy of baptism. Ellis sought to allay this concern by interpreting baptism as one significant stage in the process of salvation, in his words, "a medium of the Spirit who has already impinged on the person and led him or her to a confession of faith and a life of discipleship," which leads to "a new stage of life in the Spirit."[19] Paul Fiddes edited the volume and wrote the chapter on "Baptism and Creation," in which he argued that the sacramental nature of baptism is one specific manifestation of the general truth that God relates to humans through the "stuff" of the material world. Immersion in water is an action which is well suited to enable human participation in God's purposes, "evoking such experiences as birth, cleansing, conflict, journey, and renewal."[20] The way in which Fiddes frames his argument emphasizes baptism as a *suitable* vehicle for divine-human encounter, as opposed to a *necessary* ritual operating in a mechanistic manner.

Although the chapters by Ellis and Fiddes are both mildly apologetic in nature, neither one engages any of the traditional, anti-sacramental literature of earlier Baptists in an attempt to refute a purely symbolic view of the rite. Each "defends" baptismal sacramentalism by a positive statement of the meaning of the concept and an attempt to show how that is coherent with broader themes of creation and redemption. There is material here worthy of study, but it assumes the reformulation which is the focus of this book and addresses a new set of issues. When Ellis raises the question of Baptist uneasiness with sacramental language, his initial response is to refer to the

---

19 Christopher Ellis, "Baptism and the Sacramental Freedom of God," in *Reflections on the Water*, ed. Paul S. Fiddes (Macon: Smyth & Helwys, 1996), 31.
20 Paul S. Fiddes, "Baptism and Creation," in *Reflections*, 65.

body of literature which is analysed in this book.[21] Therefore, it seems appropriate to focus this book on the Baptist movement which culminated in the 1960's and to leave the analysis of later literature for another book.

---

21 Ellis, "Baptism," 32-33.

CHAPTER 1

The Historical Background: Baptist Views of Sacramentalism from 1600 to 1900

The Seventeenth Century

When Baptist churches emerged from the English Separatist context in the first decade of the 17th century, almost all English Christians were formally committed to the understanding of baptism expressed in the Thirty-Nine Articles of the Church of England. There the dominical sacraments were described as "not only badges or tokens of Christian men's profession," but also "effectual signs of grace, and God's good will towards us, by the which he doth work invisibly in us, and doth not only quicken, but also strengthen and confirm our Faith in him" (Art. XXV).[1] Baptism was understood to be "a sign of Regeneration or New-Birth, whereby, as by an instrument, they that receive Baptism rightly are grafted into the Church; the promises of the forgiveness of sin, and of our adoption to be the sons of God by the Holy Ghost, are visibly signed and sealed; Faith is confirmed, and Grace increased by virtue of prayer unto God" (Art. XXVII).[2] Although mainstream Anglicans and Puritans differed in their estimate of the relative significance of sacraments compared to preaching, they agreed that the sacraments both commemorated the work of Christ and communicated grace to those who received them in faith.[3] It would be clearly impossible to affirm the baptismal definition of the Thirty-Nine Articles and at the same time deny that baptism communicates grace, but the sense in which it is "effectual" and the precise way in which it functions as an "instrument" are subject to interpretation. Therefore, the English context included views that tilted in the Roman Catholic direction (emphasizing baptism as an instrument of regeneration) and views that tilted in the Calvinistic direction

---

1 John H. Leith, ed., *Creeds of the Churches*, 3rd ed. (Atlanta: John Knox Press, 1982), 274.
2 Ibid., 275-276.
3 Horton Davies, *Worship and Theology in England*, Vol. 1, *From Cranmer to Hooker, 1534-1603* (Princeton: Princeton University Press, 1970), 62-64.

(emphasizing baptism as a seal of God's promises).

The earliest leaders of those churches that would eventually be called Baptist, men like John Smyth and Thomas Helwys, lived with their congregations for some time in exile in Holland, where they were in continuing contact with Dutch Mennonites. Although the extent of Mennonite influence on the earliest Baptist churches is debatable, it can at least be said that Smyth and Helwys, along with their followers, were exposed to a non-sacramental kind of baptismal theology which may have modified their thought. At the very least, this contact gave them another option to consider as they began to formulate their own baptismal theology. However, it would be a mistake to conclude that since Baptists shared the Mennonite rejection of infant baptism, they therefore shared their non-sacramental interpretation of the efficacy of baptism. Baptists rejected other distinctive teachings of the Mennonites (e.g., pacifism), and they were capable of formulating their own distinctive doctrine of the meaning of the baptism of believers. This study will now proceed to examine this formulation in the confessions and books of the 17th-century Baptists.

Baptist Confessions of Faith

It is important to remember that there is no single statement of faith which functions normatively for Baptists in the same way as the *Westminster Confession* for many Presbyterians or the *Augsburg Confession* for many Lutherans. Most of the early confessions arose from local associations of churches, resulting in significant diversity, although some of them were later adopted by larger Baptist bodies and came to play a more dominant role. From the earliest years Baptists have also been divided into an Arminian stream going back to Smyth and Helwys in the years just prior to 1610 (General Baptist, Free Will Baptist, etc) and a Calvinistic stream going back to the late 1630's (Particular Baptist, Strict Baptist, Regular Baptist, etc.). There has also been a continuing ambivalence among Baptists about the function of confessions of faith or creeds. Many Baptists emphasize that Baptists are not a creedal people, so that confessions of faith are not binding on the individual conscience or congregation--only Scripture has final authority. At the same time, it is recognized that it is not possible to teach any conceivable doctrine on the basis of the Bible and still be a Baptist--there are some doctrinal limits, which find expression in confessions of faith voluntarily affirmed by churches and individuals. Although the following Baptist confessions of the 17th century were never considered infallible or irreformable, they are expressions of what it meant to be a Baptist in that era.

The *Short Confession of Faith in XX Articles*[4] may have been written in 1609 by John Smyth (ca. 1565-1612), General Baptist pioneer, while he was living in exile in Holland, and was apparently directed to the Waterlander Mennonites in Holland in an attempt to establish Smyth's doctrinal soundness. He indicated that one task of the church is "administering the sacraments" of baptism and the Lord's Supper (Art. 13). For him, "Baptism is the external sign of the remission of sins, of dying and of being made alive, and therefore does not belong to infants" (Art. 14). Baptism was thus seen as a "sign" of salvation, but the exact relationship was not spelled out in detail, except to deny that it is only a promise of salvation yet to come as in infant baptism. The language of this confession, as it stands, might mean that baptism is a sign of forgiveness and regeneration already experienced or a sign of such benefits presently being received. This imprecision regarding what exactly happens in baptism is characteristic of much Baptist literature of the 17th century, because the writers were in most cases concerned primarily about the question of paedobaptism, secondarily about the mode of baptism, and only to a limited degree about the sacramental issue.

A *Short Confession of Faith*[5] was apparently affirmed in 1610 by Smyth's English congregation who were living in Holland, and this too was an attempt to satisfy the Waterlander Mennonites. The origin of this confession has been debated by historians, but it appears to have been written for the English congregation by Hans de Ries, a Dutch Mennonite who had produced two earlier confessions in 1577 and 1578, and was later signed by the English proto-Baptists.[6] In that confession, baptism is one of "two sacraments appointed by Christ" (Art. 28) which are "outward visible handlings and tokens" of both God's cleansing work in the individual and the individual's obedience toward God. The conclusion of the baptismal section reads:

> Therefore, the baptism of water leadeth us to Christ, to his holy office in glory and majesty; and admonisheth us not to hang only upon the outward, but with holy prayer to mount upward, and to beg of Christ the good thing signified.

---

4   Lumpkin, *Confessions*, 97-101. The text and background information for the confessions treated here are taken from this standard source, unless otherwise noted.

5   Ibid., 102-113.

6   James Coggins, *John Smyth's Congregation: English Separatism, Mennonite Influence, and the Elect Nation* (Waterloo: Herald Press, 1991), 84-88.

This early confession of the emerging Baptist movement interpreted baptism as a visible sign of an invisible work of God, but the temporal and logical connection between the visible and invisible was not stated explicitly. Baptism was in some way a forward-looking acted prayer, a sign which requests the thing signified. The language suggested that baptism is in some way instrumental in the personal enjoyment of the benefits of Christ. There was an explicit warning against the idea that there is power in baptism as an act in itself ("the outward"), but it does in some way "lead us to Christ", in whom saving power resides.

The *Propositions and Conclusions concerning True Christian Religion*[7] were a lengthy elaboration (in 100 articles) of the 1610 confession above. The confession was published in 1612 after Smyth's death by his congregation, apparently for English readers.[8] This document articulated in some detail the way in which the sacraments work. Article 73 asserted:

> That the outward baptism and supper do not confer, and convey grace and regeneration to the participants or communicants: but as the word preached, they serve only to support and stir up the repentance and faith of the communicants till Christ come, till the day dawn, and the day-star arise in their hearts.

Article 74 further explained:

> That the sacraments have the same use that the word hath; that they are a visible word, and that they teach to the eye of them that understand as the word teacheth the ears of them that have ears to hear (Prov. x.12), and therefore as the word pertaineth not to infants, no more do the sacraments.

Article 75 related baptism to the ongoing work of Christ:

> That the preaching of the word, and the ministry of the sacraments, representeth the ministry of Christ in the spirit; who teacheth, baptiseth, and feedeth the regenerate by the Holy Spirit inwardly and invisibly.

This description of baptism as a "visible word" which functions in the

---

7   Lumpkin, *Confessions*, 123-142.
8   Coggins, *Congregation*, 109.

same way as the preached word indicated that in some way the benefits signified by baptism are given through it. The preached word both declares the finished work of Christ for our salvation and offers a personal share in it through faith; baptism as a visible word declares the same finished work and offers a share in it through faith (which is evoked, supported and expressed by baptism). There was an explicit rejection of any kind of mechanical conveyance of grace through the ritual, but at the same time the sacrament was thought of as a means through which Christ works by the Holy Spirit to accomplish his saving work.

The *First London Confession*[9] was drafted in 1644 by seven Particular (Calvinistic) Baptist Churches in London. It may have been modelled on some earlier confessions, but it was the first confession to require immersion as the mode of baptism. It described baptism as "an Ordinance of the new Testament, given by Christ, to be dispensed onely upon persons professing faith" (Art. XXXIX). It is to be administered by immersion, in order that the sign might correspond to the thing signified, namely, the cleansing of the soul, the interest of the baptized person in the death, burial and resurrection of Christ, and the future resurrection of the body (Art. XL). This confession used the term "ordinance" instead of "sacrament" and spoke more modestly than the earlier confessions of the Smyth group about the way in which baptism functions. For example, there was no comparison stated between baptism and the preached word, and nothing was said about the work of the Holy Spirit in baptism. Later Particular Baptist statements tended to imitate this choice of words, but hasty conclusions about its significance should be avoided, since the terms "ordinance" and "sacrament" were often used synonymously in the 17th century, as will be demonstrated below.

Ten years after the First London Confession, General (Arminian) Baptist Churches in the London area drafted *"The True Gospel-Faith Declared According to the Scriptures"*.[10] By that time the General Baptists had also adopted immersion as the standard mode of baptism, and thus this confession regularly used "dipped" to refer to baptism. It was a brief confession, but asserted, "That God gives his Spirit to believers dipped through the prayer of faith and laying on of hands, Acts 8.15; Acts 8.17; Acts 5.32; Ephes. 1.13,14" (Art. XII). It is not clear whether this reference to the gift of the Spirit denoted the initial baptism in the Spirit or some further empowering of the Spirit, and it is puzzling that Acts 2:38 was not used as a proof-text, but in any case some manifestation of the Spirit was

---

9   Lumpkin, *Confessions*, 144-171.
10 Ibid., 188-195.

said to be conditioned upon baptism, which embodies or is connected to a "prayer of faith."

The *Midland Confession*[11] was adopted in 1655 at the beginning of the Midland Association of Particular Baptist Churches. Article 13 asserted, "That all those who profess Faith in Christ, and make the same appear by their fruits, are the proper subjects of Baptism." This emphasis on Christian works as prerequisite to baptism seems to separate baptism from conversion by some distance and seems to indicate a non-sacramental understanding of the ordinance. At least, baptism does not seem to be viewed as instrumental in the entrance into Christian experience. Whether it may be instrumental in some further work of grace (as some other confessions indicate) is an open question.

The *Somerset Confession*[12] dates from 1656 and a Particular Baptist association in western England. It asserted the standard Baptist view of the subjects, mode, and symbolism of baptism, and then stated:

> That those that truly repent, and believe, and are baptized in the name of the Lord Jesus, are in a fit capacity to exercise faith, in full assurance to receive a greater measure of the gifts and graces of the Holy Spirit (Acts 2:38,39; Eph. 1:13).

Thus this confession envisioned some sort of bestowal of the Spirit's activity which is conditioned upon baptism, but it is not seen as the initial gift of the Spirit (even though Acts 2.38, which does refer to the initial gift of the Spirit, is used as a proof-text). Baptism, then, was interpreted as a condition of sanctification, although not (explicitly, at least) a means of regeneration or justification.

The *Standard Confession*[13] was drafted by General Baptist Churches in the greater London area in 1660, and was affirmed at the General Assembly of General Baptists in 1663 and at various later assemblies. It revealed the growing significance attached to the imposition of hands in some Baptist circles when Article XII said:

> That it is the duty of all such who are believers Baptized, to draw nigh unto God in submission to that principle of Christs doctrine, to wit, Prayer and Laying on of Hands, that they may receive the

---

11   Ibid., 195-200.
12   Ibid., 200-216.
13   Ibid., 220-235.

promise of the holy Spirit, ... whereby they may mortifie the deeds of the body. ...

Here baptism was interpreted as a prerequisite to this work of the Spirit, but not as an effective means. The effective sign is the laying on of hands, which follows baptism. It is not clear what the temporal relationship would be between baptism and imposition of hands, i.e., whether they are two parts of one event (much like the Eastern conjunction of baptism and confirmation) or two isolated events (much like the Western separation between baptism and confirmation). In this case, then, baptism was seen as a means of sanctification, but only in connection with another ritual.

The *Second London Confession*[14] was adopted by Particular Baptists in the greater London area in 1677 and became the most widely accepted Calvinistic Baptist confession. A second edition was produced in 1688, and it was adopted in 1689 by a group of messengers from over 100 churches in England and Wales. The confession was intended to show the unity that existed between Particular Baptists and their Presbyterian and Congregationalist counterparts, and so the confession is largely a reproduction of the Westminster Confession with changes made where necessary in the ecclesiological sections. Baptism and the Lord's Supper were called "ordinances of positive and sovereign institution" (Chap. XXVIII). The baptismal definition read:

> Baptism is an Ordinance of the New Testament, ordained by Jesus Christ, to be unto the party Baptized, a sign of his fellowship with him, in his death, and resurrection; of his being engrafted into him; of remission of sins; and of his giving up unto God through Jesus Christ, to live and walk in newness of Life.

Given the fact that this confession was essentially a reproduction of the Westminster Confession, any changes made must be significant. At this point, the confession used "ordinance" rather than Westminster's "sacrament," and the Westminster definition of a sacrament was omitted--indeed, there was no definition of a sacrament or ordinance as a general category. This prompted J. M. Ross to say:

> ... From about the middle of the 17th century until quite recent times the main tendency of Baptist thought has been to regard this

---

14   Ibid., 235-295.

The Historical Background

ordinance as having no more than a symbolic value. For instance, the Confession of Faith of 1677, which was modelled on the Westminster Confession of the Presbyterians, deliberately omitted all reference to the efficacy of baptism, its conferring of grace by the Holy Ghost, its being a seal of the Covenant, and its admission of the party baptized into the visible Church; . . . [15]

On the surface, then, it would seem that this confession indicated a decidedly non-sacramental view of baptism, but several facts give reason to think that this may be a premature judgment. *First*, the terms "sacrament" and "ordinance" were often used synonymously by Baptists of that era, including signatories of this confession. Given the use of "ordinance" in earlier Particular Baptist statements of faith, one would expect the same here, so that the choice of this terminology may be readily explained by historical continuity with the authors' tradition without the assumption that there is a conscious rejection of any sacramental idea. *Second*, Chapter XXX of the Second London Confession interpreted the Lord's Supper in the Westminster tradition along the lines of a "spiritual presence" of Christ which is mediated through the Supper, i.e., the Calvinistic as opposed to the Zwinglian view. The Second London term was "ordinance" in the explanation of the Lord's Supper, but the content of the explanation was a virtual duplication of the Westminster statement, which indicates that the change in terminology does not imply a modification of the concept. This shows that the thought of the signatories was still shaped by the broader Calvinistic tradition out of which the Particular Baptists arose, and if the purely memorialistic view of the Lord's Supper was rejected, then there is no reason to think that an instrumental understanding of baptism would be foreign to the mind-set of the confession. It should also be noted that there was no explicit denial of sacramental terminology or concepts in this confession. If such were the intent of the authors, it could easily have been stated. *Third*, the brevity of the baptismal chapter ought to be a caution against unjustified inferences. The stated intent of the confession was to emphasize agreement with other Calvinistic Christians and to indicate plainly disagreement where necessary. The most basic points of disagreement were the questions of the subjects and mode of baptism, and these points were stated clearly but concisely. To extrapolate beyond this is to force the confession to address issues with which it was not concerned. What was required with regard to baptism was a courteous statement of

---

15 Ross, "Theology of Baptism," 101.

disagreement with Westminster, not a statement of possible agreement on the meaning of baptism when applied to a mature person. As will be argued in this study, there is abundant evidence to show that early Baptist authors (including Benjamin Keach, a leading signatory of the *Second London Confession*) thought of believer baptism along the lines of a Calvinistic sacramentalism in which baptism "seals" the experience of saving union with Christ, but this relationship to the typical Calvinistic view is almost never stated explicitly. Therefore, it is not clear that the omissions of the *Second London Confession* imply denial.

Fourth, it must also be remembered that this confession, like others, stated the consensus of a large number of churches and pastors. Therefore, whatever was stated in the text of the confession had to satisfy all of the church representatives who approved it. By 1677 Baptists were virtually unanimous in their rejection of infant baptism and modes other than immersion, and in their affirmation of the basic symbolism of cleansing and death-burial-resurrection. This level of agreement had been reached through decades of misunderstanding and often persecution from the outside, and the intensity of the debate about subject and mode left little time to work out the nuances of what exactly happens in the immersion of believers. There was, then, no developed consensus about the right kind of "sacramental" language, and it comes as no surprise that a debate largely absent from the Baptist literature of the time would be absent from this confession. It is clear, however, that some of the signatories of the confession had thought about the efficacy of baptism, as the next paragraph will show.

The *Baptist Catechism* was prepared to be used in conjunction with the *Second London Confession*. It was commonly known as *"Keach's Catechism,"* although it was co-authored by Benjamin Keach (1640-1704) and William Collins (d. 1702). In any case, it was used to interpret and apply the Confession, and thus served as an elaboration of some of the points of the Confession. Its treatment of the "ordinances" is especially instructive:

> Q.93. What are the outward Means whereby Christ communicates to us the benefits of Redemption?
> A. The outward and ordinary Means whereby Christ communicates to us the benefits of redemption, are his Ordinances, especially the Word, Baptism, the Lord's Supper, and Prayer; all which Means are made effectual to the Elect, through faith, for Salvation.[16]

---

16 *The Baptist Catechism*, 23.

This statement should make it perfectly clear that baptism was regarded as instrumental in some sense in the personal experience of salvation. The fact that it is parallel to the Word and prayer indicates that it somehow leads to the benefits signified by it, rather than simply testifying to a prior possession of those benefits. Furthermore, it was indicated here that it is Christ himself who communicates the benefits of his saving work through the ordinances, which is to say that baptism is a means of grace as well as an act of personal confession.

The *Orthodox Creed*[17] was adopted by General Baptists in 1678. Following the lead of the Particular Baptists, this confession was loosely modelled on the Westminster Confession, but it modified the Calvinism as well as the ecclesiology. Article XXVII declared, "Those two sacraments, viz. Baptism, and the Lord's-supper, are ordinances of positive, sovereign, and holy institution." This is one example of the interchangeability of "sacrament" and "ordinance" in 17th-century thought, which should warn us not to read modern distinctions back into the expressions of our predecessors. Article XXVIII stated:

> Baptism is . . . a sign of our entrance into the covenant of grace, and ingrafting into Christ, and into the body of Christ, which is his church; and of remission of sin in the blood of Christ, and of our fellowship with Christ, in his death and resurrection, and of our living, or rising to newness of life.

This brief statement did not elaborate any definition of the relationship between the sign and the thing signified, which is not surprising, in that the burden of the baptismal article was to assert that the signification of baptism is applicable only to professed believers as opposed to infants, not to discuss the exact manner in which baptism works in such professed believers.

In summary: In the first century of Baptist life, the terms "sacrament" and "ordinance" were both used by Baptist confessions to denote baptism. General Baptists tended to use the former and Particular Baptists the latter, but the two terms were not regarded as contradictory. Their relationship is not that of opposites, but that of broader ("ordinance", which included at least the Word and prayer in addition to baptism and the Lord's Supper) and narrower ("sacrament", which described only baptism and the Lord's Supper). There was a consistent rejection of any automatic bestowal of grace through baptism, but there were various assertions in the confessions

---

17 Lumpkin, *Confessions*, 295-334.

of some kind of instrumental value of baptism in the application of the benefits of Christ. Given the Puritan-Separatist roots of Baptist churches, it would appear that the Calvinistic concept of baptism as a "seal" of union with Christ by faith continued to shape the way in which Baptists described the efficacy of the baptism of professed believers. However, this understanding was largely unelaborated, due to the necessity to focus their baptismal debates on the points at which they departed from their historical roots.

Individual Baptist Authors

Confessions of faith which speak for many churches at once do not and cannot elaborate their underlying theology in the same way as the writings of individuals, many of whom are the signatories who have shaped the confessions. This is evident in a survey of early Baptist baptismal literature, in that the language of individual writers was often much more strongly sacramental than the brief statements of the official confessions. This study will summarize the views of five representative authors who directly addressed the question of the effects of baptism.

ROBERT GARNER (ACTIVE 1640-1650)

In 1645 Garner (a Particular Baptist) wrote *A Treatise of Baptism*, in which he argued against the practice of infant baptism. In the midst of the book he attempted to show that there are great benefits attached to the baptism of believers. Specifically, he listed four privileges which are granted to baptized believers.

The *first* privilege is that, "Believers (in submitting to this Ordinance) have the name of the Father and of the Sonne, and of the holy Spirit called upon them therein."[18] This baptism into the divine name is more than a verbal formula, for "to be baptized into Christ, or into the Name of Christ, or in the Name of Christ, have one and the same sense and signification in Scripture."[19] Baptism conveys both an obligation and a benefit, since "his Name holds forth unto believers, especially two things: Authority, and Grace."[20] Baptism thus involves a voluntary submission to the authority of Christ, but also the reception of the benefits of Christ, for "in that the Lord hath commanded his servants to baptize believers in his Name, to Put or

---

18 Robert Garner, *A Treatise of Baptism* (London: n.p., 1645), 10.
19 Ibid.
20 Ibid.

Call his Name upon them in baptisme he saith Amen to it, he confirmeth the word of his servants, he performeth what he promiseth to them."[21] Garner thus saw baptism as a means by which grace is conferred in some form, at least in the experiential enjoyment of union with Christ.

The *second* privilege is that "by baptisme they do enter into the fellowship of his Body, that is his Church, with all the priviledges and liberties of the same."[22] This initiation into the church was not seen as a purely formal and regulatory matter, because "we as members of One body, are all made to drink into one spirituall benefit, or into one spirituall Communion, which believers have from Christ in his Supper."[23] Many Baptists would eventually make a sharp distinction between being in Christ and being in Christ's church, but Garner described baptismal initiation thus:

> Which sometimes is called an adding to his Church, and sometimes an adding to the Lord; both which commeth to one and the same thing: for to be added to the Church of the Lord, or the body of the Lord, is to be added to the Lord himself, in a mysticall externall union.[24]

The *third* privilege is a personal share in the saving effects of Christ's death and resurrection:

> Believers in baptisme, through the faith of the operation of God, have fellowship with Christ, in his death and resurrection: by the power of which the strength of the body of sinne is more subdued, and they are more enabled to walk in newnesse of life. Rom 6.3,4,5.[25]

From about 1640 on Baptists (especially the Particular tradition) emphasized the connection of baptism to the death-burial-resurrection of the Lord, utilizing the symbolism as an argument for immersion and the obligation to demonstrate a newness of life. In applying the Romans 6 text, Garner first gave two points of exhortation about the obligation of baptized believers to submit to the authority of Christ, but his third point of application was:

---

21 Ibid., 10-11.
22 Ibid., 14.
23 Ibid.
24 Ibid., 15.
25 Ibid., 17.

Thirdly, the Lord puts forth a glorious power to Believers in baptisme, giving in unto their hearts (in what proportion he pleaseth) the power of the death and resurrection of Jesus Christ, acting faith in them to receive the same, whereby they are in some measure enabled to perform that which their baptisme doth engage them unto.[26]

This real manifestation of resurrection power in the baptismal event was emphasized as he expounded Romans 6 and 1 Peter 3.21:

> ... like as the glory of the Father was put forth in raysing his Sonne from the dead: even so, the glory of the Father is put forth unto believers in baptisme, crucifying the power of sin in them, and raysing up their heart and minde as it were into heaven to sit with Christ, to walke with him in a holy and heavenly conversation, to live a new life, which the Scripture, calleth a newnesse of life.... Wherein, I observe, that the same operation of God which was put forth in raysing Christ from the dead, is put forth unto believers, in baptisme (in such proportion as the Lord pleaseth) acting faith in them, through which they rise with Christ, or partake with him in the power of his resurrection, in a glorious measure. And this is so cleare a truth, that Peter is bold to say, (speaking unto believers) Baptisme doth also now save us (not the putting away of the filth of the flesh, but the answer of a good conscience towards God) by the resurrection of Jesus Christ. That is the baptisme of believers must not be looked upon with a fleshly and carnall eye, as a washing of the flesh: but with a holy and spirituall eye, as a holy and pretious Ordinance of Jesus Christ: in which Ordinance, he puts forth the power of his resurrection unto believers, through faith saving them more richly than before, from the power of an inward pollution or filthynesse.[27]

Some permanent spiritual benefit is introduced in baptism, for "this grace and power of Christ in baptism, hath an influence into after times also, even so long as they continue in the estate of mortality."[28] Baptism, then, not only

---

26 Ibid., 19.
27 Ibid., 20.
28 Ibid., 21.

signifies what happened once for all in Christ and *ought* to happen in Christians, but also serves as an occasion in which God effects spiritual renewal in baptized believers.

The *fourth* privilege of baptism is the personal assurance of forgiveness, that is, "In this Ordinance, the Lord Jesus by his Spirit acting in a believers heart, doth more richly seal up or confirm to him the free and full remission of all his sinnes, through the blood of Christ."[29] Acts 2:38 is perhaps the most important scriptural text which relates baptism to forgiveness, and Garner treated it with care:

> He [Peter] doth not say, neither dare I say that baptisme is a remedy to remit sinnes: for then I should run into the mistake of such, who pleading for their infants baptisme, do say: Baptisme is a remedy to take away that sinne, which they as the sons of Adam have conveyed to them. But this Scripture, I conceive, holds forth to us especially two things. First, that repentance and remission of sins are preached & given only in the Name or through the Name of Jesus Christ. . . . Secondly, that the Lord Jesus doth in baptisme confirm or witnesse unto Believers, in some comfortable measure, the forgivenesse of their sins in his Name. And therefore he commands them to be baptized, partly for this end, that in baptisme he may confirm to them in some measure, by his Spirit, acting faith in them, the remission of their sinnes. For when a Believer is baptized in the Name of Christ, and the Spirit of God acts faith in him in his baptisme, then is his heart more sweetly assured, that through this Name all his sins are remitted, and he is at peace with God.[30]

He commented similarly on Acts 22.16:

> Not that baptisme doth wash away sinnes: for it is the bloud of Christ onely, received by us through the faith of the operation of God, that washeth or cleanseth us from all sinnes. But thus; Be baptized, and in thy baptisme call on the Name of the Lord: that is, act faith in the Lord Jesus, in whose Name thou art baptized, that through faith in his Name in this Ordinance, thy heart may be further confirmed in this assurance, that all thy sinnes are washed

---

29 Ibid., 24.
30 Ibid., 25.

away in his pretious bloud.[31]

Garner was explicit in his rejection of the notion that there is inherent in baptism the power to forgive sins. Forgiveness is thus not connected in any mechanical or necessary way to baptism; it is effected objectively in the atoning work of Christ and individually through faith. However, he was equally clear in his assertion that forgiveness becomes an experiential reality through the confession of faith in baptism. This sealing and assuring function of baptism is the essence of Calvin's view of baptism and the Reformed sacramental tradition, and is seen here in a representative Baptist author.

HENRY LAWRENCE (1600-1664)

One of the most systematic treatments of baptism in early Particular Baptist literature was Lawrence's *Of Baptism*, which appeared in its third and final edition in 1659. He began this work with a description of "the first and great end" of baptism as "the Sealing up of our Union with Christ."[32] He wrote:

> The Scripture holds forth no point with more glory and certainty, than the Oneness which we have with Jesus Christ; which Union is the rise and ground of all that is good and happy in us: This therefore is the first and great thing that is made ours by Baptism.[33]

Lawrence continued by drawing an extensive parallel between Christ's sealing by his baptism and our sealing by baptism into Christ. The implication of this sealing is:

> Let us therefore put a value and a price upon this Ordinance, more than we have done: and after being once baptized into Christ, let us know and be assured, that we have a right to what he hath, and to what he had, and to what he is.[34]

The second purpose of baptism was said to be "assuring us of our

---

31 Ibid.
32 Henry Lawrence, *Of Baptism* (London: F. Macock, 1659), 1.
33 Ibid.
34 Ibid., 7.

Justification in the remission of all our sins."[35] He explained:

> It is safe giving Ordinances that notion the Scripture gives them, which while you do, you will get the true use they afford, and you shall be sure not to err from the true nature of them: This you have, Acts 2.38. Repent, and be baptized every one of you for the remission of sins.[36]

This example of the Apostle Peter's speech to convicted sinners at Pentecost readily supports the idea that we are baptized because we are sinners, not because we are saints. Lawrence thus showed how baptism serves the needs of such sinners:

> What can be said more comfortably to a distressed soul than this? That God hath set and instituted an Ordinance on purpose, that thou maist be acquitted of every sin, to witness and seal up what is done by faith: Therefore do not languish in this condition, Why tarriest thou? Arise, and be Baptized, and wash away thy sins.[37]

The question of whether baptism is a sacramental means of appropriating Christ and his benefits or is a pure symbol pointing backward to a completed conversion through faith might be put in this form: Are we baptized because we are sinners or because we are saved? Accordingly, the fact that Lawrence could point unbelievers to baptism as a remedy for their consciousness of guilt showed his commitment to some kind of sacramentalism.

It has been shown above that Lawrence, like Garner, interpreted baptism as a "seal" of personal salvation, thus utilizing the common terminology and conceptualization of Calvinistic sacramentalism. Now if baptism "seals" faith and its effects, then it points *backward* to faith as a prior reality, and this view of baptism is easily distorted into a pure symbolism in which all the benefits follow faith but precede baptism. Lawrence, however, meant more than this when he spoke of a "seal":

> For what Baptism finds, it seals; although it doth also exhibit more of the same kinde; Baptism, and so all the Ordinances of Christ

---

35   Ibid., 8.
36   Ibid., 9.
37   Ibid., 9-10.

those we call Sacraments, seal up what is already, else how could it be a Seal, but doth also convey more of the same.[38]

One might say, then, that Lawrence understood faith as an attitude more than an act, so that while baptism presupposes faith, it also creates a strengthened and continuing faith. From this perspective, the only absolute condition of salvation is the attitude of faith, but the point at which this faith becomes definite, and thus saving union with Christ a concrete reality, is at baptism.

Lawrence's sacramental understanding of baptism was further developed when he listed and explained six ways in which the preached word and the sacraments (both baptism and the Lord's Supper) work in the same manner. Some of the agreements between Word and Sacrament are:

> ... They are both instruments in the hands of the holy Spirit for edification and salvation, the word is a dead letter without the Spirit, and so also is Baptism, it speaks no more than it is bid; ... Now if there be no vertue in the flesh of Christ, but by the personal Union, how shall bodily actions about bodily Elements confer grace, but by the mediation of the Spirit. ... They agree in the principal matter, for the same Christ with all his benefits is offered and confirmed to us in the word and Sacraments, the same Union, the same Communion in the death and the resurrection of Christ, . . . They agree in the instrument, which renders both profitable to us, both word and Sacrament are ineffectual without faith. ... They agree in the effects, They are the savour of life unto life, or the savour of death unto death, &c. So, He that believeth and is Baptized shall be saved.[39]

Having spelled out the instrumental value of both the word and the sacraments, Lawrence pointed out that one of the differences between the word and baptism is their degree of necessity:

> The word is simply necessary to actual beleevers, and so to the salvation of beleevers, and sufficient, as in Cornelius; for faith is by hearing, and hearing by the word of God; but the Sacraments are not absolutely necessary to all, nor without the word are they

---

38 Ibid., 10-11.
39 Ibid., 46-47.

sufficient to salvation, for to what purpose are seals without the writing.[40]

However, the truth that baptism has only a relative necessity does not trivialize its significance, for he wrote just prior to the above:

> They differ in the measure of their signification, the word especially teacheth, the Sacraments especially seal and confirm: the word indeed signifies and applyes spiritual things, but the Sacraments more efficaciously represent and apply.[41]

Therefore, Lawrence interpreted baptism as a "seal" of salvation in much the same way as the Reformed tradition as applied to professed believers. While baptism has only a relative necessity, and it is in any case useless apart from the preached word, it is a valuable instrument by the work of the Spirit in the application of salvation to the conscious life of the individual. It is an expression of faith from the human side and a means of assurance from the divine side.

THOMAS GRANTHAM (1634-1693)

In 1678 Grantham, a General Baptist, published his most influential book, *Christianismus Primitivus*, which included an extended defence of the Baptist understanding of baptism. But as is so often true, the book said much more about what does not happen in the purported baptism of infants than what does happen in the immersion of believers. There is, however, one passage worth considering, where he wrote:

> ... And thus was our Lord himself the chief founder of the Gospel in the Heavenly Doctrine of *Faith, Repentance, and Baptism for the remission of Sins*. . . . Now the necessity of this Sacred Ordinance to a true church-state, is further evident from the Institution or first delivery of it.
> 1. For that it is sent down from Heaven, as the first Doctrine and Ministry, to take men off from a legal confidence, and to lay the free remission of sin before them, through faith in the Gospel of God.
> 2. This Baptism is joyned with this Gospel Repentance, that as repentance being now necessary to the admission of Sinners into the

---

40 Ibid., 50.
41 Ibid.

Church of Christ, even so Baptism being joyned thereto, by the will of God, is necessary to the same end.[42]

The relevant point here is that Grantham envisioned baptism as designed to benefit those who presently are trusting in meritorious works (sinners, not saints) by offering to them salvation through free forgiveness. That is, conscious experience of the forgiveness of sins was viewed as an effect rather than a condition of baptism. The impression given in this passage is that repentance, faith, and baptism are all related to forgiveness and church membership in the same way. This would surely make baptism not merely a sign, but an effective sign.

In an earlier work, Grantham had argued that baptism is normally instrumental in experiencing the grace which is offered in the gospel:

> Baptism in the ordinary way of God's communicating the grace of the Gospel is antecedent to the reception thereof, & is propounded as a means wherein not only the Remission of our sins shall be granted to us, but as a condition whereupon we shall receive the gift of the Holy Ghost . . . [It] was fore-ordained to signifie and sacramentally to confer the grace of the pardon of sin, and the inward washing of the Conscience by Faith in the Bloud of Jesus Christ.[43]

To say that baptism effects a purification of the conscience is to say that it seals or assures the baptizand of forgiveness, and to say that it is effective "by faith" is to deny that it functions *ex opere operato* or that it is applicable to those who are not yet capable of faith. Furthermore, to say that it is the "ordinary" means of conferring these benefits is to deny that it is an absolutely necessary means of salvific union with Christ, as if the grace of God were tied to the sacrament. All these qualifications simply tell us what his sacramental language does *not* mean, but they in no way refute the idea that his thought is sacramental in concept as well as in terminology. Philip Thompson's comment that, "A non- or anti-sacramental label attaches to this view only with great difficulty,"[44] is both accurate and understated.

---

42 Thomas Grantham, *Christianismus Primitivus* (London: Francis Smith, 1678), Book 2, Chapter 1, Sect. V.
43 Thomas Grantham, *A Sigh for Peace: or The Cause of Division Discovered* (London: printed for the author, 1671), 87-88.
44 Philip E. Thompson, "A New Question in Baptist History: Seeking a Catholic Spirit Among Early Baptists," *Pro Ecclesia* 8, no. 1 (Winter 1999): 67.

BENJAMIN KEACH (1640-1704)

Keach, who was at one time a General Baptist, later had a long and influential ministry among the Particular Baptists. In a book published in 1689, he attempted to interpret baptism "in its primitive purity," and in so doing provided modest but clear evidence for a sacramental understanding of baptism. *First* of all, he referred to "the special ends of this holy Sacrament,"[45] showing that this leading signatory of the Second London Confession did not assume that baptism was an "ordinance" *as opposed to* a "sacrament." *Second,* he referred to baptism as "the Baptism of Repentance for the Remission of Sins" (with reference to Acts 2:38) and "the Washing of Regeneration" (with reference to Titus 3:5), without any apparent nervousness about the language.[46] *Third,* he indicated that baptism looks forward to salvation as its goal:

> Consider the great Promises made to those who are obedient to it, amongst other things, Lo, I am with you always, even to the end of the World. And again, He that believeth, and is baptized, shall be saved. If a Prince shall offer a Rebel his Life in doing two things, would he neglect one of them, and say this I will do, but the other is a trivial thing, I'll not do that? Surely no, he would not run the hazard of his Life so foolishly. . . . And then in Acts 2.38. Repent, and be baptized every one of you for Remission of Sin, and ye shall receive the Gift of the Holy Spirit: See what great Promises are made to Believers in Baptism.[47]

Fourth, and most clearly, Keach quoted approvingly from Stephen Charnock (1628-1680), a Puritan pastor who spoke "excellently" in Keach's opinion on the connection between baptism and regeneration:

> Outward Water cannot convey inward Life. How can Water, an external thing, work upon the Soul in a physical manner? Neither can it be proved, that ever the Spirit of God is ty'd by any Promise, to apply himself to the Soul in a gracious Operation, when Water is applyed to the Body. . . . Baptism is a means of conveying this

---

45 Benjamin Keach, *Gold Refin'd; or Baptism in its Primitive Purity* (London: Nathaniel Crouch, 1689), 78.
46 Ibid., 82-83.
47 Ibid., 173.

Grace, when the Spirit is pleased to operate with it; but it doth not work as a physical Cause upon the Soul as a Purge doth upon the Humours of the Body: for 'tis the Sacrament of Regeneration, as the Lord's Supper is of Nourishment. . . .Faith only is the Principle of spiritual Life, and the Principle which draws Nourishment from the Means of God's Appointments.[48]

The specific point at issue in this quotation is the practice of baptizing infants who cannot confess faith, so that Keach's primary concern was to argue that baptism does not accomplish regeneration in any mechanical way and is thus of no value in the case of purely passive infants. However, he argued this point, with Charnock's help, by asserting that the true way in which baptism works is as an instrument of the Spirit who sovereignly employs it in the regeneration of conscious believers. That is, although baptism has no inherent power, it is by the work of the Holy Spirit an effective sign, instrumentally conveying what it signifies. It is a sign, but not merely a sign.

WILLIAM MITCHILL (1662-1705)

In the latter part of the 17th century and until his death in 1705, Mitchill (sometimes spelled Mitchell) carried on an extensive church-planting ministry in the West of Yorkshire and the East of Lancashire. At the end of his life he wrote a work called *Jachin and Boaz*, which was designed to guide the Particular Baptist churches which he had served. This work was published in 1707 by his associate David Crosley. Included in the document was a confession of faith for the use of the churches, in which Chapter XXXI defined baptism as follows:

Baptism is an Ordinance of the New Testament instituted by Christ, to be unto the Party baptized a Sign of his Fellowship with him in his Death, Burial and Resurrection, of his ingrafting into him, of remission of Sins, and of his giving up himself unto God through Jesus Christ, to live and walk in Newness of Life.[49]

This was followed by an affirmation that immersion is the only proper mode

---

48 Ibid., 128-129.
49 "William Mitchill's Jachin and Boaz", *Transactions of the Baptist Historical Society* 3 (1912-1913): 160.

of baptism, and an affirmation that only confessing believers are appropriate subjects. Although the wording was not exactly that of the *Second London Confession*, it was very close, and the substance was identical.

There was no explicitly sacramental language in the above definition of baptism, but this definition was preceded by a general definition of sacraments in Chapter XXX of the confession, which read as follows:

> Sacraments are holy Signs of the Covenant of Grace immediately instituted by Christ, to represent him and his Benefits, and to confirm our Interest in him, and solemnly to engage us to the Service of God in Christ, according to his Word: There is in every Sacrament a spiritual Relation, or a Sacramental Union between the Sign, and the thing signified: Whence it comes to pass that the Names and Effects of the one is ascribed to the other: The Grace which is exhibited in or by the Sacraments rightly used, is not conferred by any power in them, neither doth the Efficacy of a Sacrament depend upon the Piety or Intention of him that doth administer it, but upon the Work of the Spirit, and the Word of Institution, which contains, together with a Precept authorizing the use thereof, a Promise of benefit to the worthy Receivers. There be only two Sacraments ordained by Christ our Lord in the Gospel, that is to say, Baptism and the Lord's Supper, neither of which ought to be administered but by a Minister of the Word lawfully called.[50]

This explanation of sacraments was simply a slightly abridged form of Chapter XXVII of the *Westminster Confession*. Its use by Mitchill in connection with a typical Baptist statement about baptism as an "ordinance" demonstrates the continuing impact of Calvinistic sacramentalism among Particular Baptists, and also that those who adhered to the *Second London Confession* did not necessarily (if ever) consider its statement on baptism to be anti-sacramental.

SUMMARY

Early Baptist authors consistently argued against any kind of sacramentalism which posits an automatic bestowal of grace through baptism, but they did not deny that baptism has an instrumental function in the application of redemption. It is crucial to note that Baptist refutations of baptismal

---

50   Ibid., 159.

regeneration were almost always stated in reference to *infant* baptism. The point which they insisted on is that regeneration is always connected to active faith in the recipient, so that it is meaningless to speak of the regeneration of passive infants by baptism or any other means. Therefore, Baptist protests against baptismal regeneration did not necessarily deny that baptism is instrumental in some way in the experience of spiritual rebirth by confessing believers.

Some early Baptists spoke more strongly than others, but there was among them a recurring affirmation that the reception of the benefits of Christ is in some way mediated through baptism. Their theology of baptism may not have been absolutely uniform, but they consistently asserted that God, by his Spirit, bestows spiritual benefit through baptism. Christian baptism was for them a human response to the gospel, but this human act of obedience did not exhaust the content of the event. This Baptist sacramentalism was somewhat unelaborated due to the demands of controversy about baptismal subjects and mode, but it was undeniably present. As Philip Thompson notes, interpreting early Baptists in terms of the "symbolic minimalism" which dominates much of contemporary Baptist thought is in fact a "serious misrepresentation."[51] In Thompson's terms, anti-sacramental Baptists rightly recognize that early Baptists affirmed God's "freedom from creaturely control," but they fail to see that early Baptists also affirmed God's "freedom for the redemptive use of creation."[52]

The Eighteenth Century

British Baptists in the 18th century were in many cases preoccupied with concerns other than baptismal theology, concerns which were often much more foundational than any baptismal issues. The General Baptists had drifted strongly toward Unitarianism by the middle of the century, leading to an orthodox renewal movement to form the New Connexion in the latter part of the century.[53] Particular Baptists, on the other hand, were dominated

---

51 Thompson, "A New Question," 66-67.
52 Philip E. Thompson, "People of the Free God: The Passion of Seventeenth-Century Baptists," *American Baptist Quarterly* 15, no. 3 (September 1996): 226, 231.
53 See A. C. Underwood, *A History of the English Baptists* (London: Carey Kingsgate Press, 1947), 119-128; W. T. Whitley, *A History of British Baptists*, 2nd ed., (London: Kingsgate Press, 1932), 167-174, 195-203, 211-217; H. Leon McBeth, *The Baptist Heritage* (Nashville: Broadman Press, 1987), 153-170.

The Historical Background 33

by a kind of High Calvinism[54] which tended to mute any emphasis on human religious action, baptismal or otherwise. Given the drift of the General Baptists away from orthodoxy and their numerical decline, there was virtually nothing in their literature of this period which addressed baptismal theology. Particular Baptist literature on baptism was generally devoted to a defence of the immersion of believers, but in some cases the efficacy of baptism was addressed. There were no significant Baptist confessions written during this century; therefore, the following analysis will focus on the major Baptist authors of the period.

John Gill (1697-1771)

Gill was the first great Calvinistic Baptist theologian, dominating the British context for some fifty years, during his tenure as pastor at Horsleydown, Southwark, London.[55] Indeed, his work is still seen as definitive by some modern Calvinistic Baptists.[56] His literary output included a commentary on the Old and New Testaments and a *Body of Doctrinal and Practical Divinity*, as well as many polemical tracts. His understanding of the meaning of baptism can be found in his *Body of Divinity* and in his commentary on the baptismal texts of the New Testament.

In his systematic treatment of baptism, Gill listed six "ends and uses for

---

54 The term "High Calvinism" is used here to denote what is sometimes called "Hyper-Calvinism." The latter term is particularly susceptible to abuse as a pejorative label. What is meant by High Calvinism is a kind of Calvinism which in some way denies the free, universal offer of the gospel. Normative Calvinism has always affirmed that humans are both spiritually unable to respond to the gospel and yet responsible to do so. Arminianism resolves the paradox by positing some kind of prevenient grace which restores to all the ability to respond, while High Calvinism resolves it by denying the responsibility of unbelievers to repent and believe the gospel (and the related responsibility of believers to offer indiscriminately the benefits of the gospel). A negative account of Baptist High Calvinism in this period can be found in McBeth, *Baptist Heritage*, 171-178, and a more appreciative, but still critical, appraisal in Thomas J. Nettles, *By His Grace and for His Glory* (Grand Rapids: Baker Book House, 1986), 73-107.

55 For a survey of Gill's theology, see the chapter on Gill by Timothy George in David Dockery and Timothy George, eds., *Baptist Theologians* (Nashville: Broadman Press, 1990). See also Michael A. G. Haykin, ed., *The Life and Thought of John Gill (1697-1771): A Tercentennial Appreciation* (Leiden: Brill, 1997).

56 Gill's statement of systematic theology was republished in 1989 by a group known as "Strict Old School Baptists" headquartered in Paris, Arkansas, with the purpose of calling all Baptists back to the historically distinctive doctrines as stated by Gill. See "Publisher's Foreword", in John Gill, *A Body of Doctrinal and Practical Divinity* (1769-1770; reprint Paris, Arkansas: The Baptist Standard Bearer, 1989).

which baptism is appointed." First, baptism is designed "to represent the sufferings, burial, and resurrection of Christ," according to Romans 6:4-5 and Colossians 2:12.[57] This idea of the symbolism contained in the act of immersion had rapidly become the dominant theme in the Particular Baptist doctrine of baptism, and it stood first in Gill as well.

Second, both John's baptism and apostolic baptism were "for the remission of sins, Mark i. 4. Acts ii. 38."[58] Gill qualified this apparently sacramental language as follows:

> . . .not that that is the procuring and meritorious cause of it, which only is the blood of Christ; but they who submit unto it, may, by means of it, be led, directed, and encouraged to expect it from Christ.[59]

Third, baptism is "for the washing away of sin, and cleansing from it", quoting Ananias's words to Saul in Acts 22:16.[60] It is not clear how this cleansing is to be distinguished from remission of sins at a conceptual level, but what is clear is that this biblical language demands the same sort of qualification:

> . . .this only is really done by the blood of Christ, which cleanses from all sin; baptism neither washes away original nor actual sin, it has no such virtue in it: but it is a means of directing to Christ the Lamb of God, who, by his atoning blood and sacrifice, has purged and continues to take away the sins of men.[61]

Fourth, "a salutary or saving use and effect is ascribed unto it", in that there is very clear biblical language asserting that "baptism now saves us" (1 Peter 3:21).[62] But again the force of the biblical language is qualified, in this case by the biblical text itself, indicating that this salvation is "by the resurrection of Jesus Christ". In Gill's words, "that is, by leading the faith of the person baptized to Christ, as delivered for his offences, and as risen again for his justification."[63]

---

57 Gill, *Divinity*, 914.
58 Ibid.
59 Ibid.
60 Ibid.
61 Ibid.
62 Ibid.
63 Ibid.

Fifth, as an act of obedience to God, baptism "discharges a good conscience, the consequence of which is joy and peace," with reference again to 1 Peter 3:21.[64] Here it is not the case that God rewards the baptized *for* keeping his commands, but rather that there is benefit *in* keeping those commands. The sense of having done what is right carries its own reward of a clear conscience.

Sixth, obedience to this divine command is "an evidence of love to God and Christ, 1 John v. 3", and those who love Christ in this way "may expect according to his promise, to have fresh manifestations of his and his Father's love, and to have communion with Father, Son, and Spirit."[65]

Gill's commentary on the baptismal references and possible allusions in the New Testament actually provides more extensive evidence of his thought than the above outline in his systematic theology. What follows here is a summary of his comments on the New Testament texts which are normally considered to be the strongest supports for a sacramental understanding of baptism.

Mark 16:16 speaks of faith and baptism in a way that seems to indicate that they are two elements of the human response to the gospel, and that both are necessary conditions of salvation. Gill commented that faith is *necessarily* present and baptism *normally* present in those who will be saved, but neither is a *cause* of this salvation. He wrote:

> ...faith must precede baptism, as these words of Christ, and scripture examples shew; and such as have it, ought to make a profession of it, and be baptized; and in which way it is that faith discovers itself, and works by love to Christ; namely in observing his commands, and this among the rest... not that either faith or baptism are the procuring causes of salvation; not faith, for Christ is the author of salvation: and faith is the grace that looks to him for it, receives the assurance of it now, and that will be the end of it hereafter: ... and baptism, though it is said to save by the resurrection of Christ, as it is a means of leading faith to Christ's resurrection for justification, yet has no casual influence upon salvation; it is not essential to it; the thief on the cross went to heaven without it, and Simon Magus to hell with it; but it is the duty of every one that believes, and he that truly believes, ought to be baptized, and prove the truth of his faith, by his obedience to

---

64 Ibid.
65 Ibid., 915.

Christ, . . .:⁶⁶

This text is one of several in which Gill relativized faith in the same way as baptism. Within his Calvinistic system, faith is a gift bestowed by God on all the elect and only the elect, so that for him faith ought not be called a condition of salvation. Although faith identifies the elect who will be saved, it is not the cause of their salvation. However, faith is instrumental in the present experience of salvation, in that it conveys assurance that the one who believes (by grace) is an object of God's saving purpose. Baptism is not instrumental in exactly the same way, but as the event in which "faith discovers itself," and as a means of leading faith to Christ, it is instrumental in *some* way in relation to the present assurance of salvation.

John 3:5 refers to spiritual rebirth as a birth "of water and the Spirit" and thus provides a basis for traditional references to baptism as the "sacrament of regeneration". As was noted in the preceding chapter, 17th-century Baptists often interpreted this as an allusion to baptism, although they did not connect baptism and regeneration in the same way as did the Catholic tradition. Gill, however, moved away from this traditional reading:

> By *water*, is not meant material water, or baptismal water; for water-baptism is never expressed by water only, without some additional word, which shews that the ordinance of water-baptism is intended: nor has baptism any regenerating influence in it; . . . and it is so far from having any such virtue, that a person ought to be born again, before he is admitted to that ordinance: and though submission to it is necessary, in order to a person's entrance into a Gospel church-state; yet it is not necessary to the kingdom of heaven, or to eternal life and salvation: . . . whereas by *water* is meant, in a figurative and metaphorical sense, the grace of God, as it is elsewhere; see Ezek. xxxvi. 25. John iv. 14.⁶⁷

He interpreted the phrase "water and the Spirit" as a hendiadys, so that the two words signify one idea, namely, "the grace of the Spirit of God."⁶⁸ Regeneration was interpreted as a *condition* of baptism, not as an *effect* of baptism.

---

66 John Gill, *An Exposition of the New Testament* (Philadelphia: William W. Woodward, 1811), 1:505.
67 Ibid., 1:793.
68 Ibid.

Acts 2:38 seems to indicate that baptism is a means to both the forgiveness of sins and the reception of the Holy Spirit. The text is so forceful that some modern movements tracing their origin to Alexander Campbell (1788-1866) in the mid-19th century take it as a summary of their distinctive baptismal theology.[69] Gill commented:

> *for the remission of sins*; not that forgiveness of sin could be procured either by repentance, or by baptism; for this is only obtained by the blood of Christ; but the apostle advises these awakened, sensible, repenting, and believing souls, to submit to baptism, that by it their faith might be led to Christ, who suffered and died for their sins, who left them buried in his grave, and who rose again for their justification from them; all which is, in a most lively manner, represented in the ordinance of baptism by immersion:[70]

Here he relativized repentance in the same way that he treated faith in his comments on Mark 16:16, which should again give one pause before concluding that baptism was for Gill in *no* way instrumental in the experience of forgiveness. Baptism, as an expression of repentance, is a normal part of the human experience effected by the sovereign grace of God.

The text in question also promises the "gift of the Spirit" to those who repent and are baptized. Although it would seem that this promise could be handled in the same way as the promise of forgiveness, Gill took a different approach:

> *and ye shall receive the gift of the Holy Ghost*: not the grace of the Spirit, as a regenerator and sanctifier; for that they had already; and is necessary, as previous to baptism; unless it should mean confirmation of that grace, and stability in it, as it appears from ver. 42. they afterwards had; but rather the extraordinary gifts of the Spirit, particularly the gift of speaking with tongues, . . .[71]

Acts 22:16, in the context of the conversion of Saul, connects cleansing from sin to baptism. Gill's comment was predictable:

---

69 The origin of these movements is described by Errett Gates, *The Early Relation and Separation of Baptists and Disciples* (Chicago: The Christian Century Company, 1904).
70 Gill, *Exposition*, 2:167.
71 Ibid.

... not that it is in the power of man to cleanse himself from his sins; ... nor is there any such efficacy in baptism as to remove the filth of sin; ... but the ordinance of baptism may be, and sometimes is, a means of leading the faith of God's children to the blood of Christ, which cleanses from all sin;[72]

It is not clear why Gill at this point moderated his language, so that baptism's work of pointing to Christ is only possible or occasional. His language could mean that baptism only has this effect in the case of some of the elect, with others perhaps coming to baptism with such a vivid sense of the benefits of the death of Christ as to make baptism less powerful in their experience. More likely he had in view the fact that some baptisms occur among the reprobate, and thus without effect (as was true, for example, in the case of Simon Magus [Acts 8], whom Gill mentioned in this context).

Romans 6:3-5 was a very significant text virtually from the inception of the Particular Baptist movement, in that it provides the strongest biblical evidence for the symbolism of death-burial-resurrection in the act of immersion. Although this text is obviously useful for this cherished Baptist idea, the text also seems to say that baptism effects union with Christ, which is an idea less at home in the Baptist tradition. Gill was not blind to this, but rather than accepting the conclusion that baptism is an effective sign, he suggested another way of interpreting the phrase "into Christ":

... baptized into Christ ... by which is meant, not a being brought by it into union with Christ, which is either secretly from eternity, or openly at conversion, and both before the baptism of true believers; nor a being brought by it into the mystical body of Christ the church, for this also is before it; but rather it designs a being baptized, or a being brought by baptism into more communion with Christ, into a participation of his grace and benefits; or into the doctrine of Christ, and a more distinct knowledge of it: ... though rather the true meaning of the phrase, *baptized into Christ*, I take to be, is to be baptized purely for the sake of Christ, in imitation of him, who has set us an example, and because baptism is an ordinance of his; it is to submit to it with a view to his glory, to testify our affection for him, and subjection to him, without laying

---

72 Ibid., 2:373.

any stress or dependence on it for salvation;[73]

It would seem, then, that Gill was ultimately unsure what the phrase "baptized into Christ" actually signifies. It might be a post-conversion, higher-level communion with Christ, or a leap forward in understanding the truth about Christ's work, or an act of imitation. But whatever it means, it is clear what it does *not* mean--for Gill it could not mean that baptism brings the sinner into union with Christ.

Galatians 3:27 is another Pauline text which uses the language of being "baptized into Christ." Again Gill asserted that it is "not that by baptism they are brought into union with Christ, but into communion with him."[74] Paul asserts that those baptized into Christ "have put on Christ", which Gill interpreted as follows:

> And such *have put on Christ*; both before and at baptism: before it, they put him on as the Lord their righteousness; . . . so in baptism they may also be said to put him on, as they thereby and therein make a public profession of him, by deeds as well as words, declaring him to be their Lord and King; and afresh exercise faith upon him, as their Saviour and Redeemer, and imitate and follow him in it, as their pattern;[75]

Thus baptism is not focused on Christ as the Saviour whose imputed righteousness is appropriated by those being baptized, but on Christ as the Lord who is the paradigm of obedience.

The baptismal statement of 3:27 follows a statement about faith in 3:26. In fact, it seems that the two statements are fundamentally synonymous, the one phrased in terms of the inner attitude and the other in terms of the event in which that attitude is expressed. Concerning our becoming "children of God by faith in Christ Jesus," Gill commented:

> Not that faith makes any the children of God, or puts them into such a relation; no, that is God's own act and deed; of his free rich grace and goodness, God the Father has predestinated his chosen ones to the adoption of children, and has secured and laid up this blessing for them in the covenant of grace; . . . and faith receives it, as it

---

73 Ibid., 2:479.
74 Ibid., 3:26.
75 Ibid.

does all other blessings of grace made ready to its hand; and so such persons become evidently and manifestatively the children of God by faith in Christ;[76]

Once again Gill denied that faith is efficacious, just as he denied that baptism is efficacious.

Colossians 2:12 is another Pauline text which employs the imagery of being buried and raised with Christ in baptism. For some reason Gill devoted more space at this point to an assertion that immersion is the mode of baptism and an assertion that faith is a gift from God than to an explanation of the strong language about the effects of baptism. He simply noted that baptism is a "lively representation" of spiritual resurrection, and thus it assists those who have true faith to visualize their new life in Christ.[77]

Titus 3:5 refers to God's saving work as being done by "the washing of regeneration and the renewing of the Holy Spirit." The reference to washing (like the "water" of John 3:5) has traditionally been taken as an allusion to baptism, even by many Baptists, but Gill denied the allusion. He argued that the washing denotes "not the ordinance of water-baptism; . . . but regenerating grace is meant, or a being born of water and of the Spirit; that is, of the grace of the Spirit, comparable to water for its purity and cleansing virtue."[78] He suggested several reasons why this is not a reference to baptism: it is obvious that one may be baptized but not regenerated (e.g., Simon Magus); other biblical texts indicate that the Spirit is the cause and the Word the means of regeneration; and, perhaps most importantly, this washing is contrasted with "works of righteousness", while baptism is itself a work of righteousness, according to the words of Christ himself (Matthew 3:15).[79]

1 Peter 3:21 makes the assertion that "baptism now saves us," and thus provides (at least superficially) some of the most direct evidence for baptism as an efficacious means of grace. However, Gill declared that "it saves not as a cause, for it has not causal influence on, nor is it essential to salvation." The basis for this rejection of sacramental implications was found in the phrases "answer of a good conscience" and "by the resurrection of Jesus Christ." The former phrase indicates that the heart of baptism is human obedience by one who is already committed to Jesus as Lord, and the latter

---

76   Ibid.
77   Ibid., 3:192.
78   Ibid., 3:365.
79   Ibid.

phrase indicates that baptism's task is simply "leading the faith of the baptized person, as to the blood of Christ for pardon and cleansing, so to the resurrection of Christ for justification."[80]

In summary: The baptismal theology of John Gill seems to be a significant step in a non-sacramental direction. He never used the term "sacrament" to describe baptism, nor did he refer to it as a "seal" of saving union with Christ. When confronted with biblical texts that refer to water or washing, he interpreted them in a way that eliminated any references to baptism. In all these ways he differed from leading Particular Baptists of the 17th century.

His denial that baptism is a cause of regeneration or the forgiveness of sins was not new in his tradition, but it did have a different focus. Whereas the burden of his predecessors was to deny that baptism works in any kind of mechanical way and thus is irrelevant to the salvation of passive infants, Gill wanted to deny that there is any kind of objective benefit even for the confessing believer. He appears to have rejected the typical Calvinistic view which posited both a confirming/sealing work of God and a human confession of faith in the baptismal event itself. In his view, the baptismal event has been reduced to an act of obedience with subjective benefits, the same sort of benefits which are present in any obedience to God's commands.

All of this, of course, must be seen against the background of Gill's High Calvinism, in which the significance of every human action is severely modified. As noted above, the same things that were denied of baptism were also denied of faith. Later Baptists would often contrast the (denied) efficacy of baptism to the (affirmed) efficacy of faith as an instrumental cause of salvation; however, for Gill the contrast was not between baptism and faith, but between baptism/faith and the work of Christ.

In various places he spoke of baptism as something which "leads" the faith of the elect to Christ and his work which procured their salvation, but this seems to mean merely that baptism is one way in which faith is confessed. Baptism is a sign pointing not to a divine act going on in the event itself, but to the vicarious work of Christ which is the divine act that procured the salvation of the elect. Some of Gill's statements quoted above are sufficiently strong to provide a basis for criticism from paedobaptist opponents who wanted to argue that Gill (like Baptists in general) elevated baptism to an unbiblical level of significance. William Eltringham wrote a polemical tract in which he argued that Gill was self-contradictory, in that

---

80 Ibid., 3:573.

he taught both that no human work could be a means of justification and that baptism "is of use to lead the faith of God's people to his blood and righteousness, for pardon and justification."[81] Eltringham's critique gives the impression of being a disingenuous and tendentious reading of Gill, as was pointed out by Gill's fellow High Calvinist, John Brine (1703-1765):

> I will not multiply Words, on a Matter, which is so plain, that no intelligent and attentive Person can mistake upon it, however this Writer came so grossly to mistake herein. The Spirit leads, or directs the Saints efficiently; Ministers direct them instrumentally; and evangelical Institutions, as Means appointed, by Christ, unto that important End, lead, or direct Believers to look unto his Blood and Righteousness, for Pardon, and Justification. That is the Cause of Justification, to which the Believer looks, not that by which he is directed to the Act of looking, which is most easy to be conceived of.[82]

The fact that some of Gill's language exposed him to such charges is a sign that he was driven by the language of Scripture to speak of baptism as more than simple obedience. However, the fact that he spoke of baptism as a means of looking to Christ for salvation was not an indication of an elevated significance for baptism as a means of grace, but only an indication that baptism is a normal means by which God draws the elect, those redeemed by the blood of Christ, to acknowledge the work of Christ.

Abraham Booth (1734-1806)

Booth served as Pastor of Prescott Street Baptist Church in London from 1769 to his death in 1806. He was once a General Baptist, but became a major spokesman for the Particular Baptists after his adoption of Calvinism. He wrote two major works dealing with baptism: *A Vindication of the Baptists* and *Paedobaptism Examined*. The former defended the practice of Booth and many Baptists called "close communion", i.e., the restriction of the Lord's Supper to those who have been baptized as believers by immersion; and the latter quoted and evaluated traditional paedobaptist

---

81 William Eltringham, *The Baptist Against the Baptist: or a Display of Antipaedo-baptist Self-Inconsistency* (London: J. Waugh and W. Penner, 1755), 5.
82 John Brine, *The Baptists Vindicated from Some Groundless Charges Brought against Them by Mr. Eltringham* (London: John Ward, 1756), 3.

arguments. In the process, Booth devoted hundreds of pages to a defence of believer baptism by immersion with only passing reference to what God is presumed to do in the baptismal event. However, what he did say about the effects of baptism moved strongly in an anti-sacramental direction.

One of the ironies of *Paedobaptism Examined* is the fact that Part I, over half of this large work, was devoted to the question of the *mode* of baptism, and it was in Chapter III of this section that Booth treated "the design of baptism; or the facts and blessings represented by it." What followed under that title was an emphasis on the symbolism of death-burial-resurrection and its implication that immersion is the only appropriate mode of baptism.[83] Thus the design of baptism is fundamentally to picture the death-burial-resurrection of Christ and the believer's share in the benefits associated with the work of Christ, but little was said at that point about the possibility that the experience of those benefits may occur through baptism.

For purposes of this discussion, the crucial part of *Paedobaptism Examined* is Chapter III of Part II, in which Booth reflected on "the high opinion of the Fathers, concerning the utility of baptism." One of the biblical texts which provided the basis for a strong patristic doctrine of baptismal regeneration is John 3:5, Christ's reference to a birth "of water and the Spirit." Booth's treatment of this text revealed some of the depth of his anti-sacramental opinion:

> In regard to John iii. 5, it may be observed, that had our divine Teacher, when he declared it absolutely necessary to be "born of water and of the Spirit," intended the ordinance of baptism by the term *water*; then indeed the necessity of that institution would have unavoidably followed, as being placed on a level with the renewing agency of the Holy Spirit. . . . But who can imagine that the Lord should place our immortal interests on such a footing, as neither tends to illustrate the grace of God, nor to promote the comfort of man, on such a footing as is quite inimical to the spirit of that maxim, BY GRACE YE ARE SAVED; and has no aptitude to excite virtuous tempers in the human heart? A sentiment of this kind is chiefly adapted to enhance the importance of the clerical character, and to make mankind consider themselves as under infinite obligations to a professional order of their fellow mortals,

---

83 Abraham Booth, *Paedobaptism Examined*, in *The Baptist Library*, eds. Charles G. Sommers, William R. Williams, and Levi L. Hill (New York: Lewis Colby & Co., 1846), 1:378-392.

for an interest in everlasting blessedness.[84]

Booth's antipathy toward the common patristic kind of sacramentalism is easily understandable, but given his Calvinism, one might expect him to feel greater attraction to the kind of sacramental view found in the Reformed tradition and in many of his Baptist predecessors. However, after treating the patristic evidence, he turned to the Reformers and some of his contemporaries, and the "seal of the covenant" approach to baptism was rejected by him with equal vehemence. After quoting a warning from a Walter Marshall, who said, "Beware of making an idol of baptism, and putting it in the place of Christ,"[85] he said:

> The necessity of this caution will farther appear, by the following extracts from Mr. Matthew Henry's Treatise on Baptism, lately published. When speaking about the ordinance itself, its obligation, and the privileges of baptized persons, he has the following remarkable words: . . . "The gospel contains not only a doctrine but a covenant, and by baptism we are brought into that covenant. . . .We are baptized into Christ's death; i.e., God doth in that ordinance, seal, confirm, and make over to us, *all* the benefits of the death of Christ. . . .Baptism seals the promise of God's being to *me* a God, and that is greatly encouraging; . . ."
>
> Such are the language and sentiments of Mr. Henry, respecting the utility of baptism! Upon which I would here observe, that we should not have been much surprised, if after all this he had asserted with the Council of Trent, that baptism "opens to every one of us the gate of heaven, which before, through sin, was shut;"[86]

Booth recognized that he was probably guilty of overstatement at this point in his assertion of a fundamental equivalence between Tridentine and Reformed sacramental theology, and so he said:

> Though I am far from considering Mr. Henry as avowing the natural consequences of his own positions, and equally far from charging them upon him; yet I cannot but view the positions

---

84   Ibid., 1:481.
85   Ibid., 1:485.
86   Ibid.

themselves as unwarrantable, extravagant, and of a dangerous tendency.[87]

Moving from critique to positive statement, Booth wrote:

> For no Baptist minister, without notoriously confronting the grand principle on which he proceeds in administering the solemn rite, can ever teach that baptism is a mean of producing those great effects which Mr. Henry and a thousand others have mentioned. To maintain, with a resolute perseverance, that the laws of Christ relating to a positive institution should be strictly observed, is one thing; to insist upon it, or to insinuate that baptism, to whomsoever administered, is the medium of procuring those blessings to which we advert, is another. The former is our indispensable duty; the latter is pregnant with dangerous consequences.[88]

It seems clear, then, that Booth was unwilling to think of baptism as in any sense an effective sign which leads to the things signified, and he considered his view of the matter to be inherent in Baptist theology.

Booth's *Vindication of Baptists* was an attempt to argue that Baptists are not religious bigots when they limit the Lord's Supper to immersed believers. The main thrust of his argument was quite simple: Virtually all Christian traditions agree that participation in the Lord's Supper is limited to baptized Christians, and that is the principle which is being followed by close-communion Baptists, because they understand "baptized" to mean "immersed in the name of the Trinity as a confessing believer."

One of the criticisms directed against close-communion Baptists was that they were making far too much of baptism, even "putting baptism in the place of our Lord's atoning blood and the sanctifying agency of the Divine Spirit."[89] To this charge Booth responded that it is the critics of Baptists who invest baptism with saving power, while Baptists in fact deny such power. He wrote:

> For it is too notorious to admit a plea of ignorance in any of our opponents, that we consider no one as a proper subject of that

---

87 Ibid., 1:486.
88 Ibid.
89 Abraham Booth, *A Vindication of the Baptists from the Charge of Bigotry, in Refusing Communion at the Lord's Table to Paedobaptists*, in *The Baptist Library*, 1:41.

institution, who does not profess repentance toward God, and faith in our Lord Jesus Christ; who does not, in other words, appear to be in a state of salvation. Nay, so far from making baptism a *saving* ordinance, we do not, we cannot consider anyone as a proper subject of it who looks upon it in that light.[90]

Following this disavowal of a sacramental view of baptism, he went on to show that a much higher view of baptism's significance was taught by the *Book of Common Prayer*, George Whitefield (1714-1770), and John Wesley (1703-1791), as representative of the views held by the critics of the "bigoted" Baptists.[91] It seems perfectly clear that Booth rejected *all* sacramental views of baptism, whether Catholic or Protestant. One might well argue that it is incongruous to take such a low view of the meaning of baptism and at the same time exclude from Communion persons who are recognized as genuine believers in Christ, merely because they were baptized by a defective mode. Whatever may be the coherence, or lack thereof, of such a position, what is clear is that Booth and other Baptists like him held tenaciously to a high view of church order but a low view of the efficacy of the ordinances of the church.

Anne Dutton (1692-1765)

Among Baptists in 18th-century England it was generally pastors who shaped the faith and order of the church, but Anne Dutton exerted significant influence without the benefit of such an office. Dutton's second husband became the pastor of the Particular Baptists at Great Gransden in 1732, and from that base for about thirty years thereafter she produced a stream of pamphlets, often in the form of letters to friends and signed only with her initials. One of these pamphlets dealt with the "Subject, Mode, and End" of baptism, and it provides evidence of a continuing kind of Calvinistic sacramental theology among some Particular Baptists.

Dutton asserted that the end of baptism is threefold: "1. To Represent. 2. To Seal, or Assure. And, 3. To Initiate."[92] The first purpose, to represent, denoted the standard Baptist symbolism of "the Death, Burial, and Resurrection of Jesus Christ, and of our Union and Communion with Him

---

90 Ibid., 1:42.
91 Ibid., 1:42-43.
92 Anne Dutton, *Brief Hints Concerning Baptism: of the Subject, Mode, and End of this Solemn Ordinance* (London: J. Hart, 1746), 12.

therein."[93] This first purpose was given the majority of space in her pamphlet, but the second and third addressed the sacramental question (without using the term *sacrament*).

The second purpose, to seal and assure, indicated the way in which *God* is at work in baptism. Just as there is a pictorial representation via immersion of the central facts of redemption, so also "the finish'd Work of Redemption, and the Whole of our Salvation thereby, is seal'd up, and made sure to Believers in their Baptism."[94] Since baptism is done in the name of the Trinity, it was argued that the Triune God is working through baptism:

> All the three Persons in GOD, do, as it were, solemnly engage to make good all the great Things represented therein, to a baptized Believer. They hereby set their Seal, as it were, their Amen, to all that Salvation represented in Baptism, and give the highest Assurance thereof to baptized Believers. This the Lord always gives to the *Persons* of Believers, in the due Administration of the Ordinance; and very frequently He gives this Assurance to their *Spirits* in their Submission to it. As God the Father honoured his Son, with Testimonies of his infinite Favour, upon his baptism. And as the Eunuch, after he was baptized, went on his Way rejoicing. And as the Jaylor and his House, after their Baptism, believing in God, rejoiced.--But when this is not experienced by Believers upon their Baptism, they are not to think it null and void, because, as was said, the Lord gives them a solemn Assurance in the very Ordinance of all the great Things represented therein, as it is his Appointment, and done by his Authority.[95]

It is important to note that this statement about the sealing function of baptism argued that there is an *objective* work of God in the event, whether or not it is experienced at the *subjective* level by the subject of baptism. It ought to create feelings of joy in the one who is incorporated by baptism into the people of God, the beneficiaries of Christ's redemptive work, but whatever may happen at the level of feelings, the confessing believer receives God's "Amen" in the ordinance itself.

The third purpose is to initiate, that is, "to enter Believers, into a true

---

93 Ibid., 12-13.
94 Ibid., 20.
95 Ibid., 21.

Gospel Profession of Christ."[96] Referring to Galatians 3:27 and the language of putting on Christ in baptism, she described what the subject of baptism is doing in the event:

> He hereby professeth himself to be a lost Sinner, that he believes Christ to be the only Saviour, that he looks to Him as his Saviour, and that all his Hope of Salvation stands alone in the CHRIST of GOD. He likewise hereby professeth to take Christ in all his Offices, as his Prophet, Priest and King; and to give up himself to Him, to be His for ever, to follow the LAMB, even whithersoever He goeth.[97]

In view of the fact that baptism is in the name of the Trinity, the confessor "professeth to take the Three-One GOD for his GOD."[98] This language of initiation was in the previous century a dominant motif in General Baptist rhetoric, but less so in Particular Baptist thought. The crucial point in this motif is that the subject of baptism is a sinner who is becoming a Christian through this ordinance, not a confirmed Christian who is giving testimony to past experience. As Dutton described this initiation, the language is fundamentally about the *human* act of confessing faith in Christ, but it is the human side of the initial entrance into union with Christ, not (as for Gill) some kind of second-stage entrance into a deeper communion with Christ.

Andrew Fuller (1754-1815)

Fuller served as pastor at Kettering from 1782 to his death in 1815, but his influence extended far beyond his pastorate. He was a leader in the Northamptonshire Association and one of the founders of the Baptist Missionary Society which sent William Carey (1761-1834) to India in 1793. He provided much of the theological foundation for this aggressive missionary activity with his book, *The Gospel of Christ Worthy of All Acceptation* (1785), which dethroned John Gill's version of Calvinism as the dominant outlook of Particular Baptists. His system was still very much Calvinistic, but he affirmed human responsibility to respond to the gospel, as well as the responsibility of believers to seek the response of others, thus restating Calvinistic theology in a fresh and compelling way. In many ways, then, he became the second great Calvinistic Baptist theologian. In spite of

---

96   Ibid., 22.
97   Ibid.
98   Ibid.

his stature as a Baptist thinker, very little of his extensive writing was devoted to the topic of baptism. The most relevant piece of literature is his circular letter written to the churches of the Northamptonshire Association in 1802, entitled, "The Practical Uses of Christian Baptism."

This letter assumed without argument the traditional Baptist positions on the subjects and mode of baptism, and proceeded to explore "the influence of this ordinance, where it produces its proper effects, in promoting piety in individuals, and purity in the church."[99] His summary statement was that, "The principal design of it appears to be, *A solemn and practical profession of the Christian religion.*"[100] This profession of Christian faith was described in various ways, one of which is the Apostle Paul's statement that, "As many of you as have been baptized into Christ have put on Christ" (Gal. 3:27). Fuller explained it thus:

> There is a putting on of Christ which is internal, and consists in relinquishing the former lusts, and being of the mind of Christ; but that which is here referred to appears to be an *open profession* of his name, to the renouncing of everything that stood in competition with him. It was therefore true of *as many as had been baptized*, whether they abode in the truth or not. And even their being "the children of God by faith in Christ Jesus" seems to express what they were in profession, rather than what they were in fact.[101]

This understanding of baptism as an oath of allegiance is both an early meaning of the Latin *sacramentum* and a partial description of the baptism of adult converts as conceptualized by both sacramental and non-sacramental traditions. The question that remains is whether there is an action from the divine side in the event, i.e., whether the benefits of Christ are conveyed to the elect through baptism.

As Fuller's argument unfolded, he considered the relationship between baptism and the remission of sins, and his statement of the matter communicated a common Baptist ambivalence, recognizing that Scripture points to some kind of instrumental function of baptism, but feeling the need for major qualifications. He wrote:

---

99 Andrew Fuller, "The Practical Uses of Christian Baptism," in *The Complete Works of the Rev. Andrew Fuller: with a Memoir of His Life, by Andrew Gunton Fuller*, 3rd ed. (Philadelphia: American Baptist Publication Society, 1845), 3:339.
100 Ibid.
101 Ibid., 3:340.

Hence, baptism in the name of Christ is said to be *for the remission of sins*. Not that there is any such virtue in the element, whatever be the quantity; nor in the ceremony, though of Divine appointment; but it contains a *sign* of the way in which we must be saved. Sin is washed away in baptism in the same sense as Christ's flesh is eaten, and his blood drank, in the Lord's supper: the sign, when rightly used, leads to the thing signified. Remission of sins is ascribed by Peter not properly to baptism, but to the *name* in which the parties were to be baptized. Thus also Saul was directed to WASH AWAY HIS SINS *calling on* THE NAME OF THE LORD.[102]

The crux here is the phrase, "rightly used," which must mean something like, "used as an outward and formal expression of genuine personal faith." Whatever may be the precise sense of the phrase, Fuller did see baptism as a sign which is received by a person who is *seeking* the benefits signified by it, as was true for Saul who called on the name of Christ for the removal of sin in the baptismal event. Remission of sins is "properly" ascribed to Christ, but it is clear that in *some* sense it comes through baptism; otherwise there would be nothing here to require clarification by the term "properly." It should also be noted that for Fuller, as for Gill, the contrast was not between baptism and faith, but between baptism and the work of Christ. That is, the concern was not to define the human action(s) which function(s) as the instrumental cause(s) of personal salvation, but to emphasize that any human action is at best an *instrumental* cause, a means by which God acts to apply the benefits of the work of Christ.

Fuller's statements indicate that there is some instrumental value in baptism, some way in which baptism leads to reception of the benefits of Christ, but the evidence is minimal and undeveloped. His thought seems to fit well within the context of baptism as a "seal" of union with Christ, but he did not use this language explicitly. Baptists of the 18th century generally avoided this terminology, partly because of the perceived absence of biblical precedents and partly to avoid the Reformed paedobaptist application to infants, but at a conceptual level the idea of "seal" appears to capture the essence of their thought whenever they affirm with Fuller that "the sign, when rightly used, leads to the thing signified."

---

102 Ibid., 3:341.

John Ryland, Jr. (1753-1825)

Ryland was the son of John C. Ryland (1723-1792), another noted Baptist pastor. The junior Ryland was for over thirty years the pastor at Broadmead Church, Bristol and the president of Bristol Baptist College, an influential school for the training of Baptist pastors. His baptismal theology was published in a small book, *A Candid Statement of the Reasons Which Induce the Baptists to Differ In Opinion and Practice from So Many of Their Christian Brethren*. The book was said to represent the substance of a sermon which he often preached at baptismal services, and although it was published in 1814, it represents the baptismal theology which was being taught by Ryland in the late 18th century and is thus included here.

It is abundantly clear that for Ryland, regeneration actually occurs prior to baptism. He wrote:

> With respect to those whom we baptize, we cannot search the heart, and may be mistaken in our judgment, as PHILIP was respecting SIMON, and as the strictest Independents may be respecting those whom they admit to the Lord's Table; but we dare not baptize any of whom we do not hope that they are already born of God; or that they have been renewed in the temper of their minds; that they are penitent believers, whom the love of Christ constraineth to confess him before men, in the way which he hath appointed.[103]

Later he responded to the charge that Baptists put an undue emphasis on baptism by saying:

> I know of no Baptist who ever said such strong things of the *necessity*, much less of the *efficacy* of Baptism, as many Paedobaptists have done. And let it be remembered that it is our very principle, that a man must *first* be in a state of salvation before he has a right to Baptism.[104]

In spite of this assertion that evident regeneration is a condition of baptism, the way in which Ryland described the intention of baptismal

---

103 John Ryland, *A Candid Statement of the Reasons Which Induce the Baptists to Differ in Opinion and Practice from So Many of Their Christian Brethren* (London: W. Button, 1814), 34.
104 Ibid., "Notes," xxx.

candidates pictured them as guilty sinners laying hold of Christ for salvation. For example:

> They mean hereby openly to confess their pollution and guilt. They are about to be baptized with the Baptism of Repentance, professing to be overwhelmed with shame for their inexcusable revolt from God. They are come to a place where much water is, that they may, by being washed all over, indicate a deep conviction of their entire pollution, and need of universal cleansing.[105]

In standard Baptist fashion, the baptismal candidates were "to avow their faith in Christ's death and resurrection" by their immersion in water, and thus to signify their communion in these realities.[106] Speaking to the candidates, Ryland said, "In this ordinance, you hope for that communion with him, of which infants are absolutely incapable."[107] This share in the benefits of Christ's vicarious work is *hoped for* in the ordinance, which is to say that the candidates are baptized in order to experience this spiritual death and resurrection, not simply as a testimony that it has been experienced. Similarly, "The persons about to be baptized, wish to be considered by all the spectators as hereby declaring their desire to die unto sin, and live unto righteousness."[108] Granted that some sort of spiritual reorientation has occurred in these persons to bring them to confess faith in Christ, there is nevertheless a further spiritual transformation which is anticipated through their baptism.

The same kind of dialectic which has been seen in other Baptists was present in Ryland, i.e., although the persons admitted to baptism must make a credible confession of repentance and faith, and are thus evidently in a state of grace, the benefits of salvation are being sought via baptism. This paradox is rooted in the Calvinistic theology of the Particular Baptists which affirms: (1) that regeneration is a divine act which *precedes* (logically, not temporally) and empowers faith; (2) that faith, therefore, is a means by which salvation that is actual but invisible becomes visible and experiential; and (3) that baptism is the divinely-ordained event in which the initial confession of faith occurs, so that the effects of baptism are the effects of faith.

---

105 Ibid., 35.
106 Ibid., 36.
107 Ibid., 37.
108 Ibid.

The Historical Background 53

Summary

The most significant characteristics of the baptismal theology of 18th-century Baptists would include the following:

(1) The term *sacrament* was only occasionally used to describe baptism. This had never been a common term in Particular Baptist confessions, but it had been used freely in the writings of individual signatories of those confessions. However, in the writings surveyed in this chapter, *ordinance* was the consistent label for baptism and the Lord's Supper, and *sacrament* was never the author's choice (although the term appears in some quotations).

(2) Baptism was called a *sign* but very seldom a *seal*, contrary to the usage of major 17th-century authors. There were exceptions to this rule, e.g., Anne Dutton, but the absence of such references is striking.

(3) Baptists were in general preoccupied with questions about the subjects and mode of baptism, and there was very little thought given to questions about the sense in which baptism might be a means of grace. Whereas the earliest Baptists were primarily concerned with the subjects of baptism and secondarily (indeed, only at a later point in time) with the mode of baptism, the order was often reversed in 18th-century treatments. Many pages were devoted to studies of Greek lexicography, the history of baptismal practice, and the imagery of death-burial-resurrection, but very few pages to the divine side of baptism.

(4) Whenever the effects of baptism were discussed, there was a tendency to minimize divine action in the event. There was still a recognition that God's action in forgiving sins and bestowing the Holy Spirit is in *some* way mediated through baptism, but the scriptural texts which demand this recognition (e.g., Acts 2:38; 22:16; 1 Peter 3:21; Mark 16:16) tended to be interpreted in a modest and defensive way. Other biblical texts like John 3:5 and Titus 3:5, which were admitted as allusions to baptismal water by earlier Baptists, were often reinterpreted in a way that stripped them of any baptismal reference.

Analysis

There are some obvious differences between the 17th and 18th centuries when one examines Baptist attempts to state a theology of baptism. A gap ought not be turned into a chasm, but there are differences which demand some explanation. One of the difficulties involved in analyzing the differences is the fact that the 18th-century authors seldom quoted their Baptist predecessors or explicitly interacted with their literature; therefore, the reasons for any conceptual shift may not be clear. Why did Baptists seldom quote their Baptist ancestors? Part of the answer must lie in the common Baptist assumption that each Christian can discern the meaning of divine revelation by an inductive, direct approach to Scripture alone. Another part of the answer lies in the polemical nature of so much of the Baptist literature--it was an attempt to convince paedobaptists that the Baptist practice of baptism was in fact correct, and the appeal to Baptist literature was hardly an effective appeal to recognized authority. It would be far more effective to show that illustrious paedobaptists admitted, for example, that immersion was the typical mode of baptism for thirteen centuries, or that there was no explicit reference to infant baptism prior to Tertullian (who was himself against the practice). What follows here, then, is a somewhat tentative description of some theological factors that were at work in this developing tradition.

First of all, it would be a mistake to focus on the disuse of the term *sacrament*. The terms *sacrament* and *ordinance* were never mutually exclusive, nor were they regarded as contradictions. In 17th-century Baptist usage, *ordinance* was the broader term and denoted at least prayer and the ministry of the Word in addition to baptism and the Lord's Supper, while *sacrament* was the narrower term denoting only the last two. The term *ordinance* became the standard language of the Particular Baptist confessions, but for reasons that are not entirely clear, inasmuch as leaders in the writing of the confessions (e.g., Benjamin Keach) freely spoke of baptism as a sacrament of the gospel.

One possible reason for the use of *ordinance* may well be that it better captures the sense of being commanded by the Lord, while *sacrament* has more of an ecclesiastical tone. A recurring theme in Baptist literature was that baptism is a "positive institution," that disciples of Christ ultimately do it simply because the Lord has ordained it, and that it must be done in the way that he ordained.[109] The fact that church tradition authorizes it was virtually irrelevant for the Baptists.

This sense of baptism as a "positive institution" (i.e., a precept observed simply because God has commanded it) functioned as a powerful argument for the Baptist position. For example, both sides in the paedobaptist debate generally admitted that a strong case can be made for baptizing only

---

109 For an emphatic statement of this principle, see Booth, *Paedobaptism Examined*, Part I, Chapter I.

confessing believers if the argument is based simply on the explicit narratives of Scripture. The paedobaptist case was normally rooted in inferences drawn from scriptural principles. Baptists, on the other hand, declared that in the case of a positive institution, such inferences are inappropriate; the absence of an explicit basis for baptizing infants amounts to a prohibition of the practice.[110] Therefore, even for those Baptists who were comfortable with the term *sacrament*, there was much to be gained in theological debate by using the term *ordinance*.

Another possible reason was to avoid the need for continual clarification of the term *sacrament*, in the face of the diverse usage of the term by the various Christian traditions. The use of the weaker term, *ordinance*, would not carry connotations in quite the way that *sacrament* would, and thus would eliminate potential misunderstanding.

In the end, it must be noted that although the 18th-century writers did not use the term *sacrament*, there was no explicit rejection of the term. For that very reason, one ought not infer that the choice of other terms implies that the thought patterns are anti-sacramental. That shift appears to be true in some cases, but that judgment cannot be made on the basis of terminology alone.

Second, the retreat from the designation of baptism as a *seal* is as difficult to analyse as the retreat from *sacrament*. As noted above, the retreat was not complete, for there were still some writers like Anne Dutton who used the motif of sealing/assuring to describe the effects of baptism. The most probable explanation lies in the need for Particular Baptists to distinguish themselves from Presbyterians and Independents, both of whom used the term *seal* to describe the function of baptism. However, in the case of these other Calvinistic groups, the most popularly cherished use of the term related to the incorporation of infant children of church members into the "covenant people," and this was the crucial point at which the Baptists disagreed. The other factor at work here is the attempt of Baptists to go straight to the Bible, where they did not find baptism referred to as a seal.

It seems unfortunate, though, that this terminology dropped out of the common Baptist vocabulary, because it seems well-suited to describe the significance of baptism as the event in which "faith discovers itself" (to use Gill's phrase) and conversion to Christ is ratified. It should not have been difficult to argue that the idea of a *seal* is an apt description of baptism's

---

110 Benjamin Beddome, *Baptism: Extract from a Scriptural Exposition of the Baptist Catechism; by way of Question and Answer* (London: Whittingham and Rowland, 1813), 7.

function in the case of a confessing believer, and that the application of it to infants is problematic. Both the Lutheran concept of baptism as a "visible word" which evokes and strengthen's faith and the Calvinistic concept of baptism as a "seal" which ratifies both human faith and the divine gift of salvation can easily be related to the baptism of a confessing believer, but the application to infants who cannot confess faith appears to be forced. It is not clear why the Baptists did not affirm the terminology and claim to be its rightful users, as opposed to paedobaptists.. The way in which baptism functions according to Baptist theology, i.e., as a tangible confirmation of faith and what faith receives, is precisely what the term *seal* is all about. It is a fact that the term fell out of favour, but this does not prove that the concept was no longer active at a conceptual level.

Third, the retreat from a more clearly sacramental view of baptism was due more to neglect than to positive rejection of older ideas. Baptists were involved in vigorous debate about the mode and subjects of baptism, so that little energy was devoted to a positive development. It was increasingly true that Baptists knew more about what did not happen in the sprinkling of infants than they did about what does happen in the immersion of believers.

Fourth, the impact of High Calvinism was disastrous for the development of any serious baptismal theology. At a theoretical level, such a theology minimized the significance of human acts in general, and thus of baptism in particular. At a practical level, it minimized the practice of evangelism and thus reduced the level of baptismal activity in the churches, which would reduce the incentive to reflect on baptism at a theological level.

Fifth, there are probably several reasons why Baptists tended to minimize the effects of baptism when they did move beyond the issues of subjects and mode, but none of these reasons are compelling. (1) They wanted to avoid mechanistic views of baptism's efficacy that were associated with traditional Catholic theology. They were, after all, orthodox Protestants, and furthermore, they were part of a tradition which had concluded that the magisterial Reformation had not gone far enough in its reforms. Anything that looked like a move back toward Rome would be viewed with extreme suspicion. (2) Baptists were convinced that the more one talked about the necessity of baptism, the more one would be inclined to paedobaptism and "rantism"[111] (baptism by sprinkling, from the Greek ῥαντίζω). John Ryland's interpretation of history indicated that pouring or

---

111 This "rantism" is to be distinguished from the 17th-century antinomian movement in England whose adherents were known as Ranters.

sprinkling as a baptismal mode was first accepted in the third century in the case of sick persons, due to an excessive estimate of the necessity of baptism for salvation.[112] Furthermore, they argued that in the patristic era the same doctrine of necessity was the basis for the baptism of infants, since it was assumed that unbaptized infants could not be saved any more than unbaptized adults.[113] However one may assess their reading of the history of baptismal practice, it is not hard to see the logic of their inference. (3) They minimized the effects of baptism to refute the charge that they elevated baptism to a level of undue importance. They generally practised closed membership, i.e., they accepted as church members only those persons who were immersed as confessing believers; and many of them practised close communion, i.e., they welcomed to the Lord's Supper only immersed believers. The practice of close communion was not a denial of the salvation of the irregularly baptized, but it was easily interpreted in that way, thus exacerbating the tension that already existed due to the disagreement over the practice of baptism. Consequently, Baptists emphasized that baptism was not necessary for salvation in a way that muted their Calvinistic sacramental heritage.

On balance, it seems that it would have been more appropriate to articulate carefully the kind of Baptist sacramentalism taught by Baptists like Henry Lawrence and Benjamin Keach in the 17th century. In terms of the inner logic, the Baptist practice is more understandable if there is a relative necessity for the occurrence of confessional baptism. If the baptism of confessing believers is the normal means by which God seals the individual's personal, saving union with Christ, then to neglect it is cause for serious concern. If conversion is consciously completed apart from baptism, and baptism is reduced to sheer obedience and pure symbolism, then the narrow Baptist practice is indeed mystifying, especially in its close communion form.

The Nineteenth Century

The preceding material has indicated that for the first two centuries of their existence, Baptists had shaped their baptismal theology in the midst of controversy. Usually those controversies had been focused on either the subjects or the mode of baptism, and the question of the relationship between baptism and the various aspects of salvation had been addressed for

---

112 Ryland, *Candid Statement*, 10.
113 Booth, *Paedobaptism Examined*, Part II, Chapter III.

the most part only as it came up in discussions of paedobaptism. In the 19th century, it continued to be true that Baptists shaped their doctrine of baptism in the context of controversy, but in this case the controversy dealt explicitly with baptism as a means of saving grace. In the early part of the century, Anglo-Catholic sentiment within the Church of England was powerfully expressed through what is called the Oxford Movement or Tractarianism, a movement that began as a response to theological liberalism but rapidly became a defence of Catholic views within Anglicanism, including a strong statement of baptismal regeneration. Although it was in one sense an internal debate within the Church of England, it also set the agenda for theological discussion among the dissenting churches, as Roger Hayden, a contemporary British Baptist historian, notes:

> It is almost impossible to exaggerate the impact of the Anglo-Catholic Tractarian Movement in Nonconformist churches. The word "sacrament" now became totally unacceptable in Baptist circles.... Baptists, in this period, tended to give a higher priority to what the individual believer did than to God's action in baptism. Baptists regarded this ordinance as primarily a testimony to personal faith in Christ and a disciplined following of the example of Jesus.[114]

In his discussion of the developing theology of English Baptists of the 19th century, J. H. Y. Briggs, another contemporary British Baptist historian, says:

> The context for the debate soon became that heightened sacramentalism within the established church which mid-Victorian Baptists perceived to be the fruit of the Oxford Movement, with its accompanying secessions to Rome.[115]

Such a context would seem to be the ideal time for Baptists to state their theology of baptism as a means of grace in a way that was much more explicit than their earlier literature, which tended to address the sacramental

---

114 Roger Hayden, *English Baptist History and Heritage* (London: The Baptist Union of Great Britain, 1990), 100.
115 J. H. Y. Briggs, *The English Baptists of the Nineteenth Century* (London: The Baptist Historical Society, 1994), 46.

question only indirectly. It is true that the Baptist literature of this period spoke more directly about baptism in relation to spiritual rebirth, but it was usually written in *reaction* to Anglo-Catholicism, and this reactionary process tended to formulate baptismal theology in a reductionistically non-sacramental direction. J. R. C. Perkin, a former British Baptist and later president of Acadia University, has noted that there was during this period a "minority movement within the Baptist denomination which stood for a sacramental view over against the *nuda signa* doctrine of its contemporaries," but it was a definite minority and a "fluid body of opinion."[116] There was no confessional development during this period, but there were extended treatments of baptism by individual authors, and the rest of this chapter will survey some of the most influential of those.

Robert Hall, Jr. (1764-1831)

Hall was a second-generation Baptist pastor whose contribution to baptismal theology was somewhat indirect, in that it was developed in the context of the ongoing Baptist debate about the relationship between baptism and the Lord's Supper. As noted in the previous chapter, many Baptists held to "close (strict) communion" and thus admitted to the Lord's Supper only those who had been in their opinion validly baptized. Although this view was ably defended by Abraham Booth and was probably the majority view among Particular Baptists, there was never unanimity on the point. Hall entered the debate in 1815 with his book, *On Terms of Communion*, which responded to Booth and defended "open (free) communion," in which paedobaptist Christians were admitted to the communion table in Baptist churches. This evoked a response from Joseph Kinghorn (1766-1832) in his *Baptism a Term of Communion at the Lord's Supper* (1816), which Hall countered with *A Reply to the Revd Joseph Kinghorn, being a Further Vindication of Free Communion* (1818). Several years later Kinghorn concluded the dialogue with *A Defence of Baptism a Term of Communion in Answer to the Revd Robert Hall's Reply* (1840). This debate was not explicitly about the efficacy of baptism, since debaters on both sides of the question admitted that paedobaptist believers were genuine recipients of God's saving grace, but Hall did address the sacramental question at various points in this literature.

There was an enormous amount of ambivalence in Hall's references to

---

116 J. R. C. Perkin, "Baptism in Nonconformist Theology, 1820-1920, with special reference to the Baptists" (D.Phil. thesis, University of Oxford, 1955), 10.

the efficacy of baptism. On the one hand, he interpreted Christian baptism within the New Testament as a rite with great significance and momentous effects. The context in which this occurred was his assertion of a fundamental distinction between John's baptism and the baptism instituted by Christ. One of the standard arguments for strict communion was the temporal priority of baptism relative to the Lord's Supper, given that John and Christ's disciples were baptizing prior to the institution of the Lord's Supper, which occurred only at the end of the earthly ministry of Jesus. But if Christian baptism as expressed in the apostolic commission of Matthew 28 was something radically new and not simply the continuation of John's baptism, then the temporal order of the institution of the sacraments is reversed. Hall defended the discontinuity between the two baptisms by asserting the vastly superior effects of Christian baptism:

> The baptism instituted by our Lord is in Scripture distinguished from that of the forerunner by the *superior effects* with which it was accompanied; so that, instead of being confounded they are contrasted in the sacred historians. . . . The rite administered by John was a mere immersion in water, unaccompanied with that effusion of the Spirit, that redundant supply of supernatural gifts and graces which distinguished the subjects of the Christian institute.[117]

Concerning the blessings inherent in the new covenant, and referring to the frequently-quoted promise of Peter in Acts 2:38, he wrote:

> The effusion of the Spirit, indeed, in the multifarious forms of his miraculous and sanctifying operation, may be considered as equivalent to them all; and this, we are distinctly told, was not given (save in a very scanty manner) during our Lord's abode upon earth, because he was not yet glorified. . . .[Hall describes the bestowal of the Spirit at Pentecost.] . . . In the subsequent history, we perceive that this gift was, on all ordinary occasions, conferred in connexion with baptism.[118]

---

117 Robert Hall, *On Terms of Communion, with a Particular View to the Case of the Baptists and Paedobaptists*, in *The Works of Robert Hall, A.M.*, ed. Olinthus Gregory (London: Henry G. Bohn, 1843), 1:297.
118 Ibid., 1:298.

The Historical Background

This relationship between baptism and the gift of the Holy Spirit is an indication that, "The baptism of the Holy Ghost, or the copious effusion of spiritual influences, in which primitive Christians were, so to speak, immersed, was appointed to follow the sacramental use of water, under the Christian economy."[119]

This looks like a very high view of the efficacy of baptism: it is the means by which one receives the Holy Spirit, the supreme benefit of the new covenant; baptism in water in the name of Christ is the event in which baptism in the Spirit occurs; indeed, baptism is necessary for salvation, because through apostolic teaching it was understood that a refusal to be baptized was a refusal to acknowledge Jesus as Lord and Christ, and thus a rejection of saving grace.[120]

However, this was only one aspect of Hall's baptismal theology. There was also a recurring theme which minimized the place of baptism as a means of grace and rejected the developments within the Catholic tradition: He wrote:

> It is well known that from a very early period the most extravagant notions prevailed in the Church with respect to the efficacy of baptism, and its absolute necessity in order to attain salvation. The descent of the human mind from the spirit to the letter, from what is vital and intellectual to what is ritual and external in religion, is the true source of idolatry and superstition in all the multifarious forms they have assumed; and as it began early to corrupt the religion of nature, or, more properly, of patriarchal tradition, so it soon obscured the lustre, and destroyed the simplicity of the Christian institute.[121]

There are, of course, biblical texts which suggest a high view of baptismal efficacy, some of which Hall himself had used to support his argument, but in his opinion these texts had been misused in the Catholic tradition:

> From an erroneous interpretation of the figurative language of a few passages in Scripture, in which the sign is identified with the thing signified, very similar to the mistake which afterward led to transubstantiation, it was universally supposed that baptism was

---

119 Ibid.
120 Ibid., 1:310-311.
121 Ibid., 1:317.

invariably accompanied with a supernatural effect, which totally changed the state and character of the candidate, and constituted him a child of God and an heir of the kingdom of heaven. Hence it was almost constantly denoted by the terms *illumination, regeneration,* and others, expressive of the highest operations of the Spirit; and as it was believed to obtain the plenary remission of all past sins, it was often, in order to ensure that benefit, purposely deferred to the latest period of life.[122]

Hall rejected such a "superstitious" view of baptism, asserting that Baptists, of all people, were unwilling to posit this kind of connection between baptism and regeneration:

By orthodox Christians it is uniformly maintained that union to Christ is formed by faith, and as the Baptists are distinguished by demanding a profession of it at baptism, they at least are precluded from asserting that rite to have any concern in effecting the spiritual alliance in question. In their judgment at least, since faith precedes the application of water, the only means of union are possessed by the abetters of infant-sprinkling equally with themselves; who are therefore equally of the "body of Christ, and members in particular."[123]

The tension between what he asserted to be the purpose of baptism "under the Christian economy" and what he later said about the relative insignificance of baptism is evident, and a resolution of this tension is not obvious. Apparently Hall sought to resolve this tension by limiting the high view of baptismal efficacy to the apostolic age. For example, when commenting on the Mark 16 account of the promise of miraculous gifts, he said that such "supernatural endowments regularly accompanied the imposition of the hands of the apostles on primitive converts, immediately subsequent to their baptism."[124] The account in Acts 8 of the Samaritans who believed the gospel and were baptized, but did not receive the gift of the Spirit until a later time, conflicts with other accounts of the gift of the Spirit in the same book, and interpreters have suggested various reasons for this difference. Hall suggested that the reason is that, "The apostles, to

---

122 Ibid., 1:318.
123 Ibid., 1:332.
124 Ibid., 1:298.

whom alone the power of conferring it belonged, were not present."[125] The result of all this was to posit a major distinction between the experience of baptism in the apostolic age and the experience of baptism in the present. Although this may have helped Hall to affirm the genuine Christian experience of his paedobaptist contemporaries, it created huge problems for his use of Scripture as a source for a doctrine of baptism. The New Testament assertions about faith, baptism, and spiritual rebirth were, after all, written during the apostolic age when baptism was, by his own admission, functioning as a means of God's bestowal of the blessings of the new covenant. The apostolic teaching about faith as the means of union with Christ was being communicated at the same time that baptism was mediating the experience of salvation, and indeed was being communicated by the very persons who had power to convey these blessings in connection with baptism. How is it, then, that the apostolic teaching about faith serves to minimize the role of baptism? If Acts and the apostolic epistles do not give us a Christian doctrine of baptism which is valid for the whole inter-advent age, then where would we get such a doctrine? It does not appear that Hall had the answers to these questions.

There was much in Hall's theology which pointed to a high view of baptism as a means of grace: he freely called it a *sacrament*, even though this term had fallen into relative disuse among his fellow Baptists; he also described the Lord's Supper in sacramental terms along the lines of a "spiritual presence" of Christ, as opposed to the purely memorialistic view associated with Zwingli;[126] this sacramentalism seemed to be present in his contrast between John's baptism (which effected none of the benefits of salvation) and Christian baptism (which effects what John promised). Nevertheless, in his attempt to affirm the presence of saving grace in paedobaptist Christians and their consequent right to communion at the Lord's Table in Baptist churches, he denied that the apostolic practice and doctrine of baptism are paradigmatic for the entire inter-advent age.

It would seem that a more appropriate solution can be found. This tension seems capable of resolution, if one assumes that baptism is the *normal*, though not invariable, means by which union with Christ is experientially sealed, and that faith alone is the *indispensable* instrument of this saving union. Such an approach might properly defend the laudable extension of communion at the Lord's Supper to all who give evidence of their union with Christ by obeying the commands of Christ as they

---

125 Ibid., 1:385.
126 Ibid., 1:313.

understand them, without grounding the defence in an incoherent baptismal theology.

Alexander Carson (1779-1844)

Carson was initially an Irish Presbyterian minister, who went through a change of mind about biblical teaching on church government and thus became an Independent (Congregationalist). Later he experienced another profound change of mind, this time on the subject of baptism, which led to his becoming a Baptist, and eventually an apologist for Baptist views. His *Baptism in its Mode and Subjects*, an influential polemic, was painstakingly detailed in its arguments about mode and subjects, but it devoted little space to the question of baptism as a means of grace. What he did say on the topic is stated indirectly in a brief section defending the baptism of believers only.

In that section, Carson accepted as allusions to baptism some passages which, due to their sacramental character, had been interpreted by other Baptists as having no reference to baptism at all. In this category would be John 3:5; Titus 3:5; Ephesians 5:26; and 1 Corinthians 12:13. However, he argued that each of the New Testament allusions to baptism assumes that the candidate has experienced the benefits of salvation *prior to* baptism. His summary statement was this:

> In general, it is quite apparent that baptism is not only a figure of the washing away of sin, but that it is always supposed that the sins of those who are baptized are already washed away. Now this can be supposed of none but believers. Infants dying in infancy, if saved, have their sins washed away. But millions of persons who have their sins washed away, have not had them washed away in infancy. With respect to such, then, baptism, that supposes sins already washed away, could have no proper application in their infancy.[127]

John 3:5 was accepted as a baptismal allusion, but he asserted that in this text, "The ordinance exhibits the baptized person as at the time born again."[128] Whether this meant that the person was born again in connection with baptism or was in a reborn condition at the time of baptism because of

---

127 Alexander Carson, *Baptism in its Mode and Subjects*, 5th ed. (Philadelphia: American Baptist Publication Society, 1860), 211.
128 Ibid.

a *previous* rebirth is not clear, but clarification came through his treatment of Titus 3:5. He accepted the idea that baptism is the "bath of regeneration," but also said that, "The baptized person . . . is supposed to be already born, or renewed by the Spirit."[129] With regard to Acts 22:16, he said, "Here we see baptism figuratively washes away sins, and supposes that they are previously truly washed away."[130] Concerning 1 Corinthians 12:13 he wrote, "They who are baptized are supposed already to belong to the body of Christ; and for this reason they are baptized into it."[131]

This can hardly be seen as anything other than a superficial and tendentious reading of these biblical texts. Although it may be possible to interpret these texts in a non-sacramental manner, this is anything but the obvious conclusion that he suggested. It looks as if these texts are saying that baptism is instrumental in the experience of salvation, i.e., that spiritual rebirth, cleansing from sin, and union with Christ and his church are effects of baptism. That this is the apparent meaning of the texts is evident from the common Baptist attempt to evade this conclusion by interpreting these passages in a non-baptismal sense.

The point that Carson was trying to make is that the New Testament uniformly assumes that those who have been baptized have been spiritually reborn through union with Christ, an assumption that could not be made about infants, and therefore, infant baptism must not have been the apostolic practice. This argument is meaningful and cogent as it stands, but Carson went beyond it to say not simply that those who are baptized are assumed to be saved, but also that they are assumed to have been saved *prior to* baptism. To say that baptism and salvation are assumed to be coextensive is not to specify the exact temporal or logical relationship between the two.

Charles Stovel (1799-1883)

Stovel was a pastor in various churches in England and was a respected denominational leader, twice serving one-year terms as president of the Baptist Union. In 1843 he responded to Tractarianism with a series of lectures which were published as *The Baptismal Regeneration Controversy Considered*, which is one of the most careful and thorough responses from a Baptist perspective.

Stovel's book was written against the background of Tractarianism and

---

129 Ibid.
130 Ibid., 212.
131 Ibid.

a renewed commitment to a high doctrine of baptismal regeneration, but his concern was to refute every form of baptismal theology which affirms that a spiritual gift is conferred through baptism, Tractarianism being just the most conspicuous example at that time. As examples of the kind of doctrine which he rejected, he articulated the teaching of the Canons of Trent, the Prayer Book and Thirty-Nine Articles of the Church of England, the Lutheran confessions, and the Westminster Confession of Faith.[132] The attack on the traditional Roman Catholic doctrine of conveyance of grace *ex opere operato* is understandable, as is his treatment of the Anglican tradition, given that he considered the Tractarians "to be the most full and candid expositors of the doctrines of the Church of England."[133] The language of baptismal regeneration is deeply rooted in Lutheran theology as well, although the emphasis on faith in connection with the "visible word" of baptism distinguishes it from the Tridentine theology. The most surprising aspect of Stovel's approach was his attack on the Westminster Assembly at this point; he did not simply equate it with other doctrines of baptismal regeneration, but he did argue that at the core there is a fundamental point of equivalence which must be rejected. He wrote:

> Baptismal Regeneration is only one form in which the error is stated. Where these words are rejected "with *abhorrence*," benefits are ascribed to Infant Baptism, which are quite unscriptural, and the supposition of which, have almost the same moral effect upon mankind. With some, it is "a seal of the covenant," With others, it is an "introduction into the visible Church." Some contend that "grace" is always communicated in Baptism; others, that it is not communicated invariably, but only sometimes. Some will have it to be a "regeneration;" others will not admit that term. All, however, urge the observance of this rite as a duty on parents, and plead that the infant baptized has a claim to the privilege.[134]

With regard to the teaching expressed in the Westminster Confession and Catechisms, he wrote:

> It is quite plain . . . that their whole discussion with the

---

132 Charles Stovel, *The Baptismal Regeneration Controversy Considered* (London: Houlston & Stoneman, and Dyer & Co., 1843), 72-80.
133 Ibid., 74.
134 Ibid., 17.

Episcopalians on this statement, must turn on the questions respecting an *invariable* regeneration in Baptism, and the right of others to that sacrament, besides the children of Christians. Thus much, also, ought, in justice to be said upon the case, that the question of holding or rejecting the error of baptismal grace, was never submitted to the Episcopalians in that Conference. Other terms were preferred to that of "regeneration," but the idea was retained by the objectors.[135]

On the surface, then, Stovel seemed to be resolutely non-sacramental and opposed to any thought of being the beneficiary of divine action in baptism. However, this statement that occurred early in his book must be carefully assessed in light of later statements in the same book. The crucial qualifier of this initial rhetoric is the fact that his basic target was the idea of baptismal benefit *apart from faith in the recipient*, whether in the case of infants or adults.

In his description of the varieties of baptismal regeneration doctrine quoted above, he explicitly related this to parental duty to have their infant children baptized. He was clearly against any idea of grace conveyed through baptism *per se* which is performed on unsuspecting infants, but this is not equivalent to saying that no benefit can be obtained in confessional baptism, as he noted:

> ... you will be pleased to distinguish very carefully between the *moral* effect which this Divine institution may have, when received by a believer as his own act, from the effect which is here assigned to it as a vicarious act, performed not by the wish or will of the infant, but by some one else on his behalf. In the former case, like all other acts of obedience, it may strengthen the habit of obeying. It may solemnize his engagement, as in the case of matrimony; and it may become a witness for God to all beholders.[136]

Admittedly, this statement only allowed for a benefit in baptism which is like the benefit of any act of obedience, and it did not posit any directly *divine* action in the event. That evidence will appear below.

Stovel refuted paedobaptism by both Scripture and experience. He utilized the standard Baptist apologetic to demonstrate that the patterns of

---

135 Ibid., 76-77.
136 Ibid., 18.

the New Testament consistently connect baptism to a confession of repentance and faith by the persons baptized. What is surprising is the extent to which he relied on experience in his argument. In his words:

> But though the testimony of Scripture is necessary to complete the evidence, I may yet observe here, that this is by no means the only source of evidence to which you may appeal. Do you not see, from the very nature of the case itself, that it must be *necessarily* determined by *experience*? . . . If, therefore, grace, or the spiritual gift of baptism, flow through the words or fingers of a priest, by baptism, to the child baptized; that benefit must be seen in the result. . . .--and what, after all, is the result? I answer, the experience of all nations and of all ages pronounces it a delusion, and nothing more.[137]

The experiential data invoked at this point would be obvious: baptized persons are in some cases murderers, prostitutes, thieves, and other kinds of perverse sinners. However, this argument is only valid if one assumes that regeneration invariably leads to perseverance in godly living, and although this assumption is held by Calvinistic Baptists, it would not be shared by many of the Anglicans to whom he is responding, and certainly not by Roman Catholics who would emphasize the necessity of cooperation with the grace infused in baptism.

Stovel admitted that the refutation of infant baptism is not the end of the argument. There is still the question of whether spiritual benefits are conveyed to adults in baptism. On this question also his answer was negative, but it is clear that what he was negating is the idea that baptism *in itself* is capable of conveying spiritual benefit. In his words he was attacking "promiscuous" baptism of adults, i.e., the baptism of every adult who will accept it, apart from expression of personal commitment to Christ, in the hope that grace will be imparted which will ultimately bring the person to conversion. He responded to this by summarizing the assumptions which the New Testament authors make about baptized persons:

> Hence, there can be no doubt, that these were recognized as *converted persons*. The change of heart necessary to salvation is, therefore, recognized to have taken place in them all. This is a simple, and an indisputable fact. The advocates of modern

---

137 Ibid., 36-37.

Baptismal Regeneration, however, say, that there is *no conversion in baptism*. . . . In this they are quite right. There is no such thing as conversion by Baptism spoken of in Scripture. These two facts decide our case; for, if there be no conversion by Baptism, or *in* baptism, and yet every person has been converted when baptized; then, every baptized person must have been converted *before* Baptism; and, the evidence on which these apostolical affirmations are made, must have been required and taken before the candidate was admitted to the sacrament of baptism; and, therefore, instead of supporting Baptismal Regeneration, these passages condemn the practice of *promiscuous* Baptism altogether.[138]

The argument, then, is this: In the New Testament, baptized persons are assumed to be converted persons; conversion does not happen in baptism; therefore, conversion must be complete prior to baptism. Stovel shared the second premise with his opponents and sought to turn it against them, but there was no necessity for him to accept this premise, and in fact it will be argued below that he did not in reality accept it. His real concern at this point was to reject the baptism of persons who make no confession of personal conversion, in the hope that baptism may lead to their conversion at some future point--in his words, the idea "that hypocrisy perpetrated in this Sacramental act is a step towards conversion."[139] But all that is required for this argument is the first premise, i.e., that conversion does not follow baptism. This could mean either that conversion is assumed to be complete prior to baptism (as Stovel stated it above) or that conversion is assumed to be completed in baptism (as he seems to have said later in the book). The assumption that baptized persons are converted persons still allows for some kind of work of grace in conversion-baptism, i.e., a divine work done in the baptismal event which brings the individual into the experience of saving union with Christ (as opposed to simply offering the hope of such salvation in the future).

As Stovel articulated his own theology of baptism, he conceptualized it in a way that would have to be called sacramental. At the level of terminology he did repeatedly refer to the "sacrament of baptism," but admittedly this does not settle the question at the conceptual level. However, his explanation of conversion-baptism did indicate that the person being baptized is entering into the benefits of salvation, not bearing witness

---

138 Ibid., 113.
139 Ibid., 115.

to a consciously completed union with Christ as a prior reality. For example, he interpreted the idea of being "baptized into Christ" in Galatians 3:27 in this way:

> The phrase *"into Christ"* contains an ellipsis to be supplied by a verb of motion; as in Galatians iii.27. "As many of you as *[entering]* into Christ received Baptism, have put on Christ." This distinguished the Baptism of Christ from all others. . . . But the Christian Baptism, was an immersion, received by persons *entering into Christ*.[140]

The most significant part of Stovel's baptismal theology was his treatment of John 3:5 and the idea of rebirth through baptism. At the heart of this theology was his distinction between *regeneration* and *rebirth*, the former denoting the invisible work of the Holy Spirit and the latter denoting the visible work of bringing new spiritual life to the level of conscious experience. He wrote:

> By some it has been disputed whether the case of Nicodemus, related in John iii. 1-12, refers to the sacrament of Baptism at all; but, in my opinion, the objection to this view of the passage cannot be supported. Admitting, therefore, that it does refer to Baptism, one or two points of great moment are determined by it. . . . There are, therefore, we admit, two agencies employed in that new birth; the water and the Spirit. By these, a converted man begins life anew. Not by water without the Spirit, nor by the Spirit without the water; but by the water and the Spirit. The visible action of the water, or rather of the whole sacrament, of which it becomes the instrument, is seen in the Church; where, as an authorized act of discipline, it declares the character, and seals both the privilege and obligation of every believer in the family of God. The action of the Spirit takes place in the mind and heart; and, leading and sustaining the believer, reveals itself in the effects produced upon the devoted convert. Each is essential to the support of that new life, into which a believing sinner rises and enters from the moment of his Baptism. If he seek salvation by the Baptism, without conversion to God: he acts the hypocrite, and the ceremony is reduced to a mere heathenish form. If, knowingly, he seek salvation and Church

---

140 Ibid., 114.

fellowship in the neglect of Baptism, he dispenses with the ordinance of Christ, and is reminded, that faith without works is dead.[141]

He later elaborated as follows:

> To be *born* and to be *begotten*, do not mean the same thing; . . . By *Generation*, a creature is *made to be*; and, by birth, that creature is *brought forth* into the world, to be recognized as a being, to be nourished with tenderness, and to become a partaker in the privileges and responsibilities of *human society*. So also by *Regeneration*, a new creature is *made to be*; and, in *being born again*, that new creature is *brought forth* into the Church; to be received with affection, nourished with care, and to be a partaker in all the privileges and responsibilities of *Christian society*. By his *Regeneration*, a sinner passes from darkness to light, and from the power of Satan unto God; but, by his *new birth*, he passes into recognized existence, as one who, through the Spirit which hath quickened him, aspires to the service and fellowship of his Saviour, and, is destined to overcome the world, through the guidance, and help of the Saviour to whom he is committed.[142]

This distinction between regeneration and rebirth may or may not be an accurate way to describe the use of the terms in Scripture, but it does show that in the end Stovel's theology did include the reception of spiritual benefit through conversion-baptism. In baptism, the awakened sinner seeks salvation, and in that event the Spirit who has given new life in embryo elevates that life to the level of conscious and recognized experience.

Therefore, in the end, Stovel's view of baptism was sacramental, both verbally and conceptually.[143] It was fundamentally equivalent to the Westminster understanding of baptism as a seal of union with Christ, as applied to confessing believers. His work was a potent reminder that the Baptist concern about baptismal grace is for the most part a concern about infant baptism, and certainly about the automatic bestowal of grace through the ritual apart from any faith-response on the part of the subject. He was

---

141 Ibid., 127.
142 Ibid., 129.
143 Perkin failed to see Stovel in this way, because he ignored Stovel's distinction between regeneration and rebirth, and he failed to note that what Stovel denied was that baptism is a means of grace *apart from faith in the baptizand*. See Perkin, "Baptism," 152-155.

also an example of the significance of the Tractarian movement and the extent to which 19th-century Baptist rhetoric was a reaction to Anglo-Catholic thought. If the discussion were limited to a consideration of what happens in the baptism of a repentant believer, then the rhetoric would be quite different, affirming the sacramental sense which is often present in spite of protests to the contrary.

Baptist W. Noel (1798-1873)

When Charles Stovel was arguing in 1843 that the Anglo-Catholics were the trustworthy interpreters of the official Anglican statements on baptism, an evangelical Anglican named Baptist Noel was preaching an extended series of sermons on regeneration, two of which argued that baptismal regeneration was *not* the doctrine of the Church of England.[144] By 1849, Noel had adopted Baptist views and resigned from his ministry in the Establishment, and shortly afterward he published his *Essay on Christian Baptism*, which articulated his new convictions.

Although Noel had given up his paedobaptist views, the evidence indicates that he retained his evangelical sacramentalism as applied to confessing believers.[145] This sacramentalism views baptism as a "seal of regeneration" in that it is the confession of faith which initiates the individual into the experience of salvation. It is a dialectical theology which seeks to affirm constantly both (1) that spiritual regeneration is a direct work of God which is not dependent on baptism, and (2) that baptism is the normal, divinely-ordained means by which spiritual regeneration is experientially realized.

On the one hand, Noel emphasized that the benefits of salvation are prior to baptism. For example:

All enlightened persons own the necessity of a great moral change to be effected by the Spirit of God; but why is baptism a necessary adjunct? The moral change is not effected by baptism, but before

---

144 Baptist W. Noel, *Sermons on Regeneration, with Especial Reference to the Doctrine of Baptismal Regeneration*, 2nd ed. (London: "The Pulpit" Office, n.d.). Sermons VII and VIII (72-134) argue that the Anglican formularies actually teach that whatever regeneration means, it actually precedes baptism.

145 Perkin argued that this is one way in which "Noel was always an Anglican." See Perkin, "Baptism," 333.

The Historical Background

it, as we know from Scripture and from indubitable facts.[146]

With regard to the idea of regeneration, he wrote:

> But if baptism be the sign of regeneration, an unregenerate person ought not to be baptized. If the rite is a public manifestation of spiritual life, it should be withheld from those who afford no tokens of that life. . . .Baptism can not be the baptism of regeneration except with respect to those who are previously regenerate; and as Christian baptism is the baptism of regeneration, according to the text, regenerate believers alone ought to be baptized.[147]

In a prayer of "baptismal self-dedication to God," he said:

> On the other hand, being so blessed and favored, I, as a redeemed and pardoned transgressor, desire to make a public profession of faith in thee, and publicly to dedicate myself to thy service, according to Christ's appointment, by immersion. Before which public act, I do now, therefore, first dedicate myself to thee in secret.[148]

On the other hand, there was a recurring theme in his book to the effect that baptism is an entrance into the benefits of salvation, the event in which the sinner turns to God through Christ for forgiveness and transformation. In explaining spiritual rebirth, he echoed the thoughts of Stovel:

> And when a person who has received spiritual life manifests it by confessing Christ before men by immersion, then he is born of water and of the Spirit--his new birth is complete. . . . baptism is the profession of faith, the public confession of Christ, without which confession there is no true faith and no salvation.[149]

Commenting on Peter's response to his Jewish audience at Pentecost, he said:

---

146 Baptist W. Noel, *Essay on Christian Baptism* (New York: Harper & Brothers, 1850), 97.
147 Ibid., 114.
148 Ibid., 303.
149 Ibid., 97.

They were not to expect the remission of their sins through baptism without previous repentance, nor through repentance without baptism, but through repentance and baptism. . . .It is not enough to believe in Christ, but we must also profess our Christianity, which it is the will of Christ that we should do by baptism. He who does these things is assured of the remission of his sins. Since, then, baptism is thus necessary to remission of sins, and is so closely connected with it as no mere acts of obedience ever are, baptism must be a profession of faith, and none but believers ought to be baptized.[150]

This description of baptism as "necessary" to the forgiveness of sins goes far beyond the normal Baptist sense of baptism as a primary moral obligation, and Noel appears to be the only Baptist of his era to put it in these terms.[151] Concerning the allusion to the "washing of regeneration" in Titus 3:5, he wrote:

Baptism is the washing of regeneration, or the washing which is the manifestation and completion of regeneration. By these two things, the washing and the renewing, the spiritual renovation and the baptism which manifests it, God saves his people.[152]

The intent of the subject in baptism was expressed thus:

By faith, expressed in baptism, each sincere convert confesses Christ so as to wash away his sins (Acts, xxii.,16), to receive pardon (Acts, ii.,38), to put on the robe of Christ's righteousness (Gal.,iii.,27), and to secure salvation, 1 Pet.,iii.,21. And as he confesses Christ, he will be confessed by Christ at the last day, Matt.,x.,32; Rom.,x.8-10.[153]

In his baptismal prayer he said:

Repenting of all my sins, and being about to be baptized in token of that repentance, may I have the assurance that my sins are

---

150 Ibid., 101-102.
151 Perkin, "Baptism," 329.
152 Ibid., 113.
153 Ibid., 265.

remitted, and be sealed with the Holy Spirit of promise.[154]

Both aspects of this paradox, God's saving work as both *assumed by* and *sought in* the act of Christian baptism, were present in his summary of the biblical teaching concerning the nature and effects of baptism:

> Baptism is a consecration to the Triune God, . . . and especially to Christ. . . . It is a seeking after God with a good conscience. . . . It must be preceded by true repentance. . . . It is the sign, manifestation, and completion of regeneration. . . . It is a death unto sin and a new life of holiness. . . . Those rightly baptized are in Christ. . . . Those rightly baptized have put on Christ. . . . True baptism secures pardon. . . . True baptism secures the gift of the Spirit. . . . Baptism is generally necessary to salvation. . . . True baptism saves.[155]

The emphasis which Noel gave to the idea that regeneration is prior to baptism was set in the context of his critique of paedobaptism, and was not intended to argue that saving union with Christ is completed at the experiential level apart from baptism. Indeed, he argued that baptism manifests and *completes* regeneration. Baptism mediates, for him, both the experience of forgiveness and the reception of the Holy Spirit as an empowering presence. The concept of baptism as the "seal of regeneration" conceptualizes the dialectic of biblical language about baptism, and the use of this concept locates Noel in the tradition of Calvinistic sacramentalism. It is a lamentable fact that Baptists have tended to devote their energy to a refutation of the application of this concept of sealing to infants, rather than an articulation of its suitability to describe conversion-baptism as seen in the New Testament.

John Howard Hinton (1791-1873)

Hinton was a well-educated (M.A., Edinburgh) Baptist pastor and denominational leader up to his retirement in 1868. He was a prolific author, whose seven volumes of collected works include literature on historical topics (including a history of the U.S.A.) as well as theological matters. His literary contribution to the baptismal theology debate is found

---

154 Ibid., 307.
155 Ibid., 118.

in *The Ultimatum*, a lecture given in 1850 at his church, Devonshire Square Chapel in London. In 1850 the Church of England was three years into a four-year debate known as "the Gorham case."[156] The Bishop of Exeter had refused to confirm the appointment of George Gorham, an evangelical Anglican, to funded parish ministry in Devon, because Gorham did not believe in baptismal regeneration. Ultimately the case was decided by the Judicial Committee of the Privy Council in favour of Gorham, accepting the propriety of his views as one possible reading of the Anglican formularies. Hinton used the occasion not to answer the question for the Anglicans (in fact, he believed that the Anglican statements were incapable of harmonization),[157] but to state his own views on the doctrinal issue.

Hinton expressed his view in what would have to be considered a radically non-sacramental way:

> On this ground, then, I take up the assertion that baptism is the means of conferring spiritual benefits. I totally dissent from this view. I affirm, in the most unqualified terms, that baptism is not the means of conferring any spiritual blessings whatever, and my aim this evening will be to bring forward the scriptural arguments in support of this affirmation.[158]

His basic biblical argument was a long list of texts which speak of repentance and/or faith as the instrument(s) by which the benefits of salvation are bestowed. These were seen as both necessary and sufficient, since in many places they are described as effective means of receiving salvation apart from any reference to baptism. A primary example would be the conversion of Cornelius and his household in Acts 10, in which the Holy Spirit is poured out on the members of the household while they are listening to Peter's preaching, and it is only after this manifest display of their salvation that they are baptized in water.[159] Hinton summarized:

> Now from the fact thus copiously established, that spiritual benefits are habitually spoken of in the New Testament as obtained by

---

156 For a brief survey of the Gorham case and its significance for Victorian evangelicalism, see David Bebbington, *Evangelicalism in Modern Britain* (Grand Rapids: Baker Book House, 1992), 9, 148.
157 John Howard Hinton, "The Ultimatum," in *The Theological Works of the Rev. John Howard Hinton, M.A.* (London: Houlston & Wright, 1865), 465.
158 Ibid., 466.
159 Ibid., 466-468.

The Historical Background

repentance towards God and faith in our Lord Jesus Christ, it is surely natural and just to infer that baptism is not one of the terms of their possession. Here is a proper and sufficient instrumentality fully declared. And, if baptism really be necessary to the enjoyment of spiritual benefits, then is there a great deal in this language that is incorrect and deceptive. The world thus instructed could hardly fail to have been led astray.[160]

Hinton recognized, of course, that his opponents could point to a list of biblical texts which seem to attribute spiritual efficacy to baptism. Several of those texts are references to water or washing which have traditionally been taken as allusions to baptism, although the reference is not explicit. His general treatment of these was as follows:

> Nothing more is to be found in these passages than the use of a very familiar and a very expressive metaphor, by which the "washing with water" is made representative of "sanctification by the word," and the "renewing of the Holy Ghost." That baptism is intended is a purely gratuitous assumption, without evidence, and without probability.[161]

Historically, the most prominent of the above texts has been the saying of Jesus in John 3:5, and Hinton's treatment of this text demonstrated why he was unwilling to admit a baptismal reference in these places:

> It is gratuitously assumed that this phrase, being "born of water," refers to baptism. I entertain a totally different view, but it would lead me too far from my immediate subject to enter into a full exposition; it will be sufficient for my present design to show that the text cannot refer to baptism. . . . The argument I employ for this purpose is short and simple. It is this, that you cannot interpret this passage of baptism without involving yourself in insuperable difficulties. For it is manifest that the language employed by our Lord is absolute, and that it stablishes a principle universal, and without exception. . . . It is not doing justice to these words (understanding them of baptism) to say (in the language of the Church of England) that they make baptism "*generally* necessary to

---

160 Ibid., 468-469.
161 Ibid., 471.

salvation." They make it *absolutely* necessary.[162]

There is, of course, another list of texts which refer explicitly to baptism in connection with various spiritual benefits, but Hinton took up the challenge there as well. His foundational assumption in approaching such texts was "that all such passages must be ruled by those which I have already quoted,"[163] i.e., the texts about repentance and/or faith with no reference to baptism. The apostolic commission texts (Matthew 28 and Mark 16) were set aside by pointing out that each indicates that faith precedes baptism, and thus the benefits associated with faith (salvation in all its aspects) precede baptism.[164] Acts 22:16 was handled by interpreting the command to Saul to "wash away your sins" as a demand that he live a holy life,[165] and 1 Peter 3:21 was categorized as pure metaphor.[166] The most troublesome text is Acts 2:38, which he treated thus:

> The structure of the passage clearly requires the clauses to be placed in the connexion following:--"Repent every one of you for the remission of sins, and be baptized in the name of Jesus Christ." The remission of sins is evangelically connected with repentance; a profession of repentance is required as preceding baptism. The latter is merely a test of sincerity, an act of obedience then becoming obligatory, not a term of forgiveness. . . .Upon the latter part of this passage an attempt has been made to found the doctrine that the Holy Spirit is imparted in baptism. This is clearly unsustained, however, inasmuch as the promised communication of the Spirit, whatever may be its nature, was to be after baptism, and not in it. . . . But, further, it is evident from the context that the apostle is not here speaking of the regenerating or sanctifying influence of the Spirit: first, because this must be presupposed in the exercise of repentance, which preceded baptism, and secondly, because an influence of a different kind is expressly named. . . . for by the laying on of the apostles' hands after baptism the supernatural gifts of the Spirit were conferred.[167]

---

162 Ibid., 469.
163 Ibid., 471.
164 Ibid., 472.
165 Ibid., 473.
166 Ibid.
167 Ibid., 473-474.

Hinton brought his lecture to a conclusion by arguing that if baptism is interpreted as a means of grace, then the essence of Christian proclamation is radically altered. The biblical picture is that the gospel is proclaimed to sinful humans on the assumption that they are objects of God's wrath and in need of deliverance from that condition. On the other hand:

> Let it be supposed that there is introduced into the Gospel system the element of baptismal regeneration, or the idea that baptism has an efficacy to confer spiritual benefits, and the whole scene is changed. Now the entire community is to be addressed from the first in language totally different. Instead of being solemnly told that they are sinners, and warned of the wrath to come, they must be assured that in their baptism they were justified, and brought graciously by God into his family, while at the same time that most blessed change, spiritual regeneration, took place upon them.[168]

This argument may well be applicable in relation to infant baptism within a Christianized nation like England, but it avoided the question of whether baptism might mediate the experience of regeneration in the case of confessing believers.

The preceding quotation shows that the primary concern of Hinton was to refute the concept of a *necessary* and *automatic* conveyance of grace in baptism, especially infant baptism as practised in the Church of England. Is it possible that Hinton, like Stovel, actually embraced a sacramental sense of baptism in the end, and that his initial statement was limited by the context? Probably not, because he radically reshaped the exegesis of key biblical texts (e.g., Acts 2:38) so as to remove any sacramental implications, and he divided conversion and baptism in a way that went far beyond Baptists like Stovel or Noel.

Charles Haddon Spurgeon (1834-1892)

Known for the last century as "the prince of preachers," Charles Spurgeon was easily the most famous and influential Baptist of Victorian England. He carried on a remarkable ministry as pastor of the Metropolitan Tabernacle in London from 1854 to his death in 1892, and his sermons were sold weekly around the world. Although he never functioned as a systematic theologian, his doctrinally-oriented, Calvinistic, Puritan-inspired preaching

---

168 Ibid., 477-478.

exerted a powerful influence around the world. His contribution to the baptismal debate revolves around one sermon, entitled "Baptismal Regeneration," which was preached June 5, 1864. This sermon, which initiated a relatively brief but intense debate among Christians across the theological spectrum, articulated in a powerful way the common Baptist distaste for using the terms *baptism* and *regeneration* in close proximity.[169]

The sermon was connected to Mark 16:15-16, and Spurgeon asserted that the doctrine of baptismal regeneration "is one in direct opposition to my text."[170] In response to the doctrine as he understood it, he asserted:

> We will confront this dogma with the assertion, that BAPTISM WITHOUT FAITH SAVES NO ONE. The text says, "He that *believeth* and is baptized shall be saved;" but whether a man be baptized or not, it asserts that "*he that believeth not* shall be damned:" so that baptism does not save the unbeliever, nay, it does not in any degree exempt him from the common doom of all the ungodly. He may have baptism, or he may not have baptism, but if he believeth not, he shall be in any case most surely damned.[171]

As he understood the situation, the only Protestant Church in England which actually taught the doctrine was the Church of England (described as a "powerful sect"!), and in his opinion, the doctrine was plainly taught in the Prayer Book.[172] He was aware that there were many evangelical clergy in the Church of England who did not affirm baptismal regeneration, but he questioned their morality, considering them guilty of duplicity by their sworn allegiance to doctrines which they did not believe.[173]

His attack was directed against the language of the Catechism and the Rubric for infant baptism, which asserted that the baptized child is "made a member of Christ, a child of God, and an inheritor of the kingdom of heaven," and gave thanks that in baptism, "this child is regenerate." He made it clear that he was not addressing the issue of infant baptism as such; he was aware of the different theologies of infant baptism, and he was not lumping them all together. What he was considering is "the question of

---

169 For a summary of this debate see Iain Murray, *The Forgotten Spurgeon* (London: The Banner of Truth Trust, 1966), 123-142.
170 Charles Haddon Spurgeon, "Baptismal Regeneration," in *Metropolitan Tabernacle Pulpit*, Vol. X (Pasadena, Texas: Pilgrim Publications, 1981), 315.
171 Ibid.
172 Ibid.
173 Ibid., 316.

baptismal regeneration, whether in adults or infants, or ascribed to sprinkling, pouring, or immersion."[174]

Spurgeon adduced three arguments against the doctrine that God regenerates through baptism. (1) "It seems out of character with the spiritual religion which Christ came to teach, that he should make salvation depend upon mere ceremony."[175] The argument here was that spiritual needs must be met by spiritual means, and the application of water to the physical body cannot, therefore, have any effect in the regeneration of the soul. (2) Second was an argument from experience, namely, "that the dogma is not supported by facts."[176] Baptized persons are "whoremongers, drunkards, fornicators, and murderers," and "thousands of those who were baptized in their infancy are now in our gaols."[177] In his inimitable style, he declared, "Facts, brethren, are dead against this Popish doctrine; and facts are stubborn things."[178] (3) He was convinced "that the performance styled baptism by the Prayer Book is not at all likely to regenerate and save."[179] The reasoning at this point revolved around the nature of the promises made by the sponsors in the name of the infant, i.e., to renounce the devil and all his works, and to obey constantly all of God's commands. If the sponsors were *godly*, then they would know that they could not live up to this themselves; and if they were *ungodly*, then they were clearly hypocrites. In Spurgeon's view, it is not likely that God would regenerate through a charade such as this!

Spurgeon recognized that his announced text (Mark 16:15-16) is actually a problem, inasmuch as it appears to condition salvation upon faith *and* baptism; accordingly, he imagined a listener saying, "Ah! but baptism is in the text; where do you put that?" The heart of his reply was this:

> Brethren, the baptism here meant is a baptism connected with faith, and to this baptism I will admit there is very much ascribed in Scripture. Into that question I am not going; but I do find some very remarkable passages in which baptism is spoken of very strongly. . . . I know that believer's baptism itself does not wash away sin, yet it is so the outward sign and emblem of it to the believer, that the thing visible may be described as the thing

---

174 Ibid.
175 Ibid., 317.
176 Ibid., 318.
177 Ibid.
178 Ibid., 319.
179 Ibid.

signified. . . . And so, inasmuch as baptism to the believer representeth the washing of sin--it may be called the washing of sin--not that it is so, but that it is to saved souls the outward symbol and representation of what is done by the power of the Holy Spirit, in the man who believes in Christ. . . . A man who knows that he is saved by believing in Christ does not, when he is baptized, lift his baptism into a saving ordinance. In fact, he is the very best protester against that mistake, because he holds that he has no right to be baptized until he is saved. He bears a testimony against baptismal regeneration in his being baptized as professedly an already regenerate person.[180]

It would be hard to imagine a more powerful rejection of baptismal regeneration than is found in the words of this sermon, but it needs to be carefully examined. It is crucial to note that the sermon is directed against very mechanistic conceptions of baptism, in which baptism is thought of as *invariably effective* and *absolutely necessary* for salvation. It is also clear that, in spite of his statement that he was dealing with both infant and adult baptism, the issue for him was fundamentally about the conveyance of grace to infants. At the outset, he assumed that the doctrine which he was opposing teaches regeneration in the absence of faith, and his illustrations throughout the sermon were all about infant baptism. Therefore, one should not draw hasty inferences concerning Spurgeon's attitude toward something like the baptismal theology expressed by Baptist Noel. His rhetoric does not sound as if he would feel comfortable with a concept like baptism as the "seal of regeneration," but he did not directly address the issue.

He did admit in the sermon that there are several biblical texts which posit a very close relationship between baptism and the things signified by it, sufficiently close to give the appearance of teaching the doctrine which he opposed, but these texts do not seem to have shaped his theology in any way. He approached a higher view of baptismal efficacy early in the sermon when he said:

Used by faith, had God commanded it, miracles might be wrought; but without faith or even consciousness, as in the case of babes, how can spiritual benefits be connected necessarily with the sprinkling of water?[181]

---

180 Ibid., 326.
181 Ibid., 318.

He needed to look no farther than his announced text for the sermon to find a biblical statement which seemed to indicate that God had, in fact, established a connection between baptism and salvation. This would seem to call for more attention than Spurgeon gave it.

Within the sermon Spurgeon implicitly recognized that even though regeneration is a direct and invisible work of God, the experience of salvation is mediated through human response to God's grace. Addressing listeners who were moving toward conversion, he said:

> Whoever among you can believe in the great love of God towards man in Christ Jesus, you shall be saved. If you can believe that our great Father desireth us to come to him--that he panteth for us--that he calleth us every day with the loud voice of his Son's wounds; if you can believe now that in Christ there is pardon for transgressions past, and cleansing for years to come; if you can trust him to save you, you have already the marks of regeneration. The work of salvation is commenced in you, so far as the Spirit's work is concerned; it is finished in you so far as Christ's work is concerned. O, I would plead with you--lay hold on Jesus Christ.[182]

The persons in view here were thought of as apparently (or at least, possibly) regenerate, in that they would give assent to the facts about God's love and salvation through Christ and were inclined to trust in that love; and yet, they were still exhorted to "lay hold on Jesus Christ," that is, to respond to Christ in some way so as to make this salvation a personal, experiential reality. Implicit in all this is the recognition that some kind of definite human response is instrumental in the application of redemption, and it should not be hard to see (even in the text for the sermon) that baptism admirably serves this purpose.

Spurgeon was trying to hold together all the New Testament data about the meaning of baptism, but his abhorrence of the Prayer Book doctrine (as he understood it) pushed virtually all his rhetoric to one side of the dialectic, the side which asserts that regenerating grace is not inseparably tied to baptism. In a less polemical context, Spurgeon might have provided a positive baptismal theology which affirmed both sides of the dialectic. There are brief evidences of a fuller view in the sermon, but they are relatively insignificant in the overall argument.

---

182 Ibid., 325.

Richard Ingham (1810-1873)

Ingham was a pastor in several churches of the New Connexion of General Baptists, the continuation of the Arminian Baptist tradition. Late in his life he produced a large *Hand-Book on Christian Baptism*, Part II of which dealt with the subjects of baptism, and it was in this context that he indicated his sentiments on baptism as a means of grace. The book itself was largely a collection of quotations from paedobaptists in which they make major concessions about the historic practice of the Church with regard to both mode and subjects, thus representing a literary genre widely used by Baptists throughout their history. His statements about the sacramental question were neither numerous nor lengthy, but they were reasonably clear.

Baptists have often been accused by paedobaptists of making too much of the rite, since they demand rebaptism of those baptized in infancy, which has often provided the context for a Baptist disavowal of any salvific intent in the ordinance. Ingham was one example, as he wrote:

> And, respecting those views in which they feel obliged to differ from so many whom they esteem, they wish explicitly to state,--that they do not conceive baptism to be essential to salvation, any more than they consider the Lord's Supper as essential to that end. They do not consider that men are made Christians *by* it, or cannot be Christians *without* it, for this manifest reason, that they think it ought not to be administered to any, but such as are Christians or sincere believers in Christ *first*. They do not consider it as regeneration, which they believe is a renewal of the heart by the power of the Holy Ghost, and which they believe ought to precede the administration of baptism.[183]

He attributed the doctrine of baptismal regeneration to the fact that, "It is easy to attribute to the *sign* the thing *signified*,"[184] and he asserted that this was an error into which the Church fell early on, leading to (among other things) the baptism of infants in hope that they would experience the benefits conveyed by baptism.

The denial of baptismal regeneration does not, of course, imply the denial of a sacramental view of baptism--there are other ways to describe a

---

183 Richard Ingham, *Christian Baptism: Its Subjects* (London: E. Stock, 1871), 11-12.
184 Ibid., 14.

divine activity in the event. But as Ingham's argument unfolded, he indicated his rejection of sacramentalism in general, when he wrote:

> We believe and emphatically maintain, with Paedobaptists generally, that baptism is symbolical, and with Dr. Halley, that it is symbolical only, that is, that it neither seals nor conveys the blessings that are symbolized. It symbolizes the washing away of sin, or a cleansing from its defilement and guilt. It symbolizes in its action a burial and resurrection. . . . The immersion, which may be called a burial, supposes death to have taken place, and the emersion symbolizes the rising again to newness of life, which newness of life is the precursor of a resurrection to eternal life when the risen Lord and Saviour shall return in the clouds of heaven and in his Father's glory.[185]

Later in his book he gave an extensive list of quotations from notable paedobaptists with regard to the "essence of baptism."[186] The language of the quotations is often sacramental in character, and Ingham did not express any rejection of these ideas, but there is no reason to doubt his commitment to the purely symbolic function of baptism expressed above. The purpose of his book was to refute paedobaptism, and the function of the quotations pertaining to the essence of baptism was to argue that paedobaptists ought to reject infant baptism even on the basis of their own theology of baptism. For example, the Lutheran concept of baptism as a "visible word" which evokes faith in the person baptized, and in this way effects regeneration, is meaningful in the case of confessing believers, but it is difficult to relate to infants. The difficulty is seen in Luther's suggestion that infants do in fact exercise faith in some sense. In the Calvinistic tradition, the concept of baptism as a "seal" seems meaningful and coherent in the case of a believer who has a faith to validate, but in the case of infants there is presumably no personal faith to confirm. According to Calvin and his followers, baptism confirms both God's promise and human faith, but in the case of infant baptism, only God's promise can be confirmed. The point, then, of this use of paedobaptist literature was to argue that their own premises imply the restriction of baptism to believers, not to affirm all of their premises. Ingham himself affirmed a purely symbolic view of baptism, and in so doing, spoke for many others of his day.

---

185 Ibid., 318.
186 Ibid., 354-378.

Summary

The formulation of a Baptist theology of baptism had from the beginning been articulated in reaction to the perceived errors of other churches, and this was indeed the case in the 19th century. Discussion of baptism in Victorian England was largely shaped by the context of the Tractarian movement and related Anglo-Catholic expressions. The Baptist literature, at least up to Spurgeon's time, revealed continual allusions to the *Tracts for the Times*, to J. H. Newman (1801-1890) and E. B. Pusey (1800-1882), to the "men of Oxford," to the doctrine of baptismal regeneration, and in many cases to the fear of "Popery" as a growing force in England. In Spurgeon's famous sermon, he confessed that he had been previously naive about the growth of Roman Catholicism in England, but he had come to feel great concern, and "Puseyism" was to be condemned because it was laying the foundation for "Popery."[187] As a result of this context, a large proportion of the Baptist literature was reactionary, focussing on what does not happen in the baptism of infants and attacking the idea of the automatic conveyance of grace through baptism. The controversies of the century exacerbated the Baptist tendency to define baptism negatively, and thus to affirm a minimalist understanding of what actually happens in the baptismal event.

Some Baptists continued to use the term *sacrament* to describe baptism, but in some cases this was purely semantic or was meant only in the ancient sense of an "oath of allegiance." Some others were comfortable with some sort of sacramentalism at the conceptual level (e.g., Baptist Noel), but they appear to have been a minority. The concept of baptism as a sacramental "seal" in which baptism mediates the experience (if not the fact) of saving union with Christ is largely absent from the literature. This was a departure from the foundational Baptist thought of the 17th century, and seems to have been a missed opportunity to contribute in a positive way to the debates of the century.

Conclusion

This book began by noting that paedobaptists are often surprised to find that baptismal theology is not nearly as central in Baptist thought as they would have expected. In the same way, many Baptists would be surprised to discover that earlier Baptists conceptualized baptism in a much more

---

187 Spurgeon, "Baptismal Regeneration," 322.

sacramental way than they would have anticipated. The traditional assumption that Baptists have always interpreted baptism in a purely symbolic way must be challenged and significantly modified. In the 17th century in England, the foundational period of Baptist life and thought, those Baptists who directly addressed the question often spoke of baptism in a way that was both verbally and conceptually sacramental. In the words of the *Baptist Catechism*, it was a "means whereby Christ communicates to us the benefits of redemption." The Baptist confessions were essentially silent concerning the sense in which baptism might be a means of grace, in most cases denoting it as a "sign" without specifying the exact relationship between the sign and the things signified. However, individual Baptist authors who were involved in shaping these confessions, when they spoke of the "ends" of baptism, often spoke of it as both "sign" and "seal," thus indicating that baptism mediates the conscious experience of the benefits which it signifies.

Throughout the 18th and 19th centuries, Baptist literature tended to retreat from such sacramental language. There were exceptions, to be sure, but even the moderate sacramentalism of the Calvinistic tradition, in which baptism functions as a seal of union with Christ, receded into the background and was sometimes consciously rejected. By the end of the 19th century, it was widely assumed by Baptists that baptism is an "ordinance" *as opposed to* a "sacrament," an act of human obedience *as opposed to* a means of grace. Isolating the factors which effected this shift is not a simple matter, but they would include the following.

(1) To some extent, it was simply due to neglect of the issue of *meaning*, as a consequence of the ongoing debate about paedobaptism and the increasing focus on the question of mode. Sacramental concepts easily came to be identified with the idea of conveyance of grace to passive infants, so that sacramentalism came to be dismissed along with paedobaptism.

(2) The emphasis on confession of faith as a condition of baptism focused Baptist thought on what precedes baptism and diverted attention away from the effects of baptism. This became an especially potent factor as the condition came to be not simply a credible confession of faith, but a faith evidenced by marks of obedience and articulated in a public testimony of one's experience of grace. Thus there were other means of "sealing" one's union with Christ apart from baptism, the result being a disconnection between conversion and baptism.

(3) A sacramental understanding of baptism was perceived by many as a threat to the Protestant commitment to justification "by faith alone." Many Baptist writers have interpreted baptism as a "work of righteousness," and

have thus inferred that any instrumental value of baptism in the experience of forgiveness would be in opposition to the teaching of Romans and Galatians.

(4) In the Particular Baptist tradition, the development of High Calvinism in the 18th century tended to devalue human religious action in general, and thus baptismal action in particular.

(5) The Evangelical Revival in 18th-century England demonstrated with clarity and force that God's saving grace is not tied to believer baptism. Revival did not begin among the Baptists or other Nonconformists, but within the Church of England, and Baptists were forced to admit the presence of a vast number of wholehearted disciples among those converted under the ministries of the Wesleys and Whitefield. This obvious experience of grace apart from adult baptism, when combined with the concern to preserve the "faith alone" character of salvation, provided a context in which the significance of confessional baptism was readily questioned.

(6) Most Baptist attempts to define a theology of baptism during the period in view were reactions to perceived errors on the part of other traditions. Given the fact that some of those "errors" posited a seemingly excessive sense of baptism's efficacy, the Baptist reaction resulted in a negative description of baptism, i.e., what it does *not* effect. This was particularly the case in the Victorian era, when a revived Anglo-Catholicism was the opponent.

By the end of the 19th century, there were still British Baptists who affirmed that baptism is a sacrament (i.e., that baptism in some way mediates salvific union with Christ), but they were definitely a minority. This began to change in the early part of the 20th century, when some influential Baptist leaders articulated the view that baptism is both an ordinance to obey and a sacrament of grace. The following chapter will analyse this recovery and further development of Baptist sacramentalism, tracing it from its origin in the years surrounding 1920 to its fullest statement in the 1960's.

CHAPTER 2

The Reformulation of Baptist Sacramentalism

H. Wheeler Robinson (1872-1945)[1]

The first Baptist leader of the 20th century who challenged openly the anti-sacramental consensus on baptism was Henry Wheeler Robinson, a biblical scholar and theological educator. After serving two pastorates, he began in 1906 a teaching career at Rawdon College, which lasted for fourteen years. From 1920 to 1942 he served as the principal of Regent's Park College, first in London and later in Oxford. Although he was an Old Testament specialist, his concerns were broadly theological, and he stimulated a new approach to baptismal theology through his teaching, his writing, and his denominational activities.

The major recurring theme in Robinson's writings on baptism was the connection between water-baptism and Spirit-baptism.[2] The idea of a bestowal of the Holy Spirit in a sacramental manner was rooted not only in his biblical study, but also by his own account in a profound personal experience, which he described in a third-person narrative:

> In 1913, in the course of a serious illness, he was led to ask himself why the truths of "evangelical" Christianity which he had often preached to others now failed to bring him personal strength. They remained true to him, but they seemed to lack vitality. They seemed to demand an active effort of faith, for which the physical energy was lacking. The figure that presented itself at the time was that of a great balloon, with ample lifting power,--if only one had the strength to grasp the rope that trailed down from it! He contrasted with this presentation of Christian truth that of a more "sacramental" religion, as he rightly or wrongly conceived it, in

---

[1] The contribution of Robinson and the other authors considered in this chapter to British Baptist thought and practice is detailed in Anthony Cross's *Baptism and the Baptists*. For Robinson's contribution to the sacramental question, see Cross, *Baptism*, 103-104, 108-126.

[2] For a discussion of Robinson's treatment of this theme and some of the Baptist response, see Cross, *Baptism*, 108-118.

which the priest would bring the sacred elements to the bedside, and with them the needed grace. The result of this experience was not to change a "Protestant" into a "Catholic", but to lead him to seek for the lacuna in his own conception of evangelical truth. He found it in his relative neglect of those conceptions of the Holy Spirit in which the New Testament is so rich.[3]

Thus began his quest to interpret a kind of Christian religious experience which goes beyond a purely internal, intellectualized response to the gospel to embrace the use of material means by the Spirit of God.

The application of this to baptism was declared in an address which he gave to the ministers of the London Baptist Association on June 27, 1922, which was later published in *The Baptist Quarterly* as "The Place of Baptism in Baptist Churches of To-day." Some of the concerns of the address were amplified in his later writing, but all the essential aspects of his renewal of baptismal theology were present in this earlier work.

Robinson asserted that there were serious deficiencies in the typical Baptist approach to baptism in his day. The lack of a positive baptismal theology noted in the first chapter of this book was seen in his observation that most Baptist treatments are "more concerned with showing what New Testament baptism is not, rather than what it is."[4] Most Baptists focus on baptism as an act of obedience, but he argued that as a summary of the meaning of baptism this is seriously reductionistic and easily degenerates into a kind of legalism. If others are going to be convinced that baptism is still a moral and religious obligation, then "it must be by showing that it is still intrinsically worth while."[5] Many Baptists have conceptually disconnected baptism from conversion and have seen it as simply the visible sign of entrance into formal church membership, and while it is such a sign, he suggested that any attempt to interpret *New Testament* baptism must set it in the context of the church of the apostolic age, which was primarily a "spiritual community, whose life-breath is the Spirit of Christ." In that context "water-baptism is the outward and visible sign of an inward and spiritual baptism of the Holy Spirit."[6]

---

3 H. Wheeler Robinson, *The Christian Experience of the Holy Spirit* (London: Nisbet & Co., 1928), 4. For another description of the same experience see Ernest A. Payne, *Henry Wheeler Robinson: Scholar, Teacher, Principal--A Memoir* (London: Nisbet 4& Co., 1946), 56-57.
4 H. Wheeler Robinson, "The Place of Baptism in Baptist Churches of To-Day," *The Baptist Quarterly* n.s. 1 (1922-1923): 209.
5 Ibid., 215.
6 Ibid., 210.

The Reformulation of Baptist Sacramentalism

For many British Baptists, both then and now, believer baptism[7] is not even the invariable sign of entrance into church membership, because they practise "open membership" and accept persons into membership on the basis of a verbal confession of faith alone. The practice began as an act of Christian charity toward believers whose personal faith ratified their baptism as infants, but in many cases it has been extended to those who have grown up in Baptist families. Robinson was ambivalent about the practice of open membership, not really favouring it but not fearing that it would be catastrophic, as long as the pastors of Baptist churches are convinced Baptists. But he was fearful that in fact the pastors were not convinced of the significance of believer baptism:

> I am convinced that we are reaching a point at which we must make more of baptism, if much less is not to be made of it. The chief point, indeed, of what I want to say is that baptism is not maintaining its importance in the eyes of many among us, because Baptists are not proclaiming with sufficient clearness the full doctrine of the New Testament Baptism.[8]

His practical concern was clear: if Baptists do not recover a more biblical estimate of baptism and understand it as much more than a "positive institution" and arbitrary test of obedience, then it will continue to decline in importance, and the rationale for the existence of Baptists as a distinct denomination will disappear.[9]

This concern for Baptist existence is not a sign of narrow denominationalism, but a firm belief that the Baptist doctrine of believer baptism is a valuable contribution to the universal Church. Robinson articulated three benefits of this doctrine: (1) Repentance and faith need to be embodied in a memorable act which is psychologically powerful; otherwise, these fundamental realities are less than fully conscious and personal. (2) The practice of believer baptism provides a continual reminder of the essence of the gospel, especially when done by immersion,

---

7 The practice of restricting baptism to those who are sufficiently mature to make a personal confession of faith is sometimes called "believer's baptism" and sometimes "believers' baptism." In order to avoid the confusion over the possessive form, and in order to provide an appropriate parallel to "infant baptism," this book consistently employs the term "believer baptism." Paedobaptists often refer to this practice as "adult baptism," but this misses the point of the doctrine and is not the normal term used by Baptists.
8 Ibid., 214.
9 Ibid., 215.

thus facilitating loyalty to the essence of the faith without an emphasis on the traditional language of the creeds (Robinson's liberal attitude toward traditional statements of orthodoxy being evident here). (3) Most important, the demand that baptism be connected to personal confession of faith enables us to give baptism its full meaning as a vehicle of the Holy Spirit without falling into exaggerated, "sacramentarian" estimates of the rite.[10]

Robinson recognized that paedobaptist churches have a firmer grasp on some biblical truths than many Baptists, including the idea that baptism is a divinely-appointed means of grace, in which God is at work in the experience of the baptizand. For him, then, Baptists needed to learn from others these truths, but those same truths ought to be expressed in the context of *believer* baptism:

> The uniquely ethical character of our baptism safeguards us from the risk of misunderstanding, and leaves full room for the evangelical sacramentalism of the New Testament. The moral and religious experience of repentance and faith becomes the channel of the Spirit, and is psychologically reinforced by the definite expression of this experience in water-baptism. If we teach men that water-baptism is of real value on the human side--if it is not, we have no right to practice it--may we not teach that it is in the same way of value on the divine, possibly a real occasion, always a powerful declaration, of that baptism of the Spirit which is the true secret of Christian sanctification?[11]

His indication that baptism is "possibly" the point in time at which the Spirit is bestowed shows that he was not arguing for an invariable or automatic cause-effect relationship between baptism and the gift of the Spirit. He was not arguing for faith in the power of baptism, but for baptism as the rite in which faith in Christ comes to definite personal expression. The gift of the Spirit is God's work, and thus is not controlled by human activity, but at the *experiential* level, baptism is seen as the event which mediates the gift/reception of the Holy Spirit. A rite which is reduced to sheer obedience will not survive, but a rite with this kind of meaning deserves to be perpetuated, even if it implies a distinct denominational existence.[12]

These early concerns were stated again in his small but influential book, *Baptist Principles*, first published as a book in 1925 but reissued in several

---

10   Ibid., 215-216.
11   Ibid., 217.
12   Ibid.

editions and printings.[13] In it he argued that a right attitude toward baptism "implies much more than the conservative retention of an ancient ceremony; it implies that baptism is a sacrament of grace."[14] Anti-sacramentalists are prone to ask just what it is that is supposedly conveyed through such a sacrament that has not already been conveyed through faith alone. If by faith one is forgiven, regenerated and brought into union with Christ, what can be added by baptism? Robinson's reply was that this is a fundamentally unbiblical question, because "the New Testament never considers them [faith and baptism] apart in this detached manner."[15] The disjunction between faith and baptism is what has allowed both a false kind of "sacramentarianism" (in which baptism conveys benefits apart from personal, moral action) and "the entire rejection of sacraments" (in which the full experience of conversion occurs apart from physical-sacramental action).[16]

Robinson was very far from affirming that there is power in the baptismal water *per se*. The concept of consecrated water as a material means which the Spirit uses to convey grace is the essence of what he considered a false sacramentarianism.[17] What he asserted is that the baptismal *event* (the use of water in dominically-established action) is the tangible expression of the work of the Spirit which is going on in the life of the baptizand, a work which has evoked this expression of conversion and gives assurance of a new filial relationship to God.

Robinson's view of the sacramental meaning of baptism was not so much that the benefits are given as a result of baptism, as that the benefits are being conveyed by the Spirit in a process which includes baptism as the event in which the spiritual transformation becomes a conscious reality. Thus baptism does not mediate salvation *per se* in any sort of mechanical way, but it does mediate the experience of salvation as a conscious reality. It would, in his opinion, be false both to Scripture and to experience to assume that the normal experience of moral transformation through the gift of the Holy Spirit occurs through faith in isolation from action. Although this may be the experience of many persons (in many cases because they are

---

13 This work first appeared in 1912 as a chapter in *The Baptists of Yorkshire*, ed. C. E. Shipley, a volume celebrating the centenary of the Yorkshire Baptist Association.
14 H. Wheeler Robinson, *Baptist Principles*, 4th ed. (London: Kingsgate Press, 1945), 3.
15 Ibid., 15.
16 Ibid. Robinson's language here shows that even Baptists who are comfortable with the term "sacramentalism" will often use the term "sacramentarianism" pejoratively to describe what they perceive to be an overemphasis on the physical action of the sacrament as opposed to the faith-response embodied in it.
17 Ibid., 24.

taught to expect this), this is not to be considered normative, and such a separation between the inner life and its outer expression (soul versus body) represents an unbiblical kind of dualism.

These same ideas about Baptist principles were taken up into Robinson's larger book, *The Life and Faith of the Baptists*, which was first published in 1927 but went through many printings. In his opinion, the primary contribution of Baptists to the catholic Church was "the essential and primary place of the moral within the religious."[18] Within the context of baptismal theology, this implied a firm connection between baptism and personal commitment, the denial of which is the cause of a false "sacramentarianism," which is in turn the cause of the typical Baptist reduction of baptism to a pure symbol:

> Baptists have been reluctant to recognize this "baptismal grace", just because, in their judgment, it is utterly misrepresented and distorted when ascribed to unconscious infants. The reaction from a false doctrine of divine grace in baptism has made them suspicious even of the genuine sacramentalism of the New Testament.[19]

His contention was that Baptists need to emphasize their doctrine of baptism for the benefit of the whole Church, but along the lines of a "greater spiritual content" and not simply a "literalistic appeal to the Bible."[20]

In this book he further developed the contention that baptism as a confessional act is psychologically powerful as a defining moment in discipleship. Paedobaptist churches recognize the need for some such defining moment, and for them the need must be met by confirmation or some similar vehicle for a personal confession of faith. His contention was that the need is met adequately only by believer baptism, which is the "most impressive and memorable register of the birth of a new purpose."[21]

For Robinson, then, baptism provided an identifiable and memorable declaration of conversion (from the human side) and spiritual empowering (from the divine side). Although he did not explicitly use the Reformed concept of "seal" to describe what is happening in baptism, this concept seems to be the most accurate way to summarize his baptismal theology. In

---

18 H. Wheeler Robinson, *The Life and Faith of the Baptists* (London: Kingsgate Press, 1946), 175.
19 Ibid., 177.
20 Ibid., 179.
21 Ibid., 88-89. See also Cross, *Baptism*, 123.

contrast to the Reformed tradition, he confined the seal to those who can personally declare their faith, and although the sealing is related to both the human and the divine aspects of the event, it is probably fair to say that for him the focus fell on the confirmation of human commitment to a degree that is different from the Reformed tradition.

Perhaps the most significant statement by Robinson is his 1939 article, "Believers' Baptism and the Holy Spirit," which was first given as an address to the London Baptist Association and subsequently published in *The Baptist Quarterly*. His earlier statements defended a sacramental understanding of baptism largely on the basis of general theological themes and psychological considerations, but this article developed the biblical support in a much more specific way.

The argument began with the baptism of Jesus as a paradigm for disciples of Jesus. The baptism of Jesus in water was also a Spirit-baptism, as is seen in the Gospel accounts of the descent of the Spirit on that occasion and the use of the words of Isaiah 42, "I have put my spirit upon him." Jesus was admittedly unique, but his uniqueness did not lie in any lack of genuine humanity. Therefore, he submitted to water-baptism as a believer, and that experience of believer baptism was also an experience of Spirit-baptism. We, then, as followers of the Lord may expect that our baptism in water will facilitate "a humbler, yet related, experience of the Holy Spirit" to empower us for a life of discipleship.[22]

Given the fact that the primitive church is viewed as a Spirit-filled community, it would be very strange if the rite of entrance into that community were not itself an experience of the Spirit. In fact, this is the normative expectation of the New Testament, along the lines of Peter's declaration at Pentecost that baptism is the means of both forgiveness and the gift of the Spirit (Acts 2:38). Admittedly, there are exceptions to this rule in the Book of Acts; in fact, there is no consistent pattern of cause and effect at all. However, the exceptional cases are there precisely because they are exceptions (e.g., Samaritans, Gentiles, distant disciples of John).[23]

The most important authority on this question was held to be Paul, who was believed to emphasize the connection between baptism and the Spirit. His comments in 1 Corinthians 12:13 indicate that "the ideal beginning of the Spirit-filled life is at the water-baptism of the believer."[24] The passage in Romans 6:1-6 shows Paul's assumption that by baptism "his readers have

---

22　H. Wheeler Robinson, "Believers' Baptism and the Holy Spirit," *The Baptist Quarterly* n.s. 9 (1938-1939): 390.
23　Ibid., 391.
24　Ibid., 392.

entered into such mystical union with Christ . . . that the new life to which he is calling them is already in some sense theirs."[25] Although the Spirit is not explicitly mentioned in Romans 6, the elaboration of the new life in Romans 7-8 makes it clear that the dynamic of the transformed life is the Spirit.

The connection present in Paul is even more explicit in John 3:3-8, in particular the reference to a birth "of water and the Spirit." Robinson recognized that Baptists have in many cases denied the allusion to baptism here, on the grounds that such a reference would make baptism absolutely necessary for salvation. He replied:

> If a good Baptist is troubled--as many have been--by this apparent inculcation of baptismal regeneration through water, he may comfort himself with the not unimportant fact that "born of the Spirit" in verse 6 replaces "born of water and the Spirit" in verse 5. The higher element is thus made inclusive of the lower. But this does not warrant us in trying to evade the natural meaning of the whole phrase, that a man is born of water and the Spirit. Water-baptism was in the New Testament times the natural language and occasion and experienced means of the Spirit-baptism of believers.[26]

This use of water by the Spirit was interpreted as just one example of the general principle that the spiritual is mediated by lower (physical) forms of reality, a principle demonstrated supremely in the Incarnation.[27] The key is to remember that the Spirit is the sovereign agent in the event, and the water is only an instrument utilized by the Spirit. Sacramentarian errors occur when the means is severed from the agent's control and placed in the hands of a priestly caste, resulting in a "quasi-magical control of the higher by the lower."[28]

The true paradigm for the function of water-baptism was found neither in pagan magic nor in the rituals of mystery religions, but in what Robinson called "prophetic symbolism." This was his way of denoting the connection between the prophetic word and prophetic action in some biblical accounts:

> The prophets of the Old Testament did not simply proclaim a word

---

25   Ibid., 393.
26   Ibid.
27   Ibid., 394.
28   Ibid.

of the Lord; they sometimes began to put it into operation by identifying themselves with it in a personal act, which was already a fragment, as it were, of the whole act of God which they proclaimed.[29]

An Old Testament example would be Jeremiah's breaking a flask as a symbol of God's "breaking" of Judah and Jerusalem (Jer. 19:1-15), and a New Testament example would be Agabus's binding himself as a prophecy of the binding of Paul (Acts 21:11). Inherent in this notion is the idea that the prophetic action is more than "a mere accompaniment" of the prophetic word--in some sense the prophet "is beginning what the Lord will Himself complete."[30]

Near his retirement, in an address on Baptist distinctives given in 1941, Robinson again articulated his concern that the Baptist theology of baptism needed reformulation:

> Other communions have rightly emphasized the doctrine of grace in relation to baptism, though, as we Baptists think, in a wrong and dangerous form. It should be for us, with the safeguard of personal faith, to follow the truth, avoiding the error. I believe that the future of the Baptist Church in this country does largely depend on the recovery of a lost sacramental emphasis; on our making more, not less, of believers' baptism.[31]

It is not clear whether for Robinson this "lost sacramental emphasis" was to be found in earlier Baptist thought or only in primitive Christianity. Given the absence of any references by him to specific Baptist ancestors with a high view of baptismal efficacy, he was probably thinking of his interpretation of apostolic teaching. As shown in the preceding chapter, there was in fact a Baptist tradition to which he could have appealed, but even if he wrongly assumed that Baptists had always been anti-sacramental, he was accurate in his recognition that he was proposing a baptismal theology which seriously modified that which he inherited from the 19th century.

---

29 Ibid.
30 Ibid.
31 H. Wheeler Robinson, "The Five Points of a Baptist's Faith," *The Baptist Quarterly* 11 (1942-1945): 9.

Alfred Clair Underwood (1885-1948)[32]

Principal A. C. Underwood of Rawdon College was asked to write a chapter on the Baptist view of the ministry and the sacraments for a volume related to the Faith and Order Movement and its conference at Edinburgh in 1937. It is actually the book's second chapter on Baptist views, and it was written to demonstrate that some Baptists held sacramental views that differed from what many assumed to be the only Baptist view. The first chapter, by Prof. Isaac. G. Matthews (1871-1959) of Crozer Seminary in the U.S.A. (formerly of McMaster University), asserted that for Baptists, "Baptism is considered only an outward sign of an inner experience, a symbol in which the individual pledges himself to a newness of life."[33]

Underwood responded as follows:

> While many Baptists would regard Professor I. G. Matthews' paper as an adequate exposition of their opinions on the Ministry and the Sacraments, there is an increasing number of Baptists in both England and America who could not give their assent to Professor Matthews' virtual reduction of the Sacraments to *nuda signa*.[34]

He then referred to another chapter in the book, that by Prof. J. S. Whale (b. 1896) delineating the Congregationalist view, and he affirmed that Whale's general sacramental perspective was his own, except for the Baptist distinctives about the subjects and mode of baptism.[35] This would locate Underwood's conceptual scheme within the orbit of Calvinistic sacramentalism, in which the key word is that baptism is not only a sign but also a *seal* of union with Christ. That is, baptism confirms and applies at the level of conscious experience what is done invisibly in the soul by the work of the Spirit.

In his elaboration of this framework, baptism was indeed viewed as a significant means of grace, but in the end it was still a *second*, post-conversion work of grace. He argued that Baptists are "sacramentalists though they reject sacerdotalism."[36] He affirmed that the sacraments are "efficacious symbols which mediate the grace of God," but not in any *ex*

---

32 See also Cross, *Baptism*, 105, 123-125.
33 I. G. Matthews, "Views of Modern Churches: (g) Baptist (1)," in *The Ministry and the Sacraments*, ed. Roderic Dunkerley (London: SCM Press, 1937), 221.
34 A. C. Underwood, "Views of Modern Churches: (g) Baptists (2)," in Dunkerley, ed., *Ministry and Sacraments*, 223.
35 Ibid.
36 Ibid., 225.

opere operato sense.[37] Baptism is thus "a definite religious experience, a genuine Sacrament, but only to those who submit to it in penitence and faith."[38] While he wanted to say that baptism is "not a bare symbol as of something already complete,"[39] this was in conflict with his description of the relation between conversion and baptism:

> All who proceed to baptism do so in virtue of their faith which has already welcomed the divine message of forgiveness and of new life in Christ. Apart from this faith their baptism would effect nothing. They are not baptised in order to be regenerated, for their conversion was their regeneration. Baptists adhere strictly to the New Testament doctrine of regeneration and do not, therefore, regard regeneration and conversion as separate experiences.[40]

By defining conversion in this way, the sacramental nature of baptism is severely reduced, and what is mediated through it is "a present and deeper experience of divine grace, already embraced by faith."[41] Comparing the baptisms of the New Testament to those done among Baptists today, he wrote:

> Now, as then, they surrendered to Christ at the time of their conversion, but in consciously submitting to baptism they make their surrender more complete and their consecration more absolute, and, therefore, they receive further divine power to walk in newness of life. At their conversion they received the gift of the Holy Spirit, but at their baptism they receive a further accession of the Spirit in response to their faith.[42]

In the end, then, although Underwood was compelled by the baptismal language of Scripture to interpret it as an occasion of a divine work of grace, he still severed baptism from conversion and regarded it as a testimony to a past experience of regeneration, rather than the defining moment when faith comes to tangible expression and regeneration becomes an experiential reality. He was moving tentatively away from the "mere symbol" approach

---

37 Ibid.
38 Ibid.
39 Ibid., 227.
40 Ibid., 226.
41 Ibid., 227.
42 Ibid., 228.

to baptism, but he was not far removed from it. In fact, it is probably fair to say that those who affirm that baptism is a purely symbolic testimony to a completed conversion generally agree that there is in it (as in every act of obedient discipleship) some kind of spiritual benefit along the lines of strengthened commitment. That was not explicit in the "pure symbol" view of Matthews, but neither was it denied; and it is instructive to note that Matthews did refer to renewal of commitment through the Lord's Supper, which occasioned the comment, "Only thus do Baptists consider it a Sacrament."[43] Therefore, although Underwood's rhetoric was different from that of Matthews, it is open to question whether this kind of "sacramental" view was an alternative to the other or merely an elaboration.

Robert C. Walton (1905-1985)[44]

In 1941 a group of younger Baptist ministers began meeting for corporate theological study with an ecclesiological focus. Ultimately the group numbered thirteen, and by 1944 they had arrived at certain conclusions which they desired to publish for discussion by the wider Baptist family. Robert Walton, who was serving at that time as the General Secretary of the Student Christian Movement in Schools, was commissioned to articulate these conclusions in print, and after his draft was revised by his colleagues, his statement of the matter was published as *The Gathered Community* (1946). In one sense the book was by an individual, for Walton took responsibility for its final form, but in another sense it was a group project that indicated growing ferment among Baptists about ecclesiology in general and sacramentalism in particular.[45]

There were at least three distinctive contributions which Walton made to the formulation of baptismal theology: (1) In his approach the church as a corporate entity was very important as a mediating factor in the personal experience of redemption, much more so than in Robinson's approach. (2) The sacramental view of baptism was rooted in a broader principle of sacramental action, of which the Incarnation is the supreme example. (3) In spite of a high view of the efficacy of believer baptism and the assertion of the irregularity of infant baptism, he denied the propriety of "rebaptism" for those who were baptized as infants and confessed personal faith at a later time.

---

43   Matthews, 222.
44   See also Cross, *Baptism*, 186-187.
45   Robert C. Walton, *The Gathered Community* (London: Carey Press, 1946), 8-9. This source will hereafter be noted as *GC*.

His strong sense of the church as a channel of grace can be seen in his treatment of the gift of the Holy Spirit. He argued that in the New Testament there are three essential features of Christian baptism: it is first "an act of penitence"; it is closely connected to the gift of the Holy Spirit; and it is "the door of entrance into the redeemed community."[46] Of these three elements, it would seem to be the gift of the Spirit which is nearest to the heart of the sacramental question.

Walton rejected the idea that there is any sort of invariable cause-effect relation between baptism and the personal possession of the Spirit, both on the basis of the diverse evidence of the data in Acts and on the basis of Christian experience. He admitted, though, that there is "an intimate relationship between the gift and the sacrament to which the New Testament bears witness."[47] When this new experience of the Spirit that is connected to baptism was articulated, it was in terms of initiation into the community which is corporately indwelt by the Spirit. In his words, it is "the gift of the Spirit to the Christian community, in which a man shares because he has entered that community through baptism."[48] The same sort of inner logic is seen in his treatment of the classic text in John 3:

> In this same circle of ideas is the Johannine teaching on the new birth. When a man enters the Christian community he needs the promise of a new life, lived with a new purpose, at a new pitch of intensity, with new and finer motives. This new life is the gift of the Spirit; no man can achieve it by himself. To be born again "of water and of the Spirit" is to enter the community which lives by the forthflowing of power from God.[49]

It appears, then, that this baptismal theology lacked any sense of a direct conveyance of the Spirit to the individual--it is rather the case that initiation into the church of the Spirit is the cause of the individual's empowering by the Spirit.

It is universally admitted that in the act of Christian baptism, the church is active alongside of the baptizand and God, but for Walton the role of the church is fundamental and is in fact one aspect of God's action in the event. The church is "the extension of the Incarnation" which is brought into being

---

46 Ibid., 27-31.
47 Ibid., 30.
48 Ibid.
49 Ibid., 31.

"to continue Word and Sacrament among men."⁵⁰ Both of the gospel sacraments are "acts of God through the Church," and this implied for him the rejection of the statement by Arthur Dakin (1884-1969) that "Christ is thought of in the ordinances as related not primarily to the Church as a body, but first to each believing individual, and so to the church."⁵¹ There was clearly, then, a shift by Walton away from a more traditional Baptist individualism (in which the church is created by bringing together redeemed individuals) toward a corporate focus (in which incorporation into the redeemed community facilitates the individual's experience).

Traditionally, Protestant theology has tended to emphasize the uniqueness of baptism and the Lord's Supper as sacraments, in opposition to the Roman Catholic expansion of the sacraments, but Walton argued that sacramental action in baptism is merely one manifestation of God's use of material means to convey benefit to humans. He said:

> Christianity is a supernatural religion which yet has its roots in history. . . . Christianity thus affirms that the spiritual operates through the medium of the material. . . . So God is revealed and His grace is given through things seen and temporal. . . . Of this truth the Incarnation is the supreme example. . . . The Incarnation, however, is not the only example of a principle which lies at the root of reality as Christians see it. . . . The material universe is pregnant with spiritual meaning and there is reality hidden within the "real" objects of earth and sky and sea, of man's physical body and mental life.⁵²

These sweeping assertions may or may not be justifiable inferences from Christianity's rootedness in the Incarnation, but at the very least it is imperative to distinguish among the various ways in which the invisible God works through the visible creation. For example, God works through water to sustain human life, but this is different from the way in which God works through baptismal water, however one may explain the latter. To assert that God works through baptism could mean simply that God communicates spiritual truths in symbolic form through the event, but Walton and other sacramentalists want to say much more than this. The issue is not whether God is at work in some way in the event, but whether

---

50 Ibid., 156.
51 Ibid., 161. The quoted material is from Arthur Dakin, *The Baptist View of the Church and Ministry* (London: Kingsgate Press, 1944), 34.
52 Ibid., 155-156.

God is conveying to the baptizand in baptism (at some level) the benefits symbolized by baptism. It is the nature of God's work, not the fact of God's work, that is at issue.

Walton was conscious that he was advancing views that were not in the centre of his Baptist tradition, but he overstated the difference when he chose John Smyth as a representative Baptist patriarch. Smyth defended "spiritual worship" to such an extent that he rejected the use of any printed matter before the eyes in worship, thus severing worship not only from the Prayer Book, but also from hymn books and even from Bibles (though not from biblical statements recalled from memory).[53] But this kind of extreme position was never a standard Baptist view, and as Walton admitted, Smyth in fact affirmed that Christ was at work through physical elements in both baptism and the Lord's Supper. As shown in the preceding chapter, Walton could easily have found early Baptist interpretations of the sacraments which were very similar to his own. It was his sense of a "sacramental universe" which was more distinctive, and more debatable. On that point, he could have invoked H. Wheeler Robinson's concept of the action of the divine Spirit through lower, material means, but there was no reference to Robinson's work. This is another example of the Baptist tendency to ignore the Baptist tradition.

Although Walton defended a higher view of baptism's efficacy than was common in his inherited tradition, he affirmed the Baptist refusal to baptize infants. The point at which this becomes a profoundly practical issue is the request for membership in a Baptist church by one who was baptized as an infant. If infant baptism is rejected as an unbiblical baptism, and if believer baptism is a significant means of grace as Walton passionately asserted, can it be right to admit such persons to membership without believer baptism? Walton answered in the affirmative:

> Ought we, in such circumstances, to insist upon re-baptism by immersion? . . . To insist upon re-baptism is, in our view, to unchurch everybody but ourselves, and to deny to all except Baptists the title of Christian. . . . Thus, because Christendom is divided, we could accept as members those, who, baptised as infants, have, in Confirmation, expressed in another though less scriptural form, the essential requirement of personal acceptance and personal faith in Christ and His benefits which is sacramentally

---

53   Ibid., 156.

expressed in Believers' Baptism.[54]

This is a strange piece of argumentation in two ways. First, to introduce the issue of "immersion" is to miss the point of the question, which concerns the *subjects* of baptism, not the *mode*. Second, it has never been true that Baptists who demanded believer baptism in such cases denied the genuineness of Christian faith in all those not baptized as believers, and many Baptists have accepted paedobaptist churches as genuine churches with some irregularities of practice.[55]

The difficulty of correlating a high view of baptism as a sacrament with an "open membership" policy was stated by Walton himself in relation to the practice of admission to membership on the basis of verbal confession of faith apart from any baptism (whether as an infant or as a believer). He noted that this is rooted in the idea that baptism is a "mere symbol" which is thus optional, and he replied:

> If, on the other hand, Believers' Baptism is a sacrament in which God acts, and an ordinance we are bound by our allegiance to obey, then to make it an optional extra means that the Baptist community sins grievously, misleading the flock committed to its charge, and by its neglect stops up one channel through which the divine blessing is mediated.[56]

Now, admittedly, the person baptized as an infant who later makes a personal confession of faith and the person who has never been baptized at all and now confesses faith are not in exactly the same situation. The former has been accepted as a member by a Christian church, though perhaps in an inappropriate way, while the latter is seeking initial acceptance in the

---

54 Ibid., 166-167.
55 For example, Chap. XXVI of the *Second London Confession* ("Of the Church") defines "visible saints" as "all persons throughout the world, professing the faith of the gospel, and obedience unto God by Christ according unto it, not destroying their own profession by any errors perverting the foundation, or unholiness of conversation," and asserts that "of all such persons ought all particular congregations to be constituted." Thus the visible church is defined without reference to baptism. Furthermore, the same chapter says, "The purest churches under heaven are subject to mixture and error." Other chapters in the confession define the right practice of baptism, but there is no statement conjoining baptism and the church in such a way that baptismal irregularities would invalidate a church's profession to be a genuine church of Christ. This attitude is also implicit in the fact that this Baptist confession is just a slightly modified form of the *Westminster Confession*.
56 Walton, 166.

church. Nevertheless, the repair of an inadequate baptism is still possible, and the situation in view is one in which the individual desires to be a sincere member of a church which is committed to the practice of believer baptism. Both the integrity of church membership and the value of a sacramentally-expressed confession of faith seem to demand that Baptist churches practice closed membership. This is not the way in which the reformulation of Baptist sacramentalism has unfolded--for the most part, Walton's conclusion has been affirmed, and Baptist sacramentalists have supported open membership. However, this seems to have stronger roots in the sociology of British ecclesiastical life than in the theology of Baptist sacramentalism.

There are several aspects of Baptist life in 20th-century Great Britain which have predisposed them to the practice of open membership, even though the practice is in tension with their theology. Historically, Baptists in Great Britain (especially England) have had very close relations with other Nonconformists, especially the Congregationalists. The sense of being a minority group over against the established Church of England has helped to create a desire for numerical significance, and given the serious numerical decline of the Baptist Union over much of this century, the desire to make church membership as inclusive as possible is understandable.[57] Furthermore, some of the notable leaders of the Baptist Union have been strongly committed to ecumenism, thus inclining the churches toward a less sectarian ecclesiology. In particular, the office of General Secretary was filled by J. H. Shakespeare (1898-1924) and Ernest A. Payne (1951-1967), both of whom were vigorous participants in the modern ecumenical movement.[58]

Henry Cook (1886-1970)[59]

According to Roger Hayden, Henry Cook's attempt to articulate Baptist distinctives, *What Baptists Stand For* (1947), was written as a reply to Walton, and Cook "attacked very strongly the use of the word 'sacrament' and pleaded for a return to 'ordinance'."[60] Hayden indicates that the book was widely used in the denomination for twenty years, and it may well be that the book was used by others as an antidote to a resurgent

---

57   For a description and interpretation of this numerical decline, see McBeth, *Baptist Heritage*, 507-510.
58   Ibid., 499-504.
59   See also Cross, *Baptism*, 186-187.
60   Hayden, *English Baptist History*, 163.

sacramentalism, but to do so is to overstate the contrast between Walton and Cook.

Cook did indeed explain the typical Baptist uneasiness about the term "sacrament," pointing out that it is "associated in their minds with semi-magical ideas that are utterly foreign to the New Testament."[61] This connection with sacerdotalism and traditional Roman Catholic ideas of grace, indeed the tendency among both Catholics and Protestants to associate the term with conveyance of grace in the absence of personal faith, not to mention the extension of the term to cover five other rituals in the Catholic and Orthodox traditions, has made Baptists wary of the term.

Baptists, therefore, have come to prefer the term "ordinances" to describe the two rituals of the gospel, thus emphasizing their dominical origin and binding character. However, the debate is not ultimately about terminology, and Cook was quick to note this:

> The Baptist reason for avoiding the word sacraments is thus quite intelligible, but it is at the same time unfortunate, since the word Ordinances hardly does justice to all that is involved in Baptism and the Lord's Supper. These are Ordinances undoubtedly, but they are surely very much more, and their significance lies not merely in the fact that they were enjoined upon us by Christ but that they become to the man of faith an actual means of grace.[62]

This was hardly a plea for one term over another. Cook's concern as it relates to baptismal doctrine was to argue that baptism becomes sacramental only as it is "laid hold of by the believing soul."[63] In baptism there is "a vitalizing and enriching experience of His grace and power," but there is "no magic in the sacraments, no conferring of grace independently of the will of the recipient."[64] To apply baptism to infants (or, for that matter, to anyone apart from explicit faith) is "to make a sacrament of grace into something that savours of magic."[65]

The sacramental theologies of Walton and Cook were not antithetical, but it would be accurate to say that their emphases were different, as can be seen in Cook's treatment of "the value of baptism." He treated its value by listing nine aspects of the meaning of baptism, and the focus clearly fell on

---

61 Henry Cook, *What Baptists Stand For* (London: Kingsgate Press, 1947), 87.
62 Ibid., 89.
63 Ibid., 90.
64 Ibid., 91.
65 Ibid.

the human side, the seventh aspect being the only one that implied some kind of sacramental action. Baptism was interpreted as:

(1) ... an act of obedience. ... (2) ... the acceptance of a definite challenge. ... (3) ... a witness for Christ, and experience suggests that no witness is more effective. ... (4) ... the evidence of a morally cleansing experience through the gift of Christ in the Gospel. ... (5) ... an act of initiation. ... the door of entrance into the Christian Church, ... (6) ... an expression in symbolic form of basic Gospel fact. ... (7) ... [one of the ordinances in which] the believer appropriates for himself the truths symbolized in them, and in that way enables them to become, as we say, sacramental; media, that is, through which God in saving grace is able to come to the soul. ... (8) ... a forward reference [to the future consummation of salvation]. ... (9) ... an act of dedication.[66]

This explanation of the meaning of baptism certainly put the focus on the human action in the event; even the explicitly sacramental reference was phrased in terms of the believer's act of appropriation, and this rhetoric does sound different from Walton's assertion that God is the first and primary actor in baptism. However, both Walton and Cook emphatically asserted that the operation of God's grace is such that it evokes the free response of the individual as an absolutely necessary component in the bestowal of the benefits of Christ. Grace is free and sovereign but not coercive, and baptism embodies according to each of them both divine and human action, and the grace in view both elicits and responds to the human faith. Cook's explanation may have been tilted more toward the human side, but he said of baptism that, "It is a 'high' moment of believing confession, and it is therefore a 'high' moment of experienced grace."[67]

Neville Clark (b. 1926)[68]

The years after World War II were marked by ferment in baptismal theology, much of it sparked by Karl Barth's 1943 lecture, *Die Kirkliche Lehre von der Taufe*, which was translated into English in 1948 by Ernest Payne (1902-1980), a British Baptist. One of the first Baptist contributions to this discussion was *An Approach to the Theology of the Sacraments* (1956) by

---

66 Ibid., 146-153.
67 Ibid., 153.
68 See also Cross, *Baptism*, 225-228.

Neville Clark, who was serving as a Baptist pastor in England at the time and later served as a theological educator at the South Wales Baptist College. Three years later he contributed a chapter on the theology of baptism in *Christian Baptism*, a watershed volume for British Baptists, which will be discussed below. Certain themes in his first book were further developed in a 1965 article in *Studia Liturgica*, and this discussion at this point will focus on these two pieces of literature.

Clark stated emphatically that baptism is conceptualized in the New Testament as a sacrament in which God achieves what is there symbolized. He wrote:

> There is little doubt that the New Testament view of baptism is of a rite that is effective rather than merely symbolic. It brings the disciple into a union with Christ too deep and realistic for words adequately to describe it; it has objective significance.[69]

The significance revolves around union with Christ and his vicarious action, so that, "In baptism the disciple enters into the whole redemptive action of his Lord, so that what was once done representatively for him may now be done in actuality in him."[70] On the basis of Pauline teaching in Romans 6 and Galatians 3, he asserted, "The New Testament is no less clear that the point at which redemption becomes effective for us is at baptism."[71] Contrary to most Baptist theologians, he was prepared to posit a form of baptismal regeneration:

> Baptism and new birth are inseparably bound together, for the gift of the Holy Spirit involves a radical change at the centre of man's being. The divine promises attached to the sacraments are not empty promises; what God says, "goes."[72]

In contradistinction to Robinson and Walton, Clark did not ground his sense of baptism as a sacrament in some kind of broader sacramental principle. He argued in his early book that, "The sacraments stem from historical roots; they are not adequately to be defined by means of general

---

69 Neville Clark, *An Approach to the Theology of the Sacraments* (London: SCM Press, 1956), 32. This source will hereafter be noted as *ATS*.
70 Ibid., 31.
71 Ibid., 81.
72 Ibid., 82.

concepts."⁷³ In his later article he described such general definitions as "misleading traditional understandings," to which he replied:

> We have to abandon the treatment of "sacrament" as a generic category, susceptible of abstract and *a priori* definition, which may then be regulatively imposed upon baptismal exposition. This is to liberate baptismal understanding from confining mould and unbiblical restrictive strait-jacket.⁷⁴

This appears to have been a positive step forward that was generally followed by later Baptist formulations; it avoided an unfruitful attempt to give precise definition to a term which is in fact never employed in Scripture, and it preserved the uniqueness of baptism and the Lord's Supper as signs connecting the work of Christ to human experience.

If, then, the meaning of baptism is to be determined by the biblical witness, what is the biblical evidence that supports his vigorous assertion above that there is "little doubt" that baptism is an effective sign? For Clark, the evidence is present in latent form in the Book of Acts, it is stated in an oblique way in The Gospel of John, but it is found in a clear and developed way only in Paul's epistles.

He recognized that it is necessary to look for clues in Acts as to the theology of baptism taught or assumed in the primitive preaching of the gospel, but he argued that "the picture is curiously confused," and he therefore questioned whether Luke's account will bear the weight that many want to put on it.⁷⁵ The variations within Acts in the description of the relation between baptism and the Spirit are well known (and will be treated in the following chapter), and Clark also argued that Luke "is still working with a somewhat impersonal conception of holy spirit."⁷⁶ But even though Acts does not provide the kind of system which we might desire, two general statements may be made:

> In the first place, baptism was the outward manifestation of a believing response to the proclamation of the gospel message; as such it was the appointed rite of initiation into the Church, the Spirit-filled community. Secondly, it was connected with cleansing

---

73 Ibid., 72.
74 Neville Clark, "Christian Initiation: A Baptist Point of View," *Studia Liturgica* 4 (1965): 156.
75 Clark, *ATS*, 19-20.
76 Ibid., 20.

and forgiveness of sins, and, as the obverse of this, with the reception of the Holy Spirit.[77]

Some have argued that the Gospel of John is designed to teach a high sacramental doctrine by means of multiple figures of speech and allusions. Clark was only prepared to use the Gospel in a very limited way:

> Some reference to the fourth Gospel is however appropriate, even though the difficulties of interpretation entitle us to use it only for the illustration and confirmation of conclusions already firmly grounded.... [Concerning John 3] The evangelist looks back to the baptism of Jesus himself, when water and Spirit were conjoined; but he also points forward to Christian baptism as rebirth through the operation of the Holy Spirit, the means of entrance into the Kingdom.[78]

The heart of the matter for Clark was the Pauline treatment of baptism, notably a text like Romans 6, in which Paul interprets baptism as the event in which the believer is salvifically united with Christ, or perhaps more accurately, with the whole Christ-event from Incarnation to Ascension. Baptism is "a sacrament of inaugurated eschatology," effecting the believer's entrance into the benefits presently attached to the Kingdom of God and giving hope of the consummation of this salvation at the Parousia.[79]

When Clark sought to interpret the "how" of such Pauline assertions, the Church became a major factor. He wrote:

> How is this union with Christ accomplished; how does baptism effect it? The answer is given in terms of initiation into the Church. Baptism accomplishes union with Christ because it gives entry into the Church which is his resurrection body. Into that body the baptized are incorporated as "members."[80]

With regard to the gift of the Spirit he said, "In baptism the Holy Spirit is given; for baptism is into Christ upon whom the Spirit abided, into the body of Christ which is the *locus* of the Spirit."[81] He argued that Christ is neither

---

77 Ibid., 21.
78 Ibid., 27.
79 Ibid., 26.
80 Ibid., 33.
81 Ibid., 34.

to be identified with the Body nor to be separated from the Body, so that to be united with the one is to be united with the other, the *Totus Christus* of Head and members. However, although there is no separation between "in Christ" and "in the Church", there was clearly for him a logical order such that we are "in Christ" *because* we are "in the Church."[82] Union with the ascended Christ and possession of the Holy Spirit bestowed by Christ are realities mediated through the Church which is indwelt by Christ through the Spirit. This account of the logical order was similar to Walton's treatment, but it would later be challenged by G. R. Beasley-Murray.

Traditionally Baptists have judged faith in Christ on the part of the baptizand to be an essential part of Christian baptism, so that infant baptism has been considered invalid. Even those Baptist churches which practised "open membership" did so on the basis of Christian charity and the assumption that baptism is not essential to salvation, not on the basis that infant baptism is in some sense valid. It would seem, then, that a heightened sense of the efficacy of baptism within a Baptist theology would strengthen this conclusion that infant baptism is invalid. If baptism is understood as an effective sign which unites the baptizand to Christ and all the present benefits of redemption, then it would seem that the only way to relate this kind of baptism to infants would be along the lines of traditional Catholic thought. However, Clark argued for the acceptance of infant baptism as valid, although irregular. He wrote:

> It would be arrogant, grievous, and wholly unjustifiable for any to suggest that infant baptism is no baptism. It is true baptism. The question that must constantly be posed, humbly yet searchingly, is whether it is not impaired baptism, baptism which distorts the sacramental reality, and whether with the partial disappearance of its critical assurances relative to original guilt and eternal destiny it is not increasingly a baptism in search of a theology.[83]

It is not clear what there is in Clark's baptismal theology that would justify his categorical defence of the validity of infant baptism. There may be a way to support validity in spite of irregularity, but to call the denial of this claim "wholly" unjustifiable seems to go far beyond the evidence. There are two factors in his theology which may be at work here: (1) the logical order of "in the Church" and "in Christ"; and (2) the eschatological dimension of baptism.

---

82 Ibid., 33.
83 Clark, "Initiation," 165.

With regard to the first factor, one might argue that the children of church members are in some sense "in the Church" and thus in the sphere of the Spirit's activity. If personal possession of the Spirit is a logical result of being introduced into the corporate locus of the Spirit (i.e., the Church), then it may make sense to speak of small children in Christian families as those who are "in the Spirit." In paedobaptist churches this life in the sphere of the Spirit is sacramentally signified by infant baptism. If one adds to this Clark's strong assertion of the unrepeatability of baptism, corresponding to the ἐφάπαξ of redemption, then the inference of accepting a *de facto* infant baptism may make sense. However, this leaves some major questions about the correlation between Clark's view of baptismal efficacy and the experience of infants, not to mention the problem of interpreting the relation of unbaptized infants to the Church.

With regard to the second factor, baptism as an eschatological sign embodies both an "already" and a "not yet." Just as the first advent of Christ inaugurated the kingdom of God without its immediate consummation, so it is true that our incorporation into Christ and his work has immediate effects, but the full effects await the Parousia. In Clark's words:

> In one sense, baptism effects what it signifies. In another sense, the effective realisation of its significance is the whole of life lived in the Body, that working out of union with Christ crucified and risen, in the flesh and blood of temporal existence, in corporate and corporal fashion, which is the life of eucharistic man.[84]

Christians die and rise with Christ in baptism, but the full experience of this spiritual death and resurrection is a future reality. This proleptic element in baptism is in fact a common argument for the practice of paedobaptism, as Clark noted. It may be possible to argue that since baptism effects spiritual rebirth *in principle* though not in its fullness, then those baptized as infants and those baptized as believers are not in totally different categories--in both cases the baptized persons are called to progressive actualization of what is true in principle.

These attempts to fill out the argumentation are admittedly speculative, because Clark asserted his position on the acceptance of *de facto* infant baptism without developing his case. If these factors are the relevant ones, and if there is validity to such arguments, then it is difficult to see why they would not imply the *practice* of infant baptism, not simply the *acceptance*

---

84 Ibid., 162.

of such baptism after the fact. There appears to be an incoherence in Clark's baptismal theology at this point.

The Publication of *Christian Baptism* (1959)[85]

In the summer of 1955 four Baptist ministers in London began meeting to discuss baptism, aware that the topic was near the top of the ecumenical agenda but also that Baptists had contributed very little to the discussion. They solicited the involvement of other Baptists, and ultimately ten scholars, pastors and theological educators, formed a working group in which the individuals researched specific parts of the question and submitted their conclusions for evaluation by the group. The results were published in 1959, edited by Alec Gilmore (b. 1928), under the title of *Christian Baptism: A Fresh Attempt to Understand the Rite in terms of Scripture, History, and Theology.* Ernest A. Payne, who was then the General Secretary of the Baptist Union, wrote an introductory chapter describing "Baptism in Recent Discussion" to set the historical context, but he was not a member of the working group and did not commit himself to the positions of the group. The book proved to be the watershed in the reformulation of baptismal doctrine, providing for public scrutiny the relatively advanced sacramentalism of a group of younger Baptist leaders and thus provoking public criticism from those who lamented this new departure. In Anthony Cross's words, the book proved to be "one of the most important Baptist works on baptism, and without doubt the most controversial"[86] in this process of reformulation. What follows is a summary of the sacramental contribution of the book and the criticism directed toward it. This summary is not of the book as a whole, but only of those aspects of it which argued that baptism is an efficacious sign (i.e., a sacrament) and attempted to define the benefits of baptism or the mode of their conveyance.

Stephen F. Winward (1911-1986, Baptist Minister, London--the one person who was also a member of the group that produced Walton's earlier book) launched the book with a discussion of "Scripture, Tradition, and Baptism." This chapter did not deal explicitly with the sacramental question, but it did argue for a view of the Bible and tradition which was significantly different from the typical Baptist approach. He rejected a simple biblicism which functions on the assumption that the Bible is a level collection of fully adequate insights and proof-texts, and argued that

---

85 See also Cross, *Baptism*, 196-198, 228-239.
86 Cross, *Baptism*, 196.

apostolic practice is normative only when it reflects what is essential to the gospel.[87] He accepted the idea that apostolic tradition has been perpetuated not only through the New Testament writings, but also through successive generations of the Church (although this latter transmission always stands under the judgment of the uniquely valuable apostolic deposit in the Scriptures).[88] This allows for the possible adoption of theological constructs which are legitimate developments of apostolic teaching, although not explicitly present in the New Testament, but this has more relevance for issues of subject and mode of baptism than for the sacramental question. A high view of baptismal efficacy can in fact be argued on the basis of a primitive biblicism--the long-standing Baptist reduction of baptism to a mere symbol of a completed conversion requires the assertion that key New Testament texts do not mean what they *seem* to mean when they speak, for example, of being "baptized into Christ."

Alec Gilmore (Baptist Minister, Northampton, and editor of the volume) analysed "Jewish Antecedents." In treating the relation of baptism to circumcision, which has always been at the heart of the debate, he suggested a kind of confirmatory significance for baptism:

> Under the new covenant, union with Christ did away with the need for circumcision, and created the need for something to bring home to a man his union with Christ and the realization that he was possessed by Christ's spirit. It was this need which was filled by baptism.[89]

Here the point of "bring home" seems to be that baptism mediates the conscious experience of entrance into the sphere of redemption; in other words, he interpreted baptism along the lines of a "seal" that has no efficacy in itself but does by virtue of its connection to a recognized authority or benefactor have an efficacy at the level of assurance.

At the heart of the book is the exegesis of the New Testament evidence, and R. E. O. White (b. 1914, Baptist Minister, Birkenhead) treated both "The Baptism of Jesus" and "Baptism in the Synoptic Gospels." White provided a balanced and carefully nuanced interpretation of baptism as an event embodying both a human act of obedience to the gospel and a divine

---

87 Stephen F. Winward, "Scripture, Tradition, and Baptism," in *Christian Baptism: A Fresh Attempt to Understand the Rite in Terms of Scripture, History and Theology*, ed. Alec Gilmore (London: Lutterworth Press, 1959), 51.
88 Ibid., 49.
89 Alec Gilmore, "Jewish Antecedents," in *CB*, 65.

act of grace conveying the benefits of the gospel. He posited a strong connection of this sacramental sense to the baptism of Jesus, in that the bestowal of the Spirit at the baptism of Jesus indicated that the focus of the rite was shifting from an act of obedience to a divine empowering of obedience. Although the baptism of Jesus is unique in some ways, he argued (like Robinson before him) that there is "ample suggestion and warrant for a new and vastly enriched conception of what baptism could mean also for those who followed in His steps."[90]

White expanded the significance of the baptism of Jesus along at least five lines: (1) "It lends to the practice his personal authority." (2) "It lends a note of positive enrichment, rather than of negative renunciation, to baptism." (3) It provides as a motive for baptism "personal dedication and obedience," in that this is the meaning of a baptism of "repentance" for the one sinless human. (4) It connects the rite to personal assurance of being a child of God, i.e., it has "filial overtones." (5) It links baptism to the reception of the Spirit, the promise of the Hebrew prophets for the last days, and thus "baptism becomes the sacrament for the transmission of the Spirit."[91] The last two points of this reorientation of baptism indicate something of its sacramental significance for those who "follow the Lord" in baptism. In some sense the Spirit is conveyed to the baptizand in the event, and the presence of the Spirit is an experiential reality which gives assurance that the individual is indeed accepted by grace as a child of God (not a Son of God in the same sense as Jesus, but in a related sense).

White argued that Jesus provided two kinds of warnings which relate to baptism, one against the temptation to disparage baptism as a mere ceremony that is an optional extra, and the other against the attempt to make baptism absolutely necessary for salvation. In his words:

> Unquestionably Jesus opposed any reliance upon the performance of religious acts as efficacious in themselves apart from the state of the heart which they express. . . .
> Nowhere does Jesus suggest that religion can consist in wholly inward states of soul that seek and find no expression in appropriate acts of devotion and commitment, such as baptism might provide.[92]

S. I. Buse (1913-1971, Lecturer in New Testament Studies, University College of North Wales) treated "Baptism in the Acts of the Apostles" and

---

90 R. E. O. White, "The Baptism of Jesus," in *CB*, 93.
91 Ibid., 96-97.
92 R. E. O. White, "Baptism in the Synoptic Gospels," in *CB*, 111.

"Baptism in Other New Testament Writings." In his treatment of Acts he was very hesitant to dogmatize, and he posited a very moderate kind of sacramentalism. He was only prepared to say that baptism *may* have been the normal rite of initiation into the primitive church, but "it can hardly be described as either universal or necessary for salvation."[93] He attempted to steer a middle course between Cullmann, who considered the baptizand as a passive person, and Markus Barth, who considered baptism to be a purely human act. He denied that the human activity in baptism is the whole essence of the event, thus parting company with a sizable part of Baptist tradition. The two sides of baptism are seen in the fact that the individual chooses to be baptized, but baptism is done by an administrator (not by self-baptism). Therefore, "Only when the two sides of baptism, the human and the divine, are seen together is Luke's picture viewed whole."[94]

Central to the treatment of Acts is the issue of the relation between baptism and the gift of the Spirit. Buse recognized that there is no standard description of this in Acts, and the challenge is to identify the norm (if there is one) and the exceptions. He summarized his modest conclusions thus:

"(i) There is no indication that Spirit-baptism at any stage superseded water-baptism, (ii) to assert that baptism and the gift of the Spirit always go together in Acts is to go beyond the evidence, (iii) in part of Acts there is a close connection between the gift of the Spirit and the laying-on of hands, but there are signs that this was a development later than the primitive Jerusalem church.[95]

In the end, he saw too much diversity of experience represented in Acts to draw any firm conclusions about the exact relation between baptism and the benefits signified by it.

Buse found more explicit indications of the efficacy of baptism in other New Testament texts. For example, he asserted concerning 1 Peter 3:21:

Once more we have an approximation to the kind of teaching we find in the Pauline letters: *the Christian dies with Christ in the waters of baptism, and in that experience he finds salvation* [italics his].[96]

---

93 S. I. Buse, "Baptism in the Acts of the Apostles," in *CB*, 116.
94 Ibid., 126-127.
95 Ibid., 122.
96 S. I. Buse, "Baptism in Other New Testament Writings," in *CB*, 179.

The Reformulation of Baptist Sacramentalism

Concerning the Epistle to the Hebrews he argued:

> In 10:22 the tense of the participles, "sprinkled" and "washed", justifies us in regarding them as references to baptism. Christian initiation is pictured as succeeding where the older Levitical rites failed: it gives the cleansing essential for men's approach to God. . . . *The writer of the Epistle to the Hebrews thus regards baptism as the point in Christian experience where the results of the death of Christ are made effective by entry into that close fellowship with God which is represented as the Holy of Holies* [italics his].[97]

This inference from the combination of washing imagery and an aorist participle to a baptismal reference is quite common[98] but questionable. In particular, the grammatical significance of the aorist tense is not sufficiently precise to justify the inference that these participles must refer to one specific event.

George R. Beasley-Murray (b. 1916, Principal, Spurgeon's College, London) dealt with "Baptism in the Epistles of Paul," which was in many ways the most crucial part of the book, given the dominance of Paul in the formulation of Christian theology. He began his chapter with Romans 10:9-10, which does not explicitly refer to baptism but has been interpreted as an allusion to confession of faith in Jesus in baptism. Even though the text is not explicitly baptismal, it does clearly show that Paul can treat some outward human action (verbal confession that Jesus is Lord) that goes beyond faith as instrumental in the reception of salvation, thus demonstrating that great care must be taken in drawing inferences from his *sola fide* teaching. As Beasley-Murray said:

> Since faith in Jesus as the risen Lord brings justification, and confession of His name deliverance from this world and the life of the age to come (verse 10), the baptismal act in which both are expressed is the supreme moment in the believer's experience of salvation. The enigma of the relation of the Pauline teaching on salvation by faith and his high estimate of the value of baptism come most nearly to solution in this verse. For Paul the inner and outer acts of the decision of faith and its expression in baptism form

---

97 Ibid., 183.
98 For other examples see G. R. Beasley-Murray, *Baptism in the New Testament* (Grand Rapids: Eerdmans, 1962), 163, 173. This source is hereafter noted as *BNT*.

one indissoluble event.[99]

He then proceeded to accumulate the evidence of Paul's explicit statements about baptism, the consistent tendency of which is to see it as the event in which sinners are salvifically united to Christ by faith. For example, on Galatians 3:27:

> The union was realized in baptism. It is evident that baptism *into* Christ results in being *in* Christ, which is a *putting on* Christ. . . . Baptism brings unity with Christ and His church. *And in that order of precedence* [italics his].[100]

He recognized that there is a social dimension to being in Christ, but he vigorously argued that union with Christ is the logical foundation of union with his Body. It is, he asserted, Christ who redeems, not the church.[101] In this logical order he was countering the order defended by both Walton and Clark, although without naming them.

Romans 6:3-4 and Colossians 2:12 both express Paul's conviction that what happened for our benefit objectively in the death and resurrection of Christ also happens in us subjectively at conversion, which is to say at baptism. Romans 6 is the more frequently quoted text, but Colossians 2 brings certain elements of Romans 6 to clearer expression, in particular the experience of resurrection with Christ *in the baptismal event* and the fact that what happens in baptism does so "through faith."[102]

Titus 3:5 has been interpreted in various ways by Baptists, some accepting the "washing" terminology as an allusion to baptism, while others have argued that it is a reference to spiritual cleansing and not to baptism. The underlying theological concern of the latter group has been to avoid traditional concepts of baptismal regeneration. Beasley-Murray said:

> Its central conception is that in baptism the corresponding event occurs in the life of the individual as happened to the church at Pentecost: the Spirit is "poured out" through the risen Christ--an idea in direct line with the earliest interpretation of baptism, Acts 2:33, 38. Certainly the saying implies a realistic rather than symbolic understanding of baptism, but that applies to most of the

---

99 G. R. Beasley-Murray, "Baptism in the Epistles of Paul," in *CB*, 129-130.
100 Ibid., 138.
101 Ibid., 139.
102 Ibid., 136, 140.

Pauline utterances on baptism.[103]

He described the effect of the gospel in an individual life, according to Paul, as a "radical influence" when it is received in faith, but the "decisive expression" of faith is baptism.[104] To say that baptism is "decisive" in salvation is to say that whatever may be true invisibly of the relation of the individual to God (and only God knows this), baptism is the means by which faith is translated from attitude into action, and thus the means by which salvation becomes visible and an assured personal reality. Baptism is, for Paul, an effective sign precisely because it is tied to faith. To assert that baptism saves apart from faith is to sever baptismal doctrine from Paul's teaching, but to assert that baptism saves by virtue of being the vehicle of faith is to take seriously what Paul says about both faith and baptism.

D. R. Griffiths (1915-1990, Lecturer in Biblical Studies, University College, Cardiff) treated "Baptism in the Fourth Gospel and the First Epistle of John." He recognized that there is great diversity in scholarly opinion about the extent to which sacramentalism is taught by, or even congruous with, the Johannine literature, and he concluded that the only safe path is to treat every text on its own, rather than assuming a comprehensive sacramental grid.[105] He was prepared to admit the presence of allusions to baptism in various texts about water: probably in John 13:1-11 and 19:31-37; and possibly in 1 John 5:5-8.[106] However, the important text in John is the reference to a birth "of water and Spirit" in John 3:5. Many Baptists (and others) have argued that this does not refer to baptism at all, but instead is a figurative reference to something else, perhaps the spiritual cleansing wrought by the Spirit. But Griffiths considered it impossible to imagine an early Christian writer using "water" in this way without thinking of baptism, concluding that it is both a positive statement about the significance of Christian baptism and "an underlying polemical allusion to John's baptism."[107] He summarized:

> The positive teaching of 3:5 is thus, very briefly, that *entrance into the kingdom of God is impossible except by means of the rebirth in baptism which is both a water-baptism and a bestowal of the*

---

103 Ibid., 143-144.
104 Ibid., 148.
105 D. R. Griffiths, "Baptism in the Fourth Gospel and the First Epistle of John," in *CB*, 150-151.
106 Ibid., 162, 164, 167.
107 Ibid., 156.

Spirit; [italics his] the very form of the construction suggests their indissoluble connection.[108]

This concept of spiritual rebirth (or birth from above) is the Johannine parallel to the Pauline concept of spiritual death and resurrection, and in both cases it is connected to baptism. Why does John not speak explicitly of baptism here? Griffiths followed C. H. Dodd (1884-1973) on this point, concluding that John's audience included pagans whom he wanted to bring to Christian faith, and this kind of allusive language conveys an appropriate kind of sacramentalism without misleading his readers in magical or superstitious directions with which they would be familiar.[109] As will be noted below, his relatively modest sacramental interpretation of John 3:5 was severely criticized by some fellow Baptists as a capitulation to magical ideas of baptismal regeneration.

Turning to the historical development of baptismal doctrine and practice, A. W. Argyle (b. 1910, Tutor, Regent's Park College, Oxford) surveyed "Baptism in the Early Christian Centuries." He chronicled what he interpreted as the descent of the early church into superstitious views of baptismal efficacy which depart from the New Testament, and he traced the rise of infant baptism as a corollary of this shift. He vigorously denied "the superstitious notion that water-baptism itself was regenerative."[110] For many Baptists this is equivalent to denying the sacramental character of baptism, but that was not his point. His comment was that, "The growth of infant baptism inevitably obscured the New Testament significance of baptism as a sacrament of penitence and faith in which the Holy Spirit is received."[111] Therefore, he was defending the idea that baptism is sacramental, and specifically that it mediates the gift of the Spirit, which gift is in fact at the heart of the benefits of the new covenant. What he was attacking was the idea that baptism *per se* regenerates apart from faith in the baptizand. In this regard he was like early Baptists noted in the preceding chapter who, when they denied baptismal regeneration, were not rejecting the idea that God conveys spiritual benefits (indeed, the Spirit himself) through baptism, only the idea that he conveys such benefits to infants or others who have not believed the gospel.

W. M. S. West (b. 1922, Tutor, Regent's Park College, Oxford, and later president of Bristol Baptist College) wrote on "The Anabaptists and the Rise

---

108 Ibid., 158.
109 Ibid., 156-157.
110 A. W. Argyle, "Baptism in the Early Christian Centuries," in *CB*, 217.
111 Ibid., 205.

The Reformulation of Baptist Sacramentalism 121

of the Baptist Movement." There was little in this chapter that related to the sacramental issue; the material was focused on the rise of the "believers' church" among the Anabaptists and ultimately the origin of Baptists through the application of the same ecclesiology among English Separatists in the first decade of the 17th century. The major burden of the chapter was to show the link between believer baptism and the concept of the church as a company of confessing believers voluntarily associated with one another. Unfortunately, West did not seek to interpret in any detail the baptismal language of early Baptists like John Smyth, who spoke of baptism as a "sacrament" and a "visible word" offering Christ to believing recipients.

"Baptismal Controversies, 1640-1900" were surveyed by D. M. Himbury (b. 1922, Principal, The Baptist College of Victoria, Melbourne), with a focus on Baptist debates about the subjects of baptism, the mode of baptism, and the relation of baptism to communion. The only significant reference to the sacramental question was in his suggestion that near the end of the period surveyed, i.e., in the latter part of the 19th century, some Baptists articulated a more sacramental view of baptism in the sense that, "God really acts; by it the believer enters the church and receives new power by the gift of the Spirit."[112] This assertion is a bit mystifying, because he gave no examples of this supposed trend, and in the preceding chapter it was noted that Baptist thought at that time was largely in revolt against sacramentalism, due in great measure to a reaction against Tractarianism. He indicated that he was following J. R. C. Perkin on this point, but as noted in the preceding chapter, Perkin suggested that this Baptist sacramentalism was relatively insignificant numerically. Earlier Baptists had sometimes posited an empowering work of the Spirit through baptism, often as a kind of second, post-conversion, crisis,[113] but this is not true of later Baptist thought. This chapter accurately focused on the baptismal debates that consumed the energy of Baptists, but for that very reason it did little to advance the understanding of Baptist sacramentalism.

The final chapter, "The Theology of Baptism," was authored by Neville Clark (then a Baptist Minister in Rochester) and was generally considered to be the most controversial chapter. This chapter covered much of the same ground as his earlier book (1956) which was surveyed above, but perhaps in a more aggressive tone. There is no doubt about his affirmation

---

112 D. M. Himbury, "Baptismal Controversies, 1640-1900," in *CB*, 274.
113 As noted in Chapter One above, both the *Somerset Confession* (1656) and the *Standard Confession* (1660) posit the idea of a post-conversion gift of the Spirit conditioned partly on baptism. See also the commentary on Acts 2:38 in Gill, *Exposition of the New Testament*, 2:167.

of the sacramental nature of baptism. For example:

> Grounded in the atoning work of Christ, which it applies and extends, its theology must always be an inference from Christology transposed into its true eschatological key. . . . Baptism, in this normative period, implies, embodies and effects forgiveness of sin, initiation into the church and the gift of the Holy Spirit.[114]

Again he wrote:

> Baptism effects initiation into the life of the blessed Trinity and all the blessings of the new "age," and so embodies the wholeness of redemption. It is "into Christ," into the crucified, risen and ascended Lord, into the whole drama of His redemption achievement.[115]

In fact, he was emphatic in his assertion that the divine action in baptism is the fundamental aspect of the event:

> Baptism is a sacrament of the Gospel, not of our experience of it; of God's faithfulness, not of our faithful response to Him; and any theological formulation which lends itself so readily to an interpretation of the rite primarily in terms of a public confession of faith must at once be suspect.[116]

The most significant advance beyond his earlier treatment of the sacraments was his development of the analogy between the Christ-event and the baptism-into-Christ-event. The basic point was, "Since baptism initiates into the fulness of redemption, into the crucified and glorified humanity of the Lord, the pattern of the Christ event must be interpretively decisive."[117] If baptism into Christ means a share in the vicarious work of Christ (cf. Romans 6), then the pattern of divine and human action in the work of Christ is presumed to be operative in the event of baptism into that work. One implication is that the governing action in baptism is the divine work:

---

114 Neville Clark, "The Theology of Baptism," in *CB*, 308.
115 Ibid., 309.
116 Ibid., 316.
117 Ibid., 311.

The priority is always with God, for the incarnation is rightly to be understood not in terms of Adoptionist Christology but of the *assumptio carnis*; and this principle remains regulative for the theology of baptism.[118]

However, just as the divine and human in Christ are distinguishable but not separable, this governing nature of the divine action in baptism does not imply the irrelevance of human response and thus paedobaptism:

What is, however, demanded of us is a reading of baptism in terms of the redemptive work of the God-man which fits uneasily with the Paedo-Baptist position. Salvation is not to be effected outside of, apart from, over the head of man. To deny this would be to deny both the principle of incarnation and the pattern of the life and death of the incarnate Son. But just as the baptism unto death of the Lord is constituted by the conjunction of divine action and human response, so the baptism into His death of His followers demands for its reality their ratification of His response, in obedience to the word proclaimed to them.[119]

In spite of this critique of paedobaptism, Clark argued emphatically against the rebaptism as believers of those who were baptized in infancy. He was not simply saying that rebaptism should not be demanded as a condition of church membership--he was asserting that any such rebaptism is "a blow at the heart of the Christian faith."[120] As noted above, his argument here was rooted in the once-for-allness of redemption which is reflected in baptism, the proleptic nature of every baptism (infant or believer), and the assumption that to reject the validity of infant baptism is to deny the validity of paedobaptist churches.[121] It should come as no surprise to note that this argument was widely rejected by his fellow Baptists. Many other Baptists who would defend the principle of "open membership" would at the same time allow for (and perhaps encourage) rebaptism of those whose conscience called for it, which is a reminder that "open membership" is more a practical policy than a theology of baptism.

Reviews of *Christian Baptism* show that Clark's chapter rated the

---

118 Ibid.
119 Ibid., 313-314.
120 Ibid., 326.
121 Ibid.

highest praise of all the chapters from paedobaptist critics[122] and the strongest protest from Baptists.[123] His own explanation of this was that he was writing with non-Baptists in mind and thus using conceptual categories that were much more intelligible in the ecumenical discussion of "biblical theology" than in typical Baptist circles.[124] While this may make sense at one level, concern to bring fellow Baptists along with him ought to have had some impact on the shape of his argument. It may be that his choice of rhetorical style was simply an unfortunate tactical error which diluted the potential impact of his argument among Baptists, but it may also be true, as H. H. Rowley (1890-1969) noted, that Clark was just more acute as a thinker than he was lucid as a writer.[125]

Criticisms of the Book by Baptists

Within a very short time after the publication of *Christian Baptism*, it was under attack as an unbiblical and unbaptistic capitulation to alien theologies. For several months there was a sustained flow of critical letters to *The Baptist Times*, a weekly newspaper published in London, and ultimately a critical article in that publication by J. D. Hughey (1914-1984) of the Baptist Theological Seminary in Rüschlikon, Switzerland. There was also a strongly critical review of the book by Ernest Kevan (1903-1965, Principal of London Bible College) in *The Fraternal* (July 1959). G. R. Beasley-Murray wrote two articles in *The Baptist Times* (10 December 1959 and 11 February 1960) clarifying and defending the general perspective of the book, but the critical letters continued. R. L. Child (1891-1971, Principal-Emeritus of Regent's Park College, Oxford) also contributed an article in *The Baptist Times* (4 February 1960) defending a moderate sacramentalism which posits some kind of divine action in baptism, although he was reluctant to define it very precisely. The following material is an explanation of five lines of criticism which continually recurred in the letters and articles, followed by a summary of the response by Beasley-Murray. The chief criticisms were these:

---

122 See for example John Heron, Review of *Christian Baptism*, ed. Alec Gilmore, in *Scottish Journal of Theology* 13 (1960): 102-103.
123 For a mild criticism see Norman Maring, Review of *Christian Baptism*, ed. Alec Gilmore, in *Foundations* 3 (January 1960): 91; for a strong criticism see Ernest F. Kevan, "Christian Baptism II," *The Fraternal*, no. 113 (July 1959): 10-12.
124 Neville Clark, "Christian Baptism Under Fire," *The Fraternal*, no. 114 (October 1959): 17-18.
125 H. H. Rowley, Review of *Christian Baptism*, ed. Alec Gilmore, in *The Expository Times* 70 (July 1959): 302.

First, that the sacramental view denies the "faith alone" character of salvation so clearly taught in the New Testament. Hughey, along with many others, emphasized the Pauline texts which affirm the reality of justification by faith apart from works (Ephesians 2:8; Romans; Galatians).[126] Others pointed to Acts 16 and Paul's answer to the Philippian jailor's question, which promised salvation through faith with no reference to baptism.[127] Still others pointed to Acts 10 and the salvation of Cornelius and his household, when the Spirit was bestowed on them as they received the gospel with a believing attitude, prior to any outward response.[128] One letter pointed out that if one assumes that faith is a condition of baptism (as do all Baptists, even the authors of the book in question), then there is posited some interval (short or long) between faith and baptism, so that if salvation comes to all who believe, then it must come prior to baptism.[129] One referred to Neville Clark's chapter and his three tenses of redemption (cross/resurrection, baptism, parousia) and noted that conversion is omitted.[130] This was by far the most common criticism of the book, which is understandable in view of the Baptist commitment to the Reformation principle of *sola fide.*

Second, that the book teaches baptismal regeneration in a way that is equivalent to traditional Catholic doctrine, thus viewing baptism as a kind of magical ceremony. In particular, this criticism was directed at the treatment of John 3:5 by D. R. Griffiths (quoted above). One writer asserted that this was clearly an affirmation of baptismal regeneration,[131] and another writer concurred with this judgment, adding that it was an example of an *ex opere operato* view and as such it constituted "heresy."[132] Griffiths wrote one letter to *The Baptist Times* admitting that his words, if read superficially, might be taken in that sense, but emphasizing that his assertion of the role of the Spirit in baptism safeguards his interpretation from "the materialistic and the magical," and so, "most readers would agree that this is hardly the way in which a writer arguing in favour of baptismal regeneration would put things."[133] Others phrased the criticism more generally, noting that the book betrayed an unbiblical focus on ceremony

---

126 J. D. Hughey, Jr., "The New Trend in Baptism," *The Baptist Times,* 18 February 1960, 7.
127 S. F. Carter, Letter to *The Baptist Times,* 28 January 1960, 6.
128 L. S. Jaeger, Letter to *The Baptist Times,* 24 September 1959, 6.
129 L. J. Stones, Letter to *The Baptist Times,* 10 September 1959, 6.
130 Robert Clarke, Letter to *The Baptist Times,* 8 October 1959, 6.
131 Ibid.
132 S. B. John, Letter to *The Baptist Times,* 25 February 1960, 6.
133 D. R. Griffiths, Letter to *The Baptist Times,* 10 December 1959, 6.

which is seriously at variance with the spiritual/moral tone of New Testament teaching.[134] Hughey took issue with Clark's statement that baptism not only "implies" and "embodies" the benefits of salvation, but also "effects" them. He was prepared to admit a close relation between the sign and the benefits signified, "but not one of cause and effect."[135] Thus he concluded that Clark's language was at best misleading and unfortunate, and probably fallacious.

Third, that the writers of the book misinterpret key scripture texts which are capable of non-sacramental readings. One text that looms large in any attempt to understand the role of baptism in primitive Christian preaching is Acts 2:38, which on the surface seems to clearly view baptism as a means to both forgiveness of sins and the gift of the Holy Spirit. However, Hughey and others utilized A. T. Robertson (1863-1934, the noted Southern Baptist Theological Seminary professor and Greek scholar) to argue that the preposition εἰς in that passage should be translated "because of" or "on the basis of", thus reversing the logical/temporal order of baptism and forgiveness.[136] Robertson admitted that "for" in the sense of aim or purpose would be a possible rendering of εἰς, but argued that in a few places it means "because of" (Matthew 10:41; 12:41), and the analogy of faith calls for that meaning in Acts 2:38. Hughey quoted Robertson as follows:

> One will decide the use here according as he believes that baptism is essential to the remission of sins or not. My view is decidedly against the idea that Peter, Paul, or any one in the *New Testament* taught baptism as essential to the remission of sins or the means of securing such remission. So I understand Peter to be urging baptism on each of them who had already turned (repented) and for it to be done in the name of Jesus Christ on the basis of the forgiveness of sins which they had already received.[137]

What tends to go unnoticed by those who suggest this retranslation is that even if it be accepted, the words of Peter still suggest that the gift of the Spirit is dependent on both repentance and baptism, and the "problem" of sacramental language remains.

The apparent teaching of baptismal regeneration in John 3:5 is often

---

134 S. B. John, Letter to *The Baptist Times*, 8 October 1959, 6.
135 Hughey, "New Trend," 7.
136 Hughey, "New Trend," 7; Robert Clarke, Letter to *The Baptist Times*, 7 January 1960, 6.
137 Hughey, "New Trend," 7.

dealt with by an exegesis which denies that "water" in this text refers to baptism. One writer argued, following Calvin and some others, that the καί in the statement is epexegetical, giving the sense, "of water, that is, of the Spirit."[138] Another writer suggested that "water" denotes natural birth, making the statement a declaration of the need for those who have been born physically to be born again spiritually.[139]

Romans 6:1-4 is a classic text which has always been central to any discussion of the baptismal theology of Paul, and it has played a crucial role from the beginning in the Baptist defence of immersion as the appropriate mode of baptism. However, at least one critic alleged that the text is actually a reference to Spirit-baptism, not to water-baptism at all, claiming to follow the lead of "many Spirit-filled expositors of the Word."[140] As Beasley-Murray noted, the application of this approach to Paul's epistles as a whole might well leave us with virtually no Pauline references to water-baptism at all. It should also be noted that if this reading of Romans 6 (and presumably the parallel in Colossians 2:12) is accurate, then the idea of baptism as a symbol of death and resurrection appears to be unfounded.

Kevan took the authors to task for seeing a baptismal reference in various texts which do not refer to it explicitly but do use images like "water" or "washing". Included in this list would be texts like 1 Corinthians 6:11, Ephesians 5:26, and Titus 3:5, which he argued "no one would ever have dreamed of interpreting sacramentally unless the dilemma of Paedo-Baptists had brought them into the discussion."[141] He concluded that "it is astonishing, therefore, to find that the authors are willing to concede a reference to Baptism in these passages."[142] It is difficult to understand his connecting the sacramental use of these texts to the issue of paedobaptism-- each of the texts looks more like a description of sacramental action in the case of adult converts, especially in 1 Corinthians and Titus, where in both cases the previously pagan lifestyle of the readers is assumed. Even if none of these texts is an allusion to baptism, it is still not difficult to understand why allusions to washing with water might be read that way.

Fourth, that the authors' sacramental view of baptism excludes the unbaptized from salvation and the Church. This particular criticism was rooted in an alleged inference from the basic principle of Baptist sacramentalism. One writer phrased it as a "defective definition of the

---

138 Clarke, Letter, 7 January 1960, 6.
139 John, Letter, 25 February 1960, 6.
140 Clarke, Letter, 7 January 1960, 6.
141 Kevan, "Christian Baptism II," 9.
142 Ibid.

Church as including only baptized believers and not the whole body of believing people."[143] Another argued that if baptism "results in being in Christ" (to quote from *Christian Baptism*), "then it follows that all the fine Christians who are unbaptized are still *out of Christ*."[144] These unbaptized Christians would include Quakers, members of the Salvation Army, and (from a Baptist viewpoint) those baptized in infancy. Hughey emphasized that experience, not to mention Scripture, makes it undeniably clear that saving grace is experienced by huge numbers of persons who have not been baptized as believers.[145] The critics recognized that the Baptist sacramentalists did not draw this inference about the unbaptized, but they argued that this simply represented an incoherence in their theology.

Fifth, that the teaching of the book is contrary to historic Baptist theology, so that whatever else may be said about it, it does not deserve the label "Baptist." None of the critics who made this point were saying that Baptist tradition is infallible, only that the label is not sufficiently elastic to include this kind of baptismal theology. One writer pointed out that he became a Baptist because he was assured that Baptists think of baptism as a symbol rather than a sacrament.[146] Another writer argued that the view was ostensibly rooted in ecumenical concerns, but it would in fact cause division within the Baptist family where no division presently existed.[147] Hughey suggested that the debate was actually a repetition of that between the Baptists and Disciples of Christ in North America over a century earlier, thus equating the "new view" with the Disciples' view.[148] Kevan was perhaps the most forceful critic on this point, especially in his response to Clark's chapter on the theology of baptism:

> It was an editorial blunder of the highest kind to assign this important chapter to a man who, apart from his pastoral inexperience, is an individualist in his views and does not realise how completely out of step he is with his fellow Baptists. Anything less Baptist written by an avowedly Baptist minister it will be hard to find. It is difficult indeed to recognise a Baptist in this chapter, for the magic wand of ecumenicity has been laid on his thinking. . . . The historical sense of every Baptist will rise up within him and

---

143 Stones, Letter, 10 September 1960, 6.
144 Clarke, Letter, 7 January 1960, 6; also John, Letter, 14 January 1960, 6.
145 Hughey, "New Trend," 7.
146 Stones, Letter, 10 September 1959, 6.
147 John, Letter, 8 October 1959, 6.
148 Hughey, "New Trend," 7.

say, "John Smythe I know, and Thomas Helwys I know, but who are you"?[149]

The "Preface" to *Christian Baptism* indicated that one purpose of the book was to clarify for the broader Christian world what Baptists think about baptismal issues, but according to Kevan, "No Paedo-Baptist enquirer could gather from this chapter even the remotest idea of what is normally in the mind of the Baptist minister and the believer at the time of Baptism."[150] Kevan's words were probably accurate as a description of most Baptist thinking about baptism in his day--the book in question was probably more idiosyncratic than representative.[151] However, as demonstrated in the preceding chapter, the kind of Baptist thinking represented by Kevan differs significantly from the first century of Baptist thought.

Among other things, this interchange about what can properly be called "Baptist" theology illustrates the distressing and ongoing Baptist tendency to ignore the work of previous Baptists as if there were no Baptist tradition at all. Thus John Gill wrote about baptism as if his influential predecessor, Benjamin Keach, never existed; Robert Walton wrote about baptism as one example of a broader sacramental principle with references to various Catholic and Anglican scholars, but never referred to Wheeler Robinson, even though Robinson did not retire from academic duties until after Walton's study group began their discussions; and the authors of *Christian Baptism* almost never included Baptist sources in their footnotes, except in historical chapters devoted to Baptist debates, and even there they failed to note precursors of their own viewpoint.

Beasley-Murray's Response

After a series of very critical letters about *Christian Baptism*, G. R. Beasley-Murray wrote an article in *The Baptist Times* (10 December 1959) to respond to the major criticisms. He began by dealing with the charge of teaching baptismal regeneration, noting that the phrase is "a slogan with an unpleasant odour about it," inasmuch as it tends to mean (among Baptists, at least) "automatic production of spiritual and moral ends by going through

---

149 Kevan, "Christian Baptism II," 10-11.
150 Ibid., 11.
151 This is candidly admitted by Beasley-Murray, *BNT*, vi, who refers to his thinking as "a" Baptist view with the emphasis on the indefinite article.

external motions according to prescription."[152] He vigorously denied that he and his colleagues meant anything like this in their interpretation of baptism, but he did assert that baptism is a significant means of grace as "the climax of God's dealing with the penitent seeker and of the convert's return to God."[153]

This high view of baptism was defended by showing that it is the natural way to read the actual baptismal texts of the New Testament. The baptismal commission in Matthew 28:19, by its use of εἰς τὸ ὄνομα, conceives of baptism as the event in which the baptizand hands himself over to and is appropriated by the Triune God. The "plain import" of Peter's statement in Acts 2:38 is that repentance and baptism are answered by God's bestowal of forgiveness and the Holy Spirit. Paul's account of his own baptism in Acts 22:16 does not mean that there is morally cleansing power in the water of baptism, "but it does mean that Paul and the Lord are going to have dealings on that occasion with the stated result."[154] Texts like Romans 6:1-4, Colossians 2:12, and Galatians 3:26-27 indicate that saving union with Christ, which includes a spiritual death and resurrection, is mediated through baptism. Peter's statement that "baptism now saves you" (1 Peter 3:21) indicates that through the commitment expressed in baptism God saves penitent sinners. The point of this list of texts is to show that the common Baptist idea of baptism as a mere symbol pointing backward to a completed conversion has to be read into the actual baptismal references of the New Testament.

He then emphasized that the point of the book was to articulate baptism in the "Church of the Apostles," while recognizing that it may be impossible to replicate it thoroughly today. When viewed in the light of that kind of baptismal experience and theology, current Baptist practice and theology are judged to represent a reduced and impoverished baptism. As he put it:

> This teaching relates to *baptism in the apostolic Church* [italics his], not to baptism in the average modern Baptist church. Where baptism is sundered from conversion on the one hand, and from entry into the Church on the other, this language cannot be applied to it; such a baptism is a reduced baptism. . . . My concern, along with my colleagues, is to put before Baptists the picture of ideal baptism, as it is portrayed in the apostolic writings, in the hope that we may strive to recover it or get somewhere near it. To insist on

---

152 G. R. Beasley-Murray, "The Spirit Is There," *The Baptist Times*, 10 December 1959, 8.
153 Ibid.
154 Ibid.

keeping our impoverished version of baptism would be a tragedy among a people who pride themselves on being the people of the New Testament.[155]

The authors of the book acknowledged that God's grace touches many persons today in patterns that do not correspond to the patterns assumed in the apostolic writings, but this is just to say that God is not bound to sacraments.

He concluded the article by noting that the Baptist tradition needs to be seriously examined before anyone makes sweeping statements as to who are the faithful heirs of that tradition, if in fact there is a consistent tradition.

After several more critical letters to *The Baptist Times* in response to this article, Beasley-Murray penned a second article (11 February 1960) to provide further clarification. His first, and most crucial, point was to argue that in the New Testament baptism is normatively an integral part of conversion, the climax of entrance into the Christian life. If that be the case, then the idea of being baptized in order to enjoy the benefits of Christ ought not seem strange to Baptists, because to be baptized for salvation is essentially another way to describe being converted for salvation. He wrote:

> We are not contending that God justifies by faith but gives the Spirit and unites to Christ by baptism, as though baptism was a "work" alongside faith. That would be a perversion of the Gospel. Our plea has been that in the New Testament baptism is inseparable from the turning to God in faith, on the basis of which God justifies, gives the Spirit, and unites to Christ.[156]

With regard to the exegesis of key texts like Romans 6:1-4 and Acts 2:38, he countered the arguments for a non-sacramental reading of them. He pointed out that the view that Romans 6 is talking about Spirit-baptism is "an eccentric interpretation of a few earlier commentators that will not be found in any of the great contemporary expositions of *Romans*."[157] This resort to an unnatural exegesis of Romans 6 is actually an admission that the passage is talking about baptism as the door to profound spiritual experience, not about baptism as a mere symbol. A similar response was given to A. T. Robertson's suggestion that εἰς in Acts 2:38 be translated

---

155 Ibid.
156 G. R. Beasley-Murray, "Baptism and the Sacramental View," *The Baptist Times*, 11 February 1960, 9.
157 Ibid.

"because of". Even if such a translation were possible (which he denied), it would hardly fit the context in which Peter is replying to "conscience stricken men, convicted of their part in the murder of the Messiah and *seeking* forgiveness". His assessment was that if Robertson were able to speak posthumously, he would admit that when he wrote his commentary on Acts 2:38, "he must have had his tongue in his cheek and his conscience locked up."[158]

Concerning the charge of "magic" in his sacramentalism, he was "amazed at the suggestion." He had never suggested that there is power in the rite as such, only that baptism is the vehicle of confessing faith in Christ and surrendering to him as Lord. It is because of its connection to this inner attitude that it becomes an effective symbol. This idea should not have been foreign to his critics, because such symbolic acts are common in human experience. Two examples that are readily understood are the waving of a white flag which can end hostilities, and a wedding ceremony in which saying "I will" and giving a ring can unite a man and woman in marriage. Such signs are effective symbols which by their performance say, "This here and now becomes true," (as in sacramentalism) rather than, "This has already become true" (as in mere symbolism).[159]

Finally he dealt with the charge that he made baptism necessary for salvation and thus excluded from salvation all those not baptized as believers. His essential response was to say that his baptismal doctrine was an attempt to state "what God has willed baptism to be," but this implies nothing about what happens when baptism is misunderstood or misapplied. He was prepared to recognize people of faith among paedobaptists and even among those who reject the use of sacraments entirely, but he insisted that this is not helpful in formulating a positive baptismal theology, for "we get nowhere by discussing what God can do without." In point of fact, God has given us sacraments, and "our task is not to make the least of them but to receive in gratitude whatever God has to give through them."[160] What the critics failed to note was that the Baptist sacramentalists never drew negative inferences about the spiritual condition of anyone from their baptismal theology. Although that has been true of some theological traditions historically, it was not true of the Baptists in question. This should have been perfectly clear to the critics, because it was inherent in Neville Clark's rejection of the rebaptism of those baptized in infancy--if he

---

158 Ibid.
159 For an extended treatment of this kind of symbolic act, see James W. McClendon, "Baptism as a Performative Sign," *Theology Today* 23 (1966-1967): 403-416.
160 Beasley-Murray, "Sacramental View," 10.

considered believer baptism to be necessary for salvation, then he certainly would have urged rebaptism in these cases.

R. E. O. White, *The Biblical Doctrine of Initiation* (1960)[161]

White, who later became the Principal of the Baptist Theological College of Scotland, was still in pastoral ministry when he published this *magnum opus*. As the title indicates, it explored the entirety of the Bible on the question of the means by which individuals enter into a right relationship with God. He argued for a significant degree of continuity between Old Testament prophetic religion and New Testament teaching in this area, but the bulk of the work was in reality a New Testament theology of baptism and evangelism. He interacted with a wide range of British sources, in particular the work done in the Church of Scotland in the 1950's concerning the doctrine of baptism. Some reviewers criticized the book for its lack of interaction with Continental sources,[162] its purported failure to understand contemporary Catholic thought,[163] and what seemed to some its excessively confident rejection of infant baptism.[164] However, it was widely recognized as a major contribution to the baptismal debate, a book that could not be ignored. Its long-term influence would have been greater if Beasley-Murray had not published his *Baptism in the New Testament* in 1962. This latter work interacted with a wider array of sources and demonstrated convincing exegetical judgment, and it rapidly came to be acknowledged as the crowning achievement of the Baptist contribution to the discussion of baptismal theology. Nevertheless, White's work was vigorously argued and worthy of note.

As one of the authors of *Christian Baptism*, White was well aware of the Baptist resistance to sacramentalism, but he mounted a vigorous and unapologetic counter-attack in this book. He referred to the common, purely symbolic Baptist kind of baptism as "an attenuated parable-rite in which nothing vital is even expected to happen."[165] He made a powerful plea for what he termed a "dynamic sacramentalism" which affirms baptism as the

---

161 See also Cross, *Baptism*, 198-201.
162 William E. Hull, Review of *The Biblical Doctrine of Initiation*, by R. E. O. White, in *Review and Expositor* 59 (July 1962): 403.
163 W. A. Van Roo, Review of *The Biblical Doctrine of Initiation*, by R. E. O. White, in *Gregorianum* 42 (1961): 150.
164 J. K. S. Reid, Review of *The Biblical Doctrine of Initiation*, by R. E. O. White, in *The Baptist Quarterly* 19 (January 1961): 46-47.
165 R. E. O. White, *The Biblical Doctrine of Initiation* (London: Hodder and Stoughton, 1960), 305. This source will hereafter be noted as *BDI*.

meeting-place of human acceptance of the gospel and divine regenerative power, arguing that standard concerns about baptismal regeneration are inapplicable in the context of faith-baptism.[166] One of his summaries of primitive Christian baptism was this:

> Faith-obedience in response to the kerygma's announcement remains the precondition: it is still the word heard and believed that is the operative power, and not the rite. But in the total *human* act of repentance-belief-baptism *divine* things happen; the blessings offered in the gospel are not merely assured but given to whomsoever would respond in penitence and faith to the kerygma message, and the appointed response was baptism upon confession of faith, calling upon the name of the Lord.[167]

His explanation of the fully-developed New Testament doctrine was as follows:

> The dynamic, or existential, sacramentalism of the New Testament seizes upon the fact that divine activity and human response meet in sacramental *action*. The sacramental effect--enduement, gift, remission, reception, incorporation, death-resurrection--occurs within the personal relationship which the act expresses. Thus efficacy belongs strictly neither to the element, nor to the rite, but to the action of God within the soul of the baptised who at that time, in that way, is making his response to the grace offered to him in the gospel. The sacrament consists not in the thing done, but in *the doing* of that which gives expression to faith in appointed ways. On the one side, the faith of the person doing the appointed things invests the rite at that moment, for himself, with sacramental meaning; on the other side, God, accepting this response, in fulfilment of His promise in the gospel invests the rite at that moment, for that convert, with sacramental power.[168]

Such assertions were a recurring theme throughout White's book, and they were exegetically grounded in the New Testament along the lines followed by him and his co-authors in *Christian Baptism*. There were, however, certain emphases in White which made their own special contribution to this

---

166 Ibid., 308.
167 Ibid., 274.
168 Ibid., 308.

process of reformulation.

First, he argued that this approach to initiation has firm roots in the Old Testament prophets. Many Baptists emphasize that Christian baptism is a post-Pentecost phenomenon, inasmuch as its function is to unite believers to the accomplished work of the whole Christ-event, and few want to draw bold connecting lines to anything earlier than the baptism of Jesus. Clearly the baptism of John has some relevance as a precursor, and to a lesser degree Jewish proselyte baptism and perhaps Qumran lustrations, but White saw significance in the prophetic interpretation of the covenant motif. The significance lay in the fact that although God's covenant relation to Israel was unilaterally defined from God's side, it was ineffectual apart from faithful response from the human side. The prophets recognized this and declared that the covenant was a saving reality not for Israel as a whole, but only for the believing remnant, and ultimately it was revealed that a new covenant would be established which internalized the Torah. In White's words, "Inwardness and individualism go together,"[169] which has relevance for the debate about the subjects of baptism.

Second, he emphasized the pivotal and paradigmatic nature of the baptism of Jesus. Here he expanded his argument noted above in the treatment of *Christian Baptism*, arguing that Jesus transformed the rite of baptism from a negative and candidate-centred focus into a positive and God-centred vehicle of grace and power. "Here, at any rate, the rite becomes sacramental."[170] As he later said, "Never, with Jesus' baptismal experience before us, can we reverently say that 'nothing happens' in baptism."[171]

He was, of course, not oblivious to the fact that Jesus is unique in some ways, but as was true for Robinson before him, he argued that in other respects he is imitable and paradigmatic. He summarized it thus:

> That according to our Lord's own testimony such a wealth of meaning and spiritual enrichment attended His own baptism with water at the hands of John, could not but have the most far-reaching influence upon the thoughts and expectations of all who would follow Him in undergoing the rite. Unique in many ways though His experience must be, it set the pattern for Christian baptism as the medium of spiritual confidence in divine acceptance and approval, and as the concomitant of the gift of the Spirit of truth

---

169 Ibid., 31.
170 Ibid., 96.
171 Ibid., 98.

and power. Christ's example and experience have charged the rite of baptism with immense authority and promise.[172]

The support of this assertion demands an explanation of the apparent silence of apostolic teaching about Christ's example in being baptized. White suggested that this silence is not as strange as it may seem, being grounded partly in the lack of any opposition to the rite among Christians (making such an exhortation unnecessary) and partly in the perceived distance between Jesus and those saved by him. He indicated that there may be an allusion to such imitation of Christ in Matthew's account of Jesus' saying that "it is proper for *us* to fulfill all righteousness" (Matt. 3:15).[173]

Third, he cautioned against the application of "prophetic symbolism" to Christian baptism. This attempt to explain the way in which baptism works was a contribution of Wheeler Robinson to the discussion, and although White recognized that it was attractive to those who perceive in baptism a means of great spiritual benefit, he argued that there are some major difficulties in using the analogy. First, in the Old Testament, prophetic symbolism is basically predictive of future realities, whereas Christian baptism is about present experience of the benefits signified by it. Second, the prophetic acts were never performed on persons whose cooperation was necessary to fulfill the prophecy--comparing baptism to those acts might make sense in terms of an *ex opere operato* model, but not in terms of believer baptism. Third, the normative character of such action is open to question, because "even with H. Wheeler Robinson's caveat as to its transcendence of mimetic magic, prophetic symbolism is perilously near to superstition."[174]

Fourth, he argued forcefully that faith as a precondition of baptism is compatible with baptism as a means of divine grace. All Baptist sacramentalists must agree with this statement, but some of them have tended to minimize the human action in baptism as a way of maximizing the divine side of baptism and deflecting a common paedobaptist criticism that says to make faith a condition of baptism is in effect to turn faith into a meritorious work. White, however, argued without apology that there is in baptism a work of grace which is a *response* to human faith. This does not deny the reality of a prevenient grace which draws the human to faith and baptism--it merely denies that the prevenient grace is conveyed through baptism.

---

172 Ibid., 100.
173 Ibid., 91.
174 Ibid., 82.

For example, in his treatment of the Lukan development of doctrine, he argued that although Luke goes out of his way to make it clear that it is the Lord who adds to the church those who are being saved, displaying the divine initiative in a variety of conversions, "Even so, God's will to save waits upon man's acceptance of salvation in penitent faith, of which baptism is the dramatic and appropriate expression."[175] Even though the divine initiative is sometimes expressed in predestinarian ways (Acts 13:48--". . . as many as were ordained to eternal life believed"), it is clear that in those cases the actual bestowal of salvation was an effect of human response.

One of his criticisms of paedobaptism was that it "deserts the covenantal pattern of biblical thought, the two-sidedness of spiritual initiation which is one of the constant features of scriptural religion," and in doing so it sacrifices "the truly personal nature of grace."[176] Following Emil Brunner (1889-1966) and John Oman (1860-1939), he emphasized that at the heart of human salvation is a divine-human encounter in which God, because he is a perfectly holy Person, "respects personal action above all else."[177] He inferred from the personal character of both God and humans that "man, being a person, can maintain his separateness from God, and God's relation to us being personal, He cannot overcome it merely by a grace which "irresistibly" removes it."[178] The last statement makes it reasonably clear where White stood in the Calvinist-Arminian debate, but it does not follow that his assertion of a *responding* grace in conversion-baptism demands an Arminian structure. The distinctive view of Calvinistic theology at this point would not lie in a denial that human response precedes justification, but in an affirmation that the grace which evokes this response is ultimately a special work of "irresistible" or "efficacious" grace done only in the elect. Whether this concept is consistent with responsible human agency in conversion is an issue that Calvinists and Arminians will continue to debate, but in any case it concerns the relation between prevenient grace and faith (i.e., the prelude to conversion), and in no way does it nullify White's assertion concerning the relation between faith and justifying grace (i.e., the effect of conversion).

White's contribution at this point serves to clarify the debate between Baptists and paedobaptists with regard to the implications of the prevenience of grace. There is no difference of opinion as to the reality of prevenient grace. There are essentially two questions at issue: (1) whether

---

175 Ibid., 181.
176 Ibid., 302.
177 Ibid.
178 Ibid., 303.

prevenient grace is mediated through baptism; and (2) whether divine grace is ever a response to human action. Paedobaptists answer Yes to the first question and in some cases seem to say No to the second one. White answers No to the first question, and Yes to the second one.

Fifth, he interpreted baptism as an objectification of repentance and faith, so that it mediates the fully personal experience of salvation. Both Hebrew prophetic religion and its fulfillment in the new covenant make it clear that initiation into and maintenance of a right relationship with God are ultimately about the attitude of the heart, not outward acts. But neither the old nor the new covenant supports a "gnostic idealism" (White's term)[179] which treats persons as disembodied entities and ritual acts as if they were of no value at all. Applied to baptism this means:

> The rite of water-baptism, objectifying for proselytes, for John's disciples, and for Christians, both self-cleansing repentance and divine forgiveness, does *in fact* create and express precisely that attitude, of penitence towards the past and faith towards God's grace and power in the future, which God answers with the gift of His Spirit.[180]

In his interpretation of Johannine sacramentalism, White followed C. K. Barrett (b. 1917) in his view that for John the sacraments are "extensions of the fundamental sacramental fact of the incarnate life of the Son of God."[181] Just as the Word became "flesh" (i.e., fully human), so the salvation that comes through the Incarnation touches the whole person, and adherence to this truth will help to deliver us from a kind of mystical experience which is disconnected from the historical realities of the Christ-event. In White's words:

> Men are saved by faith: but faith too can degenerate into a transient mood of the soul unless it be given body, substance, objectivity, in the overt acts of believing men. Faith needs to be "objectified" in the sacramental experience of the believer, and this involves no inconsistency, because for John, as for the whole New Testament, "sacrament" *means* "faith-sacrament".[182]

---

179 Ibid., 263.
180 Ibid., 256.
181 Ibid., 263.
182 Ibid., 263-264.

If the absolutely essential thing is the inward attitude of penitent faith, then one can talk about the possibility, indeed the reality, that individuals do enter into a right relationship with God apart from baptism. Clearly White would affirm this much, because he quite obviously affirmed the genuine Christian experience of paedobaptists who, according to his conceptual structure, entered into that relationship at some point distinct from their baptism as infants. If so, then it may be accurate to say that what baptism mediates is not the *fact* of salvation, but the *experience* of salvation, which is to say that baptism "objectifies" both the human and the divine action. But this is not to reduce in any way the significance of baptism for us, because all that we know is the visible evidence of the Spirit who "blows where he pleases," so that for us baptism mediates whatever we know about salvation.

G. R. Beasley-Murray, *Baptism in the New Testament* (1962)[183]

If the publication of *Christian Baptism* brought Baptist sacramentalism into the public view, then the publication of *Baptism in the New Testament* raised it to its highest level of visibility and provided its most articulate defence. Beasley-Murray has been in many ways a major influence in this movement being reviewed by this thesis: he defended the concept of sacraments in the Baptist context as early as 1948;[184] his literary contributions to the movement are far more numerous than those of anyone else, as the bibliography of this book will attest; when *Christian Baptism* was under attack, it was he who defended it in the Baptist press; he taught Baptist pastors not only at Spurgeon's College in London, but also at the Baptist Theological Seminary in Rüschlikon, Switzerland and at Southern Baptist Theological Seminary in the U.S.A.; he wrestled with baptismal issues as a Baptist participant in the European section of the Faith and Order Commission;[185] and finally he wrote this book, "the single most important and lasting contribution made by any Baptist this century to the baptismal debate,"[186] which has been widely quoted and respected by scholars of all traditions, as well as the smaller *Baptism Today and Tomorrow* (1966).

The major contribution of this book to sacramental theology was the thoroughness of its exegetical detail. *Christian Baptism* treated every facet

---

183 See also Cross, *Baptism*, 201-202.
184 G. R. Beasley-Murray, "The Sacraments," *The Fraternal*, no. 70 (October 1948): 3-7.
185 His appreciative comments on this ecumenical experience can be found in Beasley-Murray, *BNT*, vi.
186 Cross, *Baptism*, 202.

of its content (biblical, historical, and theological) in summary fashion, and *The Biblical Doctrine of Initiation* was strong on synthesis of biblical materials and the broad strokes of baptismal theology, and each approach had its value. But if anyone pressed the question as to whether this kind of theology is firmly rooted in the exegesis of the New Testament, then Beasley-Murray's book provided the answer. Every biblical reference or apparent allusion to baptism was studied in detail, and this was done while interacting with a wide range of sources in several languages.

After 262 pages of painstaking exegesis, he began his synthesis of baptismal doctrine in this way:

> In the light of the foregoing exposition of the New Testament representations of baptism, the idea that baptism is a purely symbolic rite must be pronounced not alone unsatisfactory but out of harmony with the New Testament itself. Admittedly, such a judgment runs counter to the popular tradition of the Denomination to which the writer belongs. . . . But the New Testament belongs to us all and we all stand judged by it. . . . The Apostolic writers make free use of the symbolism of the baptismal action; but they go further and view the act as a symbol with power, that is, a sacrament. "Whoever says sacrament says grace," wrote H. J. Wotherspoon, "for grace is the differentia of the sacrament, by which it is more than a symbol." The extent and nature of the grace which the New Testament writers declare to be present in baptism is astonishing for any who come to the study freshly with an open mind.[187]

The chapter which followed these words developed this thought in its various facets and related baptism to other soteriological realities. The thought was similar to White's book in many ways, but the following aspects were particularly important or distinctive contributions to the ongoing Baptist discussion.

First, he emphasized that baptism is fundamentally an occasion for an individual divine-human encounter. In other words, the heart of baptism, its *modus operandi*, is not the power of sanctified water, nor even the power of doing appropriate actions in the name of the Lord, but the acted prayer of a penitent sinner which is answered by a gracious God. This emphasis was very similar to that of White which was noted above, but whereas White's

---

187 Ibid., 263.

concern was to argue that both human and divine action are embodied in baptism in that order, Beasley-Murray's concern was to assert emphatically that this conjunction of prayer and response fundamentally exhausts the content of the event. In other words, baptism is efficacious only in the sense that it is the event which facilitates this personal encounter.

In his discussion of baptism in Acts he argued, "Just as baptism is an occasion of confessing faith in Christ and is itself a confession, so it is the occasion of prayer by the baptizand and is itself an act of prayer."[188] Later he asserted, "Baptism saves, not because water washes dirt from the body, but as the occasion when a man is met by the Risen Christ."[189] He rejected the idea that there is "any decisive significance imputed to water, in the sense of its possessing magical sacramental power."[190] Contrary to at least the superficial sense of much in the Catholic tradition, the grace offered in baptism is "no impersonal influence, injected through material substances, but *the gracious action of God himself* [italics his]."[191] He concluded his chapter of doctrinal synthesis with these words:

> It behoves us accordingly to make much of baptism. It is given as the trysting place of the sinner with his Saviour; he who has met Him there will not despise it. But in the last resort it is only a *place*: the Lord Himself is its glory, as He is its grace. Let the glory then be given to whom it belongs![192]

This emphasis was not entirely absent from earlier literature in this movement, but he seemed to articulate it with a unique passion and an acute sensitivity to the concerns of his fellow Baptists.

Second, he dealt directly with the issue of the necessity of baptism in an attempt to answer honest Baptist questions. As noted above, one of the major concerns of the critics of *Christian Baptism* was their claim that a sacramental understanding of baptism excluded all the unbaptized from salvation. This was a major issue for Baptists for a variety of reasons, but the earlier Baptist sacramental literature tended to ignore the concern. Whatever the reasons may have been for that apparently cavalier attitude toward the question, it should be obvious that it cannot rightly be ignored. Beasley-Murray's treatment of it was carefully nuanced. He began by noting

---

188 Ibid., 101.
189 Ibid., 265.
190 Ibid.
191 Ibid.
192 Ibid., 305.

that in the apostolic age the question would have sounded strange, given the assumption that all those who turned to Christ sealed their conversion by baptism. Paul, for example, could include "one baptism" (Eph. 4:5) in his list of commonalities of the Body of Christ, and he could assume that all those who believed in Christ were baptized into Christ (Gal. 3:26-27). But is this assumption grounded in a necessity for baptism that is the same as the necessity for penitent faith? He argued that the evidence indicates a "margin of ambiguity that exists in the New Testament with regard to baptism."[193]

One of the powerful indicators of this margin of ambiguity is the account given in the Acts of the Apostles concerning the gift of the Spirit in the apostolic age. He noted:

> The complex phenomena of the Spirit in relation to baptism in Acts compel a dual recognition: first that baptism is closely linked with the reception of the Spirit, howsoever it may be received; secondly that allowance must be made for the freedom of God in bestowing the Spirit, since *God exercises that freedom*.[194]

John 3:5 has been a text commonly used to argue for the absolute (or virtually absolute) necessity of baptism for regeneration, which has led many Baptists to deny that "water" here denotes baptism. Beasley-Murray, however, argued that while this text relates baptism to regeneration, it is only the Spirit who is described as the agent or instrument of rebirth: it is the "Spirit" who gives life, not "the water and Spirit."[195] Furthermore, the Spirit is said to be as unfathomable in his working as the air is in its movement, and if this is so, how can his regenerating activity be invariably tied to baptism? Both John 3:5 and Titus 3:5 refer to a conjunction of baptism and the Spirit's work of regeneration, but neither text argues that salvation cannot happen apart from baptism.[196]

To this list could be added Paul's treatment of justification by faith in Romans, especially the extended argument of chapter 4. There Paul argues that Abraham's experience is paradigmatic for all believers, and the assertion of Paul is that "this pattern-faith of Abraham's was wholly independent of an external rite."[197] Although Paul values baptism highly (Romans 6), it is clear that for him it is the faith expressed in baptism that

---

193 Ibid., 301.
194 Ibid.
195 Ibid., 303.
196 Ibid.
197 Ibid.

is absolutely necessary, and baptism's necessity is not in quite the same category.

In the end Beasley-Murray concluded that "it is desirable to avoid the term 'necessary' when considering the meaning of baptism,"[198] given the amount of misunderstanding and equivocation which occurs in connection with the term. It would be better "to recognize positively that God has graciously given us sacraments for our good and that it is our part to receive them gratefully."[199] This declaration that the sacramental character of baptism functions only positively ("be baptized in order to be saved by Christ"), not negatively ("if you are not baptized, then you cannot be saved"), is a crucial point which could have been emphatically stated much earlier in the reformulation of baptismal theology.

Third, he argued that we are in the Church because we are in Christ, not vice versa. In making this plea to avoid what he considered an unbiblical elevation of the role of the Church, he was responding not only to some outside his own tradition, but also to writers like Walton and Clark within the Baptist tradition. As noted above, both Walton and Clark accepted the premise that "in Christ" is fundamentally an ecclesiological formula for Paul, implying that "the convert is in the Church and consequently is in Christ."[200] Beasley-Murray dissented from this view of the matter, arguing that, "The only control over baptism that the Church or its representatives has is to grant it or withhold it, but its spiritual significance first and last is from the Lord."[201] He elaborated thus:

> Against all tendencies to a misplaced stress on the Church it must be insisted that baptism takes place in the name of the Lord Jesus, not in the name of the Church. The believer is ingrafted into the Body because he is united with the Christ in his saving work by the Spirit; the reverse is never contemplated in the New Testament. Not even the richness of the symbol of the Body must be permitted to minimize the fact that there is a Redeemer and there are the redeemed, there is a Lord and there are his servants, there is a King and there are his subjects, there is a Judge and there are those to be judged--and judgment begins at the house of God! In every symbol representing the relationship of Christ and his people, including

---

198 Ibid., 304.
199 Ibid.
200 Ibid., 280.
201 Ibid.

that of the Body, Christ dominates the scene.²⁰²

Fourth, he rejected the validity of infant baptism, even though he defended the practice of "open membership." In his treatment of "Baptismal Reform and Church Relationships," he raised the question as to whether Baptists should change their traditional practice and accept the validity of infant baptism in spite of its perceived irregularity. Many of the Baptists who had adopted a higher view of the significance of baptism also felt a heightened sensitivity about the rebaptism of those baptized in infancy, believing that such action was a functional denial of the ἐφάπαξ of redemption. As noted above, both Walton and Clark had earlier made this argument, and in 1966 Alec Gilmore would adopt the same position in his *Baptism and Christian Unity*. Beasley-Murray responded:

> I confess my inability to concur with them. For the reasons earlier made known, I find myself unable to recognize in infant baptism the baptism of the New Testament Church and nothing that my fellows have written has helped to mitigate this difficulty for me. Moreover I think it right to disabuse the minds of any who have been led by the utterances of some of my Baptist colleagues to imagine that a change of view on this matter is taking place in Baptist circles; there is strong resistance to any such change among British Baptists and the mere voicing of it is looked on with astonishment among Baptists in the rest of the world, who form the bulk of our people.²⁰³

His own position was that Baptist churches should admit to membership those who are already members of other churches, even if they were baptized as infants, but on the basis of Christian charity rather than the presumed validity of their baptism. He admitted that "this policy is open to criticism and is often misunderstood" by Baptists outside England (where it was widely accepted) and by paedobaptists, but he defended it as an appropriate "compromise in a complex ecclesiastical situation."²⁰⁴ He would suggest in general that Baptists abstain from rebaptizing those who were baptized in infancy, although he argued that it should be allowed "where there is a strong plea for it from the applicant."²⁰⁵

---

202 Ibid., 281-282.
203 Ibid., 392.
204 Ibid.
205 Ibid.

The Reformulation of Baptist Sacramentalism

This question of "open membership" and its correlation with a sacramental view of believer baptism is indeed a difficult one and will require further exploration below in Chapter Four. What is crucial here is to recognize that the theological support for the policy is not uniform. Beasley-Murray's argument would be rejected by many Baptists, but it is important to note that it is a very different kind of argument from that of Neville Clark or Robert Walton.

Alec Gilmore, *Baptism and Christian Unity* (1966)[206]

When Gilmore edited *Christian Baptism* in 1959, he had very little chance to develop his own theology of baptism, because his chapter was devoted to "Jewish Antecedents." However, in this 1966 volume he formulated his variety of sacramentalism in his continuing attempt to move Baptists beyond their cherished traditions. He was well aware that many Baptists were resistant to the "body of younger Baptist opinion"[207] which he represented, and he characterized them thus:

> Behind this self-defence there obviously lies a fear. It is the fear that Catholic and sacramentarian teaching might be accepted by the growing generation of Baptists. It is more than that: it is the fear that some Baptists might run away with the idea that in the sacraments something happens. It is more even than that: deep down, it is the fear that in the sacraments God might *do* something.[208]

He cited two examples of what he considered an excessively defensive attitude toward sacramentalism: First, he referred to Henry Cook's 1947 volume and his criticism of both Roman Catholic and Lutheran doctrines of the real presence of Christ in the Eucharist, in which he accused them of "trying to materialize something that is and must be essentially spiritual" and affirmed that the bread and wine are "merely symbolic." Second, he referred to a statement on the Eucharist by the Baptist Union Council in 1948 which said, "We hold that . . . Christ is really and truly present, *not in the material*

---

206 See also Cross, *Baptism*, 208.
207 Alec Gilmore, *Baptism and Christian Unity* (Valley Forge: The Judson Press, 1966), 40. This source will hereafter be noted as *BCU*.
208 Ibid., 41.

elements, but in the heart and mind and soul of the believer."[209]

Over against this typical Baptist kind of affirmation, Gilmore asked "whether in the light of modern scholarship it is both right and profitable to keep trying to drive this wedge between the spiritual world and the material world."[210] The modern scholarship which he adduced to affirm a correlation of the material and the spiritual worlds was both scientific and biblical.

There are several ways in which science and medicine were invoked as witnesses. He began with the observation that, contrary to the antagonistic relation between science and religion around the turn of this century, it had become increasingly true that for scientists "the worlds of matter and spirit are not nearly so clearly distinguished the one from the other as used to be imagined."[211] In the realm of medicine, especially psychiatry, "the old dichotomy of mind and spirit has at least begun finally to be resolved by an acceptance of the interdependence of the one upon the other,"[212] leading to a body of knowledge about psychosomatic medicine. The resultant assumption was that neither psychiatric illness nor physical illness could be studied in isolation from the other. Modern psychology bears witness to the power of physical actions as symbols, for example the power of parental hugs to communicate love and a sense of security to their children.[213] Both the material and the spiritual are at work in such displays of affection--a caress is more than just a certain amount of pressure being applied to the body, because a robot could not communicate the same concern even if the physical action were identical. So in the end, "The whole trend of our age is against dividing man up into body and soul, and dividing his values up into material and spiritual."[214]

Alongside this evidence from the sciences, Gilmore also noted various trends in biblical-theological scholarship. First of all, modern Old Testament scholarship "has come to see a unity in the priest-prophet controversy."[215] For some time much of Old Testament scholarship posited a contradiction between the priestly-ritualistic and prophetic-ethical kinds of religion evidenced in the history of Israel, but scholars increasingly were admitting that this distinction is about "priorities rather than alternatives."[216] Similarly, one does not have to choose between sacraments on the one hand

---

209 Ibid., 42.
210 Ibid.
211 Ibid., 45.
212 Ibid.
213 Ibid., 47.
214 Ibid.
215 Ibid., 49.
216 Ibid., 50.

and evangelical faith on the other. Some would set Jesus over against this conjunction of ritual and ethics, but this was considered misguided, inasmuch as the sacrificial system of the old covenant came to an end not because of Jesus' prophetic teaching, but because of his death. Jesus' attitude toward the temple and its cultic activity may be prophetic, but it is not anti-priestly.[217]

But what about Paul and the early church? There is indeed some tension between the "institutional" apostolate of the twelve and the "charismatic" apostolate of Paul, but the two are not in conflict. They are complementary rather than contradictory, as modern scholarship increasingly asserts. Neither the Catholic nor the Protestant style of churchmanship can lay exclusive claim to biblical roots; each needs to be modified by the other in a search for the complete picture.[218]

With regard to Paul himself, the articulate defender of justification by faith, "Modern biblical scholarship finds much of the sacramental in Paul."[219] Gilmore referred here to the work of A. Wikenhauser (1883-1960), a German Catholic New Testament scholar, on Pauline mysticism, in which he argued for baptism as the crucial objective component in Paul's concept of religious experience. Gilmore said of Wikenhauser, apparently with approval:

> He examines the relevant passages to discover what role, if any, is played by faith in the process, and concludes that though faith does not establish union with Christ, it is the indispensable condition for the establishment of this union. ". . . without faith there is no union with Christ . . . faith is the necessary condition for receiving baptism, which establishes union with Christ."[220]

If indeed he was affirming Wikenhauser's perspective, then he was expressing a relationship between faith and baptism which is significantly different from that which was present in White and Beasley-Murray. For both White and Beasley-Murray, it was the faith which is objectified in baptism that establishes union with Christ; this did not disparage the importance of baptism, but it did view baptism as important specifically because it is the definite confession of personal repentance and faith--faith is the "soul" which animates the "body" of baptism. For Wikenhauser, and

---

217 Ibid., 51.
218 Ibid., 53-54.
219 Ibid., 55.
220 Ibid., 55-56.

apparently Gilmore, faith is not the invisible content of baptism, but merely the precondition of baptism.

The final example of contemporary biblical theology which he invoked was the contribution of H. Wheeler Robinson, specifically his development of the ideas of "corporate personality" and "prophetic symbolism."[221] It is easy enough to see the significance of the latter idea, as noted above in the summary of Robinson's baptismal theology, but it is more difficult to see the point of corporate personality as a support for sacramentalism. The only illustration which Gilmore gave is the Pauline tendency to switch freely from "in Christ" to "in the Church," but while this may be relevant for certain aspects of baptismal theology, it does not seem to be relevant for the "symbol versus sacrament" question. The one possible point of relevance may be to support the idea that when the Church acts in baptizing, Christ is also acting, so that baptism embodies a "spiritual" work of grace along with the "physical" work of obedience. But if this is the inference to be drawn from corporate personality, Gilmore did not explicitly state it.

As has already become clear, one of the perplexing questions for Baptist sacramentalists, recognizing that they refuse to practise infant baptism, is whether to accept the validity of *de facto* infant baptism. The early Baptists refused to do so, but they resented being called "Anabaptists," for in their opinion infant baptism, whatever positive intentions it may express, was simply not Christian baptism. Some modern Baptists (e.g., Walton and Clark) have argued vigorously that infant baptism is genuine (though unwise) baptism, while others (e.g., Beasley-Murray) have rejected this conclusion, even though they may affirm open membership as a policy. Gilmore came down on the side of Walton and Clark, on the basis that, "if infant baptism is 'no baptism,' then the Church that practises it is 'no church.'"[222] Few Baptists affirm that narrow view at a theoretical level, and fewer still at a practical level; therefore:

> It is better to acknowledge that infant baptism, though partial in its expression of the truth and though involving serious theological distortion, is nevertheless baptism, and cannot therefore be followed by believers' baptism being administered to the same person.[223]

Thus in *Baptism and Christian Unity* Gilmore articulated a Baptist

---

221 Ibid., 56-57.
222 Ibid., 81.
223 Ibid.

sacramentalism which pressed the case for the reformulation initiated by Robinson and applied it to questions of Christian unity, but there are indications that his conceptual scheme went beyond the parameters of earlier statements. Specifically, it appears that he defended a more Catholic kind of sacramentalism in which the operations of divine grace are more localized in material elements and physical actions. The evidence for this is found in his critical appraisal of previous Baptist statements by Henry Cook and the Baptist Union Council, as quoted above. Both of these statements dealt directly with the Eucharist and the relation of Christ to the material elements; however, it was in the context of an attempt to articulate the nature of sacraments in general, so that explicit statements about the bread and wine of the Eucharist carry implicit meaning for the water of baptism.

His use of Cook revolved around Cook's criticism of the doctrines of transubstantiation and consubstantiation as explanations of the presence of Christ in the bread and wine of the Eucharist. He took issue with Cook's assertion that both doctrines are illegitimately translating spiritual realities into the material realm, which implies that he was prepared to accept a genuinely material presence of Christ in the elements. If he were unwilling to accept this, then what would be the point of his criticism of Cook? As shown above in the summary of Cook's thought, he was open to the term "sacrament" when carefully explained, and he viewed both baptism and the Lord's Supper as means of grace to those who receive them in faith; therefore, his assertion that the elements are "merely symbolic" does not imply a Zwinglian, purely memorialistic, view of the Eucharist, only that the elements are vehicles of a work of the Holy Spirit rather than carriers of the physical body and blood of Christ. As applied to baptism, Gilmore's approach would seem to imply that God acts through the water *per se*, rather than in a direct personal encounter occasioned by the water-based ritual.

Similarly, Gilmore suggested that the Baptist Union Council was driving a "wedge between the spiritual world and the material world" in its statement that the presence of Christ in the Eucharist is "not in the material elements." But if this qualification was objectionable to him, it can only be because he affirmed what the statement denied, which would be the actual physical presence of Christ in the elements. The historical referent of the Council statement is not really in question, given that the intent of the statement was to position British Baptists in relation to the ecumenical Church. The statement affirmed that Christ is "really and truly present" (and presumably active) in the celebration of the Lord's Supper, so that the only thing lacking (from Gilmore's standpoint) would be activity in the elements themselves.

It is one thing to affirm that God is actively conveying the benefits of redemption to the believing person in the baptismal event, but quite another thing to say that God conveys this benefit through the water as such. Although Gilmore may not explicitly say the latter, it seems to be implicit in his thought.

Denominational Statements

The Baptist Union of Great Britain has been from its inception a relatively non-credal body, but there have been periodic statements adopted by either an annual Assembly as a whole or by the Council elected to govern the Union. Some of these statements have discussed the doctrine of baptism and thus illustrate the shape and direction of Baptist thought. The relevant statements for this century indicate that the Union is willing (despite the reservations of some of its members) to use the term "sacrament" to describe baptism, that baptism is thought of as a means by which God's grace affects human experience, but that the grace which is mediated is perhaps only a "second" kind of grace connected to post-conversion experience.

In April 1918, the Baptist Union Assembly, under the influence of its ecumenically oriented Secretary, J. H. Shakespeare, approved a doctrinal basis for a projected Free Church Federal Council, which included the following paragraph:

> The Sacraments--Baptism and the Lord's Supper--are instituted by Christ, Who is Himself certainly and really present in His own ordinances (though not bodily in the elements thereof), and are signs and seals of His Gospel not to be separated therefrom. They confirm the promises and gifts of salvation, and, when rightly used by believers with faith and prayer, are, through the operation of the Holy Spirit, true means of grace.[224]

Although this statement did not originate with the Baptist Union, its approval by the Assembly indicated that it qualified as a Baptist assertion. It was highly general in tone, using the term "sacrament" in the sense of a "means of grace," but without defining the precise sense in which grace is at work in the event. It was, no doubt, this lack of precision that allowed the

---

224 Ernest A. Payne, *The Baptist Union: A Short History* (London: Carey Kingsgate Press, 1958), 276. The full text of the doctrinal statement is "Appendix VIII" of this book. See Cross, *Baptism*, 42-52 for a commentary on the Baptist discussion concerning membership in the Free Church Council.

approval of the statement.

In 1920 the Lambeth Conference of the Anglican Communion issued an "Appeal to all Christian People" concerning Christian unity. After a delay to allow for clarifying conversations between Anglican bishops and Free Church leaders, a Baptist Union reply was adopted unanimously by the Assembly in May 1926, which said at one point:

> Christian Baptism and the Communion of the Lord's Supper are duly received by us not only as rites instituted and hallowed by our Lord Himself, but as means of grace to all who receive them in faith.[225]

The paragraph following the above explained the continuing Baptist refusal to practise infant baptism and the normative role of immersion as the mode of baptism, and in so doing it used the terminology of "the ordinance of baptism." Later it dissented from "the place given to Sacraments by the Lambeth Appeal," but it did not reject the term "sacrament."[226]

The most explicit affirmations are found in a statement called "The Baptist Doctrine of the Church," which was approved by the Council of the Baptist Union in March 1948 as a part of their involvement in the founding of the World Council of Churches.[227] The statement asserted, "We recognize the two sacraments of Believers' Baptism and the Lord's Supper as being of the Lord's ordaining," and it affirmed that "both are 'means of grace' to those who receive them in faith."[228] It expressed a belief "that Christ is really and truly present" in the sacramental action of the believing community, although not in the material elements.[229] The manner in which baptism functions sacramentally was stated thus:

> As a means of grace to the believer and to the church and as an act of obedience to our Lord's command, we treasure this sacrament. The New Testament clearly indicates a connection of the gift of the Holy Spirit with the experience of baptism which, without making the rite the necessary or inevitable channel of that gift, yet makes it

---

225 Payne, *Baptist Union*, 280. See also Cross, *Baptism*, 52-67 for a discussion of the Baptist response to the Lambeth Appeal.
226 Payne, *Baptist Union*, 281.
227 See Cross, *Baptism*, 152-158 for a commentary on Baptist response to Faith and Order and the World Council of Churches.
228 Ibid., 288.
229 Ibid.

the appropriate occasion of a new and deeper reception of it.[230]

This concept of baptism as a means of a "deeper" experience of the Spirit echoed the comments of Underwood a decade earlier and still posited an experience of conversion and the Spirit which is completed prior to baptism. This was even more explicit in their statement about the conditions of church membership:

> The basis of our membership in the church is a conscious and deliberate acceptance of Christ as Saviour and Lord by each individual. There is, we hold, a personal crisis in the soul's life when a man stands alone in God's presence, responds to God's gracious activity, accepts His forgiveness and commits himself to the Christian way of life. Such a crisis may be swift and emotional or slow-developing and undramatic, and is normally experienced within and because of our life in the Christian community, but it is always a personal experience wherein God offers His salvation in Christ, and the individual, responding by faith, receives the assurance of the Spirit that by grace he is the child of God. It is this vital evangelical experience which underlies the Baptist conception of the Church and is both expressed and safeguarded by the sacrament of Believers' Baptism.[231]

Given the later admission that they were divided on the question of whether baptism is a precondition of church membership, this "vital evangelical experience" was clearly thought of as occurring apart from and prior to baptism; i.e., this experience is "expressed" by baptism as something which has already occurred, not as something which happens in the act of baptism itself. Later developments in Baptist sacramentalism argued that although personal experience cannot be made uniform, the normative expectation is that this response to the offer of grace occurs in baptism, rather than prior to it, i.e., that the "personal crisis" occurs in baptism.

Baptist Service Books

Since the theology of baptism is expressed in the practice of baptism, one evidence of a shift in theology might be found in printed liturgies of

---

230 Ibid., 289.
231 Ibid., 285.

baptism. Although there is no uniform "Prayer Book" in the British Baptist tradition, there have been various outlines for the conduct of worship and the sacraments that have been widely used. For most of the period in view the most widely used service book was *The Minister's Manual*, published in 1927 by M. E. Aubrey (1885-1957), who later became the General Secretary of the Baptist Union, but it was eclipsed by the publication in 1960 of *Orders and Prayers for Church Worship* by Ernest Payne and Stephen Winward. The developing Baptist theology is reflected in the differences between the two books.

In Aubrey's book there were guidelines for a pastoral homily which clarifies what is presumed to happen in the baptismal event. Baptism is interpreted as (1) an act of obedience to the command of Christ and his apostles; (2) an open confession of faith in God and devotion to the service of Christ; (3) the act by which the individual joins himself to the community of believers; and (4) an imitation of Christ. Only after this four-fold focus on the human expression of commitment is there a stated recognition that the act symbolizes God's work in Christ, and that there is some experience of grace to be anticipated.[232]

In the later book by Payne and Winward, published just one year after *Christian Baptism* and in the same year as *The Biblical Doctrine of Initiation*, the emphasis was decidedly reversed. After reading selected baptismal texts from the New Testament, the minister says, "Let us now set forth the great benefits which we are to receive from the Lord, according to his word and promise, in this holy sacrament." The benefits are then declared as follows:

> In baptism we are united with Christ through faith, dying with him unto sin and rising with him unto newness of life.
>
> The washing of our bodies with water is the outward and visible sign of the cleansing of our souls from sin through the sacrifice of our Saviour.
>
> The Holy spirit, the Lord and giver of life, by whose unseen operation we have already been brought to repentance and faith, is given and sealed to us in this sacrament of grace.
>
> By this same Holy Spirit, we are baptized into one body and made

---

[232] Cited by Michael J. Walker, "Baptism: Doctrine and Practice among Baptists in the United Kingdom," *Foundations* 22, no. 1 (1979): 75-76.

members of the holy catholic and apostolic Church, the blessed company of all Christ's faithful people.

These great benefits are promised and pledged to those who profess repentance toward God and faith in our Lord Jesus Christ.[233]

This attitude of repentance and faith is then described as coming to expression in baptism, and prior to the act of immersion the minister prays that the baptizands "may by faith be united with Christ in his Church, and receive according to thy promise the forgiveness of their sins, and the gift of the Holy Spirit."[234]

The earlier and later service books were not contradictory in any explicit way, but the focus of the later book was clearly on God's action in a way that was not true of the earlier book. This is reflective of the growing sense that baptism is not merely a means of some sort of "second" work of the Spirit that strengthens an assurance of salvation which has already been experienced, but instead the normative means by which entrance into the benefits of Christ becomes an assured, experiential reality. To put it another way, the earlier and milder form of sacramentalism conceived of baptism as an act of an obedient disciple by which she is empowered for further steps in the Christian life, but the later and stronger form thought of baptism as an act of a penitent sinner by which she consciously responds to the offer of grace in the gospel and becomes a disciple of Christ.

Summary

At a *descriptive-historical* level, the 20th-century reformulation of a Baptist-sacramental view of baptism would be characterized as follows: (1) It originated in a context of concern for denominational identity. Baptists in England had always existed as an uncomfortable minority over against a state Church and paedobaptist Free Churches, and it was not clear that a purely symbolic view of baptism was sufficient to undergird a distinct denominational existence. (2) It was marked by collegiality. Two of the major books, *The Gathered Community* (1946) and *Christian Baptism* (1959), were products of group discussion with a view to consensus. (3) It was rooted in ecumenical concern. Much of the literature was a conscious attempt to be involved meaningfully in the baptismal debates which marked

---

233 Ernest A. Payne and Stephen F. Winward, *Orders and Prayers for Church Worship* (London: Kingsgate Press, 1960), 171-172.
234 Ibid., 173.

most denominations after World War II. Several of the major contributors participated in Faith and Order Commission discussions of baptism, notably Ernest Payne, G. R. Beasley-Murray, and Morris West; and Neville Clark was involved in the Joint Liturgical Group in Great Britain. (4) The contributors were aware that they were seeking to reform Baptist thought and practice, but they showed only a limited knowledge of the Baptist tradition. They were in general much more concerned to interact with scholars of other traditions than to interact with earlier Baptist literature. Consequently, they failed to demonstrate that they were legitimate heirs of an early Baptist tradition, and at times they failed to anticipate Baptist objections to their conceptual structure. (5) The movement was very much rooted in biblical theology, to the neglect of systematic theology. Their interaction with scholars of other traditions was generally in the area of New Testament exegesis (where there was a high degree of ecumenical consensus), not the area of systematic formulations.

At a *theological* level, there were two key principles at work: (1) Whatever may be the Baptist tradition, an accurate interpretation of the Bible demands that baptism be viewed as an effective sign, i.e., a sacrament. At the heart of the movement was a cherished Baptist principle: the unique authority of Scripture and the corresponding possibility of error in all creeds and extra-biblical traditions. It was assumed that the Church is *semper reformanda*, and the reshaping of baptismal theology is part of the process. (2) As human beings we function holistically; therefore, it is important that an attitude of commitment to Christ be objectified in personal action. Baptism is the divinely-ordained context in which attitude is translated into action. Although many persons enter into genuine Christian discipleship apart from believer baptism, this is in biblical terms an anomaly, and something is missing when conversion is not sacramentally sealed.

There was in general a high degree of consensus in this collegial modification of Baptist theology, but there were some internal points of tension and lingering questions. (1) To what extent is this understanding of baptism rooted in a general principle of sacramental action? (2) What is the exact significance of the baptismal water and action? Is the divine bestowal of grace mediated through the water or the action as such, or is the water-based action simply the occasion for a direct divine-human encounter? (3) What is the significance of the Church in baptism? Is it simply the community entered as the result of baptism into Christ, or is it a related means by which the individual is united with Christ?

In what follows, Chapter Three will examine the biblical exegesis which has informed this conceptual shift, and Chapter Four will analyse the theological meaning and coherence of this new Baptist paradigm.

CHAPTER 3

An Analysis of
The Biblical Foundations

As George Beasley-Murray has noted, the reformulation of British Baptist sacramentalism has been rooted to a great degree in a fresh exegesis of New Testament baptismal texts. This is not to say that the system is grounded in a naive, proof-texting biblicism which ignores issues of historical criticism and assumes *a priori* that all the biblical data constitute a fully unified picture.[1] It is to say that at the heart of the movement is the conclusion that the New Testament statements about baptism, in spite of their diversity of expression, do consistently view baptism as instrumental in the application of redemption to the individual. Indeed, it would not be an overstatement to say that the validity of this baptismal theology depends ultimately on the accuracy of the exegesis which informs it. For these Baptists, as for Baptists in general, no ultimate appeal can be made to ecclesiastical tradition—only Scripture can be the basis for such an appeal. Accordingly, an analysis of this Baptist sacramentalism demands above all else an assessment of this exegetical foundation.

The Baptist sacramental exegesis represents an alignment of this Baptist thought with the consensus of the historic churches. Although other denominations have articulated their sacramentalism in divergent ways, they have agreed that the biblical statements about baptism imply that baptism is more than a symbol, that it is in some way a means of conveying what it signifies. Historically, the idea that baptism is merely a symbol giving testimony to a conversion already completed has been formally accepted only in the Anabaptist and Baptist traditions. Therefore, it would be of little

---

1 The British Baptist authors examined in this book held divergent views concerning some of the critical issues about the date and authorship of the New Testament books. However, this made no significant difference in their theological conclusions, because they were all attempting to discover the meaning of baptism in the canonical New Testament as it has come to us, on the assumption that this is at least the starting point for any genuinely Christian theology. Accordingly, this book is concerned with the meaning of the biblical text, not with critical questions about how it came to exist in its present form. References to authorship are normally phrased in traditional terms, but these are not intended as answers to critical questions.

value in this chapter to compare Baptist exegesis to that of the historic churches--the two are fundamentally equivalent. What is relevant is to assess this exegesis in relation to the non-sacramental interpretations of other Baptists (and "baptists" who share the basic theology without the denominational label). The balance of this chapter, then, will take the following form: first, a summary of the exegetical foundations of Baptist sacramentalism; second, a summary and evaluation of the Baptist challenge to this exegesis; third, a summary and evaluation of a Baptist hermeneutical critique which accepts most of the exegetical details but challenges the sacramental synthesis; and fourth, an analysis of the critique of sacramentalism put forward by Karl Barth (1886-1968) in his *Church Dogmatics* IV/4. Although he never became a Baptist in terms of denominational affiliation, Barth adopted a "baptist" view of the subjects of baptism in his provocative lecture of 1943; therefore, his rejection in 1967 of the sacramental character of baptism may be seen as a criticism of Baptist sacramentalism from within its tradition, theologically if not ecclesiastically. In any case, given Barth's status as arguably the most significant Protestant theologian of the 20th century, his critique can hardly be ignored.

Baptist Sacramental Exegesis

The biblical texts which speak of John's baptism are of limited value here, inasmuch as Christian baptism is assumed to be distinct from John's baptism, but the two are related if not equivalent. Therefore, it is significant that John's baptism is an act of repentance which is done "for the forgiveness of sins" (εἰς ἄφεσιν ἁμαρτιῶν--Mark 1:4; Luke 3:3). This forgiveness of sins is sought as a way of avoiding the eschatological wrath associated with the inauguration of the kingdom of God (Luke 3:7). Although there is no power in the rite apart from genuine repentance (Luke 3:7-14), the act of baptism is done as a plea for eschatological salvation, which is to say that the rite is in some way sacramental.

The baptism of Jesus has traditionally played a large part in Baptist rhetoric about baptism, as in the typical language about "following the Lord in baptism." However, the exact relationship between the baptism of Jesus and Christian baptism is a matter of ongoing debate; it is therefore impossible to define confidently the nature of Christian baptism on the basis of the Gospels' witness to the baptism of Jesus. Some Baptists, notably R. E. O. White, have seen great significance in the experience of Jesus, arguing that the description of his baptism is an indication that what had been a sacrament of anticipation is becoming through him a sacrament of realization.² In his baptism Jesus received an assurance of his divine sonship and the empowering gift of the Holy Spirit, and the vicarious character of his humanity readily leads to the inference that there is some sort of parallel between his baptism and ours. Other Baptists have been more reluctant to draw inferences from the baptism of Jesus, noting both the uniqueness of his baptism and the fact that no New Testament writer uses the baptism of Jesus as a basis for exhortation.³ What can be said is that *if* the Lord's baptism is paradigmatic, then Christian baptism should be thought of as containing both a human act of commitment and a divine bestowal of spiritual benefit.

The baptismal commission of Matthew 28:19 was discussed by these Baptist writers mostly to assess the genuineness of the saying and its relevance for the dominical institution of baptism. There was significant variety of opinion among them about the extent to which the saying comes from the mouth of Christ, but there was general agreement that the text represents a valid Christian inference that baptism is to be done in obedience to Christ.⁴ They did not emphasize this text as a support for the sacramental sense of baptism, but it may in fact be useful in that regard. There is general agreement that the idea of baptism "into the name" (εἰς τὸ ὄνομα) of the Trinity signifies being brought into the possession or ownership of the Triune God,⁵ and thus into the sphere of salvation wrought by God. But if baptism establishes this sort of relationship between the individual and God, then it can hardly be thought of as a mere symbol.

One of the crucial issues in interpreting the significance of baptism in this commission is that of the syntactical connection between the imperative "make disciples" (μαθητεύσατε) and the participles "baptizing" and "teaching" (βαπτίζοντες and διδάσκοντες). Although many Baptists have assumed a chronological relationship (make disciples, then baptize the disciples, then continue to teach them), this is not a self-evident interpretation.⁶ It may well be that the participles are instrumental or modal

---

2   White, *BDI*, 90-109.
3   Beasley-Murray, *BNT*, 63-67.
4   For a negative assessment of the authenticity of the saying, see Clark, *ATS*, 16, 19. For a positive assessment, see White, *BDI*, 338-345 and Beasley-Murray, *BNT*, 87-88.
5   Beasley-Murray, *BNT*, 90-91; D. A. Carson, *Matthew*, in *The Expositor's Bible Commentary*, Vol. 8, ed. Frank E. Gaebelein (Grand Rapids: Zondervan, 1984), 597; Donald A. Hagner, *Matthew 14-28*, Vol. 33B, *Word Biblical Commentary* (Dallas: Word Books, 1995), 888; Craig L. Blomberg, *Matthew*, Vol. 22, *The New American Commentary* (Nashville: Broadman Press, 1992), 432.
6   Beasley-Murray, *BNT*, 88.

in force, describing the way in which the nations are to be brought into Christian discipleship (make disciples by baptizing them and teaching them).[7] In that case, a disciple of Christ would be one who has signified commitment by baptism and entered into the process of learning and obeying the commands of Christ, which is to say that baptism makes one a disciple of Christ rather than testifying that one has already become a disciple. The instrumental sense of βαπτίζοντες and the reference to baptism *prior to* teaching have sometimes been combined as a support for infant baptism, but this is not a necessary inference.[8]

The book of Acts is a source of sacramental teaching about baptism, although the evidence is not as consistent as one might like. When the text gives an account of what might be called didactic baptismal language, the sacramental sense is strong. For example, Acts 2:38 records Peter's instructions to Jews who have come to recognize their rejection of the Messiah, and the apparent sense of his instructions is that repentance (and the implied faith in Jesus as Lord and Christ) is to be expressed in baptism, with the result of their baptism being their forgiveness by God and the bestowal of the Holy Spirit upon them. Acts 22:16 records Ananias' exhortation to Saul to "wash away" his sins as he calls on the name of the Lord in baptism. While the reference to invoking the name of the Lord indicates that the power at work is that of the Lord, and not baptism *per se*, it is equally clear that this spiritually cleansing power of God is conceived as operative in the context of baptism. The enigmatic account of the twelve "disciples" in Ephesus (Acts 19:1-7) provides both narrative and didactic evidence for sacramentalism. At the narrative level, it is at the time of their Christian baptism that these men receive the gift of the Spirit (vss. 5-6); and at the didactic level, Paul's probing question about their reception of the Holy Spirit (vs. 2) is rooted in his assumption that they ought to have received the Spirit through their faith-baptism (vs. 3).

The narratives of Acts, however, make it clear that there is no simple cause-effect relation between baptism and the gift of the Spirit. In the

---

7   For a confident assertion of this exegesis, see R. C. H. Lenski, *The Interpretation of St. Matthew's Gospel* (Minneapolis: Augsburg Publishing House, 1943), 1173. For the acceptance of a loosely-defined modal interpretation, see Beasley-Murray, *BNT*, 89; Carson, *Matthew*, 597; Blomberg, *Matthew*, 431; Hagner, *Matthew 14-28*, 886; R. T. France, *The Gospel According to Matthew: An Introduction and Commentary* (Grand Rapids: Eerdmans, 1985), 414; Robert H. Gundry, *Matthew: A Commentary on His Literary and Theological Art* (Grand Rapids: Eerdmans, 1982), 597.

8   For a paedobaptist rejection of this particular argument, see William Hendriksen, *Exposition of the Gospel According to Matthew* (Grand Rapids: Baker Books, 1973), 1000-1001.

Cornelius episode of Acts 10, the Spirit is poured out on the Gentile household as they are listening to Peter's preaching, thus prior to any visible response on their part. But even here it is clear that baptism in the Spirit does not nullify the significance of baptism in water, for Peter calls for the immediate baptism in water of those who have received the Spirit, thus affirming the normative link between baptism and the benefits of Christ. It is assumed that in the normal pattern of God's salvific work, baptism and the gift of the Spirit occur together, although the precise linkage is a function of God's free activity and not of human manipulation.

The Samaritan episode of Acts 8 provides an example of another way in which baptism and the Spirit may be experienced, and in this case it involves a post-baptismal delay in the gift of the Spirit. Although this narrative clearly implies that there is no power inherent in baptism such that baptism automatically conveys the Spirit, it would be unwarranted to construct a baptismal paradigm from such an exceptional case. The narrative itself appears to assume the exceptional character of the events in Samaria. For example, vs. 16 indicates that the Samaritans had "not yet" (οὐδέπω) received the Spirit; they had "only" (μόνον) been baptized "into the name of the Lord Jesus." The use of οὐδέπω here, rather than the simple negative οὐ indicates that there is an expected connection between two things (in this case, Christian baptism and the bestowal of the Spirit), which for some reason are disconnected.[9]

The evidence of Acts does not allow for easy harmonization, but the data do not support in any way a non-sacramental reading which posits a normative bestowal of the benefits of salvation through a calling on the name of the Lord prior to and apart from baptism. The only evidence in the book for the bestowal of salvation prior to Christian baptism is in Acts 10, and in that case the Spirit comes prior to any kind of outward response, including prayer, which is not the paradigm of non-sacramental Baptist thought. The initial movement of the gospel into the Gentile world can hardly be a timeless paradigm; its revolutionary character is the reason for its unusual form, and even in that case it is clear that baptism and the Spirit go together. In the end it seems clear that if there is a normative understanding of the relation between baptism and the Spirit in Acts, then it is to be found, not in narrative accounts of what *did* happen in diverse experiences, but in statements declaring what is *expected* to occur. A statement like Acts 2:38 would then acquire special significance, as noted

---

9   Frederick Dale Bruner, *A Theology of the Holy Spirit* (Grand Rapids: Eerdmans, 1970), 177-178.

by Richard Longenecker:

We should understand Peter's preaching at Pentecost as being theologically normative for the relation in Acts between conversion, water baptism, and the baptism of the Holy Spirit, with the situations having to do with the Samaritan converts, Cornelius, and the twelve whom Paul met at Ephesus (which is something of a case all to itself) to be more historically conditioned and circumstantially understood.[10]

The evidence of the narratives of Acts may be ambiguous, but the references to baptism in the Pauline epistles seem to give clear support for a sacramental sense of baptism. The *locus classicus* is Paul's reference to baptism εἰς Χριστὸν in Romans 6:3-4. Baptism is there viewed as the event in which believers were effectively united to Christ and thus to the benefits of his redemptive work--baptism εἰς Χριστὸν results in the condition of being ἐν Χριστῷ. For centuries Baptists have relied on this text as a support for the mode of immersion, but while the imagery of immersion may underlie Paul's words, the text itself seems to assert much more than a pictorial significance for baptism. This language of burial with Christ in baptism occurs also in Colossians 2:12, where Paul clarifies that this occurs "through faith" and not simply through a ritual act, and where he explicitly refers to being "raised" with Christ in baptism (as opposed to the more guarded language about resurrection in Romans 6). The language of baptism εἰς Χριστὸν appears also in Galatians 3:27, where it explains the condition of being ἐν Χριστῷ Ἰησοῦ (vss. 26, 28). The conjunction of εἰς Χριστὸν and ἐν Χριστῷ seems to indicate that the former phrase means something more than simply "with reference to Christ"--it is indicative of movement into saving union with Christ.

If Romans 6 is the crucial Pauline reference to baptism as a means of union with Christ, it might also be said that the crucial reference to the Spirit and the Church is 1 Corinthians 12:13. Baptist sacramentalists almost universally have interpreted this as a reference to water-baptism and an indicator that water-baptism is also a baptism in the Spirit, and thus a means of union with the body of Christ. It is clear that whatever baptism is in view here initiates individuals into union with the body of Christ, which is to say into union with Christ himself (vs. 12).

---

10   Richard N. Longenecker, *The Acts of the Apostles*, in *The Expositor's Bible Commentary*, Vol. 9, ed. Frank E. Gaebelein (Grand Rapids: Zondervan, 1981), 285.

Pauline texts such as 1 Corinthians 6:11, Ephesians 5:25-27, and Titus 3:5 may allude to baptism via metaphors related to washing. If so, then justification, sanctification, and regeneration are all connected in Pauline thought to the baptismal event, although these texts give little help in defining the precise causal relation between baptism and these concepts.

On the surface 1 Corinthians 1:10-17 seems to contradict this Pauline respect for the significance of baptism. There Paul draws a sharp distinction between baptism and the preaching of the gospel, indicates that his commission is to preach rather than to baptize, and gives thanks that he baptized so few of the Corinthian converts. Although some use this text to modify the force of the other baptismal references in Paul's epistles, this is not the only solution. The apparent disparagement of baptism is stated in the context of Paul's anguish over divisions within the church at Corinth, divisions which were rooted in appreciation for one minister of the gospel over another. Part of the Pauline reply to this division is expressed in the rhetorical question, "Were you baptized in /εἰς/ the name of Paul?", which of course demands a negative answer. The fact that baptism is brought into the discussion at this point indicates that the rite was the common experience of all to whom Paul wrote and that in some way it was central to Christian identity. Baptists have argued that although it may appear that Paul was indifferent to the rite, this is a false inference.[11] At most the text is a reminder that the gospel embodied in baptism is the heart of the matter, not baptism *per se*. Paul's thanksgiving that he personally baptized so few Corinthians simply points to a division of ministry among Paul and his colleagues, and his concern that those baptized by him might make too much of this may point precisely to the great significance attached to baptism.

Interpreters of the Gospel of John hold widely varying views of the Johannine attitude toward sacraments, some seeing in the Gospel a pronounced sacramentalism couched in references to water, flesh and blood, while others see in it a corrective to excessive sacramentalism.[12] Baptist sacramentalists have been generally reluctant to base their theology on any of these general schemes, given the uncertainty of their assumptions.[13] At the heart of the Johannine contribution is the reference to spiritual rebirth

---

11 Beasley-Murray, *BNT*, 180-181.
12 Griffiths, in *CB*, 150 refers to Albert Schweitzer and Oscar Cullmann as proponents of a high sacramentalism in John, and to Rudolf Bultmann and Amos N. Wilder as defenders of the anti-sacramental view of John.
13 Clark, *ATS*, 27; Griffiths, in *CB*, 151; White, *BDI*, 247-264; Beasley-Murray, *BNT*, 216-226.

as a birth "of water and Spirit" (John 3:5). Although several alternatives have been suggested, Christian interpreters have traditionally understood this "water" as a reference to baptism, and Baptist sacramentalists normally have shared this opinion. Suggestions that the saying is actually about two births, one ἐξ ὕδατος and the other ἐκ πνεύματος are not compelling, because in fact the two nouns are governed by one preposition (ἐξ ὕδατος καὶ πνεύματος), pointing to one birth which is related to both water and the Spirit. Some have suggested that "water" here is purely figurative, denoting the spiritual cleansing and transformation wrought by the Spirit, as promised by the prophets (Ezek 36:25-27). Although this is possible, it is difficult to read John 3:5 in its context without thinking of baptism (cf. 1:24-34; 3:22-23; 4:1-2).

However, even if it is assumed that "water" in this saying refers to baptism, there are various ways of interpreting the systematic implications of this reading of the text. Some see in it a polemical reference to John's baptism, an emphasis that John's baptism is inadequate in itself to effect entrance into the kingdom of God. Others see a reference to Christian baptism, an indication that through the work of Jesus Christ baptism will become not simply an expression of repentance but an occasion for the transforming gift of the Holy Spirit. Given this Gospel's frequent use of terms that are pregnant with meaning, it may well be that there is both a backward and a forward reference in the word.[14] It is crucial to note that the emphasis in John 3 is on the fact that this birth is ἐκ τοῦ πνεύματος (vss. 6 and 8, as well as 5), which is to say that although this birth is related to both water and the Spirit, it is not related to both in the same way. Water has a role to play, but its significance is found not in itself but in its connection to the Spirit. Nevertheless, in a real (though secondary) sense water (baptism) is a vehicle of spiritual rebirth, which is to say that baptism is sacramental in character.

In the rest of the New Testament, the most significant text is 1 Peter 3:21 and its reference to "baptism which now saves you." If, as several interpreters have suggested, all or most of 1 Peter is a baptismal sermon, then all the references within the book to God's salvific work can be related in some way to baptism. Baptist writers generally have agreed (with various degrees of confidence) that much of the epistle is rooted in a baptismal context,[15] but this cannot be dogmatically asserted. Therefore, the focus

---

14 This idea of a double allusion to John's baptism and to Christian baptism is suggested by Griffiths, in *CB*, 156; White, *BDI*, 253-255; and Beasely-Murray, *BNT*, 229-230.

15 Buse, in *CB*, 171-175; White, *BDI*, 228; Beasely-Murray, *BNT*, 251-258.

must remain on the one explicit statement about baptism within the epistle. This statement occurs in a passage with all sorts of exegetical difficulties, but it clearly asserts that baptism effects salvation now in some way which is analogous to the ancient deliverance of Noah and his family from divine wrath. Peter's language emphasizes that the salvific role of baptism is not due to any power inherent in the physical act of baptism--instead it saves ultimately "by the resurrection of Jesus Christ" and proximately by "an appeal to God for a good conscience." This last phrase is translated in various ways, depending on whether ἐπερώτημα is taken to denote a "request" or a "pledge," and whether the genitive συνειδήσεως ἀγαθῆς is taken to be subjective or objective. In any case, the attitude toward God which comes to expression in baptism is the fundamental concern and the basic instrumental cause of salvation from the human side. Nevertheless, it is assumed that this attitude comes to expression *in baptism*, and thus baptism is instrumental in the application of salvation to the individual.

In summary, although there is diversity of expression, and some of the exegetical details do not allow for dogmatism in interpretation, the New Testament consistently views baptism as a means of entrance into the eschatological salvation wrought by Jesus Christ. Although the crucial factor from the human side is penitent faith in Christ, this faith is not normally thought of as fully formed apart from baptism. However laudable may be the common Baptist insistence on salvation by faith alone, the idea of faith apart from baptism with its corollary of baptism as merely a symbolic testimony to a past experience of salvation is foreign to the New Testament.

Baptist Exegetical Criticisms

The sacramental exegesis summarized above is challenged at every point by some within the Baptist tradition. This book will not investigate every detail of this dispute, but instead will focus on the three major aspects of it: (1) the assertion that Matthew 28:19-20 teaches that entrance into Christian discipleship precedes baptism, thus refuting the claim that union with Christ is mediated through baptism; (2) the assertion that Acts 2:38 does not view the forgiveness of sins as the result of baptism; and (3) the assertion that the key Pauline texts about baptism are actually talking about Spirit-baptism and not water-baptism.

Matthew 28:19-20

A dominant stream of Baptist thought has interpreted the Great Commission along these lines: "Go (to all the world) and make disciples of all the nations, then baptize (these who have become disciples) as a sign of their (previous) entrance into union with the Triune God, and then go on teaching them how to live in obedience to the commands of Christ." Interpreters going back to John Gill have argued on the basis of the Greek text that the objects of this baptizing and teaching must be *disciples*, not *the nations*. The object of the discipling, πάντα τὰ ἔθνη, is neuter in gender, while the object of both βαπτίζοντες and διδάσκοντες is *αὐτούς*, which is masculine in gender. Thus it is argued that the two objects cannot be the same, and it is concluded that αὐτούς must denote the disciples (μαθηταί) who are the implied result of the discipling (evangelizing) of the nations.[16] Within this interpretation, a "disciple" is one who has indicated a positive response to the gospel, and this response is confirmed prior to baptism.

Although this conceptual structure may not be impossible, the switch from the neuter *ἔθνη* to the masculine αὐτούς does not prove the point. The same switch occurs in Matthew 25:32, where in a description of final judgment by Christ it is said that πάντα τὰ ἔθνη will be assembled before him, and he will separate them (αὐτούς) into two groups, and it is quite clear that the two terms denote the same persons. The distinction is that of people-groups *(ἔθνη)* versus the individuals who constitute those groups *(αὐτούς)*, not that of the whole versus the part. Restricting baptism to those who respond positively to the gospel is biblically defensible, but not on the basis of gender shifts in Matthew 28:19.

The syntactical relation between the imperative (μαθητεύσατε) and the participles (βαπτίζοντες and διδάσκοντες) in this text cannot be dogmatically defined. Such adverbial participles modify the action of the main verb (in this case the imperative), but the exact force is determined by the context. Whatever may be the exact relation between the imperative and the participles, it seems clear that the verbs for baptizing and teaching are not grammatically coordinate with the verb for discipling, making it very unlikely that the statement means, "Make disciples, then baptize them, and then teach them." Rather the actions of baptizing and teaching are subordinate to that of discipling, and the natural conclusion is that in terms of this text, a Christian disciple is one who has signified faith in Christ by

---

16 Gill, *Divinity*, 901. Carson, *Matthew*, 597 sees this as a possibility but does not commit himself to it.

baptism and entered into the process of learning how to live out this baptismal commitment.[17] But this implies that baptism is instrumental in the entrance into discipleship, not that it bears witness to a previous entrance into discipleship.

Acts 2:38

On the surface, it would seem that Peter's exhortation recorded here plainly indicates that baptism is done for the purpose of personal salvation, but there are two distinct ways in which baptistic interpreters have sought to deny this inference. The first is the assertion that εἰς ἄφεσιν τῶν ἁμαρτιῶν ὑμῶν means "on the basis of the forgiveness of your sins," rather than "for the purpose of the forgiveness of your sins," and the second is the assertion that the entire baptismal clause is parenthetical, so that forgiveness of sins is connected to repentance and not to baptism.[18]

Defenders of the *first* approach tend to rely on the argument of A. T. Robertson, a Southern Baptist scholar and author of a widely used grammar of New Testament Greek. With regard to this key phrase he wrote:

> This phrase is the subject of endless controversy as men look at it from the standpoint of sacramental or of evangelical theology. In themselves the words can express aim or purpose for that use of *eis* does exist as in I Cor. 2:7 *eis doxan hemon* (for our glory). But then another usage exists which is just as good Greek as the use of *eis* for aim or purpose. It is seen in Matt. 10:41 in three examples *eis onoma prophetou, dikaiou, mathetou* where it cannot be purpose or aim, but rather the basis or ground, on the basis of the name of prophet, righteous man, disciple, because one is, etc. It is seen again in Matt. 12:41 about the preaching of Jonah (*eis to kerugma Iona*). They repented because of (or at) the preaching of Jonah. . . . One will decide the use here according as he believes that baptism is essential to the remission of sins or not. My view is decidedly against the idea that Peter, Paul, or any one in the New Testament taught baptism as essential to the remission of sins or the means of securing such remission. So I understand Peter to be urging baptism on each of them who had already turned (repented) and for

---

17 Carson, *Matthew*, 597; Gundry, *Matthew*, 596; Hendriksen, *Matthew*, 1000.
18 Both approaches are suggested by B. H. Carroll, *An Interpretation of the English Bible: Acts* (1948; reprint Grand Rapids: Baker Book House, 1986), 76-77, 89-93.

it to be done in the name of Jesus Christ on the basis of the forgiveness of sins which they had already received.[19]

Robertson's argument, then, takes this form: the Greek preposition εἰς may indicate either cause or purpose; its meaning here must be determined by theological principles; therefore, biblical soteriology demands that it indicate cause here. Given Robertson's stature as a Greek scholar, it is not surprising that his reasoning has commanded wide assent among Baptists, but in the end his case is not convincing.

The major premise of his argument, the existence of a recognized causal use of εἰς, is disputed by lexicographers and grammarians. The contemporary lexicon of Arndt and Gingrich lists it only as a possible but disputed meaning,[20] and although J. R. Mantey tried to establish such a meaning in Hellenistic Greek,[21] Nigel Turner stated that "hardly any of the Hellenistic parallels brought forward by Mantey are convincing."[22] Robertson listed as New Testament examples only Matthew 10:41 and 12:41 (parallel in Luke 11:32), but each is capable of more than one sense. While Matthew 10:41 may mean something like "receive a prophet because he is a prophet," it may also mean "receive a prophet into the treatment appropriate to a prophet" or "receive a prophet in the name of a prophet" (the latter if εἰς is equivalent to ἐν as it often is).[23] Similarly Matthew 12:41 may mean "repented because of the preaching of Jonah," but it may also mean "changed their mind in the direction of what Jonah preached" or "repented when Jonah preached" (again if εἰς is equivalent to ἐν). There is no unanimity among interpreters concerning the precise use of εἰς in these texts, and there is doubt about the causal use of εἰς in Hellenistic literature, which indicates the doubtful character of this major premise of Robertson's argument.

One recent writer has defended Robertson's argument by pointing to

---

19 A. T. Robertson, *Word Pictures in the New Testament* (Nashville: Broadman Press, 1930), 3:35-36.

20 William Arndt and F. Wilbur Gingrich, *A Greek-English Lexicon of the New Testament and Other Early Christian Literature*, 2nd ed. (Chicago: University of Chicago Press, 1979), 230.

21 J. R. Mantey, "The Causal Use of *eis* in the New Testament," *Journal of Biblical Literature* 70 (1951): 45-48.

22 Nigel Turner and James Hope Moulton, *A Grammar of New Testament Greek* (Edinburgh: T. & T. Clark, 1963), 3: 266.

23 A. T. Robertson, *A Grammar of the Greek New Testament in the Light of Historical Research* (Nashville: Broadman Press, 1934), 593; Lenski, *Matthew*, 421-422.

Matthew 3:11, which describes John's baptism as one done εἰς μετάνοιαν as further evidence for the causal use of εἰς.[24] The context narrates John's rebuke of Pharisees and Sadducees as they presented themselves for baptism and his demand that they must "bring forth fruit in keeping with repentance." It is argued, then, that "John demanded repentance as a prerequisite for his baptism," implying that "one could not undergo John's baptism without first showing evidence of repentance."[25] It would seem, then, that John's baptism εἰς μετάνοιαν is a baptism based on a prior repentance, which amounts to a causal use of εἰς.

Although this may be plausible, it is not convincing. This reading of John's words would demand that he personally examine the life of every person coming to him for baptism prior to enacting the ritual, and given the contextual indications that large numbers were coming to him, this seems humanly impossible. Furthermore, the context (Matt 3:6) indicates that those coming to him for baptism were not declaring the evidence of their moral transformation, but were instead "confessing their sins," the intent of which is surely to experience forgiveness. It seems, then, that the demand placed on the religious leaders is not to prove moral transformation prior to baptism, but to be aware that their baptism will demand that they live differently afterward. That would mean that εἰς looks forward to a repentant way of life, not backward to a previous transformation.

A more profitable study of εἰς would consider other occurrences of the preposition in connection with the forgiveness of sins. There are only four occurrences of εἰς ἄφεσιν ἁμαρτιῶν in the New Testament apart from Acts 2:38. Matthew 26:28 uses the phrase to modify Christ's blood of the covenant, indicating that it is poured out "for the forgiveness of sins," clearly denoting purpose. Luke 24:47 (in a variant reading) refers to the preaching of the gospel to all nations "for the forgiveness of sins," and this forgiveness is clearly the result (not the condition) of the preaching. Both Mark 1:4 and Luke 3:3 describe John's baptism as a βάπτισμα μετανοίας εἰς ἄφεσιν ἁμαρτιῶν, and given Luke's statement that the baptizands are seeking deliverance from eschatological wrath, the forgiveness of sins here is something experienced through baptism rather than a condition of baptism.

In the end, then, Robertson's reconstruction of Peter's comments is flawed in several ways: (1) The causal use of εἰς is very rare at best and perhaps unsubstantiated. (2) When the phrase εἰς ἄφεσιν ἁμαρτιῶν occurs

---

24 R. Bruce Compton, "Water Baptism and the Forgiveness of Sins in Acts 2:38," *Detroit Baptist Seminary Journal* 4 (Fall 1999): 30-31.
25 Ibid., 31.

elsewhere in the New Testament, it indicates purpose, not cause. (3) Robertson himself admitted that his conclusion was determined by theology and not grammar, and his theology failed to note that other baptismal texts are in fact very similar to Acts 2:38 and demand a similarly strained explanation if they are to fit his system. (4) Even if the causal use of εἰς be granted in Acts 2:38, the text would still appear to say that the gift of the Spirit occurs through both repentance and baptism, and this would create just as much difficulty for anti-sacramentalists as the phrase concerning forgiveness of sins.[26]

The *second* way to minimize the force of Acts 2:38 recognizes the improbability of a causal εἰς but still sees in the text a threat to the idea of salvation by grace through faith alone. The proposed solution is to connect the purposive εἰς to repentance (μετανοήσατε) rather than baptism, thus making the baptismal clause a parenthesis. Support is found within the text in the shift from the plural μετανοήσατε to the singular βαπτισθήτω ἕκαστος ὑμῶν and outside the text in Acts 3:19 where relief from sins is promised on the basis of repentance without reference to baptism.[27] One form of this argument focuses on the plural ὑμῶν which modifies the sins which are to be forgiven, inferring that, "The concord between verb and pronoun requires that the remission of sins be connected with repentance, not with baptism."[28]

Although this exegesis may be possible, there are several weaknesses in the argument: (1) The shift from plural to singular is explicable without disconnecting baptism from forgiveness. The plural imperative for repentance is appropriate in view of the fact that all the members of the crowd could change their mind about Jesus simultaneously, but their baptisms could only occur individually and sequentially. In any case, the exhortation to be baptized is coextensive with the exhortation to repent (each addressed to all persons in the group listening to Peter), and this explains why the pronoun modifying "sins" is plural rather than singular.[29] (2) As the narrative continues, it is baptism which is noted in describing the conversion of 3,000 persons (vs. 41), thus indicating its crucial character.

---

26 For an extended critique of this approach to Acts 2:38, see J. C. Davis, "Another Look at the Relationship Between Baptism and Forgiveness of Sins in Acts 2:38," *Restoration Quarterly* 24 (1981): 80-88.
27 Stanley D. Toussaint, "Acts," in *The Bible Knowledge Commentary: New Testament*, eds. John F. Walvoord and Roy B. Zuck (Wheaton: Victor Books, 1983), 359.
28 Luther B. McIntyre, Jr., "Baptism and Forgiveness in Acts 2:38," *Bibliotheca Sacra* 153 (January-March 1996): 55.
29 Compton, "Water Baptism," 26.

(3) Even if this parenthetical interpretation be accepted, repentance and baptism are coordinated in a way that seems to view both as means to the reception of the Spirit, thus supporting the sacramental nature of baptism. (4) This exegesis is rooted in the same sort of theological concerns as those in Robertson's approach, but these concerns are phrased in a way that fails to account for the actual baptismal language of the New Testament and thus draws a false contrast between the "sacramental" and the "evangelical."

In the case of those who seek to explain away the obvious sense of Acts 2:38, there is a persistent inability to see or accept the distinction between baptism as the *normative* means of the experience of personal salvation and baptism as the *essential* means of such salvation. Baptist sacramentalists assert that the natural and obvious sense of Acts 2:38 is that one submits to baptism as a repentant sinner seeking salvation, but they do not take that to imply that one who has come to repentance and faith in Jesus as Lord but for some reason has not been baptized is therefore damned. They rightly refrain from drawing this negative inference, because the biblical text in question does not envision an unbaptized but repentant person and accordingly states no conclusion about such a person.

Water versus Spirit

Traditional Christian exegesis has assumed that Pauline references to being "baptized into Christ" (Rom 6:3; Gal 3:27) refer to water-baptism as the event in which personal union with Christ is effected, and that Paul links possession of the Holy Spirit and membership in the Church to water-baptism (1 Cor 12:13), but some modern interpreters have argued that each of these texts is actually a reference to baptism in the Spirit.

Many baptistic interpreters argue that the language of baptism "into Christ" (εἰς Χριστὸν) is simply too strong to be referred to water-baptism, their assumption being that such language would teach baptismal regeneration, which is believed to be impossible.[30] Some see a reference to a symbolic water-baptism in Romans 6:4 (and the parallel Col 2:12) as the element of personal experience which corresponds to the burial of Christ, so that baptism confirms the person's previous (spiritual) "death with Christ" at conversion, just as the burial of Christ confirmed his previous (physical) death, even though the language of Romans 6:3 about baptism into Christ

---

30 John A. Witmer, "Romans," in *Bible Knowledge Commentary*, 461; Donald K. Campbell, "Galatians," in *Bible Knowledge Commentary*, 600; Norman L. Geisler, "Colossians," in *Bible Knowledge Commentary*, 677.

and thus into his death is limited by them to Spirit-baptism.[31]

Some interpreters outside the Baptist tradition have argued that Romans 6:3-4 implies nothing at all about any pictorial significance of water-baptism and speaks exclusively of Spirit-baptism. The argument can be easily developed: Paul speaks in Romans 6 of union with Christ and a baptism which effects this; Paul elsewhere minimizes the significance of water-baptism (1 Cor 1), but he affirms explicitly that believers are baptized by the Spirit into Christ and his Body (1 Cor 12:13); therefore, "To argue that the Apostle has water baptism in his mind in any shape or form here is to give a prominence to baptism that the Apostle Paul never gives to it."[32]

Although he does not disconnect baptism from conversion in exactly the same way as much of the Baptist tradition (in fact he criticizes the Pentecostal type of baptistic thought at this very point), James Dunn (b. 1939) has argued that βαπτίζειν εἰς Χριστὸν should be read as a metaphorical reference to Spirit-baptism as the means of incorporation into Christ, while βάπτισμα denotes only the water ritual.[33]

Although this interpretation is argued skillfully, especially by Dunn, it is less than convincing. *First*, given the compressed nature of Paul's argument in Romans 6, it seems highly unlikely that "baptized into his death" in vs. 3 would denote only baptism in the Spirit, while "baptism into death" in the next sentence would denote only baptism in water. Granted that the spiritual realities in view may demand that *more* than water-baptism is in view in vs. 3, it is still unlikely that water-baptism is absent from view there if it is admittedly present in vs. 4. Since about 1640, Baptists have wanted to see in Romans 6 a basis for the mode of immersion, due to the symbol of burial and resurrection, while at the same time they have often been nervous about the apparent indication that baptism actually unites the individual to Christ, but they cannot have it both ways. If water is in view in this text, then it is more than a symbol.

Second, the imagery of baptism in the Spirit, as found in the Gospels and in Acts 1:5, points to Christ as the baptizer who brings his people into the sphere of the Spirit, but in both Romans 6:3 and Galatians 3:27 Christ is the goal of the baptism rather than the baptizer. Although some fluidity

---

31 Witmer, 462; Geisler, 678.
32 D. M. Lloyd Jones, *Romans: The New Man* (Grand Rapids: Zondervan, 1972), 34. See also James Montgomery Boice, *Romans, Vol. 2: The Reign of Grace, Romans 5-8* (Grand Rapids: Baker Books, 1992), 660.
33 James D. G. Dunn, *Baptism in the Holy Spirit* (London: SCM Press, 1970), 109-112, 140-141; idem, *Romans 1-8*, Vol. 38A, *Word Biblical Commentary* (Dallas: Word Books, 1988), 311-313, 327-330.

of language is allowable in the use of metaphors, the use of εἰς Χριστὸν appears to connect Romans 6 to Matthew 28:19 (εἰς τὸ ὄνομα) more naturally than to the language about baptism ἐν πνεύματι.

Third, the connection between baptism in water and baptism in the Spirit is sufficiently close to question this bifurcation of water and Spirit which is being suggested. Although Christ's baptizing in the Holy Spirit is contrasted to John's baptism, it is never contrasted to Christian baptism. In fact, both Acts 2:38 and Acts 19:1-6 seem to assume that the norm is that Christ would baptize in the Spirit in connection with baptism in water. If this is true, then allusions to Spirit-baptism in Romans 6 or Galatians 3 would not imply that water-baptism is absent from view.

The use of 1 Corinthians 12:13, on the other hand, presents more problems, and the critique at this point may be well-founded. In that text Paul explicitly names the Spirit as the element in which Christians are baptized, and the goal of the baptism is incorporation into the body of Christ, the Church. Going back to the ministry of John, when the Holy Spirit is named in relation to baptism it is by the phrase ἐν πνεύματι, which corresponds to ἐν ὕδατι in the water-baptism of John. The text in question uses the phrase ἐν ἑνὶ πνεύματι, emphasizing that there is only *one* Spirit shared by all Christians, but apart from the numerical adjective, the language is precisely that of the Johannine promise about the work of the Messiah. What Paul affirms here as the experience of all Christians is what was promised through John, and that experience is phrased in language that displaces water as the medium of baptism.

It should be noted that the dominant theme of 1 Corinthians 12 is the Holy Spirit. The entire context of the debated verse focuses on the Spirit, both in terms of the unity located in the common possession of the same Spirit and the appropriate diversity located in the manifestations of the Spirit. Even if there is an allusion to water-baptism in vs. 13, the locus of unity in this passage is the Spirit, not baptism.[34] Accordingly, in vs. 13 ἐν ἑνὶ πνεύματι stands first for emphasis, and the verb ἐβαπτίσθημεν comes only at the end of the clause. Paul's point in this passage does not depend on any reference to water-baptism.

It might be argued that even though the primary reference in this text is to baptism in the Spirit, the very use of the term "baptize" points to a normative connection between water-baptism and Spirit-baptism, in which case this text would affirm that water-baptism is also the occasion for the

---

34 As argued convincingly by Gordon D. Fee, *God's Empowering Presence: The Holy Spirit in the Letters of Paul* (Peabody: Hendrickson Publishers, 1994), 179-180.

An Analysis of the Biblical Foundations

gift of the Spirit. However, this connection between water and Spirit cannot successfully be established simply on the basis of the term "baptize," because there is evidence for a purely metaphorical use of the term going back to Jesus (Mark 10:38; Luke 12:50). Dunn's point here is well-taken: the terminology is sometimes metaphorical, and 1 Corinthians 12:13 may well be one example, especially in view of the fact that the medium of the baptism in view is explicitly named as the Spirit. It should also be noted that the verse in question refers to the gift of the Spirit in *two* ways: the first in terms of baptism, and the second in terms of drinking (ἐποτίσθημεν). The second manner of description clearly does not arise from baptism and is thoroughly metaphorical, which lends support to the metaphorical sense of the first description as well.[35]

Some have argued that if Paul is to achieve his purpose of teaching the unity of the body of Christ, then he needs to provide for his readers a clear and tangible marker of their unity, which would be found in their common experience of acknowledging Jesus as Lord in water-baptism, an experience noted in vs. 13. The argument assumes that water-baptism provides a tangible, public sign of unity in contrast to the invisible and somewhat nebulous Spirit-baptism, but this would be an anachronistic approach to Paul's argument. Dunn is accurate when he asserts that within the New Testament the gift of the Spirit is viewed as essential evidence of being a Christian and an experienced reality which can be known as a fact.[36] For example, it was recognized as a fact that the Samaritans had not received the Spirit at their baptism and that they did later receive him (Acts 8), and Paul asked the Ephesian "disciples" whether they had received the Spirit when they believed, assuming that they knew the answer (Acts 19). However strange it may seem to modern Christian experience, the implication of New Testament language about the Spirit is that the indwelling presence of the Spirit is an identifiable reality, even apart from its connection to baptism. Therefore, although it appears that Paul believed that there was a normative connection between baptism and the Holy Spirit (Acts 19), he also seemed to believe that baptism in the Spirit was just as definite an experience as baptism in water, so that his appeal to baptism in the Spirit in this text may be perfectly meaningful apart from baptism in water.

Although Baptist sacramentalists have referred repeatedly to 1 Corinthians 12:13 as support for their theology of baptism, the same conclusions can be reached without this support. It may be that this Pauline

---

35 Ibid., 180.
36 Dunn, *Baptism in Spirit*, 229.

statement links water and the Spirit in a way that was clear to his original readers, but at this distance in time this is not self-evident.

Baptist Hermeneutical Criticisms

Most Baptist criticisms of a sacramental view of baptism lie in the exegetical areas as noted above, but at least one Baptist scholar has accepted the exegetical conclusions without affirming the theological synthesis. In 1968 William E. Hull (b. 1920), a Southern Baptist scholar, wrote a critique of Beasley-Murray's *Baptism in the New Testament* which was intended to be a response to "a significant new development in the study of New Testament baptism," as seen in "the findings put forth recently by a group of British Baptists," of which Beasley-Murray's work is taken to be the outstanding statement.[37] Accordingly, Hull's critique, although focused on Beasley-Murray, was directed at the entire reformulation of baptismal theology which is being analysed in this study.

Hull summarized the recent British view in terms of three fundamental contentions: that baptism is a confessional act of the baptizand; that baptism is an integral part of conversion; and that baptism is sacramental, an effective symbol embodying God's gracious action. His initial response was this:

> We may begin with a surprising concession: most of the exegesis of the relevant passages is thorough and accurate. Beasley-Murray is at his best as an interpreter of the Greek text and I doubt if his findings at this level should be seriously modified.[38]

Although this would be the final word for some interpreters (especially Baptists), he asserted that "exegetical findings are but the indispensable raw materials out of which the house of meaning must be built."[39] Beyond the details of exegesis of particular texts, there are broader issues to be addressed which "raise the very questions which Beasley-Murray must answer before we can accept his exalted claims for the place of baptism in the New Testament."[40] There were three crucial issues to be considered.

(1) The relation between the Old Testament and the New Testament.

---

37 William E. Hull, "Baptism in the New Testament: a Hermeneutical Critique," *Review and Expositor* 65, no. 1 (Winter 1968): 3.
38 Ibid., 4.
39 Ibid., 5.
40 Ibid.

An Analysis of the Biblical Foundations

Any genuinely Christian perspective must recognize both continuity and discontinuity between the Testaments, but Hull claimed that Beasley-Murray overstated the discontinuity between the Testaments and was able to exalt baptism only by questioning the reality of religious experience under the old covenant. To refer as Beasley-Murray does to the old covenant in terms of "death...flesh...old creation... and life of this age" seemed to be seriously out of balance, given that these realities are also present in new covenant experience, and their opposites are present within the Old Testament. Hull argued:

> From a unified biblical perspective, the normative elements in man's relation to God are those fundamental spiritual realities characteristic of true religion in both Testaments, not the variety of rites employed in different periods to express them.
>
> Thus I am uncomfortable with sweeping generalizations to the effect that baptism is a unique vehicle of the divine encounter, because this emphasis minimizes, or may even radically call into question, the quality of religious experience in the Old Testament.[41]

Hull concluded this criticism by noting Beasley-Murray's concession that Paul's classic description of faith in Romans 4 is that of Abraham's faith prior to circumcision, that is, faith which is "wholly independent of an external rite."[42]

In response to Hull, it should be noted that the locus of continuity between the covenants lies not only in certain timeless elements of religious experience, but also in the theme of promise and fulfillment. When Hull attempted to demonstrate that New Testament themes like "life, Spirit, new creation, and age to come" occur in the Old Testament as well, all but one of his proof-texts came from the latter part of Isaiah and looked forward to these as anticipated rather than realized, and the other text (Deut 30:15) envisioned only the *possibility* of "life" through obedience to the covenant stipulations. By the time of the exile the prophets had concluded that a radically new, internalized work of God would be necessary if Israel would ever fulfill its destiny (Jer 31:31-34; Ezek 36:24-27). Whatever may be the nature of the continuity between the covenants, it is not an equivalence of religious experience in the two cases.

The continuity between the covenants may in fact support

---

41 Ibid., 6.
42 Ibid., 6-7, quoting Beasley-Murray, *BNT*, 303.

sacramentalism as much as it seems to question it. While Paul's exposition of Abraham's faith does indicate that no ritual act is ultimately decisive in a person's acceptance before God, it is equally true that the patterns of the old covenant show that ritual acts (when they are the vehicles of faith) are not insignificant in the nurture of the divine-human relationship. Baptist sacramentalism tries to maintain this balance, recognizing that great effects are predicated of baptism in the New Testament not because baptism is more powerful than Old Testament rituals, but because the benefits experienced by the new covenant community (to which baptism unites believers in Christ) are greater than those of the old covenant.

(2) The historical Jesus and the kerygmatic Christ. As far as one can tell from the Gospel accounts, Jesus had very little to say about baptism, and he and his disciples practised baptism only briefly in an early Judean ministry. If the message and mission of the historical Jesus are to be determinative for Christian thought, then it would appear that baptism's significance may be minimal. To magnify its significance, then, as Beasley-Murray did, was in Hull's view to exaggerate the discontinuity between Jesus and the Church and "to suggest the inferior situation of the disciples during the earthly ministry, when Christian baptism was not yet available, as compared with their superior situation following the earthly ministry, when baptism was freely administered."[43] This is not simply an argument from silence, because Jesus' attitude toward baptism is seen not only in his virtual silence on the subject, but also in "the way in which he offered forgiveness *without recourse to any cultic apparatus* (e.g., Mk. 2:5; Lk. 7:47; 8:48). *He* was the visible organ of mediation; neither sacrificial animals nor Jordan waters were needed."[44] How, then, can baptism take on the significance which Beasley-Murray gave to it?

In response, it may be said that there are various factors which might account for the (apparently) minimal practice of baptism during Jesus' earthly ministry. To begin with, whatever baptism was authorized by Jesus was essentially a continuation of John's preparatory baptism, so that the only candidates for his baptism were those who had not responded to John's appeal. Perhaps the most significant factor is the relativizing of all ritual approaches to God which follows from the personal, visible presence of God in Christ. If a major purpose of sacred rituals is to provide a tangible sign of God's presence and action, then such rituals can hardly have their normal significance when the Incarnate Lord is visibly present. To take an analogy,

---

43 Ibid., 7.
44 Ibid., 8.

the spiritual discipline of fasting was relativized by the personal presence of Christ, even though he recognized that after his earthly ministry the practice would again be relevant (Mark 2:18-20).

Hull was accurate in his claim that Beasley-Murray asserted the superiority of the post-Pentecostal experience of Christ's disciples, but this agrees with the Fourth Gospel's account of Jesus' teaching, in which he indicates that his departure will be to the advantage of his disciples (John 16:7), inasmuch as the bestowal of the Spirit awaits the glorification of the Son (John 7:37-39). In New Testament terms, those who became disciples during Jesus' earthly ministry were at that time in transition toward the new covenant, but their experience was not equivalent to what it became after Easter and Pentecost. It is true that Beasley-Murray asserted that baptism "assumed a transformed meaning" after Pentecost,[45] but this was not an affirmation of new power in baptism as such; it was instead an affirmation of the new benefits conveyed by the risen Lord to his disciples, and a recognition that baptism initiates into this discipleship. The continuity between the historical Jesus and the risen Christ retains an element of promise and fulfillment.

(3) Unity and diversity in the New Testament church. Hull argued that Beasley-Murray was excessively confident about his ability to speak of *the* doctrine of Christian baptism in the New Testament, as if there were a consistent emphasis on baptism throughout the apostolic witness. He noted:

> When I read Beasley-Murray's cumulative exegesis of baptismal passages lifted out of their original settings and strung together, the effect is very different from a reading of each New Testament document separately with an eye to the importance which baptism has within it.[46]

For example, it may be true that Colossians 2:11-12 is Paul's commentary on his treatment of baptism in Romans 6:1-4, but neither the Colossians nor the Romans were able to read Paul's teaching in this canonical fashion. It is also true that more than half of the Pauline epistles do not mention baptism, and that the subject is missing from most of the General Epistles and the Apocalypse as well. One is forced, therefore, to ask whether baptism is so important after all. Perhaps it is only a flat, simplistic reading of the New Testament which will support this exalted view of baptism.

---

45   Ibid., 7, quoting Beasley-Murray, *BNT*, 280.
46   Ibid., 9-10.

This criticism has some merit, especially in view of the fact that most of the New Testament references to baptism occur only as subordinate propositions used to teach other truths. For example, Romans 6 and Colossians 2 are fundamentally about the present ethical impact of union with Christ, and Galatians 3 is focused on the equality of Jews and Gentiles in the people of God. At the very least, this ought to serve as a reminder that baptism derives its significance from the gospel realities to which it points. As Hull noted, "Baptism depends for its validity upon such factors as grace and faith, but grace and faith do not depend on baptism."[47]

But having accepted this valuable caution against magnifying baptism out of biblical proportion, it is still necessary to interpret the baptismal texts which we do have, and they do seem to speak of baptism as more than a symbol of salvation already experienced. Given the relative paucity and brevity of the baptismal texts, but given also the strength of these texts, one possible inference is that they imply the existence of a widely taught and well understood doctrine of baptismal efficacy which needed little explanation. Perhaps the words with which Paul begins his baptismal statement in Romans 6:3, ἢ ἀγνοεῖτε ("Or are you ignorant . . ."), assume a well known doctrine of union with the death of Christ through baptism which is not evidenced elsewhere in the biblical canon. In the end, our understanding of the apostolic doctrine of baptism must be derived from apostolic references to baptism, whether those be many or few, and the extant references are sacramental in tone.

At the end of his critique, Hull admitted that his assessment of Beasley-Murray's work was much more positive than negative, and his differences with the British reformulation were "of *degree* rather than *kind*," although he was convinced that this British spokesman "has overstated his case for the centrality of baptism in the canon, in conversion, and in the church."[48] However, to say that baptism is not as central to biblical religion as Beasley-Murray thought it to be is not to say that baptism is not sacramental. It is just to say that sacramental doctrine is not the central core of biblical religion, and that it is farther from the centre than some think.

Karl Barth's Critique of Sacramentalism

When Karl Barth attacked infant baptism in 1943, he still held to an essentially Calvinistic conception of baptism as a means of *cognitio salutis*,

---

47 Ibid., 10.
48 Ibid., 11.

steering a middle course between the Catholic tradition and the purely symbolic view of Zwingli and the Anabaptists.[49] But in 1951 his son, Markus, published his book *Die Taufe--ein Sakrament?*, which gave a negative answer to the question of the title. The elder Barth was persuaded by his son's research and lamented the fact that his arguments had been largely ignored.[50] Therefore, in the final part-volume of the *Church Dogmatics* (IV/4), which appeared in 1967 in German and in 1969 in English, this exegesis was summarized and restated in support of a non-sacramental view of baptism. In view of Barth's shift to a baptistic view of the subjects of baptism, his critique of sacramentalism may have special relevance for Baptists. Although he did not interact directly with the British Baptists, his treatment of the subject is one of the most sustained arguments against sacramentalism in print, and its exegetical focus makes it especially relevant as a critique of the Baptist position.

Barth argued in his final statement on baptism that it is the foundation (first step of obedience) in the Christian life. It is "the first step of the life of faithfulness to God, . . . the binding confession of his obedience, conversion and hope, made in prayer for God's grace, wherein he honours the freedom of this grace."[51] Baptism with water bears witness to the divine work in Jesus Christ, but it is not itself a divine work. Although a sacramental view of baptism purportedly affirms the significance of the rite, Barth argued otherwise:

> The praise of baptism is not served but fatefully damaged if the sanctity of this action is sought, not in the true and distinctive thing which characterises it as a human action, but in a supposedly immanent divine work.[52]

He recognized that the label "sacramental" covers a wide range of concepts from the *ex opere operato* view of the Catholic tradition to the Reformed view of baptism as a means of conveying the knowledge and assurance of personal salvation (Barth's earlier view), but he rejected this entire spectrum of views. As he saw it, the common error of all these concepts was the assumption that there must be a divine work concealed in the humanly-

---

49 Karl Barth, *The Teaching of the Church Regarding Baptism*, trans. Ernest A. Payne (London: SCM Press, 1948), 25-30.
50 Karl Barth, *Church Dogmatics IV/4*, trans. G. W. Bromiley (Edinburgh: T. & T. Clark, 1969), x.
51 Ibid., 2.
52 Ibid., 101.

administered event.[53]

This rejection of sacramentalism and the description of baptism as the initial step of obedience in the Christian life superficially looks like just one more statement of the traditional (non-sacramental) Baptist view, but Barth emphasized that this is not the case. Baptists tend to focus on a definitive experience of conversion, a personal crisis of the soul, in which experience of repentance and faith there is an assurance of God's grace with its effects of forgiveness of sins and the bestowal of the Holy Spirit. In the aftermath of this experience, baptism occurs as a testimony not only to the objective work of Christ, but also to a prior experience in which the gospel has been assuredly appropriated. With regard to such views Barth said:

> There is a certain similarity in so far as this understanding, too, carries with it an explicit criticism of the sacramental interpretation. On closer examination, however, it will not be overlooked that this is the only point of agreement, and that the context and meaning of this criticism are obviously very different from ours. If in this understanding the sacramental view of water baptism is rejected or avoided--often far too hastily and critically--the price which is blatantly paid is that the external work of water baptism, robbed of its glory as a sacrament, is replaced by an "inner work" in the form of experiences, inspirations, illuminations, exaltations or raptures. This work as such is then invested with the sacramental interpretation denied to water baptism, and it is thus identified with the baptism of the Spirit.[54]

Accordingly, Barth's criticism of sacramentalist exegesis must be considered separately here. This book will examine his treatment of New Testament texts normally used to support sacramentalism, and seek to isolate the crucial theological factors which are inherent in his exegesis. It should be noted that there are some surprising omissions from the list of texts considered. For example, although he alluded at various points to both Acts 2:38 and 1 Corinthians 12:13 (the latter accepted as a reference to water-baptism), neither text was treated in the list of proof-texts for sacramentalism. 1 Corinthians 6:11, which connects a "washing" to both justification and sanctification and is commonly taken as an allusion to baptism, was ignored even though some more obscure references were

---

53 Ibid., 102-107.
54 Ibid., 106.

considered (e.g., 1 John 5:5-8; John 19:33-37). But having pointed out these omissions (which are not insignificant), this study will now consider the texts which Barth does discuss, using his own order for this analysis.

Acts 22:16

Paul's account of his own conversion, in which Ananias exhorted him to "wash away" his sins by "calling on the Lord" in the act of baptism seems to represent baptism as a vehicle of the forgiveness of sins. Barth's reply to this inference was centred on the fact that a resolute *human* act is demanded of Saul: "This appeal and the use of the middle βάπτισαι show that no wonderful experience of grace is held out to Saul."[55] The central issue here is the petition ("calling on his name"), Saul's active prayer that God will forgive him for his sins. Such a petition presupposes an acknowledgment of the truth about Jesus Christ, so that Saul "has already experienced the grace" of the Lord, "the One by whom his sins are already washed away."[56]

It is difficult to feel the force of Barth's reading of this text. First, the reminder that a human act is in view here is accurate but beside the point. All would agree that the baptism of a confessing believer is a human act of the baptized person, but the question is whether a *divine* act is thought to occur also in the event. Second, Barth recognized that the forgiveness which is in view is in some sense the "goal" of Saul's action, the object of his prayer. When Barth said that Saul had *already* experienced the grace of forgiveness, he must have been using "experienced" in an abnormal way to describe the objective reconciliation achieved in the work of Christ. The forgiveness here to be prayed for must be a subjective cleansing not yet accomplished. But this is connected to baptism, which is another way of saying that the baptism is sacramental, a means by which the divine act of forgiveness is mediated. In Beasley-Murray's words, baptism here is "the supreme occasion and even vehicle of his yielding to the Lord Christ,"[57] and the conscious appropriation of Christ's vicarious work.

Hebrews 10:22

This text uses Old Testament imagery to describe believers under the new covenant as those whose hearts are "sprinkled" and whose bodies are

---

55 Ibid., 112.
56 Ibid.
57 Beasley-Murray, *BNT*, 102.

"washed with pure water." Although there is no explicit reference to baptism, Barth agreed that the reference to water is so vivid "that there is actual allusion to water baptism."[58] But all this must be related to the major theme of the epistle, i.e., the uniqueness and finality of the priestly work of Christ. Barth wrote:

> According to the whole tenor of Hebrews there are no cleansings apart from that which took place in the death of Jesus Christ; neither that of the old covenant nor any new ones which might replace it.[59]

Granted the finality and perfection of the death of Jesus Christ, it was argued that baptism can be nothing more than a *reminder* of the once-for-all cleansing effected in the atonement, not a means of cleansing itself.

The allusion to baptism is difficult to deny, not only because of the references to water, but also because the exhortation of vs. 23 is "almost certainly an appeal to maintain the confession made in baptism."[60] But there is no reason to limit the force of the allusion as Barth did. It is true that a major theme of the epistle is the truth that the death of Christ was the sufficient and final cleansing sacrifice, but the question remains: how does that sacrifice become operative in the individual? How does one enter into the "full assurance of faith" noted in vs. 22? Apparently this occurs through the event indicated in the last clause of the verse, i.e., baptism. To quote Beasley-Murray, "The meeting place of the sanctifying power of Christ's death and the individual is the baptism wherein the believer turns to God in faith for cleansing through Christ."[61] As Barth noted in his treatment of Acts 22:16, there is both an objective cleansing which occurred in the past in the atoning death of Christ and a subjective cleansing for which the believer prays in the act of baptism. Baptism is indeed a reminder of the objective cleansing, but the allusion in this text seems to say what other texts say more explicitly, that baptism is not *merely* a reminder.

Ephesians 5:25-56

Jesus Christ's sanctification of the church is here said to occur "by the

---

58 Barth, *IV/4*, 112.
59 Ibid., 113.
60 Beasley-Murray, *BNT*, 250.
61 Ibid.

washing with water through the word." Barth conceded that the reference to water makes it impossible not to think of baptism when reading the text. But did the readers think of baptism as the occasion of their cleansing or as the vivid reminder of the death of Christ which was their real cleansing? Barth argued that the crux of this interpretive question is whether there are two acts of Christ in view (his sacrificial death and a subsequent cleansing of the church) or only one (his death which effectively cleansed the church). He concluded that if these are two distinct things, then "this sentence or clause undoubtedly ascribes a sacramental character to the cleansing and thus to the act of baptism."[62] Having admitted that the λουτρὸν τοῦ ὕδατος clearly brings baptism to mind, he conceded that the sacramental interpretation is possible and understandable, but he denied that it is necessary. He suggested instead that this sanctification-cleansing is simply a restatement of what happened in the love and self-sacrifice of Jesus Christ. The sacrifice of Christ is the "true cleansing of the community . . . the goal of water baptism, which is reflected in its technical administration, but which naturally does not take place in and with this."[63] But why should this reading be accepted rather than the sacramental one? The one reason that Barth gave is that this interpretation construes the "word" (ῥῆμα) as the work of Christ which is a "living and present" word still at work, and this is supposedly a "much more natural and fruitful interpretation" of ἐν ῥήματι than any of the interpretations connected with the baptismal confession.[64]

In reply it may be said that Barth has simply suggested an alternative exegesis of this text, but his alternative is not compelling. His exegesis pointed in two directions, in that he wanted to read the cleansing of the text as a reference to the objective work of Golgotha, but at the same time to see it as the "*goal* of water baptism." Now to say that the cleansing is the goal of baptism is surely to say that we are talking about the application of the atonement to individuals, but this is what Barth needed to avoid to sustain his exegesis. It is also not clear that ῥῆμα most naturally refers to the work of Christ; it is generally conceded that ῥῆμα, as opposed to λόγος, tends to denote a *spoken* word, indicating the natural connection between this term and the verbal confession and invocation of the Lord in baptism. In the end, it seems that Barth was straining to avoid the obvious in this passage. If this reference to water points to baptism, but without implying a sacramental significance, then the language of the text can only be called confusing.

---

62 Barth, *IV/4*, 113.
63 Ibid., 114.
64 Ibid.

Titus 3:5

This text refers to a "washing" or "bath" (λουτρόν) which is related to "regeneration and renewal of the Holy Spirit," and Barth admitted that this is probably an allusion to baptism. He added, "If this λουτρόν is identical with the act of baptism, then, since it can be taken only instrumentally and causatively, a sacramental meaning has uncontestably to be ascribed to baptism."[65] He argued that a *direct* reference to baptism here faces at least five serious difficulties: (1) This would make the two words διὰ λουτροῦ the focus of the whole extended statement about God's saving grace. (2) This would make baptism as such the primary goal of the epiphany of Jesus Christ. (3) This posits a second cleansing distinct from the cleansing death of Christ referred to in Titus 2:14. (4) This gives to παλιγγενεσία an individualistic meaning different from its cosmic reference in its other New Testament occurrence (Matt 19:28). (5) This makes the baptism with the Spirit identical to or coincident with baptism with water, contrary to the Gospels and Acts.[66]

What, then, is this λουτρόν? Based on Old Testament prophetic language about eschatological purification and the Spirit, Barth asserted:

> The cleansing bath ... is the purifying and renewing outpouring of the Holy Spirit which has taken place on the basis of the new creation ushered in by the Saviour God in the history of Jesus Christ.[67]

This exegesis allows "regeneration" to be understood as cosmic renewal as in Matthew 19:28, interprets the "cleansing" in the spiritual sense clearly present in the prophets, and thus reduces baptism to no more than a vague allusion here. Although this is a possible interpretation of the text, it is necessary to ask whether the allusion might be more than a glance in the direction of baptism. Specifically, one needs to examine each of Barth's five reasons for denying the direct reference to baptism.

(1) Identifying the λουτρόν as baptism does not make διὰ λουτροῦ the central point of the passage any more than any other interpretation. The *fact* of God's saving mercy toward foolish sinners is clearly the point of the passage, whatever the *means* may be. (2) The second argument is open to the same criticism as the first; in fact it is essentially a restatement of the

---

65 Ibid., 114.
66 Ibid., 114-115.
67 Ibid., 115.

first argument. It may well be true that some sacramentalists exalt baptism unduly, allowing it to usurp the role of Christ himself, but this is not inherent in the baptismal exegesis of this text as long as baptism is merely an instrument utilized as a vehicle of God's action. (3) Concerning Titus 2:14 two points may be made. First, that statement indicates that Christ's self-sacrifice was for the *purpose* of cleansing sinners, but this does not in itself indicate the *temporal* relationship between the two, i.e., whether the cleansing follows immediately or at some length. Second, there is no real problem with the idea of two cleansings related to the atonement, one an objective fact provided once-for-all and the other an individual-subjective cleansing appropriated by faith. Barth himself accepted this duality in his treatment of Acts 22:16, as noted above. Furthermore, even if the λουτρόν of Titus 3:5 is, as Barth asserted, the objective and cosmic outpouring of the Holy Spirit, this is still a *second* reality dependent on, but different from, the self-sacrifice of Christ. (4) There is no reason why the idea of "regeneration" could not have both an individual and a cosmic application. The text to which Barth pointed (Matt 19:28) is the only other occurrence of this word in the New Testament, and this is hardly enough evidence to establish a pattern which would govern Titus 3:5. (5) The radical disjunction which Barth posited between baptism with water and baptism with the Spirit is not supported by the New Testament evidence. The contrast which he noted in the Gospels and Acts is between *John's* baptism with water and *Jesus'* baptism with the Holy Spirit. This is a contrast between preparation and fulfillment, but whether the contrast still applies in the case of post-Pentecostal water-baptism is another matter and must be decided on the basis of post-Pentecostal apostolic witness. As argued above, the evidence seems to point to a normative, though not invariable, connection between water and the Spirit.

Galatians 3:27

This passage serves to illustrate the general New Testament truth that the effects ascribed to faith and those ascribed to baptism are the same. A statement about the readers' faith (vs. 26) is explained in terms of their baptism (vs. 27), which is the basis for Beasley-Murray's representative conclusion:

> Baptism is the baptism of faith and grace, so that in it faith receives what grace gives. Above all grace gives Christ, for Christ is the

fullness of grace; faith therefore receives Christ in baptism.[68]

Barth saw this text as more than an allusion; it is rather a statement about the fundamental meaning of baptism. As such, "It could lend support to a sacramental view of baptism,"[69] but this was rejected as out of harmony with the general argument of the epistle. Barth argued that if baptism is the initiation into salvation (as opposed to circumcision), then one would expect more than this one isolated reference to it in an epistle devoted to the refutation of Judaizing tendencies. But rather than emphasizing baptism as the alternative to circumcision, Paul grounds human salvation in the work of Christ with only faith and the work of the Spirit "as the condition of its subjective actualization."[70]

This minimal reference to baptism in Galatians, as opposed to the focus on faith, does make it clear that baptism has no independent power to convey the benefits provided in Christ, but its relative importance cannot be so easily refuted. The fact that Paul can so naturally shift from faith in 3:26 to baptism in 3:27 should warn us not to drive a wedge between them. Similarly, Paul does not mention *repentance* at all in Galatians (and only a few times in any of his epistles), but surely this does not negate the essential place of repentance in Christian conversion, and indeed in Paul's preaching (Acts 17:30; 20:21; 26:20). Faith is opposed to circumcision as interpreted by the Judaizers, but faith is not opposed to baptism, and Galatians 3:27 seems to clearly indicate that for Paul baptism is the event in which faith is expressed and Christ is consciously appropriated, which is to say that baptism is in some sense sacramental.

Romans 6:3-4

This Pauline text may well be the *locus classicus* for a sacramental conception of baptism, but Barth denied that this passage teaches a spiritual dying and rising with Christ as a result of baptism. He noted that what Paul does say is that we were *buried* with Christ through baptism. "This verse does not say, however, that baptism was the change in which this dying (not to speak of their entry into new life) took place."[71] For Jesus his burial was "the final confirmation that he truly died."[72] This confirmatory function

---

68 Beasley-Murray, *BNT*, 151.
69 Barth, *IV/4*, 116.
70 Ibid.
71 Ibid., 117.
72 Ibid.

applies also to Christian baptism:

> This burial with him, their baptism . . . is the regular confirmation of the fact that they have died with Him and in Him. It is not the actual conclusion of their existence as sinners, but the dramatic concluding line which denotes it.[73]

Baptism, according to this reading of the text, confirms and signifies that we died with Christ *when he died* and looks forward to our resurrection *at the Parousia*. Baptism, like the burial of Christ, stands *between* death and resurrection. What saves us is the once-for-all vicarious work of Jesus Christ. "Baptism cannot be--as though this were necessary--a repetition, extension, re-presentation or actualisation of the saving event which is the true theme of the argument in v. 2-10."[74]

There are two major problems with Barth's reading of this important text. First, it is impossible to evade the reference of the text to a present, experiential entrance into new life which is rooted in the prior, historical death and resurrection of Christ. Vs. 11 exhorts Christians to consider themselves already "dead to sin but alive to God," which assumes that they have not only "died" with Christ but also have been "raised" with him. There is to be sure a future share in the resurrection of Christ at the Parousia (vs. 5), and the language of resurrection is not explicitly applied to the present in vs. 4, but the connection there between Christ's being "raised from the dead" and the Christian's "walk in newness of life" points to a kind of "resurrection" now in anticipation of the eschaton. Vss. 15-23 describe this present transformation of human existence in terms of release from slavery to sin and entrance into slavery to God and righteousness, and the transformation is linked to the time when the readers "became obedient from the heart to the form of teaching" embodied in the gospel (vs. 17). This memorable response to the gospel which marks the transfer from the sphere of sin/death to that of righteousness/life must be included in the event to which the readers have already been recalled (vss. 3-4), i.e., their baptism. What baptism into Christ signifies, then, is not merely what happened at the first advent and will happen at the Parousia, but also the present manifestation of salvation.

Second, Barth's denial that baptism is viewed in this text as a means of grace does not follow from his assertion that baptism is viewed there as a

---

73   Ibid.
74   Ibid., 118.

human Yes to God's work in Christ. His understanding of baptism as a genuinely human, and thus morally significant, act is fully compatible with a doctrine of baptism in which the divine work in baptism includes a *response* to the human obedience of faith. In fact, if the human faith expressed in baptism is answered by a work of grace in baptism that makes the vicarious obedience of Christ effective in individual experience, then the human act of baptism is clearly significant in its effects. Therefore, it may be argued that Barth's denial of a divine act mediated through baptism serves to reduce the significance of the human response embodied in the event, in spite of his protests to the contrary.

Colossians 2:12

This text echoes Romans 6 in its assertion of a link between baptism and the entrance into new life in Christ, but all this is here subordinate to a description of salvation in terms of a "circumcision of Christ" which is "not a circumcision done by human hands." This is commonly interpreted as an equation between baptism and the circumcision of Christ (or "Christian circumcision"), thus making baptism the means of "putting off the body of flesh" (i.e., moral renewal), but Barth challenged this view. He pointed out that baptism can hardly be called an act which is done without human hands, and beyond this it would be strange to put this kind of emphasis on any ritual in an epistle which is largely devoted to a refutation of Jewish-Gnostic ritualism.[75] He proposed instead that the "circumcision of Christ" is not a circumcision *done by* Christ, but a circumcision *done to* Christ by putting off *his* "body of flesh" in his crucifixion.[76] This is admittedly an unusual way to describe the crucifixion, but it is very appropriate in this epistle which is an attack on a heresy in which false ideas of circumcision were significant.

This is an interesting and plausible exegesis of this text, but it fails to refute the sacramental character of baptism, because sacramentalism does not depend on identifying baptism with "the circumcision of Christ." Beasley-Murray, for example, agreed with Barth's equation of "circumcision of Christ" with the crucifixion, but still inferred sacramentalism from the text.[77] Barth's exegesis put the focus on the objective work of Christ, but the text also seems to denote the subjective realization of this work with the

---

75 Ibid., 119.
76 Ibid.
77 Beasley-Murray, *BNT*, 152-153.

An Analysis of the Biblical Foundations

statement, "In him you were also circumcised" (vs. 11), an experience which is explained by the words, "having been buried with him in baptism" (vs. 12). The most natural way to read the passage seems to be that baptism is the event in which this "circumcision of Christ" affects the individual "through faith."

John 3:5

Jesus' declaration to Nicodemus that personal "rebirth" is ἐξ ὕδατος καὶ πνεύματος has served as a classic proof-text for a sacramental view of baptism, but Barth turned it into a refutation of sacramentalism. He admitted that this reference to water must denote baptism, given that this chapter is part of the story of John's baptism and its relationship to Jesus (and his baptism--4:1-2). Other meanings have been suggested for this "water," but as Barth noted, the reference to baptism can be denied only by disconnecting it from its immediate literary context.[78] But how exactly is baptism treated here?

> Might it not turn out that there is here a protest against the idea of a work or revelation of salvation in baptism and thus against the baptismal belief which was held in the surrounding world and which was perhaps widespread, or was just arising, in certain circles in the community itself?[79]

Barth supported this inference by comparing "water and Spirit" to other "pairs-in-tension" in the Gospel of John, such as "grace and truth" (1:17), "spirit and truth" (4:23), "resurrection and life" (11:25). He interpreted this form as follows:

> The second word, connected by a καί, certainly refers to the same thing as the first. Hence it does not set a second thing alongside that first mentioned. The accent, however, is always on the second, so that the order is not reversible. In this irreversible order a step is taken, a critical synthesis made, in which the second member totally explains the first, absorbs it, and thus completely replaces it.[80]

---

78 Barth, *IV/4*, 120.
79 Ibid., 121.
80 Ibid.

When this methodology is applied to John 3:5, the "Spirit" absorbs the "water," which is attested by the Gospel's reference to the Spirit as the "living water" (4:10-11; 7:38). The Spirit's baptism is thus the only truly effective baptism, the only one that regenerates. The Gospel thus lodges a protest against any tendency to slip into a magical view of baptism, a Christianized form of Hellenistic religion. All this is intimated in John 3 in that when the new birth is referred to again in vss. 6 and 8, it is simply ἐκ πνεύματος, the water having disappeared.[81]

This may well be an insightful look at this text in some ways, but Barth seems not to have proved all that he wanted to prove. In the first place, he seems to have overstated the degree to which the second member of a Johannine pair-in-tension absorbs the first. Does truth really replace grace (1:17) or minimize the importance of spirit (4:23)? Does the water from the Lord's side nullify the blood (19:34)? His description of such pairs does not really seem adequate to explain the data. Second, while the focus on "Spirit" rather than "water" in John 3 does seem to indicate that the former is necessary and effective in a way that the latter is not, virtually all sacramentalists would agree. But the fact remains that "water" *is* mentioned, although in a way that denotes a kind of necessity which is admittedly secondary and not absolute. The text may well be a polemic against magical, pagan views of baptism, emphasizing the ultimate necessity of the sovereign work of the Spirit of God, but this does not rule out a carefully nuanced sacramentalism, certainly not a Reformed sacramentalism which was once Barth's view.

Mark 16:16

Although the consensus of textual critics would deny the originality of Mark 16:9-20, Barth ignored this detail and considered it as a possible sacramental proof-text. "He who believes and is baptized will be saved" clearly lends itself to such use. Barth first noted that when the New Testament refers to "salvation" in either nominal or verbal form, both the meaning and the subject are ambiguous and must be determined by the context. The salvation in view may be either eschatological liberation from death or a present manifestation of liberation. The subject is in most cases God, but in other cases it is the gospel, the preacher, faith, or the recipient. Now the meaning is quite clear here; it is a reference to eschatological acceptance by God, since the alternative in this text is to disbelieve and be

---

81 Ibid.

An Analysis of the Biblical Foundations

condemned (the verb is κατακρίνω). This leaves baptism in view as a means to final salvation, but Barth argued that baptism's connection with faith diminishes the sacramental force:

> Baptism saves because, like faith and with it, it is an element in the action God has entrusted to and enjoined upon those who will be saved by God and who are saved already in hope in Him. It is a human work which is, like faith, wholly appropriate and indispensably proper to their position.[82]

If Barth was right in his suggestion that faith and baptism stand in essentially the same relation to salvation, then he conceded the case for sacramentalism. If anything is clear in the New Testament, surely it is that faith is a means by which salvation is individually received, not a meritorious *basis* of salvation, to be sure, but a *means* of entrance into salvation nevertheless. If this is also the case with baptism, then baptism seeks salvation as its goal, and this is sacramentalism.

1 Peter 3:21

This text is even more explicit than Mark 16:16, in that it straightforwardly says that "baptism now saves you." Barth treated the text in two places, first as a parallel to Mark 16:16 and later at the end of his volume in his positive development of the meaning of baptism. The first stage of his treatment is open to the same objection as above for Mark 16:16. In the second stage he suggested that this is the clearest definition of baptism in the New Testament. Baptism is here described as a *prayer*, assuming that the positive part of the statement should be rendered "request to God for a good conscience." The significant thing about baptism, then, is not the administration of the ritual, but the human act of prayer (ἐπερώτημα) embodied in it. Barth found support for his anti-sacramentalism in the negative part of the description, "not the removal of the filth of the flesh":

> Baptism is not their cleansing and renewal, their justification and sanctification, their regeneration, their endowment with the Holy Spirit. All this takes place through God's work and word in Jesus

---

82 Ibid., 122.

Christ, not through any work of man, even though the man be a Christian and the work baptism. What takes place in baptism is neither the work of salvation nor the revelation of salvation. There could be no clearer rejection of every sacramental understanding of baptism than that given here.[83]

If Barth was right in his exegesis of the positive part of Peter's statement, i.e., if baptism is an acted prayer for salvation, then it is difficult to understand the sense in which this is non-sacramental. From that perspective salvation is at least conveyed *through* baptism, although not necessarily in the very act of baptism, but this is simply to affirm that God is not manipulated by human action (even divinely-mandated human action). Any denial of sacramentalism in this text would have to be located in its negative aspect concerning the "removal of the filth of the flesh." Barth defended the exegesis which reads this as a reference to the moral renewal of human nature under the conditions of this age, which is based on one possible meaning of σάρξ.[84] Although this would be its common meaning in Pauline literature, it is not at all clear that it means this here. The word σάρξ is used five other times in 1 Peter 3:18-4:6, and there it consistently seems to mean simply "body," especially when it refers to the sufferings of Christ as "in the flesh" (σαρκὶ–3:18; 4:1). It seems clear that Peter is not referring to Jesus Christ as one who would in any way need moral renewal. Now if σάρξ here means simply "body," then the meaning of the negative phrase in vs. 21 would be "not the removal of dirt from the body," and the point would be to deny that the crux of baptism is the physical ritual itself.[85] Thus the effect of the baptismal definition would be to emphasize that there is no power in the rite *per se*, but that spiritual renewal is mediated through the commitment (prayer) expressed in baptism. In the end, however one interprets the negative phrase, the positive thrust of the text indicates that "through the resurrection of Jesus Christ" there is salvation for those who call on him, and this calling on him is assumed to occur in baptism.

---

83 Ibid., 212.
84 For another defense of this exegesis, see J. Ramsey Michaels, *1 Peter*, Vol. 49, *Word Biblical Commentary* (Dallas: Word Books, 1988), 216.
85 See, for example, Dunn, *Baptism in Spirit*, 218.

Conclusion

The most that can be said for Barth's exegesis of New Testament baptismal texts is that he provided a *possible* exegetical basis for a non-sacramental view of baptism. However, it cannot be said that he offered a *natural* interpretation of these texts, and it must be said that his failure to interpret Acts 2:38 and 1 Corinthians 12:13 left two of the most significant texts without extended comment. Repeatedly in his exegesis he admitted that a sacramental reading of a text would be very natural, after which he proceeded to offer an alternative reading; although this is allowable when dealing with obscure texts in light of clear texts, it was for him a consistent pattern applicable to all kinds of texts.

Barth was unable to let the baptismal texts speak naturally, because his interpretation was controlled by certain theological concerns which, though in some cases valid in their own way, were inaccurately applied to the baptismal statements of the New Testament. Three concerns are paramount: (1) the objectivity and finality of the work of Christ in his death and resurrection; (2) the significance of human moral action; and (3) the distinction between baptism with water and baptism with the Spirit.

The objectivity of the death and resurrection of Christ is indeed a legitimate concern. It is helpful to be reminded that whatever it may mean to say that baptism (or faith) "saves," it is still the case that only the vicarious work of Christ saves in the ultimate sense. But having said this, it is important to note that this is a false issue, because no form of sacramentalism asserts that baptism saves apart from, or in the same sense as, the events of the gospel. The debate over sacramentalism is not about the ultimate cause of human salvation; it is about the instrumental cause(s), specifically the role of baptism as an instrument. It is not clear that Barth took seriously the whole question of applying the saving work of Christ in personal experience, because he appeared to relativize the response of faith in much the same way as he relativized baptism.

In the multi-faceted debate about the relation between divine action and human action, there is always the danger of an extreme view which completely envelops the human act in the divine, and Barth directed this concern toward baptism in order to preserve the integrity of the human decision which it embodies. He was jealous for the dignity of this foundational human response, and he denied that baptism's significance has to be located in a divine act. However, to say that God acts in baptism is not to say that the human person does not act, especially if the context is conversion-baptism and it is assumed that there is a divine act which *responds* to penitent faith in the human. If it is the human who repents, and it is God who forgives and bestows the Spirit, then baptism may serve as an event in which there is action from both sides.

Barth's concern to separate baptism with water from baptism with the Spirit was grounded in the freedom and sovereignty of God, with its corollary that God's work of salvation is not manipulated by any human action. He inferred from this that the assertion of a temporal coincidence of water and Spirit is disallowed--baptism is a prayer for the gift of the Spirit, but not a means to achieve it, for the gift of the Spirit is God's prerogative. Although this is an appropriate warning, it is a warning that is articulated by sacramentalists themselves, especially in their treatment of the narratives in Acts. Nevertheless, to deny the propriety of a declaration that the gift of the Spirit occurs invariably in water-baptism is not to deny that there is a *normal* connection between the two. If the Spirit is given to all those who believe, as both Jesus (John 7:37-39) and Paul (Rom 8:9) affirm, and baptism is the vehicle by which faith comes to expression, then it is appropriate to think in terms of the bestowal of the Spirit through baptism.

In spite of his statements to the contrary, it appears that in the end Barth was unable to escape the sacramental significance of baptism in the New Testament witness.[86] As opposed to all kinds of "enthusiasts" who locate their assurance of God's grace in some subjective religious experience, Barth recognized that baptism adds a necessary objectivity to this awakening to grace. He thus wrote at the end of his part-volume on baptism:

> In the light of their baptism Christians can regard themselves as saved, and they can be comforted and admonished thereby, since baptism is an asking and praying which is empowered and set in motion by the resurrection of Jesus Christ, and as such it is the proper counteravouchment of Christians to the avouchment of the Lord that He will be their God.[87]

In view of his comments about assurance of grace coming through baptism, it seems that Barth was still very close to the cognitively-oriented sacramentalism of the Reformed tradition. His disavowal of sacramentalism was fundamentally a rejection of certain kinds of sacramentalism, in particular those which stress the divine act in baptism to the virtual exclusion of any human act and those which posit an invariable connection

---

86 As argued by Herbert Hartwell, "Karl Barth on Baptism," *Scottish Journal of Theology* 22 (1969): 29.
87 Barth, *IV/4*, 212-213.

between the sign and the thing signified. Sacramentalism is a spectrum of views, and Barth's critique was in fact directed only at part of the spectrum, certainly not consciously or effectively at Baptist sacramentalism.

Summary

This chapter has demonstrated that a Baptist-sacramental exegesis of the New Testament references to baptism is readily defensible. Baptists who reject sacramentalism admit that these New Testament texts do seem to say that baptism is instrumental in the application of the work of Christ to individuals, but they argue that broader theological principles demand another interpretation of the texts. This would be acceptable, *if* the broader principles do in fact clearly (though implicitly) address the issue of baptism, and *if* there are plausible ways to read the baptismal texts in a non-sacramental manner. However, neither of these conditions seems to be true.

If, as argued in this chapter, it is true that Baptist sacramentalism can be defended on an exegetical basis, there are still questions to be answered about the precise meaning of this sacramentalism and its relation to other theological themes. Chapter Four will be devoted to an examination of the connections between this baptismal theology and the related themes of systematic theology.

CHAPTER 4

An Analysis of the Theological Formulation

As the previous chapter indicates, there is in the exegetical area a high degree of agreement among sacramentalists, whether Baptists or others, as to the teaching of the biblical texts. However, this agreement that the biblical texts, taken as a whole, give an essentially consistent affirmation that the saving union with Christ signified by Christian baptism is in some way conveyed through the rite does not eliminate the fact of disagreement in the context of systematic theological formulation. To say that baptism is instrumental in the application of redemption to the individual is not to say exactly how baptism conveys grace or what may be the nature of that grace, nor does it define the precise relationship between baptism and the faith of the individual. Sacramentalists draw various inferences about the connection between water-baptism and Spirit-baptism, the relationship between baptism and communicant church membership, and the status of the unbaptized. The purpose of this chapter, therefore, is to articulate further the ways in which Baptist sacramentalists answer these systematic questions and to assess the coherence of their system(s). In particular, this will involve an attempt to demonstrate that "Baptist sacramentalism" is not an oxymoron, but instead is a valid synthesis of the necessity of divine initiative in redemption and the related necessity of human response.

Creation, Incarnation and Baptism

Although the Baptist case for a sacramental view of baptism is grounded fundamentally in the New Testament references and allusions to baptism, some Baptists claim that there are valid sacramental inferences to be drawn from the doctrines of the Incarnation and/or creation. For Robinson the ultimate principle was found in the nature of the created order, specifically in the divinely-established role of the physical world as a vehicle of the spiritual realm. In his words, "In all our life and thought the spiritual is

An Analysis of the Theological Formulation

directly or indirectly mediated by that which is lower than itself."[1] This function of the physical order is "the very principle of the Incarnation, when the Word became flesh."[2] Thus the Incarnation, far from being a thoroughly unique event, becomes the supreme manifestation of an even more basic principle. Walton followed the same line of thought, arguing on the basis of Romans 1 that Christian theology "affirms that the spiritual operates through the medium of the material," and that "God is revealed and His grace is given through things seen and temporal."[3] This is one aspect of the biblically rooted combination of transcendence and immanence in the Christian view of God, which distinguishes Christianity from other religions which are grounded in abstract speculation and from materialistic philosophies like Marxism which fail to rise above history. The Incarnation was interpreted as the supreme, but not the only, example of "a principle which lies at the root of reality as Christians see it," and "the sacraments are another example of this principle."[4]

Clark's approach did not rely on any assumed relation between the physical world and a general realm of "spirit," but he did argue that God's action in history follows a pattern which supports sacramentalism. In response to Baptist criticism of his alleged overestimate of baptism's efficacy, he wrote:

> We are persuaded that, in accordance with the whole principle of divine dealing with humanity in creation, incarnation, resurrection, the spiritual gift and reality is "embodied" (in this case, sacramentally); that it is reality for us only as embodied reality; that fidelity to scriptural witness forbids any separation of sign and signification.[5]

Similarly, Gilmore accepted as a valid insight the emphasis by many modern theologians on the conjunction of "word" and "flesh," arguing that Baptists have been prone to focus on "word" apart from "flesh," thus illegitimately positing a conversion experience divorced from sacramental expression.[6]

This sort of general principle was largely insignificant in the arguments of Beasley-Murray, but he did write, "The sacramental principle is rooted in

---

1 Robinson, "Believers' Baptism and the Holy Spirit," 394.
2 Ibid.
3 Walton, *GC*, 155.
4 Ibid., 156.
5 Clark, "Christian Baptism Under Fire," 17.
6 Gilmore, *BCU*, 11.

life as God has created it."⁷ He argued that due to our existence as embodied creatures we "need baptism," not in any absolute sense, but in the sense that a tangible, physical action like baptism is an appropriate provision of divine grace which seals and assures us of our reconciliation to God through Christ. This reference to creation as a basis for sacramentalism was merely a brief part of his treatment of the necessity of baptism, and its significance for him seemed to be limited to the embodied nature of human existence and the consequent relevance of physical action for spiritual experience.

White affirmed a connection between the Incarnation and the sacraments, but the logical order in his conceptual scheme is from Incarnation to sacraments, not from sacramental principle to Incarnation. Following C. K. Barrett in his treatment of Johannine sacramentalism, he argued that the sacraments are "extensions of the fundamental sacramental fact of the incarnate life of the Son."[8] Whereas both Robinson and Walton interpreted the Incarnation and baptism as two examples of a more fundamental principle, White argued that both the Gospel of John and the First Epistle of John were calling their readers away from a dangerous reliance upon "spiritual experience" in general to the message about "the historic life and words of the divine Master."[9] Therefore, there was for him no sacramental principle more ultimate than the Incarnation--baptism is effective not because it is one example of a sacramental universe, but because it objectifies the faith-response to the historical action of God in Christ.

Although the doctrines of creation and Incarnation *may* have some relevance for sacramentalism, there are various reasons for caution in drawing inferences. *First*, it should be noted that the Johannine declaration that "the Word became flesh" (John 1:14) is not simply an assertion about the physical nature of Christ, but rather is an affirmation of his full *humanity*. John 1:13 refers to "the will of the flesh," and this attribution of "will" to "flesh" indicates that the author thinks of σάρξ as inclusive of the total human person. To limit the assertion to his physical nature would be to fall into the ancient error of Apollinarianism, which denied the presence of a human, rational soul in the person of Christ[10]. Therefore, one may not

---

7 Beasley-Murray, *BNT*, 304-305.
8 White, *BDI*, 263.
9 Ibid.
10 For a translation of the extant writings of Apollinaris of Laodicea and a description of his teaching, see Richard A. Norris, Jr., trans. and ed., *The Christological Controversy* (Philadelphia: Fortress Press, 1980), 21-23, 103-111.

safely generalize about the significance of the Incarnation for the physical world as a whole, because it is specifically oriented toward the redemptive assumption of complete humanity by the Logos.

Second, even if one accepts the general principle that God works in us through the material world and physical action, this does not explain precisely *how* he works in baptism. Baptists who resist sacramentalism do not in general deny that there is some kind of spiritual benefit connected to the event, but they argue that it is the same kind of benefit which is contained in other acts of obedience to divine commands. The debate concerns whether baptism should be thought of as an event which mediates salvific union with Christ, and this question is not answered by a general assertion that God relates to humans through the material world. There is nothing incoherent in the non-sacramentalist interpretation of baptism as a means of strengthening commitment through testimony to an already completed conversion, and this interpretation does not deny the presence of spiritual benefit in the physical act of baptism. The problem with such a view is that it does not seem to give an adequate account of the biblical witness to the nature of the spiritual benefit attached to baptism.

Third, if the term "sacramental" is applied to the entire material world, then the assertion that baptism is a "sacrament" is emptied of distinctive content. The intra-denominational debate among Baptists would then concern only the *mode* of baptism's sacramental function, not the *fact* of it. To speak of a sacramental universe in no way settles the baptismal debate--it merely shifts the terms of the debate.

Baptist sacramentalists have generally utilized inferences from creation and the Incarnation only to support and explain what they have already formulated on the basis of the explicit biblical witness to baptism. There may be some value in such support, but it is far from clear.

Baptism and Faith

Baptist sacramentalists generally have affirmed that baptism is a "symbol with power" precisely because of their understanding of the connection between baptism and faith.[11] True to their Baptist heritage and what they consider to be a proper kind of individualism, they have affirmed that the crucial factor in the divine-human relationship is moral, not ritual. Robinson, for example, argued that the primary contribution of Baptists to the Church is "the essential and primary place of the moral within the

---

11   White, *BDI*, 274, 308; Beasley-Murray, *BNT*, 272-273.

religious."[12] One biblical way to state this is to say that the instrumental cause of personal salvation is personal faith in Christ, inasmuch as all the benefits of salvation are promised to those who believe in Jesus as Lord. The biblical texts which are invoked here may use terms other than "faith" to describe this reality (repentance, confession of sins, turning to the Lord, etc.), but in each case the reference is to a positive response to the gospel which might be subsumed under the label of "faith." In various ways the witness of the New Testament is that God promises to all who believe in Jesus Christ all the benefits of salvation, specifically forgiveness of sins (1 John 1:9; Acts 15:9); union with Christ (Eph 3:18; Gal 2:20; 3:26); possession of the Holy Spirit (Gal 3:2,14; Acts 5:32); membership in the Church (Acts 4:32 ["the group of those who believed"]; Acts 5:14 ["believers were added to the Lord"]); eternal life or inheritance of the kingdom of God (John 3:14,16,36); and justification (Rom 3-4; Gal 2-3).

Alongside this list of biblical texts about faith can be placed another list of texts which indicate that the same benefits are seen as the effects of baptism.[13] For example, forgiveness of sins is promised to baptism in Acts 2:38, and the related metaphor of cleansing from sin is a baptismal effect in Acts 22:16. Saving union with Christ is the result of baptism in the classic text of Romans 6:1-11 and the parallel in Colossians 2:11-12, and the union with Christ of believers mentioned in Galatians 3:26 is explained as the result of baptism in Galatians 3:27. The possession of the Holy Spirit is promised along with forgiveness of sins in Acts 2:38, and the spiritual rebirth which the Spirit effects is located in the context of baptism in Titus 3:5 and John 3:5. Membership in the Church is mediated through baptism, whether the imagery is that of the body of Christ (1 Cor 12:13) or the seed of Abraham (Gal 3:27-29). Eternal life or entrance into the kingdom of God is related to baptism according to John 3:5, and the same can be said for the eschatological dimension of salvation according to Mark 16:16, if the long ending of Mark's Gospel is a genuine witness to the mind of Christ. Justification occurs in the baptismal context if the washing imagery of 1 Corinthians 6:11 is in fact an allusion to baptism.

There is, then, an essential equivalence between the things promised to faith and the things promised to baptism in the New Testament texts, and in some cases these two kinds of promises exist within the same text. For example, Paul's sustained argument in Galatians for justification by faith

---

12 Robinson, *LFB*, 175.
13 This parallelism between faith and baptism is developed at length in Beasley-Murray, *BTT*, 27-37.

apart from works leads to his statement that all who believe in Christ are by that fact the children of God, but this is immediately explained in terms of baptism as the instrument of union with Christ (3:26-27). In 1 Peter 3:21 we read that "baptism now saves us," although the instrument of this salvation is not the physical act itself, but the "appeal to God for a good conscience" which is expressed by the act.

Baptists have always insisted that the natural inference from such biblical data is the equation between the baptized and confessing believers, i.e., the restriction of baptism to those who can confess faith for themselves; but the same data also imply that baptism is related to the benefits of Christ in the same way as faith, i.e., that baptism looks toward saving union with Christ as its goal. This is not to say that faith seeks some benefits, and baptism seeks a further complement of benefits, but rather that faith and baptism seek the *same* benefits.

Thus Baptist sacramentalism is generally rooted in the concept of baptism as the vehicle of faith, the means by which faith becomes a conscious, tangible reality. Faith *per se* is an internal attitude by definition, whether one thinks of mere belief of the truth (*assensus*) or trusting commitment (*fiducia*). The consistent biblical picture is that genuine faith in Christ is marked by external action. This is perhaps stated most forcefully in James 2:14-26, with its assertion that we are justified by faith *and* works. Although at a superficial and purely verbal level this contradicts the Pauline argument of Romans and Galatians, Paul himself makes the similar assertion that what is crucial is "faith working through love," and he does so in the Galatian epistle (5:6) which is focused on justification by faith apart from works of the Law. Therefore, for Paul as for James and other New Testament writers, genuine faith always shows itself and demands ongoing witness in a life of love for God and others. Just as true faith which brings justification demands ongoing evidence of good works, so also true faith demands initial expression in baptism. To ask whether salvation is promised to faith or to baptism is, in New Testament terms, a meaningless question, since the former is initially expressed in the latter.

Baptist sacramentalists have not located the connection between faith and baptism simply in an arbitrary divine command to that effect, but rather in a holistic view of the human person.[14] This is not to say that God could not have chosen some other act to serve as the embodiment of faith, but it is to say that *some* act is needed if response to the gospel is to be fully

---

14   See for example G. R. Beasley-Murray, "Baptism in the New Testament," *Foundations* 3 (1960): 17, 27-29; Gilmore, *BCU*, 43-48.

personal, inasmuch as we do not act simply as "souls" apart from bodies. At a theoretical level, Wheeler Robinson asserted that a biblical-Hebraic view of the person is not dualistic, and this provided the context for his view of baptism as integral to conversion.[15] Neville Clark argued that the doctrines of creation and Incarnation both imply that God's encounter with human beings occurs in the realm of the physical as well as the spiritual.[16] R. E. O. White emphasized the need for an objectification of faith in baptism, and rejected the disconnection between faith and baptism as "gnostic idealism."[17]

If conversion were to be marked as a definite reality apart from baptism, what could serve as an adequate marker? Some might argue for supernatural phenomena (e.g., glossolalia) which accompany the gift of the Spirit in Acts, but to look for such signs as standard markers of conversion would contradict the Pauline perspective in 1 Corinthians 12-14, which interprets such signs as occasional rather than universal. Some would suggest the evidence of good works, but while this is relevant as an ongoing evidence of convertedness (James 2), the demand for works that are sufficiently specific to serve as evidence of the point of entrance into salvation tilts toward a legalism that is perilously similar to what Paul rejects in his battle with Judaizers. Some would argue for a relatively standard kind of religious feeling or interior experience which serves as a sign of salvation, but this is as difficult to correlate with 1 Corinthians 12-14 as is the demand for external phenomena. Commonly in Baptist and other evangelical contexts, faith comes to focus in a definite act of prayer, in which repentance and faith are expressed and God is asked to provide the benefits of salvation. At one level this is theologically appropriate, in that prayer is at the heart of human movement toward God, but the New Testament evidence indicates that this prayer (calling on the Lord) inheres in the event of baptism (Acts 22:16; 1 Peter 3:21), which is itself an acted prayer. Within the New Testament it seems to be assumed that those who believe in Christ are an identifiable group, which implies the existence of some definitive mark of identification, and baptism is apparently that mark. That explains why the apostle Paul, in the process of stating the commonalities of the members of the body of Christ, mentions "one Lord, one faith, one [expression of this faith in] baptism" (Eph 4:5).

---

15 Robinson, *LFB*, 85. This is developed at length in his *The Christian Doctrine of Man*, 3rd ed. (Edinburgh: T. & T. Clark, 1926).
16 Clark, "Christian Baptism Under Fire," 17.
17 White, *BDI*, 263-264.

An Analysis of the Theological Formulation

This construction of the relation between faith and baptism is criticized from two sides: non-sacramental Baptists allege that it compromises the *sola fide* character of justification/salvation, and some paedobaptists argue that to make personal faith a condition of baptism is to transform faith into a meritorious work. Each criticism is concerned to apply the insights of Romans and Galatians to this question, and it is assumed that those insights are threatened by the assumption that faith and baptism (in that order) are normatively inseparable.

The *Baptist* critique is quite straightforward, although it may be expressed in several ways.[18] One form would be: Romans and Galatians teach that justification is by faith alone, apart from good works; baptism is a work of righteousness (as seen in the example of Jesus, Matt 3:15); therefore, justification does not occur through baptism.[19] Alternatively it could be phrased: faith is demanded prior to baptism; justification is by faith alone; therefore, justification occurs before baptism.[20] The paradigm for justification by faith, according to Paul in Romans 4, is Abraham, and Abraham was justified by bare faith in the divine promise, and only later was this sealed by circumcision--although Baptists reject a simple

---

18 A representative sample of such Baptist statements would include the following: James Robinson Graves, *The Relation of Baptism to Salvation* (Texarkana: Baptist Sunday School Committee, 1881), 8; Jeremiah B. Jeter, *Campbellism Examined* (New York: Sheldon, Lamport, & Blakeman, 1855), 230-237; Walter T. Conner, *Christian Doctrine* (Nashville: Broadman Press, 1937), 276-278; idem, *The Gospel of Redemption* (Nashville: Broadman Press, 1945), 208-209; Dallas M. Roark, *The Christian Faith* (Nashville: Broadman Press, 1969), 293-294; J. M. Cramp, *A Catechism on Baptism* (Philadelphia: American Baptist Publication Society, 1865), 71; August Hopkins Strong, *Systematic Theology* (Valley Forge: Judson Press, 1967 [orig. pub. 1907]), 821; Herschel H. Hobbs, *Fundamentals of our Faith* (Nashville: Broadman Press, 1960), 117-119; Ralph E. Knudsen, *Christian Beliefs* (Philadelphia: Judson Press, 1960), 124-125; Thomas Polhill Stafford, *A Study of Christian Doctrines* (Kansas City: Western Baptist Publishing Company, 1936), 533-534; Edgar Young Mullins, *The Christian Religion in Its Doctrinal Expression* (Philadelphia: Judson Press, 1917), 382-384; B. H. Carroll, *Baptists and Their Doctrines* (Nashville: Broadman Press, 1913), 20-23; Edward Charles Dargan, *The Doctrines of Our Faith*, rev. ed. (Nashville: Sunday School Board of the Southern Baptist Convention, 1920), 151; George Duncan, *Baptism and the Baptists* (London: Baptist Tract and Book Society, 1882), 73.
19 For an example of this use of Matt 3:15 see Gill, *Commentary on the New Testament*, 3:365.
20 This focus on temporal succession can be seen in Stones, Letter to *The Baptist Times*, 6. The chronological/theological argument is summarized by Christopher Ellis, "Baptism and the Sacramental Freedom of God," in *Reflections on the Water*, ed. Paul S. Fiddes (Macon, GA: Smyth & Helwys Publishing, 1996), 30-31, although Ellis rejects the anti-sacramental inference.

equivalence between circumcision and baptism, there is a sufficiently analogous relation to infer that baptism is no more than a backward-looking witness to an assured justification.[21] There are many examples of this Baptist critique of a sacramental view of baptism, one of which is the following statement by W. T. Conner (1877-1952) about the apparently sacramental biblical texts:

> Moreover, to interpret these passages literally, i.e., in such a way as to make baptism a condition of salvation, is to make the New Testament fundamentally a self-contradictory book. This would introduce an inconsistency into the very heart of its doctrine of salvation. This is evident if we look at the numerous passages in the New Testament where it is plainly taught that the only conditions of salvation are spiritual. It is abundantly set forth in the New Testament that repentance and faith are the only conditions of salvation--conditions that are primarily and only spiritual. Salvation is a spiritual transaction and depends on spiritual conditions alone.[22]

Historically, the assertion that a sacramental view of baptism threatens or denies the *sola fide* character of justification (or salvation, to use the more comprehensive term favoured by Baptists) must be blind to the facts of the magisterial Reformation. Some Baptists recognize that virtually every other Protestant denomination affirms in its confessional documents that baptism in some way conveys or seals what it signifies,[23] but this affirmation stands alongside the confession of justification by faith alone. It could easily be argued that among the Reformation traditions, Lutheran theology has taught both the strongest form of justification by faith alone and the highest view of baptismal efficacy. The idea that salvation by faith alone is incompatible with sacramentalism is at least historical nonsense.

Exegetically, this Baptist critique fails to interpret Pauline thought within the parameters of the first-century context and thus draws unwarranted inferences. One cannot read Romans and Galatians without seeing the contrast drawn there between faith in Christ and trust in the works of the Mosaic Law, but nowhere in Paul does one find the same sort of contrast drawn between faith and baptism. One might just as well argue

---

21 See, for example, Cramp, *Catechism*, 72-73; Conner, *Christian Doctrine*, 277.
22 Conner, *Christian Doctrine*, 276.
23 Carroll, *Baptists*, 20; Graves, *Relation of Baptism*, 10-19.

that Paul denies the crucial character of *repentance* (since repentance is distinct from faith, and faith is the only condition for salvation) as to argue the same sort of thing concerning baptism. "Faith alone" for Paul means faith as opposed to meritorious works, not faith as opposed to baptism. In point of fact, when Paul does refer to baptism (e.g., Rom 6; Col 2; Gal 3:27), his language seems to indicate that baptism is instrumental in effecting saving union with Christ, and the statements are sufficiently strong to cause some Baptists to deny that such texts refer to *water*-baptism at all. According to Luke's account (Acts 22:16), Paul submitted to baptism in order to be cleansed from his guilt. Paul's theology of baptism ought to be derived from an exegesis of his references to baptism, not from his references to the works of the Law.

Theologically, the Baptist critique tends to misinterpret the intention of Baptist sacramentalism. As can be seen in the quotation from Conner above and in other Baptist literature, it is assumed that sacramentalists understand baptism as a rite which is fundamentally a *sine qua non* of salvation, a kind of human achievement which is absolutely necessary to secure divine favour.[24] This, however, is not the way in which baptism was conceptualized by the Baptists being analysed in this book. As was shown in Chapter 2, they interpreted baptism as the normal, though not invariable (and certainly not absolutely necessary), vehicle by which faith in Christ comes to tangible expression and God meets the penitent sinner in grace. Baptism was for them no more an extra "condition" for salvation than is the prayer for salvation which other Baptists would ask of a convert. It is the separation of baptism from conversion by many Baptists which creates the impression of multiple conditions of salvation.

A common *paedobaptist* critique accepts the idea that baptism is the sacrament of justification but argues that justification is to be thought of as preceding faith rather than following it as in the Baptist construction. Such critics allege that to posit personal faith as a condition of baptism is to turn "faith" into a "work," a human achievement which merits justification, and thus to invert the biblical order of the gospel. John Heron (b. 1928), a Scottish theologian, went so far as to suggest that the Baptist order of faith and baptism "springs from a Pelagian view of human nature, which imagines that unregenerate man can choose whether to sin or not," and he suggested that the Baptist anthropology is the same as that which "underlies

---

24 Dargan, *Doctrines*, 151; Carroll, *Doctrines*, 21-22; Conner, *Redemption*, 208; Hobbs, *Fundamentals*, 117-118; Stafford, *Doctrines*, 532-534.

theological liberalism,"[25] namely, a naively optimistic estimate of human potential.

This perspective of faith-by-justification over against justification-by-faith was stated with clarity by Alan Richardson (1905-1975), a New Testament scholar at the University of Nottingham:

> The central truth of the Gospel which infant baptism enshrines is that faith is the response to God's saving act, not the condition of it. I am not baptized because I have decided to believe; I believe because I have come to know that I have already been admitted to the sphere of Christ's redemption.... This is the NT doctrine of baptismal justification: I am not justified by my faith: I believe because I have been justified.... Our faith is not the condition of our baptism but the response to it, made possible by our having already received the Holy Spirit (cf. 1 Cor. 12.3).... Baptism is the sacrament and effective symbol of justification...[26]

Justification, then, for Richardson denotes what God has done for all humankind objectively in the Christ-event, in particular in the death of Christ which was "the baptism of the *whole* human race."[27] The objectivity and priority of God's act in Christ, his "baptism" for all on the cross which was prefigured by his literal baptism in the Jordan, find their answer in individual human experience in the baptism of humans before they are capable of personal response. Personal faith as a response to one's prior baptism parallels the fact that individual faith is a response to the prior work of Christ declared in the gospel.

T. F. Torrance (b. 1913) of the University of Edinburgh has been one of the most forceful critics of the idea that faith is a condition of justification. Although he recognized (as all must) that the thought of justification *by faith* is indeed biblical, and that the faith in view is in some sense *our* faith in response to the gospel, he was concerned to maintain that faith is an empty vessel with no value in itself, not a human contribution to our redemption. In his words, "We do not rely, then, upon our act of faith, but upon the faith of Christ which undergirds and upholds our faith."[28] He

---

25 John Heron, "The Theology of Baptism," *Scottish Journal of Theology* 8 (1955): 44.
26 Alan Richardson, *An Introduction to the Theology of the New Testament* (New York: Harper & Row, 1958), 362-363.
27 Ibid., 363.
28 Thomas F. Torrance, *Theology in Reconstruction* (Grand Rapids: Eerdmans, 1965), 159.

expanded this as follows:

> Therefore when we are justified by faith, this does not mean that it is *our* faith that justifies us, far from it--it is the faith of Christ alone that justifies us, but we in faith flee from our own acts even of repentance, confession, trust and response, and take refuge in the obedience and faithfulness of Christ -- "Lord I believe, help thou mine unbelief." That is what it means to be justified by faith.[29]

Torrance argued that any emphasis on the nature of the human response to Christ as the instrumental cause of justification easily leads to a subtle form of self-justification and tends to turn faith into a kind of work which merits human salvation, a condition capable of being met by autonomous human action.[30]

Torrance was unsparing in his criticism of what he called "conditional grace," i.e., the idea that individuals are justified *if and only if* they believe the gospel. He judged that this idea has "permeated Protestantism, Lutheran pietism, and the Federal Theology of the Calvinists, Puritanism and Anglicanism alike," and that this effectively denies the ultimacy and finality of the vicarious work of Christ and introduces "a new legalism."[31] Although he did not mention Baptists specifically at this point, his treatment of baptismal doctrine makes it clear that he considered the doctrine of faith as a condition of baptism to be a particularly flagrant example of "conditional grace." But what of the urgency of gospel preaching? He admitted that the apostolic kerygma is: Christ has lived, died, and been raised for you; therefore, repent and believe in him; but according to Torrance, "Never does it say: This is what God in Christ has done for you, and you can be saved on condition that you repent and believe."[32]

To say, as these critics do, that humans believe because they are justified, rather than believing in order to be justified, may superficially magnify the objectivity of the work of God in Christ, but it does so by nullifying the significance of the imperative which accompanies the declarative in the apostolic kerygma. In the case of Baptist sacramentalism, baptism is the context in which the individual sinner confesses something like this: "I repent of my sins against God and others, and I acknowledge in

---

29 Ibid., 159-160.
30 Thomas F. Torrance, *God and Rationality* (London: Oxford University Press, 1971), 56.
31 Ibid., 57.
32 Ibid., 58.

Jesus Christ the answer to my need for forgiveness and transformation; I confess that he died and was raised from the dead for me; in this act of baptism I say 'Yes' to the good news about him, and I appeal to him for forgiveness and the gift of his Spirit, on the basis of his finished work." Now, assuming that such an attitude toward Christ is a condition of salvation, in what sense does this sort of faith become a work? Such a confession affirms the lack of any personal claim on God's grace; it affirms the priority of God's action in Christ; and it locates the source of salvation outside the baptizand. The only apparent basis for interpreting such faith as a "work" is the fact that it is the faith of *this individual*. But to say that my *faith* is *my* faith is not to say that it is meritorious, nor to say that it is possible apart from divine grace.

To discuss the biblical doctrine of the justification of the individual sinner is essentially to discuss the *Pauline* doctrine of justification, inasmuch as it is Paul alone for whom this terminology represents a regulative concept. At the purely verbal level, at least, Paul consistently refers to justification by faith (Rom 3:22,28,30; 4:11; 5:1; 10:10; Gal 2:16; 3:8,11,24), not to faith by justification. It may be theologically appropriate to speak of an objective justification wrought in the work of Christ, in that the vicarious obedience of Christ is called a δικαίωμα (Rom 5:18), but when Paul speaks explicitly of the justification of sinners, what is in view is the application of the objective obedience of Christ to the individual condition of believers, and in that context faith is logically prior to justification. The issue, then, concerning faith and baptism is *not* whether there is some kind of objective justification inherent in the Christ-event, or whether our faith terminates on that fact which is prior to our response, but instead is whether baptism functions only to declare that objective justification (Richardson, Torrance) or both to declare that objective reality and to seal the personal acceptance of it (Baptists).

Speaking from within a Reformed context, G. C. Berkouwer (b. 1903) of the Free University of Amsterdam commented:

> We must not allow ourselves, in reaction to the doctrine of faith's meritoriousness, to become too timid to speak of its necessity. This is a very real hazard. It would be possible for us, upon consideration of *sola gratia* in its truly exclusive and radical sense, to conclude that an emphasis on the singular necessity of faith tends to relativize grace. The Holy Scriptures point with weighted

decisiveness to this necessity.[33]

Although he did not accept a Baptist doctrine of baptism, Berkouwer was prepared to admit that the rejection of Baptist doctrine could not be based on a denial that faith is a condition of saving grace. According to him, the implication of the necessity of faith is this:

> Let it be written in capitals, put in italics that salvation is God's salvation, coming to us in the miracle of redemption, God's salvation which has been devised by no human mind and has risen from no human heart. None of this changes a letter of the fact that this sovereign grace *must* be accepted in faith.[34]

Apart from the desire to defend paedobaptism, it would be difficult to imagine the idea that a Baptist theology of baptism is essentially Pelagian and compromises the sacramental character of baptism. Paedobaptists also posit a personal confession of faith as a condition of baptism in the case of adult converts, and if there are no Pelagian assumptions in such practice, then it can hardly be said that the Baptist restriction of baptism to such cases is a Pelagian denial of Pauline teaching about faith and baptism.

Baptism and Grace

To say that baptism is a sacrament is to say that it is a "means of grace," but this is an assertion that demands definition, for all "means" do not function in exactly the same way, and "grace" is a somewhat elastic concept. In many cases Roman Catholic theology has spoken of grace almost as if it were a kind of substance which is physically infused into the recipient. Although this reification of grace has not been an explicit assertion, it has been argued that there are differing amounts of grace conveyed in the sacraments corresponding to the degree of receptivity in the individual,[35] and all such rhetoric is at least substantialist in tone. At least since Vatican II, Catholic theologians have sought to clarify the issue by describing grace as the personal action of God, whose action is in some cases mediated through

---

33 G. C. Berkouwer, *Faith and Justification*, trans. Lewis E. Smedes (Grand Rapids: Eerdmans, 1954), 185.
34 Ibid.
35 Ludwig Ott, *Fundamentals of Catholic Dogma*, 2nd ed., trans. Patrick Lynch, ed. James Bastible (Cork: Mercier Press, 1957), 330.

sacraments just as it is always mediated through Christ who is the fundamental sacrament, the Word become flesh.[36] The recent *Catechism of the Catholic Church* (1994) teaches that the primary content of grace is the gift of the Holy Spirit himself, along with his work of empowering individuals for service to God and others.[37] It would appear, then, that the traditional Catholic language about grace ought to be interpreted in light of these modern clarifications, but the need for clarity remains.

Baptists who interpret baptism as a means of grace tend to emphasize that grace is one way of describing the personal action of God as he shows unmerited favour to sinful humans through Jesus Christ.[38] In the context of baptism, their argument is that according to the apostolic witness God has connected various divine gifts (e.g., forgiveness, adoption, the Holy Spirit) to baptism, which amounts to a pledge by God that he will be active in the baptismal event, conveying these gifts to penitent sinners who seal their turning to Christ in confessional baptism. Ultimately, then, it is not that baptism conveys any benefits through any power inherent in itself, but that God, by the Holy Spirit, effects a genuine encounter with the baptizand in which he unites the baptized believer with Christ and thus with the benefits of Christ.

This concept of faith, baptism and grace implies that baptism is the normal venue for the introduction of the individual into the sphere of redemption, although this is neither invariably nor automatically true. But this is just to say that the gospel proclaimed sacramentally functions as does the gospel proclaimed verbally. The verbal proclamation of the gospel is the normal means by which individuals are brought into the sphere of salvation, but this does not mean that everyone who hears the gospel receives its benefits, nor does it mean that everyone who affirms a positive response is thereby saved, for some professions of faith are spurious or short-lived. It is also true that some are saved apart from any proclamation by a contemporary (e.g., by reading the gospel in Scripture), and many would argue that some are saved through the work of Christ though they have not heard the gospel and had the opportunity to come to explicit faith in Christ. Similarly, some who are baptized are not in fact saved, and some are saved apart from baptism, but the normal way in which grace meets faith is in a believer's baptism.

---

36 For example, Edward Schillebeeckx, *Christ the Sacrament of the Encounter with God*, trans. Paul Barrett, Mark Schoof and Laurence Bright (New York: Sheed and Ward, 1963), 76-78.
37 *The Catechism of the Catholic Church* (New York: Doubleday, 1995), 538-540.
38 Beasley-Murray, *BNT*, 265.

Is this baptismal grace a grace of justification and sanctification, or is it merely a grace of confirmation-assurance? That is to say, are the benefits of Christ *actually* bestowed by God through baptism, or are they *symbolically* ratified as benefits given to faith? The language of Baptist sacramentalists has been varied on this point, depending on what facet of theology they wanted to emphasize at any given time. However, assuming that we can never know with certainty the invisible work of God, these two approaches are in the end functionally equivalent. To say that these benefits of Christ are actually bestowed in baptism is to say that as far as our perception of them is concerned, they are bestowed in this context. As R. E. O. White put it, "Where the kerygma is presented and faith is awakened, *cognitio salutis* and *causa salutis* coincide."[39] What differentiates between Baptist sacramentalism and the anti-sacramental Baptist tradition is the fact that for sacramentalists the confirming/assuring/sealing function of baptism concerns the confirmation that saving union with Christ is *here and now* a reality, not that such union with Christ has become a reality at some earlier time through some other means.

Grace and paedobaptism

If God acts in baptism, so that the event is more than a human confession of faith and discipleship, then the human response may be relativized in a way that questions the traditional Baptist refusal to baptize infants. If the most fundamental reality in baptism is God's gracious action of uniting the individual to Christ (as some Baptist sacramentalists emphasize), and if, as Walton said, "It is God who first acts in Christian baptism,"[40] then there may well be a solid case for paedobaptism. If baptism as a means of grace follows the contours of divine grace, then it may be that it should precede the individual's confession of faith. The argument from the priority of grace to the baptism of infants has become perhaps the most popularly cherished argument for paedobaptism in the latter half of this century, and its challenge needs to be considered. Is it perhaps true that a strong sense of divine action in baptism relativizes the human response to such an extent that Baptist sacramentalism becomes incoherent? Does genuine sacramentalism demand paedobaptism?

Much of the contemporary paedobaptist argument from the priority of grace depends on the work of Oscar Cullmann (b. 1902), a professor at both

---

39 White, *BDI*, 293.
40 Walton, *GC*, 31. See also Clark, in *CB*, 316.

the University of Basel and the Sorbonne, who responded to Karl Barth's 1943 lecture on baptism. His thought focused on the "baptism" of Christ accomplished in his vicarious death and resurrection (Mark 10:38-39 and Luke 12:50 record this use of baptismal imagery), an act to which Jesus was committed by his baptism at the hands of John, and which is recalled at every occurrence of Christian baptism. This vicarious baptism of Christ was provided independently of (indeed, in spite of) human response, and thus it is argued that Christian baptism which corresponds to this ought to signify the priority of the grace of baptism. Cullmann wrote:

> Everything that the New Testament implicitly teaches concerning a *gratia praeveniens* (Romans 5:8-10; John 15:16; 1 John 4:10 and 19) applies in heightened measure to Baptism as reception into the Body of Christ. The Grace of Baptism is not only a "picture" of *gratia praeveniens* which God has applied to us at Golgotha. It is more; a once-for-all event entirely dependent on Golgotha, and also a new and special manifestation of the same *gratia praeveniens*. The divine act of salvation advances into the time of the Church.[41]

But how does all this correlate with the New Testament passages which call for faith prior to baptism? Cullmann understood baptism as an act which, among other things, places one into the Church, the "inner circle" of the kingdom of God, and indicates that the one baptized is "commissioned for special duty."[42] That is, what is demanded by baptism is *subsequent* faith, the performance of the duty to which one is committed by baptism. In the case of adults, the sign that such obedience will occur is the faith confessed by the baptizand, but in the case of infants, the requisite sign is the birth of the child in a Christian family.[43] In this way Cullmann sought to apply consistently his understanding of faith as a response to divine grace which has been manifested primarily at the Cross and secondarily in baptism. The faith which ultimately matters is thus the continuing post-baptismal faith, as Paul wrote to the Corinthians on the basis of Israel's example (1 Cor 10:1-13).

Pierre Marcel (1910-1992), a French Reformed theologian, grounded infant baptism primarily in the unity of the covenant of grace, but one aspect

---

41 Oscar Cullmann, *Baptism in the New Testament*, trans. J. K. S. Reid (London: SCM Press, 1950), 33-34.
42 Ibid., 36.
43 Ibid., 50-51.

of this covenant is its sovereign and unilateral character; it is a gracious promise given and an obligation imposed by God alone, not a contract between equals. "God's decision and the offer of the blessings of the covenant precede the faith of the child. . . . It is because he is taken hold of by God that the child is able to believe."[44] He argued that the sequence of God's action followed by human response is operative in both adult and infant baptism. "In both cases faith is the response of man to the initiative of God."[45] In adult baptism the human response is included in the baptismal event, while in infant baptism the individual response is anticipated and demanded by the baptismal event; each points to the prior grace of God, but infant baptism does so in a more striking way.

To the objection that infant baptism fails to respect the freedom of the baptizand and affirm the human side of the covenant, Marcel responded:

> We reply that such a requirement, which at first sight manifests such a concern for the child's heart and his liberty and personal decision, is stamped with the mark of philosophical idealism, of the individualism and subjectivism which we have already so often unmasked; and that it does not sufficiently take into account what the Bible teaches us concerning our personal corruption from birth, nor its manner of regarding children and Christian education.[46]

He contended that, "In the history of the Church every attack against paedobaptism has involved either implicit or explicit alterations of the biblical notion of grace,"[47] alterations which are allegedly rooted in *a priori* individualistic assumptions without biblical foundations.

The British Methodist W. F. Flemington (b. 1901) wrote a significant study of baptism in the New Testament which said nothing about infant baptism in the mostly exegetical body of the work, but devoted a brief excursus at the end to justify the practice on theological grounds, primarily on the basis of the prevenience of grace. Assuming that "the sacraments of the Gospel should exhibit that which is characteristic of the Gospel itself,"[48] and that the essence of the Gospel is that God has acted for us in Christ prior

---

44 Pierre Ch. Marcel, *The Biblical Doctrine of Infant Baptism*, trans. Philip Edgcumbe Hughes (London: James Clarke & Co., 1953), 191, 204.
45 Ibid., 203.
46 Ibid., 204.
47 Ibid., 247.
48 W. F. Flemington, *The New Testament Doctrine of Baptism* (London: S.P.C.K., 1953), 136.

to any faith-response on our part, he wrote:

> Here surely is something which forms part of the meaning of infant baptism no less than of believers' baptism. The validity of the Gospel does not depend on human faith. The Church's practice of infant baptism witnesses to this "objective givenness" of the Gospel. The primary significance of such a baptism is not that we dedicate the child to God, but that God has done something for the child.[49]

If the priority of grace is the primary thing to be emphasized by baptism, then infants are not only suitable subjects for baptism, but *especially* suitable subjects, in that their helplessness is "eloquent of man's universal need for the divine grace."[50]

Although he admitted that it is impossible to ground paedobaptism in a directly exegetical approach to biblical texts on baptism, he argued that there is a proleptic aspect to all baptisms, whether of adults or infants, in that baptism promises more than it immediately effects in all cases. Infant baptism simply says in a more extreme way that Christians must paradoxically "become what they are."[51] He thus concluded that infant baptism embodies all that is essential in baptism, indeed, that it does so in a superior manner:

> Infant baptism, so far from being less evangelical than believers' baptism, is in reality more so, because it even more unmistakably embodies the primary truth of the Christian gospel, namely that the grace of God comes before everything else, and that man's only hope of salvation rests upon that act of God in Jesus Christ, from which (as the chief writers of the New Testament so clearly and so unanimously demonstrate) this sacrament of the gospel draws all its meaning and efficacy.[52]

It has been common for Baptists to criticize paedobaptists for their alleged departure from evangelical truth to ritualism, but by this focus on the priority of grace Flemington and others have turned the argument around.

---

49 Ibid., 137.
50 Ibid., 138-139.
51 Ibid., 143.
52 Ibid., 146-147.

The Lutheran Edmund Schlink (1903-1984) displayed an awareness that Baptists have in many cases begun to recover a sense of baptism as a means of grace, but he argued that, "The more the New Testament witness to God's saving action in Baptism is again perceived, the more difficult it becomes to maintain a rejection of infant Baptism as valid Baptism."[53] For him baptism is not merely a symbol pointing to the priority of grace; it is also a means by which God, through the church, acts graciously toward the baptizands, "helping them attain to the freedom of faith."[54] He argued that a biblical estimate of the human condition and the grace of God leads to the conclusion that, "Just as the resurrection of the dead occurs without the assistance of the dead, so also the new creation of man whose life is forfeit to sin and death is accomplished through Baptism."[55] If the new creation and resurrection motifs concerning salvation are to be pressed in the baptismal context, then it is not difficult to appreciate the inference that infant baptism is an appropriate vehicle of grace.

In summary: many contemporary paedobaptists have argued that Baptist sacramentalism is incapable of giving grace its proper place in baptism, because the pattern of God's grace is one in which grace precedes faith, rather than following it. Even in the case of adult baptism, the promises made by the baptizand are essentially concerned with the faith that will follow baptism, not with a demonstration that there is already a faith of sufficient quality to justify baptism. The conclusion is that if Baptists are going to take seriously the divine action in baptism, then they will have to surrender their opposition to the baptism of infants.

Baptist sacramentalists have not rejected this paedobaptist criticism as if it were totally lacking in substance. There has been a widespread admission that traditional Baptist attitudes need a major adjustment in the direction of a focus on God's grace in baptism, thus giving up the common Baptist focus on human commitment as if it were the only word to be spoken about baptism.[56] However, it is one thing to recover the awareness of God's action in the event, and quite another to infer that the sacramental character of baptism validates its application in the absence of any action from the side of the baptizand.

Neville Clark agreed with Cullmann that there is an inner logic

---

[53] Edmund Schlink, *The Doctrine of Baptism*, trans. Herbert J. A. Bouman (St. Louis: Concordia Publishing House, 1972), 149.
[54] Ibid., 160.
[55] Ibid.
[56] For a direct acknowledgment of valid insights in this particular paedobaptist argument, see White, *BDI*, 280, 292, 295 and Beasley-Murray, *BNT*, 379.

connecting the "baptism" of Christ in his passion and the baptism of individuals, but he came to the opposite conclusion about the application of baptism to infants. Whereas Cullmann interpreted the death of Christ as a "general baptism" offered for all humans prior to their turning toward God, and drew the inference that this finds its echo in the baptism of individuals prior to their own faith, Clark argued on the basis of Chalcedonian Christology that "the baptism unto death of the Lord is constituted by the conjunction of divine action and human response," with the consequence that our baptism demands both God's grace and our ratification of Christ's vicarious human response.[57]

The most fundamental weakness of the paedobaptist argument on this point is the logical leap from the fact of prevenient grace to the conclusion that this is what baptism is intended to signify. In one sense all baptisms signify the prevenience of grace, in that they visibly proclaim the gospel and testify to the death and resurrection of Christ, which occurred long before we were even alive, but to recognize this still leaves us with the question whether baptism is intended to signify a divine work of prevenient grace in the life of the individual baptizand. Granting that such a work of prevenient grace is a reality, it is also true that a personal faith-response to God's offer of grace is crucial in the teaching of the apostles. Although infant baptism might admirably signify the truth of prevenient grace, the restriction of baptism to confessing believers would better signify the necessity of personal faith. The question, then, revolves around the divine intention for the signification of baptism, and this must be answered by an appeal to the apostolic witness.

The New Testament evidence seems to point consistently to baptism as the locus for the actual, personal experience of Messianic salvation, not merely the hope that such salvation may someday be experienced. Thus, as the occasion for faith in the gospel from the human side and grace from the divine side, baptism serves to signify both the priority of grace (in the work of Christ) and the necessity of faith for a personal interest in the benefits of Christ's work. As Paul Jewett (1919-1991), of Fuller Theological Seminary, put it:

> While granting the Paedobaptists' emphasis on the primacy of God's action over that of man's, and while acknowledging the corrective sought for infant baptism in the rite of confirmation, it must be affirmed that for the writers of the New Testament the new age has

---

57 Clark, in *CB*, 313-314.

begun. The Christian knows that his sins are forgiven and that he has received the Spirit; in the New Testament baptism is always linked with this knowledge. Hence apostolic baptism is a sacrament of eschatological realization. He who is baptized is one who has received the good news, acknowledged Christ as Lord, and begun the Christian life. To baptize one as a sign of things hoped for (and only hoped for) is to make it a sacrament of *anticipation*, whereas in the New Testament it is always the sacrament of *fulfillment*.[58]

Among paedobaptists, G. C. Berkouwer was prepared to admit that the argument from prevenient grace to infant baptism is a faulty argument to prove what was for him a valid point. He argued that the Reformers defended infant baptism on the basis of the unity of the covenant of grace, not on the basis of the priority of grace, and at a much more fundamental level, he argued that Scripture does not support the modern argument. Concerning the relevant biblical texts (e.g., Romans 6) he wrote:

> The prevenient aspect of the grace of God lies not in the temporal priority of the acts of God in baptism in comparison with the conscious acceptance of the divine promise, but in the temporal priority of the cross of Christ with respect to the baptized person, whether child or adult. Therein--and certainly not in infant baptism only--we see the predestinational motif which undoubtedly is of great significance in baptism.[59]

As Berkouwer noted, if prevenient grace in the life of the baptizand is at the heart of baptism, then "less value would have to be attached to the baptism of adults, with whom baptism follows upon faith,"[60] which ironically amounts to a devaluation of the only kind of baptism explicitly described in Scripture.

Another major problem with the modern paedobaptist argument from prevenient grace is its implication of indiscriminate baptism. An illustration of this can be found in a dialogue between two German New Testament scholars: Kurt Aland (b. 1915), whose work on infant baptism has been

---

58 Paul K. Jewett, *Infant Baptism and the Covenant of Grace* (Grand Rapids: Eerdmans, 1978), 158.
59 G. C. Berkouwer, *The Sacraments*, trans. Hugo Bekker (Grand Rapids: Eerdmans, 1969), 176.
60 Ibid.

mostly of an historical nature, has argued (against Joachim Jeremias [1900-1979]) that the early church did not baptize infants.[61] In spite of his historical conclusions, he argued in the end that the delayed commitment of the church to infant baptism was in fact a theologically accurate deduction.[62] The spiritual renewal associated with infant baptism is a purely divine work in the infant and thus reminds us of the priority of grace, and from his perspective the demand for conscious faith prior to baptism turns faith into a work which displaces God's promise as the basis of trust.[63] He further argued that the priority of grace and the universality of the gospel demand that we baptize all who do not explicitly reject it, which would certainly include all infants whose parents are willing to allow their baptism.[64] This is admittedly a more indiscriminate approach to baptism than is common among paedobaptists (at least principially), but it is a logical inference. If the death of Christ was in fact a "general baptism" for all humans, and the essence of Christian baptism is to translate this into an offer of grace to those for whom Christ died, then why would we not give visible witness to the gospel by baptizing in a manner as indiscriminate as the death of Christ?

Although many paedobaptists utilize both the "priority of grace" argument and the "seal of the covenant" argument, it appears that these two arguments are in fact contradictory. The former logically leads to baptizing everyone in the world as an offer of the gospel to all for whom Christ died, while the latter leads to the restriction of baptism to those who are called out from the mass of humanity as the holy, covenant people. In terms of infants, the former would imply the baptism of all infants whose parents would allow it, while the second would restrict baptism to the infant children of professed believers. It is possible that one of these arguments might be valid, but not both simultaneously.

It is not true that the restriction of baptism to confessing believers is a functional denial of the priority of divine grace. That would be true only if *every* work of divine grace were prevenient, but such is not the testimony of Scripture. For example, the grace of forgiveness follows confession of sins (1 John 1:9), and the grace of justification follows faith in Christ (Rom 5:1). As important as the reality of prevenient grace may be, the testimony of Scripture is that there are other kinds of grace as well. The objective

---

61 Kurt Aland, *Did the Early Church Baptize Infants?*, trans. G. R. Beasley-Murray (London: SCM Press, 1963). Cf. Joachim Jeremias, *The Origins of Infant Baptism*, trans. David Cairns (Philadelphia: Westminster Press, 1960).
62 Ibid., 113.
63 Ibid., 115.
64 Ibid.

manifestation of grace in the Christ-event and the subjective manifestation of grace in the application of redemption to the individual do not stand in the same relation to the faith of the individual. Faith looks back to the one in order to experience the other. Baptist sacramentalists are neither unbiblical nor incoherent in their assertion that the grace which is active in baptism is the grace of applied redemption, a grace which has effects that cannot realistically be posited of any but confessing believers.

Baptism and the Holy Spirit

Baptist sacramentalists have recognized that there is some kind of normative connection between baptism and the reception of the Holy Spirit, although they have placed varying degrees of emphasis on this linkage and have seen varying degrees of consistency in the New Testament witness. The connection could hardly be denied, for if baptism unites the individual to Christ and thus to the benefits of Christ's redemptive work, and if the gift of the Holy Spirit is central to the benefits of the Messianic salvation (as envisioned by the Hebrew prophets and John the Baptist), then any act which accomplishes union with Christ must be presumed to mediate the presence of the Spirit. As noted in Chapter 2, this connection between baptism in water and baptism in the Spirit was central to the concerns of Robinson in his pioneering efforts to rejuvenate a dynamic, Baptist sacramentalism; for White the bestowal of the Spirit via baptism was implied in the paradigmatic experience of Jesus in his baptism; and for Beasley-Murray one of the ways in which the sacramental significance of baptism could be expressed was, "The Spirit is there." Some Baptists have argued for the laying on of hands as an integral part of the baptismal rite, in order to signify this aspect of initiation into Christ,[65] but it should be noted that the incorporation of this act into the baptismal event and the affirmation that the Spirit is given in baptism are logically distinct.

Some Baptists have seen great significance in the bestowal of the Spirit at the baptism of Jesus,[66] but others have emphasized the discontinuity between Jesus and those who believe in him.[67] Varying degrees of significance have been attached to the conjunction between water and the

---

65 For a brief survey of Baptist attitudes toward the laying on of hands, see Ernest A. Payne, "Baptism and Christian Initiation," *Baptist Quarterly* 26, no. 4 (October 1975): 150-153.
66 White, *BDI*, 98.
67 Beasley-Murray, *BNT*, 63-64.

Spirit in John 3:5--the saying is too cryptic to serve as any kind of regulative text. The major support for the conjunction of baptism and the bestowal of the Spirit has been found in the theology of Paul. On the assumption that 1 Corinthians 12:13 refers to baptism in water, this text indicates that baptism is an event in which the individual is brought within the sphere of the Holy Spirit. Similarly, on the assumption that the λουτρόν of Titus 3:5 denotes baptism, the sacrament is interpreted as an event that is instrumental in the regenerating/renewing work of the Spirit. The classic text in Romans 6 views baptism as the event in which the baptizand is united to Christ, and thus as the point at which the saving work of Christ becomes effective in the individual and inaugurates in a proleptic way the life of the resurrection. This present experience of "resurrection" implies a deliverance from destructive slavery to sin through a constructive slavery to God and righteousness. As the argument unfolds it becomes clear that the dynamic of this transformed present existence is the empowering presence of the Holy Spirit (Rom 7:6), and this is the experience of all who belong to Christ--to belong to Christ is to have the Spirit of Christ (8:9). Therefore, it is baptism in the Spirit, an act of the risen Christ, which makes the redemptive work of Christ transformative in the individual, and this encounter with Christ and the Spirit is assumed to occur in baptism.

Relating this systematic perspective to the narratives of Acts is admittedly problematic, but this is true for every systematic perspective, given the obvious diversity of the narratives. However, the diversity is not inexplicable, given the special character of the narrated receptions of the Spirit, and the narratives are compatible with the view that baptism is the *normal* context for the gift of the Spirit. At the "Gentile Pentecost" in Acts 10, the Spirit is poured out prior to baptism, but the account records Peter's insistence on immediate baptism, based on his assumption that the Spirit and the water belong together. In the Acts 19 account of the enigmatic "disciples" at Ephesus, the point at which the Spirit is given is in fact their Christian baptism at the hands of Paul. The only context in which there appears to be a genuine disjunction between Christian conversion-baptism and the gift of the Spirit is in the Acts 8 account of the Samaritan mission, and even there the "not yet" (8:16) language of the narrative seems to imply that the disjunction is exceptional rather than paradigmatic.[68] Luke's

---

68 Bruner, *A Theology of the Holy Spirit*, 177-178. For the view that Luke represents the Samaritans as lacking genuine, saving faith prior to the descent of the Spirit, see Dunn, *Baptism in the Holy Spirit*, 63-68. Either approach concludes that Acts 8 is exceptional in some way.

account of apostolic *teaching* about baptism is to be found in a text like Acts 2:38, which views baptism as instrumental in both forgiveness and the bestowal of the Spirit. Narratives of what occurred on specific occasions are *descriptive* of the freedom of the grace of God, who is not bound to his appointed means, but Acts 2:38 is *prescriptive* of the assumed effects of conversion-baptism. The narratives of Acts indicate that we are mistaken if we think that there is some sort of automatic cause-effect relation between baptism and the Spirit, but taken as a whole the book is compatible with Pauline theology. Both affirm that entrance into the life of the kingdom of God includes repentance, faith and baptism from the human side, and forgiveness of sins and the gift of the Spirit from the divine side, and that baptism is the normal point at which the action of each side is focused.

Sacramentalists with a high doctrine of Confirmation often deny the normativity of this connection between baptism and the gift of the Spirit, arguing instead that the crucial factor in the gift of the Spirit is the ministry of apostles or their successors.[69] Much of the support for this perspective comes from patristic teaching, but it is argued that this patristic thought is grounded in the patterns of the Acts of the Apostles, specifically the significance attributed to the laying on of apostolic hands. It is recorded in Acts 8 that the Spirit came upon the Samaritans when Peter and John prayed for them with the laying on of their hands, and likewise in Acts 19 the Spirit was bestowed upon the twelve men at Ephesus when Paul laid hands on them.

The ongoing relevance of such apostolic ministry would depend on some sort of doctrine of apostolic succession, which is a large question outside the parameters of this study. But even if such succession were granted, Baptists (and others) have rightly argued that the Acts of the Apostles will not bear the weight of this doctrine of apostolic hands. For example, in the Acts 19 episode, the laying on of Paul's hands occurs in the context of the Christian baptism of the twelve men, and the account of Paul's dialogue with the men indicates that the fundamental reason for their lack of the Spirit has everything to do with the nature of their baptism and nothing to do with the laying on of hands. Acts 8 does indeed indicate that it was the ministry of the apostles Peter and John that brought about the gift of the Spirit, but to infer a doctrine of apostolic/episcopal confirmation from

---

69   For example, see Arthur James Mason, *The Relation of Confirmation to Baptism: As Taught in Holy Scripture and The Fathers* (London: Longmans, Green & Co., 1891) and Dom Gregory Dix, *The Theology of Confirmation in Relation to Baptism* (London: Dacre Press, 1946). For a critique of this approach by a fellow Anglican, see G. W. H. Lampe, *The Seal of the Spirit* (London: Longmans, Green & Co., 1951).

this one text is an unwarranted extrapolation. Acts 9 points to the bestowal of the Holy Spirit in the conversion of Saul through the hands of Ananias, who is not an apostle, and Acts 10 shows the pouring out of the Spirit prior to Peter's imposition of hands and indeed prior to the baptism of Cornelius and his household. When all this evidence is considered, it seems that Acts 8 is included in the Lukan account precisely because it is exceptional, not because it is normative.

None of this is to deny that many Christians have in fact experienced a filling/empowering of the Holy Spirit in connection with their confirmation, episcopal or otherwise. But this is easily explained on the basis of Baptist assumptions, inasmuch as confirmation embodies a personal confession of commitment to Jesus Christ, and it is that kind of μετάνοια to which the gift of the Spirit is promised (Acts 2:38). On Baptist assumptions the normative context for that confession is baptism, but the crucial factor is the confession and not the context. The narratives of Acts demonstrate that God exercises his freedom in the granting of the Spirit, and the present gift of the Spirit outside the baptismal context would be a continuing display of that freedom.

Non-sacramentalist evangelicals (as well as some who interpret baptism as a sacramental means of grace in *some* sense) challenge this link between the Spirit and baptism by affirming as normative an experienced indwelling of the Spirit connected to conversion prior to baptism.[70] This is understandable within the Baptist context, in which faith is considered to be a condition of baptism and the Spirit is considered to be given to all who believe in Christ. However, it is simply another variation on the theme of conversion apart from baptism, and it is subject to all the criticisms expressed above in the discussion about faith and baptism. To posit the bestowal of the Spirit prior to baptism may be true to the experience of many Baptists, but the view that this is normative is rooted in a conscious distinction between conversion and baptism and the consequent provision of some other vehicle to confirm conversion (perhaps a verbal confession, even a ritualized one). There is no need to deny the reality of such experience, but what can be denied is that this is the theologically normative construction of the matter.

---

70 H. Clarkson, "The Holy Spirit and the Sacraments," *Baptist Quarterly* 14 (1951-1952): 269; D. S. Russell, "Ministry and Sacraments," *Baptist Quarterly* 17 (1957-1958): 72. Russell is an example of those who affirm a sacramental view of baptism but deny that it normatively mediates the personal experience of the initial gift of the Spirit. He argued that baptism is an experience in which "The Spirit, who was given to us at our conversion, deepens still further our experience of God's grace."

The truth in the non-sacramentalist perspective is the affirmation that the gift of the Spirit is God's answer to faith in Christ, but the error lies in the disjunction between faith and baptism. The biblical norm is not simply that there is some fresh experience of the Spirit in baptism, but rather that this is in fact the initiation into the life of the Spirit, inasmuch as it is initiation into Christ. But God's bestowal of the Spirit is not limited by human misperception of sacramental purposes, and the witness to the gift of the Spirit apart from and prior to baptism is simply a witness to the freedom and richness of the grace of God, whose normal instruments of grace are not the only venues in which he is prepared to meet penitent sinners.

Baptism and the Church

In Pauline terms, to be baptized into Christ is to be baptized into the Body of Christ, the Church as a universal entity (1 Cor 12:12-13). However, the equation of "in Christ" and "in the Church" does not specify the *logical* order between the two concepts: are we in the Church because we are in Christ, or are we in Christ because we have been introduced into the Church which is the Body of Christ? As noted in Chapter Two, Baptist sacramentalists have opted for each of these logical orders. Both Walton and Clark interpreted "in Christ" as primarily an ecclesiological formula, and they argued that incorporation into the Church is the means by which union with Christ is achieved.[71] Beasley-Murray, on the other hand, took issue with this logical order and emphatically argued that it is union with Christ which effects entrance into the Church.[72] The view of Walton and Clark appears to be driven by a desire to avoid an excessive individualism for which Baptists have often been criticized, the kind of perspective which views individual discipleship as the heart of salvation in a way that makes the Church necessary only insofar as it supports individual concerns. The view of Beasley-Murray seems to be shaped by his concern for the headship of Christ relative to the Body and his desire to avoid an undue exaltation of the Church as an instrument of salvation.

It is not clear that either of these valid concerns about a false theological emphasis actually settles this question. As long as it is assumed that all who are in Christ are also in the Church, and that vital participation in the life of the Church is an essential part of Christian discipleship, it is theologically

---

71 Walton, *GC*, 30-31, 161; Clark, *ATS*, 33-34.
72 Beasley-Murray, *BNT*, 281-282.

illegitimate to relativize the Church to support an excessive individualism. There is a genuine, biblically-grounded, individualism which Baptist theology has always sought to articulate, which asserts that entrance into the Church presupposes a voluntary commitment of the individual to Christ. On the other hand, as long as it is assumed that the Church is merely an instrument utilized by God, and that the salvific work of God is not bound to or controlled by the Church, there is no basis for exalting the Body above the Head. Positing the Church as an instrument which God uses to effect union with Christ does not necessarily diminish the glory of Christ any more than does the concept of baptism as an instrument of union with Christ.

Although it may be impossible to settle this debate with finality, it would appear that the general tenor of both Scripture and Baptist theology would point toward the logical priority of union with Christ. For example, Paul's flow of thought in Galatians 3 seems to assume that it is union with Christ (the individual "seed of Abraham") by faith-baptism which effects union with the people of God (the corporate "seed of Abraham"). Within the parameters of Baptist ecclesiology (or in a broader sense what is sometimes called "believers' church" ecclesiology), which assumes that individual confession of commitment to Christ is a condition of church membership, visible union with Christ is logically prior to visible union with the Body of Christ.

Although the debate about the logical order of Christ and the Church may be interesting and may carry certain implications, insofar as the debate is carried on within the Baptist context, it is *only* about logical order, and not about temporal order. The debaters on both sides agree that all those who are in Christ are in the Church (universal), and vice versa, and both agree that in biblical terms baptism is the context in which the individual is joined to both Christ and the community of Christ.

The more perplexing question for Baptist sacramentalists is that of the relation between baptism and membership in the church (local), and this question is the most difficult test for the coherence of the system. This question has always been a point of contention among Baptists in general, even among those who hold a lower view of the efficacy of baptism. There are essentially three views among Baptists as to the precise relation between baptism and church membership: *First*, some have argued that individuals become members of the local church by the act of baptism, so that there is no distinction between those who are being baptized and those who are being received as formal members of the church. This view was dominant among the early General Baptists, for whom initiation into the church was perhaps the primary meaning of baptism;[73] it has also been widely held by Particular Baptists;[74] and it lies at the heart of Landmarkism, a radical view formulated in the southern United States in the 19th century affirming that the only true church is a local Baptist church, and the only valid baptism is one administered by such a church.[75] *Second*, some have argued that baptism is prerequisite to, but not constitutive of, church membership.[76] This approach emphasizes the connection between conversion and baptism and may allow for baptism on the basis of approval by the administrator, while church membership requires approval by the church meeting as a whole. *Third*, some have argued that although all believers ought to be baptized, church membership is for all who credibly profess conversion, and baptism may precede or follow church membership.[77] At the heart of this option is the assumption that membership in the church is for all who give evidence of being in the Church, and that such evidence is located in visible discipleship, i.e., a lifestyle which is oriented toward obedience to Christ according to one's understanding of his commands.

Generally Baptist sacramentalists have affirmed at a theoretical level the first option, i.e., that initiation into the church ought to coincide with initiation into the Church, both being mediated through the same act of believer baptism. Several of the major participants in this movement have argued that baptism, official reception into membership, and first communion ought to be integrated not only theoretically but practically into one service of worship.[78] However, this Baptist sacramentalism has for the most part arisen among English Baptists who affirmed the practice of "open membership," accepting as church members both those baptized as believers and those who profess faith after being baptized as infants, and in some cases admitting persons into membership on the basis of verbal confession

---

73 See The Standard Confession, Article XIV in Lumpkin, *Confessions*, 229, where baptism is described as the "order of constituting Churches." See also Michael Walker, "Baptism: Doctrine and Practice among Baptists in the United Kingdom," *Foundations* 22, no. 1 (January-March, 1979): 73-74.

74 For example, Garner, *Baptism*, 14.

75 James Robinson Graves, *The Act of Christian Baptism* (Texarkana: Baptist Sunday School Committee, 1881), 6.

76 Gill, *Body of Divinity*, 896.

77 This approach is defended at length in John Bunyan, "A Reason of My Practice in Worship," and "Differences About Water Baptism, No Bar to Communion," in *The Whole Works of John Bunyan*, ed. George Offor (Glasgow: Blackie and Son, 1863), 4:602-647.

78 Beasley-Murray, *BNT*, 394-395; Gilmore, *BCU*, 58-74; Clark, in *CB*, 324; Payne, "Baptists and Christian Initiation," 154-156.

of faith apart from any baptism. For some this practice of open membership is simply an act of Christian charity toward those who are clearly disciples of Christ but are not convinced of the invalidity of their infant baptism,[79] while for others the refusal to rebaptize those who were baptized in infancy is a matter of theological principle.[80]

The question is, therefore, whether a Baptist-sacramental view of baptism can be reconciled with the practice of open membership. In this theological context baptism is understood to be the divinely-ordained way to say "Yes" to the gospel; baptism is conceptualized as the normal means of entrance into saving union with Jesus Christ; the view that baptism is merely symbolic and declaratory is rejected; and infant baptism is considered to be incapable of bearing the weight of a New Testament theology of baptism, and therefore ought not be practised. All of this is equivalent to saying that the idea of conversion and discipleship apart from believer baptism is highly anomalous, and it thus comes as no surprise that the vast majority of Baptists have been committed to closed membership restricted to those baptized as believers. For many Baptists this closed membership is rooted only in concepts of church order and baptism as mere obedience, but for Baptists committed to a sacramental view of baptism the significance of the rite is elevated into the soteriological realm. Is it logically possible to accept this heightened significance of believer baptism but declare such baptism optional for church membership?

There are only two ways to justify open membership in the Baptist context: (1) to admit persons to membership on the basis of confession of faith, even though they have not been validly baptized; or (2) to accept infant baptism as valid, although irregular. These approaches will now be examined in turn.

The *first* approach, which has roots as far back as John Bunyan (1628-1688) in the 17th century, draws a sharp distinction between conversion and baptism, arguing that verbal confession of repentance and faith which is corroborated by lifestyle is all that is required to be considered as a Christian and therefore all that is required for church membership. Some would see a closer connection between conversion and baptism, but they would argue that although baptism is the normal means of formally expressing faith and

---

79 Beasley-Murray, *BNT*, 392-393. More recently Beasley-Murray has signified an openness to affirming the validity of at least some forms of infant baptism; see his article, "The Problem of Infant Baptism: an Exercise in Possibilities," in *Festschrift Gunter Wagner*, ed. Faculty of Baptist Theological Seminary, Rüschlikon/Switzerland (Bern: Peter lang, 1994), 1-14.
80 Walton, *GC*, 166; Clark, in *CB*, 325; Gilmore, *BCU*, 76-78.

An Analysis of the Theological Formulation

entering into Christian discipleship, due to the confusion which has arisen in the Church about baptism, many persons have entered Christian experience in what the New Testament would judge to be an abnormal way. Nevertheless, they give evidence of the possession of the Holy Spirit, and their Christian status cannot be denied. Christian charity, therefore, would accept those whom Christ has accepted, recognizing that the solution to this anomaly is baptismal reform, not closed membership which functionally denies the unity of all believers in Christ. This latter approach was affirmed by H. W. Robinson at the beginning of the movement under consideration and by Beasley-Murray at the culmination of it in the 1960's.

Although this approach may be meaningful within a non-sacramental Baptist theology, it is hard to see it as anything other than a functional denial of a sacramental view of baptism. Granted that such "rebaptisms" which may be severely disconnected from conversion are not true to the full New Testament picture, it would seem to be less anomalous to repair an invalid attempt at Christian baptism than to admit to full membership in the church apart from valid baptism. In no case can one infallibly identify the precise temporal relation between the attitude of faith and the act of confessional baptism, because no one is capable of knowing the mind of another--but in any case baptism serves to seal and focus the meeting of faith and grace. Accordingly, however short or long the time between the first awareness of faith and its sacramental expression in baptism, the ritual act can still serve its purpose of translating faith into act. Baptist sacramentalists from Robinson to Beasley-Murray have lamented the large number of persons who grow up in Baptist families and churches and request church membership apart from baptism, but as long as others are admitted to membership without a valid baptism, it is hard to avoid the extension of the principle to these persons.

The *second* approach assumes that valid baptism is a condition of church membership, but argues that a *de facto* infant baptism should be accepted as valid in spite of its irregularity. Accordingly, those who were baptized as infants and have subsequently confessed faith in Christ and been accepted as members of some church are accepted into Baptist church membership on that basis. Baptism and faith are seen as the essential conditions of church membership, and as long as both are present the conditions are considered to be met, even though they may have occurred in an irregular order. There are two standard principles employed to defend the validity of such infant baptisms: (1) the once-for-all character of Christian baptism; and (2) the validity of paedobaptist churches.

The "once-for-all" argument. The work of Christ is ἐφάπαξ, a once-for-all redemptive event, never to be repeated. Furthermore, the Pauline understanding of baptism, stated most fully in Romans 6, indicates that baptism decisively unites the individual to that redemptive activity of the death and resurrection of Christ, so that what happened in the Christ-event happens in an analogous and derivative way in individual experience through baptism into Christ. Therefore, what happens in baptism is of the same nature as the work of Christ. Since Christ died once for all (ἐφάπαξ-- Rom 6:10), never to die again (6:9), it is also the case that we are united with Christ by baptism once only.

Baptist theologians in general have agreed with the principle that baptism ought not be repeated in the life of any individual, even though in some circles pastoral practice has allowed for multiple experiences of believer baptism due to doubts about the genuineness of faith expressed in an earlier baptism.[81] But the meaning of the principle that baptism is ἐφάπαξ depends on the definition of baptism, and traditionally most Baptists have argued that personal confession by the baptizand is essential to baptism, so that the baptism as a believer of one "baptized" in infancy is not a rebaptism at all. Therefore, from their beginning in the first decade of the 17th century in England, Baptists have normally rejected the label "Anabaptists."

Contrary to this tradition, some Baptist sacramentalists have argued that although baptism ought not be applied to infants, when in fact it has been done, this is a real baptism, however tenuous its connection to biblical baptism. But what factors might constitute the validity of such (irregular) baptisms? (1) Is it simply the fact that it is called "baptism" and is intended to fulfill the demands of Christian baptism? If so, would absolutely anything that is called "baptism" qualify? What if the rite were performed without water or anything like water, say, by means of a dipping or sprinkling motion without substance? What if it were done with no reference to the Godhead? Few theologians would be prepared to accept the mere label as a basis for validity. (2) Is it the fact that such baptism incorporates the infant into the Christian community for spiritual nurture? If so, would not the same thing be true of a service of infant blessing and dedication in a baptistic context? (3) Is it the fact that it declares the gospel and signifies the work of Christ? That may well be true, but to say that this is the heart of Christian baptism is to reduce baptism to a purely declaratory or kerygmatic function, which is the very thing that Baptist sacramentalists

---

81 Timothy George, "The Southern Baptists," in *Baptism & Church: A Believers' Church Vision*, ed. Merle D. Strege (Grand Rapids: Sagamore Books, 1986), 48.

have been seeking to refute within their own ecclesiastical context. The ἐφάπαξ argument in Romans 6 assumes that baptism is the point at which the work of Christ becomes effective in the individual, not that baptism merely proclaims what may happen in the individual. Therefore, to apply the argument of Romans 6 to an event which is merely declaratory and hopeful is to confuse categories.

The burden of Baptist sacramentalism has been to assert that baptism is an event in which God truly acts and effects spiritual change in the baptizand, and that this is so because it is the event in which there is a genuine and conscious divine-human encounter, a meeting of grace and faith. To ridicule fellow Baptists for their "attenuated parable-rite in which nothing is even expected to happen"[82] while defending infant baptism as valid baptism is at least problematic if not contradictory.

The valid church argument. For some Baptists, to deny the validity of infant baptism is to "unchurch" paedobaptists, and it is assumed that this cannot be done. These Baptist sacramentalists share with (non-sacramentalist) Landmark Baptists the view that the validity of a church and the validity of the baptism practised by that church stand or fall together. In the Landmark tradition, what is assumed to be clearly true is that the baptism practised by paedobaptist churches is not valid baptism, and consequently such "churches" are such in name only--they may be "societies" of sincere but misguided Christians, but they are not valid churches.[83] For the Baptist sacramentalists, on the other hand, the argument assumes that paedobaptist churches are true churches, and infers from this that the baptism practised by such churches must be valid baptism.[84]

Now this assumption that a church is a valid church if and only if its baptismal practice is valid is by no means shared by the whole Baptist tradition. Both of these perspectives differ from a major stream of Baptist thought, which affirms that valid churches exist in spite of serious irregularities, even in the practice of baptism. This other stream of Baptist thought may be seen in the influential Second London Confession (1677 and 1689), in which the lengthy Chapter XXVI ("Of the Church") makes no reference to the practice of baptism at all. Churches are defined as communities of "visible saints," that is, persons who make a credible profession of faith in the gospel and obedience to Christ. It is admitted that,

---

82 White, *BDI*, 305.
83 Graves, *Act of Baptism*, 54-56. See also Robert George Torbet, "Landmarkism," in *Baptist Concepts of the Church*, ed. Winthrop Still Hudson (Chicago: Judson Press, 1959), 170-195.
84 Walton, *GC*, 166; Clark, in *CB*, 326; Gilmore, *BCU*, 81.

"The purest Churches under heaven are subject to mixture, and error." It is true that the church members are said to covenant with one another "in professed subjection to the Ordinances of the Gospel," and baptism would be comprehended under the label of "Ordinances," but no specific pattern of baptismal practice is indicated at that point. The statement of the distinctively Baptist doctrine of baptism is reserved for Chapters XXVIII and XXIX.[85] The logic of the confession, then, is this: a visible Church is defined as a community of visible saints, an organized congregation made up of individuals who evidently belong to Christ by faith; following this definition of a Church, there is a statement of the way in which baptism *ought* to function in this Church. But there is no assertion that errors in baptismal practice render invalid the claim to be a Church--indeed that could hardly be the mindset of the authors of the confession, because the confession is a virtual replica of the Westminster Confession. In the preface to the Second London Confession (1677), the authors state that by using the very words of the Westminster Confession (1646) and its Congregational modification, the Savoy Confession (1658), as far as possible, they intend to "manifest our consent with both, in all the fundamental articles of the Christian religion."[86] The Baptist confession quite clearly asserts that the only valid baptism is believer baptism by immersion, but this assertion is not used as a litmus test to determine the validity of a church.

It is true, of course, that some other Baptist confessions do define a church as a community of *baptized* believers. Such is true of the First London Confession, Chapter XXXIII (Particular Baptist-1644),[87] the Standard Confession, Chapter XI (General Baptist-1660),[88] and the Orthodox Creed, Chapter XXX (General Baptist, 1678).[89] In some cases, notably the Standard Confession which denies Christian fellowship with paedobaptists ("the unfruitful works of darkness"),[90] this is clearly an intentional assertion that paedobaptist churches are not valid churches, but it is not clear that the same is true in other cases. It may well be that definitions of the church which include baptism are simply statements of the biblical pattern as the authors understand it, and inferences concerning the extent to which the pattern must be followed in order to qualify as a valid church must be done with care. Whatever may be the intent of the First

---

85 Lumpkin, *Confessions*, 285-291.
86 Ibid., 245.
87 Ibid., 165.
88 Ibid., 228.
89 Ibid., 319.
90 Ibid., 228-229.

London Confession in this regard, the developing thought of the Particular Baptists moved in the direction of affirming their close ties with Presbyterian and Congregational churches even as they denied the validity of their sprinkling of infants.

The foundational assumption of Baptist sacramentalists in this argument is that paedobaptist churches are valid churches, but on what basis can this assumption be made? It cannot be assumed on the basis of a valid baptism which constitutes the church, because that is the very point in question. The assumption must be based on some demonstrable Christian commitment, some visible evidence of spiritual life, what Paul would call the "fruit of the Spirit." But the same thing can be said for other churches that do not practise baptism at all (the Friends and the Salvation Army) and for individuals in various churches (including many Baptist churches) who have never been baptized in any form. The logical inference from these facts is that while baptism is the biblically normative means of joining the Church and its local manifestation, it is not the invariable means or the *sine qua non* of a valid church. The irreducible constitutive factor is the presence of the Holy Spirit, the giver of new life, the one who joins the members of the Body to the Head, the one whose presence makes the community of believers the temple of God. Accordingly, a congregation of disciples of Christ, indwelt by the Spirit and committed to the manifestation of the kingdom of God may be considered a valid church, even though that congregation's practice may be highly irregular in certain ways.

In the end, then, a Baptist church which is committed to the theology and practice of believer baptism may demand the "rebaptism" of those not baptized as believers, on the basis of its sealing the conversion which is already apparent in other ways. This in no way denies the work of the Spirit which has occurred apart from baptism, nor does it deny the validity of the church in which infant baptism occurred. Liturgically, such "rebaptism" could be constructed in such a way that it formally affirms what was started in an irregular manner and repairs a discipleship which lacks its appropriate sacramental expression.[91]

The failure to connect theory to practice on this point is the major deficiency of modern Baptist sacramentalism. If (as this theology asserts) the only theologically justifiable practice of baptism is that of a confessing believer, and believer baptism has the kind of sacramental character affirmed in this theology, then it seems that to counsel willful neglect of this

---

91 This concept of baptismal "repair" is elucidated by James McClendon in his *Systematic Theology*, Vol. 2, *Doctrine* (Nashville: Abingdon Press, 1994), 395-397.

sacrament is to contradict the theology that is affirmed and to withhold from many Christians the conscious experience associated with believer baptism. On the basis of Christian charity, the effect of open membership may be to attenuate the Christian experience of many disciples of Christ.

The Baptist debate about open versus closed membership is multi-faceted and complex. Baptismal theology is only one of several ecclesiological issues which must be elucidated and prioritized in the process of this debate. Perhaps it is possible to construct an argument for open membership which is based on giving a higher priority to the biblical principle of the visible unity of Christians than to the biblical principle of baptism as the normative means of union with Christ and the Church. Such an approach, if it seeks to preserve the sincerity and integrity of church membership, would call into question any church confession of faith which exceeds minimal content, but perhaps such could be defended (especially by Baptists, who have always displayed some ambivalence about creeds and confessions). However, even if some such approach may be possible, what seems impossible is to claim that open membership logically follows from a Baptist-sacramental understanding of baptism. It may be defensible *in spite of* such a baptismal theology, but the British practice of open membership appears to be grounded in the complexities of the British ecclesiastical context and in other ecclesiological principles, not in a logical inference from Baptist sacramentalism.

The Necessity of Baptism

One of the common criticisms of Baptist sacramentalism from within the Baptist tradition has been that it makes baptism necessary for personal salvation, which elevates baptism to an unbiblical and unbaptistic level of significance and disqualifies the unbaptized from salvation. As noted in Chapter Two, this criticism was especially directed toward *Christian Baptism* when it was published in 1959. It is surprising that the authors of that volume did not anticipate the force of this criticism and attempt to deal with it preemptively, but in any case satisfactory answers have been given after the fact.

The most basic point is to note that Baptist sacramentalists have been trying to interpret the doctrine of baptism which underlies the New Testament writings, without any illusions that present reality always matches biblical theory or that we can readily duplicate the experience of the apostolic age in all its details. It might be said that this Baptist reformulation was an exposition of "ideal baptism," not in an idealistic

An Analysis of the Theological Formulation

manner assuming that the paradigm can easily be translated into the present, but in the hope that the biblical paradigm will function as a norm to be approximated to the greatest possible degree.[92]

Baptist sacramentalists have also emphasized that baptism is conversion-baptism, so that to ask whether baptism is necessary for salvation is at one level to ask whether conversion is necessary for salvation. Baptists in general would argue that the latter is a meaningless question in biblical terms. However, Baptist experience has in various ways disconnected baptism from conversion, leading to the assumption that a completed and assured conversion must occur prior to baptism, and this has created a pre-understanding which makes a sacramental view of baptism sound like an attempt to multiply the conditions of salvation. When baptism is conceptually reconnected to conversion as the way in which a penitent sinner says "Yes" to the gospel, the question of necessity ceases to be so problematic.

Baptist sacramentalists have clearly affirmed the salvation of paedobaptist believers, and indeed of all believers, even those not baptized in any form. This has been demonstrated in their affirmation of open membership as well as their ecumenical involvement in the Faith and Order Commission, the British Council of Churches, the Joint Liturgical Group, etc. When pressed to explain the status of the Friends or The Salvation Army, they have affirmed the presence of the Spirit in those contexts, although they have lamented the impoverished nature of churches without sacraments.[93]

At the heart of this particular issue is the distinction between *normal* and *necessary* means of conveying the benefits of redemption. To say that baptism is the normal means of bringing individuals into a redemptive encounter with Christ is to say that it is relatively necessary in two ways: (1) It is a *preceptive* necessity in that it is the dominically-appointed way to express the response of faith in relation to the kerygma.[94] In any case in which the individual understands the gospel and perceives that baptism is the appropriate way to affirm the gospel, the refusal to be baptized would take on great significance, not because of the mere absence of baptism, but because of the rejection of what is embodied in baptism. (2) It is what might be termed a *holistic* necessity, in that we exist as embodied persons

---

92 Beasley-Murray, *Baptist Times*, 10 December 1959, 8.
93 Beasley-Murray, *Baptist Times*, 11 February 1960, 10.
94 Beasley-Murray, *BNT*, 304. Earlier examples may be found in Keach, *Gold Refin'd*, 173; and Hall, *Works*, 1:310-311.

and therefore respond as more than minds or "souls."[95] It would be an overstatement to assert with Alan Richardson that salvation apart from baptism is, due to its disjunction between body and spirit, "sheer Christian Science"[96] when judged by biblical standards, but it would be closer to the truth to say that a non-sacramental norm of conversion would be grounded in an unbiblical dualism. Just as we need actions and symbols to convey truth adequately, so also we need them to facilitate human response to Christ who confronts us in the gospel. If it is true that "the body without the spirit is dead," it may also be said that "the spirit without the body" is at best an anomaly.

Baptist sacramentalists would contend that to ask whether baptism is necessary is to ask the wrong question. If the question is pursued to the end and the answer is that baptism is not absolutely necessary, then what is gained by the discovery? To assert that spiritual benefit can be obtained apart from baptism is not to say that there is no spiritual benefit in baptism. Baptist sacramentalists would not assert that God is gracious to sinners only in baptism, but rather that one may expect him to be gracious in baptism. Their theology represents a positive statement of what may be normatively expected in baptism, not a negative statement of what may not be obtained in any other way. If this is not comprehended, then the whole discussion of baptismal necessity will be misdirected and fruitless.

Baptists and Other Sacramental Traditions

Although Baptist sacramentalists have interacted with the broader world of Christian scholarship in their reformulation of baptismal theology, they have not explicitly identified their views with any other traditions. There are several reasons for this lack of explicit connection to the historic baptismal doctrine of other denominations: (1) Most of this Baptist reformulation has been focused on New Testament exegesis and biblical theology, rather than systematic theology. Although the larger systematic questions have been addressed in some ways in ecumenical discussion, notably in the work leading up to the *Baptism, Eucharist and Ministry* document (1982), the scholarly literature which was contemporary with the Baptist reformulation generally focused on biblical theology and was marked by a lack of denominational content. Thus Beasley-Murray was able to say in the

---

95 White, *BDI*, 263; Beasley-Murray, *BNT*, 138, 305; Gilmore, *BCU*, 43-47; Clark, "Under Fire," 17.
96 Richardson, *Theology of the New Testament*, 348.

preface to his *magnum opus* that the bulk of it could have been written by a scholar of any denomination.[97] (2) Most of the other traditions are paedobaptist, thus ruling out any strict equivalence between those systems and the developing Baptist thought. (3) The other traditions have been in flux as well, making it difficult to identify the precise character of the baptismal theology of whole denominations. Nevertheless, it is appropriate to compare Baptist sacramentalism with the interpretation of the baptism of confessing believers in other streams of sacramentalism, in order to describe more precisely the systematic structure of the Baptist thought. Although the practice of the historic churches has been predominantly the baptism of infants, the stated paradigms have often been constructed in terms of believer baptism, thus facilitating comparison with Baptists at the theological level.[98]

The Roman Catholic Tradition

Although there are superficial similarities to traditional Catholic categories of baptismal theology, even to the point of viewing baptism as the context in which regeneration occurs, there are major differences between the traditions.

First, there are different understandings of the nature of the grace conveyed in baptism. Although modern Catholic scholars have clarified older language which seemed to reify grace and have conceptualized grace as fundamentally gracious *action* by God, and have thus agreed with Baptist conceptions, there remains the question as to the precise nature of this gracious action in baptism. Both traditions affirm that this grace includes the gift of the Holy Spirit to empower moral transformation (i.e., sanctification), but most Baptists also affirm that this grace includes a radical declaration of forgiveness (i.e., justification) along traditional Protestant lines. This traditional difference has never been finally resolved,

---

97   Beasley-Murray, *BNT*, vi.
98   In the years since the period of reformulation being examined in this book, various groups of Baptists have engaged in formal dialogue about baptism with other traditions, and in some cases entire issues of Baptist journals have been devoted to the topic. Baptist-Roman Catholic dialogues are displayed in *Foundations* 12, no. 3 (July-September 1969) and *Southwestern Journal of Theology* 28, no. 2 (Spring 1986). Baptist-Lutheran dialogue can be found in *American Baptist Quarterly* 1, no. 2 (December 1982). Unfortunately, these dialogues postdate the British reformulation era being considered here, and most of the Baptists involved are not strongly sacramental in orientation.

although some Roman Catholic theologians have made major concessions in a Protestant direction,[99] and some Baptists have suggested that the Protestant distinction between justification and sanctification requires major revision if not rejection.[100]

Second, and perhaps most important, there are different views of the nature of the faith expressed in baptism. In the Baptist system the faith in view is active and fiducial, it is consciously directed toward Christ and his work in death and resurrection, and this fiducial faith is the heart of the baptismal event from the human side. However, Catholic theologians make it clear that the faith expressed in baptism may be merely predispositive and not yet fiducial.[101] It appears that this predispositive faith may be directed simply toward the assumed power which will be at work in the baptismal event, and the heart of the event is doing the right action with the right intentions.[102] One contemporary Roman Catholic theologian has argued that both White and Beasley-Murray have responded to outdated notions of the meaning of *ex opere operato*,[103] but although modern Catholics may have clarified the concept in a way that avoids crassly mechanistic notions, there is still a significant distinction between faith in divine action pledged to accompany baptism (Catholic) and faith in Christ which is met by divine grace as that faith is expressed in baptism (Baptist). Christ is the object of faith directly in the Baptist approach, but much more indirectly in the Catholic approach.

Third, there remains a major difference in the degree of necessity which is attributed to baptism. In the Baptist approach, baptism is "necessary" only in the preceptive sense as the divinely-ordained event which focuses and objectifies the faith-response to the gospel, but the absence or even

---

99 See, for example, *Salvation and the Church: An Agreed Statement by the Second Anglican-Roman Catholic International Commission* (London: Church House Publishing, 1987).

100 This is apparently asserted by Robert G. Torbet, "The Nature and Communication of Grace: The Baptist Perspective," *Foundations* 12, no. 3 (July-September, 1969): 222. Torbet cites as a major Baptist proponent of this revision Arthur B. Crabtree, *The Restored Relationship: A Study in Justification and Reconciliation* (Valley Forge: Judson Press, 1963).

101 Joseph Pohle, *The Sacraments: A Dogmatic Treatise*, trans. Arthur Preuss (St. Louis: B. Herder, 1915), 1:123; Ott, *Catholic Dogma*, 329; Schillebeeckx, *Christ the Sacrament*, 109.

102 Ott, *Catholic Dogma*, 329; Schillebeeckx, *Christ the Sacrament*, 89, 109.

103 W. A. Van Roo, Review of *The Biblical Doctrine of Initiation*, by R. E. O. White, in *Gregorianum* 42 (1961): 150; idem., Review of *Baptism in the New Testament*, by G. R. Beasley-Murray, in *Gregorianum* 44 (1963): 134.

neglect of baptism in the case of one who is a evidently a disciple of Christ is not interpreted as a sign that saving grace has not been conveyed. In the Catholic view, there are to be sure exceptions to the normative necessity of baptism, but these exceptions are for cases in which there is in fact a desire for baptism which has not yet been fulfilled.[104] In Baptist thought faith is the fundamental reality and baptism the normal vehicle of expression, but in Catholic thought baptism is the fundamental reality, and the idea of a fully-formed faith apart from baptism is essentially untenable.

The Lutheran Tradition

At the heart of Lutheran baptismal theology is the idea of baptism as a *verbum visibile*, a visible and tangible proclamation of the Word of the Gospel. As a proclamation of the gospel in dramatic form, baptism both offers and conveys the benefits of Christ to those who receive it. It serves to evoke and strengthen faith which lays hold of Christ for spiritual rebirth, and in this sense (as a facilitator of fiducial faith) it is a means of regeneration.[105] The terminology of "visible word" has not been as central in Baptist thought as in Lutheranism, but it was used (under the influence of John Smyth) in the 1612 confession of the emerging General Baptist movement.[106]

Perhaps the crux of the Lutheran-Baptist comparison is the sense in which baptism "evokes" faith in the baptizand. If "evoke" here means to bring an existing though undeveloped faith to a definite, focused expression in the sacramental ritual, then the two views appear very similar. If, however, "evoke" means to create faith where none presently exists, then there is a significant difference between the two. The question that must be answered, then, concerns the nature of the faith that is presupposed in the baptism of a mature person.

Baptists assume that the baptizand is prepared to confess faith in Christ in a way that embodies both *assensus* and *fiducia*. Baptist sacramentalists recognize that this faith may be relatively undeveloped, and they do not assume that a conscious assurance of grace has already occurred, but they do posit a genuine faith to be concretely expressed in baptism. Lutherans, on the other hand, exhibit great diversity on this question. Francis Pieper

---

104 Ott, *Catholic Dogma*, 340-341.
105 Francis Pieper, *Christian Dogmatics*, 3 vols. (St. Louis: Concordia Publishing House, 1953), 3:264.
106 Lumpkin, *Confessions*, 138.

(1852-1931), a conservative and traditional theologian of the Lutheran Church–Missouri Synod, interpreted baptismal faith as strongly cognitive in character, arguing that an adult baptism presupposes conscious awareness of the content of the gospel and honest (though immature) commitment to Christ and the gospel.[107] Indeed, he recognized that in some cases of adult conversion, this faith may be sufficiently formed to lead to regeneration prior to baptism, in which case baptism (though it always possesses regenerative power) may in fact *confirm* or *strengthen* an existing regeneration.[108] Regin Prenter (b. 1907), a Scandinavian Lutheran, agreed that baptismal faith contains some sort of cognitive element, but he argued that we must allow for a minimal amount of cognition. This is a concern especially in the case of infants, but even in the case of adult baptism, he argued that the priority of grace minimizes the need for concern regarding the precise nature or content of the faith of the baptizand.[109] Gustaf Aulen (1879-1978), a Swedish Lutheran, stood at the opposite end of the spectrum from Pieper, arguing that there is no need to posit any kind of faith at the point of baptism, because baptism is fundamentally a symbol and means of prevenient grace, the vehicle by which the grace that appeared in history in Christ advances into the history of the individual.[110]

Baptist formulations of the relationships among faith, baptism and regeneration are quite similar to the conceptual scheme of Pieper. Both approaches posit a genuinely cognitive though immature faith as the condition of adult baptism; both interpret baptism as the event in which regeneration becomes a confirmed reality; and both agree that regeneration may very well be a reality prior to baptism, even though our perception of this reality is normatively mediated through baptism. However, when Baptist interpretations are compared to the schemes like those of Prenter and Aulen, the differences are prominent. Those Lutheran views interpret faith as fundamentally the effect of baptism, and whatever differences there may be among Baptist sacramentalists, that is to them a foreign concept.

The Reformed/Calvinistic Tradition

The heart of the Reformed view of baptism is that it is not only a "sign," but

---

107 Pieper, *Dogmatics*, 3:277.
108 Ibid., 3:264.
109 Regin Prenter, *Creation and Redemption*, trans. Theodor I. Jensen (Philadelphia: Fortress Press, 1967), 465-470.
110 Gustaf Aulen, *The Faith of the Christian Church*, trans. Eric M. Wahlstrom (Philadelphia: Muhlenberg Press, 1960), 341.

also a "seal" of personal incorporation in the covenant of grace. In the language of the Westminster Confession, baptism is for the baptizand "a sign and seal of the covenant of grace, of his ingrafting into Christ, of regeneration, of remission of sins, and of his giving up unto God, through Jesus Christ, to walk in newness of life."[111] In this conceptual scheme, therefore, baptism ratifies both the human confession that Jesus is Lord (the "giving up" to a new life of discipleship) and the divine work of remission and regeneration (effecting both justification and sanctification). Baptism is conceptualized as a symbol, but more than a symbol, in that "by the right use of this ordinance the grace promised is not only offered, but really exhibited and conferred by the Holy Ghost"[112] to the elect.

In many ways, the concept of baptism as a "seal" appears to be the ideal way to describe the Baptist idea of baptism as a sacrament, and it has been shown earlier in this book that this language is explicitly used by some early Baptists. In this view baptism is both secondary (pointing beyond itself to the divine promise which it confirms and apart from which it has no power) and effective (applying the promise of the gospel to the realm of holistic personal experience). Indeed, this concept of baptism as a seal appears to be more applicable in the Baptist framework than it is in a paedobaptist Reformed context, in that the ratification of the divine establishment of the covenant is present in both systems, but the ratification of the human side of the covenant (faith as the evidence of the divine call) is consistently present only in the Baptist context.

It may be, then, that the Baptist sacramental view is equivalent to the traditional Reformed view as applied to confessing believers. The one qualification of this equation may be that the Baptist view seems to tie the assurance which is effected by this "sealing" more closely to the baptismal event itself than is true in the Reformed tradition. For example, the Westminster Confession states, "The efficacy of baptism is not tied to that moment of time wherein it is administered." Instead, the grace which is "conferred" through baptism is actually given to the elect "in his appointed time."[113] Now while this may have special relevance for the baptism of infants, this explanation is given in reference to baptism as such, not simply the baptism of infants. Both the Baptist and the Reformed sacramental traditions affirm that baptism is both declaratory and effective, but in terms of what is presumed to happen in the baptismal event itself, Baptist

---

111 *Westminster Confession of Faith*, XXVIII, I.
112 Ibid., XXVIII, VI.
113 Ibid.

sacramentalism tends to emphasize its effective character and Reformed sacramentalism the declaratory aspect. This difference may, of course, be due to the reactive nature of each system: the Baptists reacting against the dominant non-sacramental stream of their denominational tradition, and the Reformed confessions reacting against medieval Catholic sacramentalism.

Both the Lutheran sense of baptism as a "visible Word" and the Calvinistic sense of baptism as a "seal" have been utilized by some Baptists in their verbalization of sacramental theology. These two concepts are not mutually exclusive, both emphasizing the inherent connection between the Word of the gospel and the sacrament which dramatizes it, and both asserting that the sacrament is effective only in those who receive it in faith. The description of the baptism of confessing believers in each system fits easily into the Baptist conceptual scheme. Perhaps the best way to describe the relationship is to say that the Baptist approach is like the traditional Lutheran approach, but with a somewhat weaker sense of necessity, and that the Baptist approach is like the traditional Reformed approach, but with a somewhat stronger sense of grace conferred in the baptismal event itself.

The Disciples/Restorationist Tradition

The tradition which is closest to Baptist sacramentalism is that which was developed by Alexander Campbell (1788-1866) and others in the first half of the 19th century, primarily on the North American frontier but also in Great Britain.[114] Although Campbell was largely responsible for the mature baptismal theology of this tradition, some aspects of his thought were derived from the work of John Glas (1695-1773) and Robert Sandeman (1718-1771) in Great Britain. In particular, Glas contributed an anti-creedal mentality, and Sandeman developed a reductionistic interpretation of faith as mere assent.[115] Some have claimed that this tradition and Baptist

---

114 Campbell's writings are voluminous, but his mature thought on baptism can be found in his *Christian Baptism* (Bethany, VA: by author, 1853). Relevant excerpts from his many articles and books can be found in Royal Humbert, ed., *A Compend of Alexander Campbell's Theology* (St. Louis: Bethany Press, 1961). The relationship of this tradition to Baptist thought is assessed by Errett Gates, *The Early Relation and Separation of Baptists and Disciples* (Chicago: The Christian Century Company, 1904) and E. Roberts-Thomson, *Baptists and Disciples of Christ* (London: Carey Kingsgate Press, 1948).

115 See the articles on Glas and Sandeman by R. E. D. Clark in *The New International Dictionary of the Christian Church*, 2nd ed., gen. ed. J. D. Douglas (Grand Rapids: Zondervan, 1978), 415, 877. See also Melvin Breakenridge, "The Scottish Connection:

An Analysis of the Theological Formulation

sacramentalism are indistinguishable, in that both baptismal theologies restrict baptism to confessing believers and embody a high view of baptismal efficacy.

The American form of this movement originated among Presbyterians (Barton Stone [1772-1844] and Thomas Campbell [1763-1854], Alexander's father), then existed briefly within the Baptist context, but soon became ecclesiastically distinct, largely due to disputes over baptismal theology.[116] Its institutional form is called (pejoratively) "Campbellism" by its opponents, due to Alexander Campbell's role as the dominant theologian of the movement, while its proponents refer to it as Restorationism, the Stone-Campbell tradition, or the Disciples movement. The related movement in Great Britain had diverse origins among small groups known as Glasites, Sandemanians, and Scotch Baptists, but since their first annual conference in 1842 they have existed as an organized body with explicit ties to the American movement.[117] The vast majority of such churches are found in North America, but the British Churches of Christ, although quite small, have played a significant role in ecumenical discussions of this century, notably through William Robinson (1888-1963), their leading theologian.[118]

Campbell and his associates in the early years of the movement affirmed both the unity of the Church and the restoration of primitive Christianity (as they saw it), with primitivism conceived as the means to unity, but it was not long before the tension between the two principles was obvious. The Christian Church (Disciples of Christ) and the British Churches of Christ emphasize the unity principle and are committed to ecumenism, while the American congregations called Churches of Christ or independent Christian Churches emphasize the restoration principle and remain apart from most

---

John Glas, 1695-1773," in *The Campbell-Stone Movement in Ontario*, ed. Claude E. Cox (Lewiston: Edwin Mellon Press, 1995), 43-59.

116 For examples of the intensity of the Baptist reaction to Campbell, see Graves, *Relation of Baptism to Salvation*, 16-56; idem., *Act of Baptism*, 44, 56; Jeter, *Campbellism*, 191-281.

117 William Robinson, *What Churches of Christ Stand For* (Birmingham: Berean Press, 1959), 21-24.

118 The previously cited work by Roberts-Thomson deals with the issue in the British context. Relevant works by William Robinson include *The Biblical Doctrine of the Church*, rev. ed. (St. Louis: Bethany Press, 1955); *The Shattered Cross* (Birmingham: Berean Press, 1948); and *What Churches of Christ Stand For* (Birmingham: Berean Press, 1959). See also his contribution to Faith and Order discussion, "The View of Disciples or Churches of Christ," in *The Ministry and the Sacraments*, ed. Roderic Dunkerley, 253-268.

ecumenical relationships.[119]

The baptismal doctrine of the Disciples/Restorationist tradition includes the following elements: (1) Baptism is the act of a confessing believer in Christ, and represents the culmination of the conversion of a sinner to discipleship. Repentance and faith precede baptism, which is undergone for the purpose of the remission of sins. (2) There is a concern for objectivity in religious experience, and baptism provides the objective action through which one enters into an assured relationship with Christ, as opposed to the subjectivity of other religious traditions which locate assurance of salvation in some kind of internal awareness. (3) Within the movement there are varying views of the necessity of baptism: some see it only as the normal means by which individuals express repentance and faith, and thus receive the "formal" remission of sins, but some argue that both "formal" and "actual" remission of sins come only through baptism. This difference has existed since the early years of the movement.[120]

The similarities between the Baptist-sacramental and Disciple doctrines are obvious. Each tradition asserts that baptism is properly restricted to confessing believers, those who can affirm for themselves their repentance and faith. Each tradition thinks of baptism as the act of a penitent sinner who is turning to Jesus Christ for forgiveness, not as the act of a confirmed disciple--i.e., baptism is integral to conversion and initiates the baptizand into the visible community of believers. Each tradition also teaches that in some way God conveys through baptism the benefits which are signified by it.

The two traditions are clearly very similar to one another, and it is no doubt true that the baptismal theologies of individual theologians from the two sides would in many cases be judged essentially equivalent. However, when the two traditions are assessed as a whole, there are differences, among which are the following.

(1) Human condition versus concursive action. The Disciples tradition has from the beginning interpreted baptism as the final human condition which must be met before entrance into salvation, as part of the terms of surrender which evoke divine acceptance, but Baptists have placed a greater emphasis on the grace of God which has been at work in the individual evoking the faith-response and is at work in the baptismal event itself. The

---

119 William D. Carpe, "Baptismal Theology in the Disciples of Christ," *Review and Expositor* 77 (1980): 90-91.
120 For a chart which surveys the range of views in the Disciples tradition, see Joseph Belcastro, *The Relationship of Baptism to Church Membership* (St. Louis: Bethany Press, 1963), 215-216.

precise relation between grace and human action varies among Baptists according to their Calvinistic or Arminian orientation, but in either case there is a sense of a continuing stream of concursive action which differs from most Disciples thought. Robinson claims that in the tradition going back to Campbell, "They proclaimed, against both Calvinism and Arminianism, that man was a *free agent* in accepting Christ as his Saviour."[121] This difference manifests itself in the significance attached to the term "sacrament" in the two traditions. The term is very important for Baptists who have recovered a high view of baptismal efficacy, because of its connotation of divine action in the event; in the Disciples tradition the term may be accepted, but it is not a crucial concept.[122]

(2) The nature of baptismal faith. From its beginning the Disciples tradition has been concerned with the formulation of a rational approach to religion which is able to make "faith" easily understandable and readily identifiable. Believing the gospel has in some cases been reduced to mere assent "that Jesus Christ is the Son of God" (based at least partially on Acts 8:37 in the Latin manuscripts and the Textus Receptus). Faith has been interpreted as believing revealed facts and obeying revealed commands, so that the conditions of divine acceptance are assent to the facts of the gospel and obedience to the baptismal command.[123] Baptists, on the other hand, have consistently emphasized that the apostolic sense of faith involves both *assensus* and *fiducia*, so that the faith confessed in baptism is both belief in the facts about Christ and an attitude of trust and commitment.

(3) Objectivity versus subjectivity. The early Disciples movement was driven to a large extent by a desire for objectivity in religious experience, as opposed to the search for subjective signs of grace which prevailed on the American frontier.[124] This subjectivity had roots in the Puritan search for assurance of personal election and in the revivalism of the 18th and 19th centuries. In the Baptist context, the acceptance of the individual for baptism was conditioned on the baptizand's ability to articulate a personal experience of grace and give tangible evidence of prior regeneration, but the Disciples reacted to this both because of the personal despair which many

---

121 Robinson, *Churches of Christ*, 57.
122 Ibid., 81.
123 Richard T. Hughes, "Are Restorationists Evangelicals?", in *The Variety of American Evangelicalism*, ed. Donald W. Dayton and Robert K. Johnston (Downers Grove: Inter-Varsity Press, 1991), 116, 124.
124 L. Edward Hicks, "Rational Religion in the Ohio Western Reserve (1827-1830): Walter Scott and the Restoration Appeal of Baptism for the Remission of Sin," *Restoration Quarterly* 34 (1992): 211-212, 215, 217; Robinson, *Churches of Christ*, 56-57.

experienced in this search for signs of grace and because the New Testament did not seem to support this approach to baptismal conditions.

Early Disciples argued that the biblical doctrine of baptism indicated that God had provided the rite as the objective confirmation of human faith and the divine act of forgiveness. The assurance of divine acceptance comes in the external event of baptism, not in some sort of internal experience, which implies that there is no necessary recitation of religious experience which must come prior to baptism--all that is necessary is belief in the facts of the gospel and willingness to submit to the command of baptism.

Baptist sacramentalists grant a kernel of truth in this Disciples perspective, in that they recognize that baptism is in biblical terms the defining moment in conversion, the objectification of the human response to the gospel. However, they have still retained the concept of some sort of subjective experience of grace prior to baptism, although this experience will be heightened and intensified via baptism. As noted in Chapter 2, the 1948 statement of the Baptist Union, although referring to baptism as a sacrament and a means of grace, still posited a prior "personal crisis in the soul's life."[125] In some cases they have retained the demand for a personal testimony of the experience of grace and approval by the church meeting prior to baptism, which posits a level of subjectivity in conversion that differs markedly from the Disciples tradition.[126]

(4) The degree of necessity. As demonstrated above, Baptist sacramentalists do not teach an absolute necessity of baptism for personal salvation. Instead, they argue that the link between baptism and salvation is normal and experiential, but not strictly necessary. What is absolutely necessary is the personal response to God in Christ that is termed "repentance" or "faith" in the New Testament. Baptism is conceptualized as a means by which God works in grace to confirm in us the reality of a saving encounter with Christ, but it is not thought of as a *sine qua non* of salvation. This is a corollary of the distinction between baptism as final human condition (Disciples) and baptism as a divine-human act (Baptist). For Baptists, then, the absence or even the neglect of baptism does not in itself imply that the unbaptized person is in a state of damnation, although willful neglect may be symptomatic of a deeper problem.

The history of Disciples/Restorationists on this point is marked by

---

125 Cited in Payne, *Baptist Union*, 285.
126 For a brief account of the various ways of conducting this assessment of religious experience, see Gilmore, *BCU*, 65-69.

significant diversity, but in any case the degree of necessity attached to baptism by early Disciples was a major cause of the division between them and the Baptists. Alexander Campbell's treatment of the question was perhaps inconsistent, as even his followers admit, sometimes asserting that both the "formal" and the "actual" remission of sins come only in baptism, but on other occasions apparently asserting that baptism mediates the "formal" *as opposed to* the "actual" remission.[127] An early and ongoing debate within the conservative wing of Restorationism concerns the status of Baptists (and others) who have been baptized by immersion as believers, but as a testimony to prior conversion and not intentionally for the remission of sins. Some have gone so far as to render a negative judgment on the status as Christians of those baptized in this way, while others have been more charitable.[128] Some anti-sacramental Baptists have reciprocated by rejecting the validity of "Campbellite" baptism due to its erroneous intention,[129] but sacramental Baptists have never taken this approach.

In many cases Baptist sacramentalists and those in the Disciples tradition seem to affirm indistinguishable theologies of baptism. In particular, British Baptists and those in the British Churches of Christ hold very similar views, the distinctions probably lying more in emphasis than in substance. Such was the judgment almost fifty years ago of Robinson from the Disciples side and Roberts-Thomson from the Baptist side.[130] Another Baptist, R. L. Child, was prepared to concede a large measure of truth in this conclusion, but he also noted that "differences of emphasis can be extremely important."[131] In particular, distinctive emphases concerning the nature of baptismal faith and the place of subjective experience in conversion may affect the proclamation of the gospel and the practice of baptism far beyond what might be expected on the basis of the subtle differences at the theoretical level.

However one may assess the relation between Baptists and the ecumenically-inclined Disciples tradition, in the self-styled Restorationist part of the tradition there is a widespread view of baptismal necessity which is radically different from Baptist sacramentalism. In terms of a positive statement of what happens in baptism, Baptist sacramentalism and the

---

127 Humbert, ed., *Compend*, 196-197; Earl West, "The Churches of Christ," in *Baptism & Church*, ed. Strege, 85-88.
128 West, "Churches of Christ," 92-96.
129 For example, Graves, *Act of Christian Baptism*, 56.
130 Robinson, *Shattered Cross*, 41; Roberts-Thomson, *Baptists and Disciples*, 123.
131 R. L. Child, "Baptists and Disciples of Christ," *The Baptist Quarterly* 14 (1951-1952): 189.

Restorationist tradition may seem very close, but any negative implication ("no valid baptism" implies "no salvation") is at home only within the Restorationist movement.

Summary

The Baptist variety of sacramentalism which has been developed in this century by British Baptists is not only defensible as an explanation of the biblical statements about baptism, but is also coherent as a system of baptismal theology. Although it is similar in various ways to the baptismal theologies affirmed by Roman Catholics, Lutherans, Calvinists and Disciples in their explanations of the baptism of confessing believers, it cannot be identified completely with any of those constructions of baptismal theology. The Baptist paradigm does not arise from any contradictory imposition of an alien theology onto Baptist practice. On the contrary, traditional Baptist emphases can be correlated readily with this kind of sacramentalism. Specifically, the traditional Baptist emphasis on the centrality of personal, fiducial faith is retained, in that such penitent faith is conceived as the absolutely necessary content of baptism, and apart from such faith (evoked by prevenient grace) there is no grace conveyed in baptism. The Baptist restriction of baptism to confessing believers is not threatened by the idea that God conveys grace through baptism, because a biblical theology of grace implies that while there is such a thing as prevenient grace, it is also true that some operations of grace are conditioned on a human faith-response. The traditional Baptist affirmation that salvation is not tied to ceremonies is retained, even though the reformulation affirms a higher relative necessity of baptism than is true in most Baptist theology, because the necessity is only relative and not absolute. The traditional assertion that all who have faith in Christ also have the Spirit of Christ is affirmed as well, the only modification being the assertion that baptism is the normative event in which faith receives both Christ and the Spirit at the level of conscious experience.

The one aspect of this theology which seems incoherent is the tendency of some to accept *de facto* infant baptism as valid baptism, which stands in opposition to historic Baptist theology and does not seem to follow from the premises inherent in the sacramental theology of baptism. If believer baptism has the kind of significance which is affirmed in this theology, then it is difficult to see how infant baptism can be accepted as its equivalent without affirming either that there is power in the ritual apart from personal faith or that baptism is purely declaratory-symbolic. The former alternative would make this theology something other than *Baptist*, and the latter would make it something other than *sacramental.* This tendency to affirm infant baptism after the fact appears to be inconsistent with the general theology being affirmed, but this calls into question only this one inference from the theology, not the theology itself.

CHAPTER 5

The Significance of Baptist Sacramentalism

A promising new model for baptismal theology in the Baptist tradition has been developed by British Baptists in the 20th century. Grounded in the exegesis of the New Testament and stimulated by ecumenical discussions, these Baptists have formulated a theology of baptism which is both Baptist and sacramental, emphasizing that baptism in biblical terms is a divine-human encounter in which there is significant action from both sides, a conjunction of grace and faith. It has been widely assumed by Baptists that the New Testament teaching about salvation by grace through faith demands a rejection of all sacramental views of baptism, and it has been widely assumed by those of other Christian traditions as well as Baptists that such anti-sacramental theology has always been the norm for Baptists. A study of both the biblical theology of baptism and of Baptist history indicates that both assumptions are false.

Baptist churches arose in the first decade of the 17th century when some English Separatists came to a revised view of the church and baptism. Baptist theology departed from its Puritan-Calvinist heritage in its assertion that Christian baptism must be restricted to those who can personally confess faith in Christ for themselves. After some three decades of Baptist life, some Particular Baptists concluded that baptism must be done by immersion, and this rapidly became the viewpoint of the whole Baptist tradition. The demands of controversy over these two issues of subject and mode of baptism consumed most of the literary energy of the Baptists, so much so that the early Baptist literature devoted little space to developing a doctrine of baptism as a means of grace. However, some early Baptist literature did address this question, and the dominant view was very much like the Puritan-Calvinist understanding of baptism as both sign and seal of entrance into salvific union with Christ, the only difference being the

Baptist application of the concept to confessing believers alone. At both verbal and conceptual levels, Reformed sacramentalism was the essence of the mainstream baptismal theology of 17th-century English Baptists.

Although this Reformed sacramentalism was still evident in major Baptist writers at the end of the 17th century, it was either ignored or rejected by most Baptists in the following two centuries. Although there were some exceptions, the idea that baptism is a sacrament, a means of grace, came to be associated with high doctrines of baptismal regeneration or at least with paedobaptism. As a result, by the beginning of the 20th century, British Baptists (indeed, Baptists everywhere) commonly thought of baptism as a purely symbolic ritual bearing witness to a previously confirmed union with Christ, and sacramentalism was rejected both verbally and conceptually.

However, some Baptists were convinced that such a reduced theology of baptism did not adequately interpret either Scripture or experience. Starting with H. Wheeler Robinson in the years surrounding 1920 and culminating in the extensive work of G. R. Beasley-Murray in the 1960's, British Baptists formulated a Baptist-sacramental theology of baptism which (unconsciously) built upon and advanced the foundational Baptist thought of the 17th century and modified the one-sided view inherited from the 19th century. Without surrendering the distinctive doctrine of believer baptism, this theology also postulated a divine work of grace within the event. This Baptist variety of sacramentalism is defensible as an exegesis and synthesis of the New Testament baptismal texts, and it coherently relates baptism to the broader themes of soteriology and ecclesiology. The one point at which the movement falters is its tendency to deny the necessity of believer baptism for local church membership, but this appears to be a failure to draw a logical inference, not a deficiency in the foundational theology of baptism.

This ferment among British Baptists is only one example of the general rethinking of baptism which has characterized most denominations in the 20th century, especially in the era since Emil Brunner's (1938) and Karl Barth's (1943) pointed attacks on infant baptism. The theologians and doctrinal commissions of various traditions have admitted that infant baptism has been a practice in search of a theology, and some of the concessions made by them in the process of fresh study have been quite significant. Even the Roman Catholic Church in the post-Vatican II era has refocused its baptismal theology in the direction of an adult paradigm with the publication of its revised *Rite for the Christian Initiation of Adults* (1972), and some Roman Catholics have argued that infant baptism ought to be terminated.[1]

In spite of these changes in paedobaptist churches and the transdenominational respect for the work of Beasley-Murray in particular, there has been no widespread defection in the Baptist direction. One major factor, as noted at the beginning of this book, is the apparent lack of a coherent Baptist theology of baptism to undergird the Baptist practice that is so vigorously defended. In particular, the common Baptist assertion that baptism is a *nudum signum* is difficult to correlate with the actual biblical language about baptism, and it seems to be an inadequate basis for the typical Baptist willingness to perpetuate division from other Christians on the basis of baptismal practice. Perhaps Baptist sacramentalism would offer a more compelling alternative.

Whatever may be the significance of this British Baptist sacramentalism for inter-denominational dialogue, the greater significance would lie in its potential to reshape Baptist thought on a wider scale. Although the British reformulation has some parallels among Baptists in continental Europe,[2] there is only minimal evidence of it in North America. For example, in a recent book analysing shifts in Southern Baptist thought over the 150 years from 1845 to 1995, there is no chapter devoted to baptism and only a few passing references to baptism in the entire book.[3] There is some evidence in recent Baptist discussions of baptism that the "act of obedience/pure symbol" concept of baptism is perceived to be less than adequate as a synthesis of biblical theology, but the conceptual shifts are usually rather tentative, and there is no sustained interaction with the British paradigm shift.[4]

The British paradigm could be useful for Baptists in general at both theoretical and practical levels. At the theoretical level, it provides a way to formulate a baptismal theology on the basis of the biblical statements

---

[1] Paul F. X. Covino, "The Postconciliar Infant Baptism Debate in the American Catholic Church," in *Living Water, Sealing Spirit: Readings on Christian Initiation*, ed. Maxwell E. Johnson (Collegeville, Minnesota: The Liturgical Press, 1995), 327-349.

[2] For example, Johannes Schneider, *Baptism and Church in the New Testament*, trans. Ernest A. Payne (London: Carey Kingsgate Press, 1957).

[3] Paul A. Basden, ed., *Has Our Theology Changed? Southern Baptist Thought Since 1845* (Nashville: Broadman & Holman, 1994).

[4] Clark H. Pinnock, *Flame of Love: A Theology of the Holy Spirit* (Downers Grove: Inter-Varsity Press, 1996), 119-129; Stanley J. Grenz, *Theology for the Community of God* (Nashville: Broadman & Holman, 1994), 670-675; Wayne Grudem, *Systematic Theology: An Introduction to Biblical Doctrine* (Grand Rapids: Zondervan, 1994), 953-954; Robert H. Stein, "Baptism and Becoming a Christian in the New Testament," *Southern Baptist Journal of Theology* 2, no. 1 (Spring 1998): 6-17.

about baptism, as opposed to the common tendency to develop a theology of conversion based on biblical texts about faith and/or repentance in isolation. Such a theology of conversion may appear to contradict the natural synthesis of the baptismal texts, with the result that the baptismal language is frequently minimized to resolve the contradiction and baptism is thus marginalized.

At the practical level, the British paradigm facilitates the practice of Christian initiation by providing in baptism an objective seal of conversion and spiritual rebirth. When baptism is not allowed to function in this way, the typical result is an introspective approach to the experience of conversion, a search for signs of grace in one's own private psychological experience. The natural result of such subjectivism is either personal despair over the ambiguity of experience or a judgmental attitude toward others who cannot articulate the "right" kind of experience.[5] Many evangelists in Baptist and other evangelical contexts have perceived this problem (either consciously or unconsciously), and they have provided substitutes for baptism in the form of tangible physical responses known in the middle of the 19th century as the "anxious seat" and more recently as the "altar call." Charles Finney (1792-1875), a father of such modern techniques, articulated the connection between such measures and baptism:

> In the days of the apostles *baptism* answered this purpose. The gospel was preached to the people, and then all those who were willing to be on the side of Christ were called on to be *baptized*. It held the precise place that the anxious seat does now, as a public manifestation of their determination to be Christians.[6]

It is thus recognized in practice that if union with Christ is to be an experiential reality, then the entrance into that union calls for some event which translates the attitude of faith into a personal act. Baptism admirably serves this purpose according to both Scripture and experience, and only a perverse anti-sacramentalism prevents the recognition of this. Baptism not only serves to objectify the faith-response of the baptizand, but also affirms the divine action of grace, in that baptism is fundamentally something done *to* the individual rather than *by* the individual.

One of the major emphases of the Baptist tradition has always been the

---

5   Hicks, "Rational Religion," 212.
6   Charles Grandison Finney, *Lectures on the Revivals of Religion*, ed. William G. McLoughlin (Cambridge, MA: Harvard University Press, 1960), 268.

unique authority of Scripture, with all that is thus implied about freedom to rethink all traditions, including Baptist traditions. As noted in this study, one of the key elements in the British Baptist reformulation of baptism along sacramental lines was a reassessment of the New Testament baptismal language. If other Baptists in the world are true to their historic principles, then they should at least admit that the non-sacramental paradigm which has dominated their baptismal theology for some time may be inadequate and in need of modification. If that can be admitted, then the British Baptist voices deserve a hearing.

In a recent article a leading Southern Baptist theologian has surveyed Baptist monographs on baptism from the latter half of the 20th century, and this review includes significant summaries of the literature which is the focus of this book. However, near the end of the article he notes the absence of trans-Atlantic dialogue:

> British Baptist writings on baptism and Southern Baptist practice of baptism have been like two ships passing in the night during the last third of the twentieth century. The dawn of the new century has exposed the genuine and persistent differences.[7]

The conclusion of the article raises questions which, in the writer's opinion, need to be addressed by Southern Baptists in the 21st century:

> Why have recent Southern Baptists been reluctant to produce a positive theology of Christian baptism? Will they continue to say more about what baptism is not than what it is? Has recent affinity with American Evangelicals dulled the blade of the importance of baptism? Ought Southern Baptists to apply the term "sacrament" to baptism? If so, with what meaning?[8]

These are in fact the questions which have received sustained attention in the British Baptist recovery of baptismal sacramentalism, and the answers which have resulted from this study of baptism appear to provide a natural synthesis of the biblical witness to baptism and a coherent theology of baptism which could enrich the theology and experience of Baptists and other Christians. If the answers suggested in this British reformulation were

---

7 James Leo Garrett, Jr., "Baptists concerning Baptism: Review and Preview," *Southwestern Journal of Theology* 43, no. 2 (Spring 2001): 67.
8 Ibid.

accepted by the Southern Baptist Convention (the largest Protestant denomination in the world), then it would hardly be necessary to demonstrate the significance of this Baptist sacramentalism. Whatever may be the reasons for the lack of trans-Atlantic dialogue in the past, there are abundant reasons to facilitate it in the future.

BIBLIOGRAPHY

Primary Sources

Argyle, A. W. "'Outward' and 'Inward' in Biblical Thought." *The Expository Times* 68, no. 7 (April 1957): 196-199.

Ballard, Paul. "Baptists and Baptism: A Socio-Ecumenical Issue." *The Baptist Ministers' Journal*, no. 260 (October 1997): 18-22.

Bampton, T. A. "The Sacramental Significance of Christian Baptism." *The Baptist Quarterly* 11 (1942-1945): 270-276.

Baptist Revival Fellowship. *Liberty in the Lord: Comment on Trends in Baptist Thought Today*. London: Carey Kingsgate Press, 1964.

Beasley-Murray, George R. "The Authority and Justification for Believers' Baptism." *Review and Expositor* 77 (1980): 63-70.

_____. *Baptism in the New Testament*. Grand Rapids: Eerdmans, 1962.

_____. "Baptism in the New Testament." *Foundations* 3 (1960): 15-31.

_____. "Baptism and the Sacramental View." *The Baptist Times*, 11 February 1960, 9-10.

_____. *Baptism Today and Tomorrow*. London: Macmillan, 1966.

_____. "Baptist Interpretation of the Place of the Child in the Church." *Foundations* 8 (1965): 146-160.

_____. "The Case Against Infant Baptism." *Christianity Today* 9 (1964): 11-14.

_____. "Church and Child in the New Testament." *The Baptist Quarterly* 21 (1965-1966): 206-218.

_____. "The Church and the Child." *The Fraternal*, no. 50 (April 1943): 9-13.

_____. "The Church of Scotland and Baptism." *The Fraternal*, no. 99 (January 1956): 7-10.

_____. "Confessing Baptist Identity." In *A Perspective of Baptist Identity*, ed. D. Slater, 75-86. London: Mainstream, 1987.

_____. "Faith in the New Testament: a Baptist Perspective." *American Baptist Quarterly* 1 (1982): 137-143.

_____. "Holy Spirit, Baptism, and Body of Christ." *Review and Expositor* 63 (1966): 177-185.

_____. "I Still Find Infant Baptism Difficult." *The Baptist Quarterly* 22 (1967-1968): 225-236.

_____. "John 3:3,5: Baptism, Spirit, and the Kingdom." *The Expository Times* 97 (1985-1986): 167-170.

_____. "The Problem of Infant Baptism: An Exercise in Possibilities." In *Festschrift Gunter Wagner*, ed. Faculty of Baptist Theological Seminary, Rüschlikon/Switzerland, 1-14. Bern: Peter Lang, 1994.

_____. "The Sacraments." *The Fraternal*, no. 70 (October 1948): 3-7.

_____. "The Second Chapter of Colossians." *Review and Expositor* 70 (1973): 469-479.

Bibliography

_____. "The Spirit Is There." *The Baptist Times*, 10 December 1959, 8.
_____. "The Theology of the Child." *American Baptist Quarterly* 1 (1982): 197-202.
Beasley-Murray, Paul. "Celebrating the Faith in Baptism." *Baptist Ministers' Journal*, no. 244 (1993): 11-14.
Beattie, N. Letter to *The Baptist Times*, 4 February 1960, 6.
Beattie, W. Letter to *The Baptist Times*, 18 May 1961, 6.
Bottoms, Walter W. "Christian Baptism." *The Fraternal*, no. 78 (October 1950): 40-43.
Bridge, Donald and David Phypers. *The Water that Divides*. Downers Grove: Inter-Varsity Press, 1977.
Bryan, F. C., ed. *Concerning Believers Baptism*. London: The Kingsgate Press, 1943.
Burnish, Raymond. *The Meaning of Baptism: A Comparison of the Teaching and Practice of the Fourth Century with the Present Day*. London: SPCK, 1985.
Burrows, E. W. "Understanding of Baptism in Baptist Traditions, with Special Reference to Modern Trends." *Indian Journal of Theology* 26 (1977): 12-28.
Campbell, R. Alastair. "Jesus and His Baptism." *Tyndale Bulletin* 47, no. 2 (November 1996): 191-214.
Carter, S. F. Letter to *The Baptist Times*, 28 January 1960, 6.
Champion, L. G. *Baptists and Unity*. London: A. R. Mowbray, 1962.
_____. *The Church of the New Testament*. London: Carey Kingsgate Press, 1951.
Child, R. L. "Baptists and Disciples of Christ." *The Baptist Quarterly* 14 (1951-1952): 188-190.
_____. "The Biblical Doctrine of Initiation." *The Fraternal*, no. 118 (October 1960): 18-23.
_____. "The Church of Scotland on Baptism." *The Baptist Quarterly* 16 (1955-1956): 244-251.
_____. *A Conversation about Baptism*. London: SCM Press, 1963.
_____. "The Ministry and the Sacraments." *The Baptist Quarterly* 9 (1938-1939): 132-138.
_____. "What Happens in Baptism?" *The Baptist Times*, 4 February 1960, 8, 10.
Clark, Neville. *An Approach to the Theology of the Sacraments*. London: SCM Press, 1956.
_____. "Christian Baptism Under Fire." *The Fraternal*, no. 114 (October 1959): 16-18.
_____. "Christian Initiation: A Baptist Point of View." *Studia Liturgica* 4 (1965): 156-165.
Clarke, Paul et al. *Our Baptist Heritage*. Leeds: Reformation Today Trust, 1993.
Clarke, Robert. Letter to *The Baptist Times*, 8 October 1959, 6.
_____. Letter to *The Baptist Times*, 7 January 1960, 6.
Clements, K. W., ed. *Baptists in the Twentieth Century*. London: Baptist Historical Society, 1983.
Cook, Henry. *What Baptists Stand For*. 3rd ed. London: Carey Kingsgate Press, 1958.
Cranefield, D. L. Letter to *The Baptist Times*, 24 September 1959, 6.
Cross, Anthony R. *Baptism and the Baptists: Theology and Practice in Twentieth-Century Britain*. Carlisle: Paternoster Press, 2000.
_____. " Baptists and Baptism: A British Perspective." *Baptist History and Heritage* 35, no. 1 (Winter 2000): 104-121.
_____. "Dispelling the Myth of English Baptist Baptismal Sacramentalism." *The Baptist Quarterly* 38, no. 8 (October 2000): 367-391.
Dakin, Arthur. *The Baptist View of the Church and Ministry*. London: Kingsgate Press, 1944.

Dunning, T. G. "A Baptist Oxford Movement." *The Baptist Quarterly* 11 (1942-1945): 411-416.
Edwards, A. David. Letter to *The Baptist Times*, 27 April 1961, 6.
Ellis, Christopher J. "Relativity, Ecumenism, and the Liberation of the Church." *The Baptist Quarterly* 29 (1981-1982): 81-91.
Ennals, J. E. "Our Baptist Witness: Baptism in Practice." *The Baptist Quarterly* 20 (1963-1964): 183-186.
Evans, P. W. "The Baptismal Commission in Matt. xxviii.19." *The Baptist Quarterly* 15 (1953-1954): 19-28.
_____. *Sacraments in the New Testament.* London: Tyndale Press, 1947.
_____. "Sealing as a Term for Baptism." *The Baptist Quarterly* 16 (1955-1956): 171-175.
Fiddes, Paul S. *Charismatic Renewal: a Baptist View.* London: Baptist Union of Great Britain, 1980.
_____, ed. *Reflections on the Water: Understanding God and the World through the Baptism of Believers.* Macon, GA: Smyth and Helwys Publishing, 1996.
Ford, S. W. Letter to *The Baptist Times*, 5 November 1959, 6.
Gilmore, Alec. *Baptism and Christian Unity.* Valley Forge: The Judson Press, 1966.
_____, ed. *Christian Baptism: A Fresh Attempt to Understand the Rite in Terms of Scripture, History and Theology.* London: Lutterworth Press, 1959.
_____. "Leenhardt on Baptism." *The Baptist Quarterly* 15 (1953-1954): 35-40.
_____. Letter to *The Baptist Times*, 24 September 1959, 6.
_____, ed. *The Pattern of the Church.* London: Lutterworth Press, 1963.
_____. "The Scottish Report on Baptism (a Study Outline)." *The Fraternal*, no. 102 (October 1956): 16-19.
_____. "Some Baptismal Problems." *The Fraternal*, no. 109 (July 1958): 12-15.
_____. "Some Recent Trends in the Theology of Baptism." *The Baptist Quarterly* 15 (1953-1954): 310-318, 338-345; 16 (1955-1956): 2-9.
Griffiths, D. R. "An Approach to the Theology of Baptism." *The Expository Times* 63, no. 5 (February 1952): 157-159.
_____. Letter to *The Baptist Times*, 10 December 1959, 6.
_____. "Study Outline on Baptism." *The Fraternal*, no. 90 (October 1953): 21-28.
Hastings, B. Gordon. "An Outline of the History of Baptism." *The Fraternal*, no. 90 (October 1953): 28-32.
Haymes, Brian. "Baptism: A Question of Belief and Age?" *Perspectives in Religious Studies* 27, no. 1 (Spring 2000): 121-126.
Hayward, Victor E. W. "Can Our Controversy with the Paedobaptists Be Resolved?" *The Baptist Quarterly* 22 (1967-1968): 50-64.
Hulse, Erroll. *The Testimony of Baptism.* Sussex: Carey Publications, 1982.
Jaeger, L. S. Letter to *The Baptist Times*, 24 September 1959, 6.
John, S. B. Letter to *The Baptist Times*, 8 October 1959, 6.
_____. Letter to *The Baptist Times*, 14 January 1960, 6.
_____. Letter to *The Baptist Times*, 25 February 1960, 6.
_____. Letter to *The Baptist Times*, 27 April 1961, 6.
_____. Letter to *The Baptist Times*, 15 June 1961, 6.
Jones, N. B. "Christian Baptism III." *The Fraternal*, no. 115 (January 1960): 18-23.
Kevan, Ernest F. "Christian Baptism II." *The Fraternal*, no. 113 (July 1959): 8-12.
Kingdon, David. *Children of Abraham: A Reformed Baptist View of Baptism, the Covenant, and Children.* Sussex: Carey Publications, 1973.

Kreider, Alan. "Baptism, Catechism, and the Eclipse of Jesus' Teaching in Early Christianity." *Tyndale Bulletin* 47, no. 2 (November 1996): 315-348.

Kreitzer, Larry. "Baptism in the Pauline Epistles, With Special Reference to the Corinthian Letters." *The Baptist Quarterly* 34 (1991-1992): 67-78.

Lane, Eric. *I Want to Be Baptised.* London: Grace Publications, 1986.

Law, A. E. Letter to *The Baptist Times*, 4 February 1960, 6.

Maoz, Baruch et al. *Local Church Practice.* Haywards Heath, Sussex: Carey Publications, 1978.

Martin, Hugh. "Baptism and Circumcision." *The Baptist Quarterly* 14 (1951-1952): 213-221.

_____. "Baptism in the Fourth Century." *The Baptist Quarterly* 13 (1949-1950): 370-372.

_____. "Baptism as Cleansing." *The Baptist Quarterly* 16 (1955-1956): 378-381.

Mason, Rex A. "The Theology of Baptism." *The Fraternal*, no. 90 (October 1953): 7-11.

Matthews, A. J. Letter to *The Baptist Times*, 14 January 1960, 6.

Matthews, John F. *Baptism: a Baptist View.* London: Baptist Union of Great Britain, 1976.

Nicholson, J. F. V. "Baptism in Context: Further Reflections on Louisville 1979." *The Baptist Quarterly* 28 (1979-1980): 275-279.

Noble, Frank J. Letter to *The Baptist Times*, 10 March 1960, 6.

Norgaard, Johannes. "Shall Our Interpretation of Baptism Be Allowed to Divide Baptists?" *The Fraternal*, no. 91 (January 1954): 27-31.

Norman, J. G. G. Letter to *The Baptist Times*, 31 December 1959, 4.

Parratt, J. K. "The Seal of the Holy Spirit and Baptism." *The Baptist Quarterly* 23 (1969-1970): 111-113, 125.

Payne, Ernest A. "Baptism and Church Membership among the Baptists." *Theology* 55 (1952): 170-173.

_____. *The Baptist Movement in the Reformation and Onwards.* London: Kingsgate Press, 1947.

_____. *The Baptist Union: A Short History.* London: Carey Kingsgate Press, 1958.

_____. "Baptists and the Laying on of Hands." *The Baptist Quarterly* 15 (1953-1954): 203-215.

_____. "Baptists and Christian Initiation." *The Baptist Quarterly* 26 (1975-1976): 147-157.

_____. "Believers' Baptism in Ecumenical Discussion." *Foundations* 3 (January 1960): 32-39.

_____. *The Fellowship of Believers: Baptist Thought and Practice Yesterday and Today.* London: Kingsgate Press, 1944.

_____. *Henry Wheeler Robinson: Scholar, Teacher, Principal--A Memoir.* London: Nisbet & Co., 1946.

_____. "Implications of Baptism for Christian Unity." *Encounter* 21, no. 3 (Summer 1960): 311-316.

_____. "Professor Oscar Cullmann on Baptism." *The Baptist Quarterly* 14 (1951-1952): 56-60.

_____. "Professor T. W. Manson on Baptism." *Scottish Journal of Theology* 2 (1945-1950): 50-56.

_____ and Stephen F. Winward. *Orders and Prayers for Church Worship.* London: Kingsgate Press, 1960.

Peacock, Heber F. "Baptism and the Holy Spirit." *The Fraternal*, no. 85 (July 1952): 17-20.

Quicke, M. J. "Baptists and the Current Debate on Baptism." *The Baptist Quarterly* 29 (1981-1982): 153-168.

Read, L. A. "The Ordinances." *The Fraternal*, no. 67 (January 1948): 8-10.
Reiling, J. "The Holy Spirit in Baptism." *The Baptist Quarterly* 19 (1961-1962): 339-351.
Robinson, Henry Wheeler. *Baptist Principles*. 4th ed. London: Kingsgate Press, 1945.
_____. "Believers' Baptism and the Holy Spirit." *The Baptist Quarterly* n.s. 9 (1938-1939): 387-397.
_____. *The Christian Experience of the Holy Spirit*. London: Nisbet & Co., 1928.
_____. "The Five Points of a Baptist's Faith." *The Baptist Quarterly* 11 (1942-1945): 4-14.
_____. *The Life and Faith of the Baptists*. London: Kingsgate Press, 1946.
_____. "The Place of Baptism in Baptist Churches of To-Day." *The Baptist Quarterly* n.s. 1 (1922-1923): 209-218.
Rowley, H. H. "Dr. G. R. Beasley-Murray on Baptism." *The Baptist Times*, 30 August 1962, 6.
_____. "The Origin and Meaning of Baptism." *The Baptist Quarterly* 11 (1942-1945): 309-320.
_____. *The Unity of the Bible*. London: Carey Kingsgate Press, 1953.
Russell, D. S. "Christian Baptism I." *The Fraternal*, no. 113 (July 1959): 5-8.
_____. "The Ministry and Sacraments." *The Baptist Quarterly* 17 (1957-1958): 67-73.
Scott, William. "The Spiritual and the Sacramental in the Theology of Baptism." *The Fraternal*, no. 137 (July 1965): 22-28.
Shackleton, G. Elwin. Letter to *The Baptist Times*, 22 October 1959, 6.
Snell, R. J. Letter to *The Baptist Times*, 10 March 1960, 6.
Stones, L. J. Letter to *The Baptist Times*, 10 September 1959, 6.
Trent, H. W. "Ourselves and the Ordinances." *The Baptist Quarterly* 17 (1957-1958): 10-22.
Underwood, Alfred Clair. "Conversion and Baptism." In *The Faith of the Baptists*, by J. H. Rushbrooke et al. London: The Kingsgate Press, 1926.
_____. *Conversion: Christian and Non-Christian, A Comparative and Psychological Study*. London: George Allen & Unwin Ltd., 1925.
_____. *A History of the English Baptists*. London: Carey Kingsgate Press, 1947.
_____. "The Place of Conversion in Christian Experience." *The Baptist Quarterly* 6, no. 4 (October 1932): 157-163.
Walker, Michael J. "Baptism: Doctrine and Practice among Baptists in the United Kingdom." *Foundations* 22, no. 1 (1979): 72-80.
_____. *Baptists at the Table: The Theology of the Lord's Supper amongst English Baptists in the Nineteenth Century*. Didcot: The Baptist Historical Society, 1992.
_____. "The Relation of Infants to Church, Baptism and Gospel in Seventeenth Century Baptist Theology." *The Baptist Quarterly* 21 (1965-1966): 242-262.
Walton, Robert C. *The Gathered Community*. London: Carey Press, 1946.
Weaver, John D. "Reconsidering Believers' Baptism." *Baptist Ministers' Journal*, no. 257 (January 1997): 3-7.
West, W. M. S. "Towards a Consensus on Baptism? Louisville 1979." *The Baptist Quarterly* 28 (1979-1980): 225-239.
_____. "Toward a Possible Agenda." *Review and Expositor* 77 (1980): 13-20.
Whilding, W. E. "Conversion, Baptism, and Church Membership." *The Fraternal*, no. 90 (October 1953): 11-14.
White, R. E. O. "Baptism: the Domestic Debate." *The Fraternal*, no. 118 (October 1960): 14-17.
_____. *The Biblical Doctrine of Initiation*. Grand Rapids: Eerdmans, 1960.

_____. *Invitation to Baptism*. London: Baptist Union of Great Britain and Ireland, 1962.
_____. "New Baptismal Questions." *The Baptist Times*, 13 April 1961, 9.
_____. "New Baptismal Questions--II." *The Baptist Times*, 24 August 1961, 2.
_____. "Some Important Issues for Baptismal Theology." *Expository Times* 61 (1949-1950): 108-111.
Winward, Stephen F. "The Administration of Baptism." *The Fraternal*, no. 123 (January 1962): 8-11.
_____. *The New Testament Teaching on Baptism*. London: Carey Kingsgate Press, 1952.
Wright, Nigel. "The Influence of the Charismatic Movement on European Baptist Life and Mission: Theological Reflections." *EPTA Bulletin* 13 (1994): 5-18.

Secondary Sources

Aland, Kurt. *Did the Early Church Baptize Infants?* Trans. G. R. Beasley-Murray. London: SCM Press, 1963.
Aldwinckle, Russell F. "Believer's Baptism and Confirmation." *The Baptist Quarterly* 16 (1955-1956): 123-127.
_____. "The Fellowship of Believers and the Nature of Belief." *Foundations* 23 (1980): 6-21.
_____. "Infant Baptism or Believers' Baptism: A Reply to D. M. Baillie." *Foundations* 2 (1959): 153-160.
_____. *Of Water and the Spirit*. Brantford: Baptist Federation of Canada, 1964.
Appéré, Guy. "Le Baptisme et les Baptistes Devant L'Avenir." *Baptist Review of Theology/La Revue Baptiste de Théologie* 6, no. 1 (Spring 1996): 7-22.
Arndt, William and F. Wilbur Gingrich. *A Greek-English Lexicon of the New Testament and Other Early Christian Literature*. 2nd ed. Chicago: University of Chicago Press, 1979.
Aulen, Gustaf. *The Faith of the Christian Church*. Trans. Eric H. Wahlstrom. Philadelphia: Muhlenberg Press, 1960.
Averbeck, Richard E. "The Focus of Baptism in the New Testament." *Grace Theological Journal* 2 (1981): 265-301.
Baillie, Donald M. *The Theology of the Sacraments and Other Papers*. New York: Charles Scribner's Sons, 1957.
Bancroft, Emery H. *Christian Theology: Systematic and Biblical*. Grand Rapids: Zondervan, 1949.
Barth, Karl. *Church Dogmatics*, Vol. IV/4. Trans. G. W. Bromiley. Edinburgh: T. & T. Clark, 1969.
_____. *The Teaching of the Church Regarding Baptism*. Trans. Ernest A. Payne. London: SCM, 1948.
Barth, Markus. *Die Taufe--ein Sakrament?* Zollikon-Zurich: Evangelischer Verlag, 1951.
_____. "Weakness or Value of the Baptist Position." *Foundations* 1, no. 4 (1958): 62-68.
Basden, Paul A., ed. *Has Our Theology Changed?: Southern Baptist Thought Since 1845*. Nashville: Broadman & Holman, 1994.
Bebbington, David. *Evangelicalism in Modern Britain*. Grand Rapids: Baker Book House, 1992.
Belcastro, Joseph. *The Relationship of Baptism to Church Membership*. St. Louis: Bethany Press, 1963.

Berkhof, Hendrikus. *Christian Faith: An Introduction to the Study of the Faith.* Trans. Sierd Woudstra. Grand Rapids: Eerdmans, 1979.

Berkhof, Louis. *Systematic Theology.* 4th rev. ed. Grand Rapids: Eerdmans, 1949.

Berkouwer, G. C. *The Sacraments.* Trans. Hugo Bekker. Grand Rapids: Eerdmans, 1969.

Best, Ernest. *One Body in Christ: A Study in the Relationship of the Church to Christ in the Epistles of the Apostle Paul.* London: S.P.C.K., 1955.

Bjornard, Reidar B. "Important Works on Baptism from Continental Protestants." *Foundations* 3 (January 1960): 40-45.

Blomberg, Craig L. *Matthew.* Vol. 22, *The New American Commentary.* Nashville: Broadman Press, 1992.

Boice, James Montgomery. *Romans, Vol. 2: The Reign of Grace, Romans 5-8.* Grand Rapids: Baker Books, 1992.

Brackney, William H., ed. *Baptist Life and Thought: 1600-1980.* Valley Forge: Judson Press, 1983.

_____. *The Baptists.* New York: Greenwood Press, 1988.

Bromiley, Geoffrey W. *Children of Promise.* Grand Rapids: Eerdmans, 1979.

_____. *Sacramental Teaching and Practice in the Reformation Churches.* Grand Rapids: Eerdmans, 1957.

Brooks, Oscar R. *The Drama of Decision: Baptism in the New Testament.* Peabody, MA: Hendrickson Publishers, 1987.

Brow, Robert. *"Go Make Learners": A New Model for Discipleship in the Church.* Wheaton: Harold Shaw Publishers, 1981.

Bruce, F. F. *The Book of the Acts.* Revised edition. In *The New International Commentary on the New Testament.* Grand Rapids: Eerdmans, 1988.

Bruner, Frederick Dale. *A Theology of the Holy Spirit.* Grand Rapids: Eerdmans, 1970.

Brunner, Emil. *The Divine-Human Encounter.* Trans. Amandus W. Loos. Philadelphia: Westminster Press, 1943.

Buswell, James Oliver, Jr. *A Systematic Theology of the Christian Religion.* 2 vols. Grand Rapids: Zondervan, 1962-1963.

Calvin, John. *Institutes of the Christian Religion.* 2 vols. Ed. John T. McNeill. Trans. Ford Lewis Battles. Philadelphia: Westminster Press, 1960.

Carpe, William D. "Baptismal Theology in the Disciples of Christ." *Review and Expositor* 77 (1980): 89-100.

Carr, Warren. *Baptism: Conscience and Clue for the Church.* New York: Holt, Rinehart and Winston, 1964.

Carroll. B. H. *An Interpretation of the English Bible: Acts.* Grand Rapids: Baker Book House, 1986 reprint.

Carson, D. A. *Matthew.* In *The Expositor's Bible Commentary*, Vol. 8. Ed. Frank E. Gaebelein. Grand Rapids: Zondervan, 1984.

Catechism of the Catholic Church. New York: Doubleday, 1995.

Church of Scotland. *The Biblical Doctrine of Baptism.* Edinburgh: The Saint Andrew Press, 1958.

Compton, R. Bruce. "Water Baptism and the Forgiveness of Sins in Acts 2:38." *Detroit Baptist Seminary Journal* 4 (Fall 1999): 3-32.

Conner, Walter T. *Christian Doctrine.* Nashville: Broadman Press, 1937.

_____. *The Gospel of Redemption.* Nashville: Broadman Press, 1945.

Cullmann, Oscar. *Baptism in the New Testament.* Trans. J. K. S. Reid. London: SCM Press, 1950.

Cummins, John S. "The Nature and Communication of Grace: The Roman Catholic Perspective." *Foundations* 12, no. 3 (July-September 1969): 223-231.

Davis, J. C. "Another Look at the Relationship Between Baptism and the Forgiveness of Sins in Acts 2:38." *Restoration Quarterly* 24 (1981): 80-88.

Dean, Eric. "Baptism in the Denomination: A Rationale for Infant Baptism." *Encounter* 21, no. 3 (Summer 1960): 279-286.

Deterding, Paul E. "Baptism According to the Apostle Paul." *Concordia Journal* 6 (1980): 93-100.

Deweese, Charles W., ed. *Defining Baptist Convictions: Guidelines for the Twenty-First Century.* Franklin, TN.: Providence House Publishes, 1996.

Dobbie, Robert. "The Validity of Sacramentalism: An Analysis of Recent Claims." *Encounter* 21, no. 3 (Summer 1960): 287-298.

Dix, Dom Gregory. *The Theology of Confirmation in Relation to Baptism.* London: Dacre Press, 1946.

Dockery, David S. "Baptism in the New Testament." *Southwestern Journal of Theology* 43, no. 2 (Spring 2001): 4-16.

_____ and Timothy George, eds. *Baptist Theologians.* Nashville: Broadman Press, 1990.

Duffy, Stephen J. "Southern Baptist and Roman Catholic Soteriologies: A Comparative Study." *Pro Ecclesia* 9, no. 4 (Fall 2000): 434-459.

Dunkerley, Roderic, ed. *The Ministry and the Sacraments.* London: SCM Press, 1937.

Dunn, James D. G. *Baptism in the Holy Spirit.* London: SCM Press, 1970.

_____. "The Birth of a Metaphor: Baptized in Spirit." *The Expository Times* 89 (1977-1978): 134-138, 173-175.

_____. *Romans 1-8.* Vol. 38A, *Word Biblical Commentary.* Dallas: Word Books, 1988.

Eagen, Joseph F. "The Authority and Justification for Infant Baptism." *Review and Expositor* 77 (1980): 47-61.

Edgren, John Alexis. *Fundamentals of Faith.* Trans. J. O. Backlund. Chicago: Baptist Conference Press, 1948.

Eller, Vernard. *In Place of Sacraments: A Study of Baptism and the Lord's Supper.* Grand Rapids: Eerdmans, 1972.

England, Stephen J. *The One Baptism: Baptism and Christian Unity, with Special Reference to Disciples of Christ.* St. Louis: Bethany Press, 1960.

Erickson, Millard J. *Christian Theology.* 3 vols. Grand Rapids: Baker Book House, 1983-1985.

Estep, William R. *The Anabaptist Story.* Revised edition. Grand Rapids: Eerdmans, 1975.

Faith and Order Commission, ed. *Baptism, Eucharist and Ministry.* Geneva: World Council of Churches, 1982.

_____. "Report of the Consultation with Baptists." *Review and Expositor* 77 (1980): 101-108.

Fee, Gordon D. *God's Empowering Presence: The Holy Spirit in the Letters of Paul.* Peabody: Hendrickson Publishers, 1994.

Flemington, W. F. *The New Testament Doctrine of Baptism.* London: S.P.C.K., 1953.

Forsyth, P. T. *The Church and the Sacraments.* London: Longmans, Green and Co., 1917.

France, R. T. *The Gospel According to Matthew: An Introduction and Commentary.* Grand Rapids: Eerdmans, 1985.

Garrett, James Leo. "Baptists concerning Baptism: Review and Preview." *Southwestern Journal of Theology* 43, no. 2 (Spring 2001): 52-67.

_____. *Systematic Theology: Biblical, Historical, & Evangelical.* 2 vols. Grand Rapids: Eerdmans, 1990-1995.

_____. "The Theology and Practice of Baptism: a Southern Baptist View." *Southwestern Journal of Theology* 28, no. 2 (1986): 65-72.
Gill, Athol. *A Bibliography of Baptist Writings on Baptism, 1900-1969*. Rüschlikon-Zurich: Baptist Theological Seminary, 1969.
Green, Michael. *Baptism: Its Purpose, Practice and Power*. London: Hodder & Stoughton, 1987.
Grenz, Stanley J. "Baptism and Church Membership in a Post-denominational Context." *Atlantic Baptist* 167 (March 1993): 17-19.
_____. *Theology for the Community of God*. Nashville: Broadman & Holman, 1994.
Gritz, Paul L. "The Decline and Recovery of Believers' Baptism." *Southwestern Journal of Theology* 43, no. 2 (Spring 2001): 32-51.
Gundry, Robert H. *Matthew: A Commentary on His Literary and Theological Art*. Trand Rapids: Eerdmans, 1982.
Hagner, Donald A. *Matthew 14-28*. Vol. 33B, *Word Biblical Commentary*. Dallas: Word Books, 1995.
Hammond, T. C. *In Understanding Be Men: A Handbook of Christian Doctrine*. 6th ed. Ed. and rev. David F. Wright. Leicester: Inter-Varsity Press, 1968.
Hardon, John A. "Believers' Baptism and the Sacrament of Confirmation." *Foundations* 11, no. 2 (April-June 1968): 127-135.
Hartwell, Herbert. "Karl Barth on Baptism." *Scottish Journal of Theology* 22 (1969): 10-29.
Harvey, Thomas. "Baptism as a Means of Grace: A Response to John Stott's 'The Evangelical Doctrine of Baptism..'" *Churchman* 113, no. 2 (1999): 103-112.
Hastings, C. B. "The Lima Document: A Southern Baptist View." *Ecumenical Trends* 12 (1983): 24-27.
Hendricks, William L. "Baptism: A Baptist Perspective." *Southwestern Journal of Theology* 31, no. 2 (1989): 22-33.
_____. "Baptists and Children: the Beginnings of Grace." *Southwestern Journal of Theology* 28 (1986): 49-53.
Hendriksen, William. *Exposition of the Gospel According to Matthew*. Grand Rapids: Baker Books, 1973.
Hendrix, Scott H. "The Sacraments in Lutheranism." *American Baptist Quarterly* 1 (1982): 179- 187.
Heron, John. "The Theology of Baptism." *Scottish Journal of Theology* 8 (1955): 36-52.
Hine, Leland D. "A Second Look at the Baptist Vision." *American Baptist Quarterly* 4 (1985): 118-130.
Hobbs, Herschel H. *Fundamentals of Our Faith*. Nashville: Broadman Press, 1960.
Hoedemaker, L. A. "Toward a Consensus on Baptism, Eucharist and Ministry." *Review and Expositor* 77 (1980): 7-11.
Hughes, Richard T. "Are Restorationists Evangelicals?" In *The Variety of American Evangelicalism*, ed. Donald W. Dayton and Robert K. Johnston. Downers Grove: Inter-Varsity Press, 1991.
Hughey, J. D., Jr. "Baptism in Baptist Theory and Practice." *Foundations* 3 (1960): 7-14.
_____. "The New Trend in Baptism." *The Baptist Times*, 18 February 1960, 7.
Hull, William E. "Baptism in the New Testament: a Hermeneutical Critique." *Review and Expositor* 65 (1968): 3-12.
Jeremias, Joachim. *The Origins of Infant Baptism*. London: SCM Press, 1963.
Jewett, Paul K. *Infant Baptism and the Covenant of Grace*. Grand Rapids: Eerdmans, 1978.
Johnson, Maxwell E., ed. *Living Water, Sealing Spirit: Readings on Christian Initiation*. Collegeville, Minnesota: The Liturgical Press, 1995.

Kalin, Everett R. "New Birth and Baptism: An Exegetical Study." *Covenant Quarterly* 41 (1983): 11-17.
Kavanagh, Aidan. *The Shape of Baptism: The Rite of Christian Initiation*. New York: Pueblo Publishing Company, 1978.
Kerr, Hugh Thomson. *The Christian Sacraments: A Source Book for Ministers*. Philadelphia: Westminster Press, 1944.
Knudsen, Ralph E. *Christian Beliefs*. Philadelphia: Judson Press, 1947.
Kuhrt, Gordon W. *Believing in Baptism: Christian Baptism--Its Theology and Practice*. London: Mowbray, 1987.
Lampe, G. W. H. *The Seal of the Spirit*. London: Longmans, Green and Co., 1951.
Lawson, John. *Introduction to Christian Doctrine*. Wilmore, KY: Francis Asbury Publishing Company, 1980.
Leenhardt, Franz J. *Le Baptême Chrétien: Son Origine, Sa Signification*. Neuchâtel: Delachaux & Niestle, 1946.
Lenski, R. C. H. *The Interpretation of St. Matthew's Gospel*. Minneapolis: Augsburg Publishing House, 1943.
Lloyd-Jones, D. M. *Romans: The New Man*. Grand Rapids: Zondervan, 1972.
Longenecker, Richard N. *The Acts of the Apostles*. In *The Expositor's Bible Commentary*, Vol. 9. Ed. Frank E. Gaebelein. Grand Rapids: Zondervan, 1981.
Lorenzen, Thorwald. "Baptism and Church Membership: Some Baptist Positions and Their Ecumenical Implications." *Journal of Ecumenical Studies* 18 (1981): 561-574.
_____. "Baptists and Ecumenicity with Special Reference to Baptism." *Review and Expositor* 77 (1980): 21-45.
Lotz, Denton. "Baptist Identity in Mission and Evangelism." *Foundations* 21 (1978): 32-49.
MacNeil, Genna R. *A Study Guide for Baptism, Eucharist and Ministry*. Valley Forge, PA: Judson Press, 1986.
Macquarrie, John. *Principles of Christian Theology*. 2nd ed. New York: Charles Scribner's Sons, 1977.
Manson, T. W. "Baptism in the Church." *Scottish Journal of Theology* 2 (1949-1950): 391-403.
Mantey, J. R. "The Causal Use of *eis* in the New Testament." *Journal of Biblical Literature* 70 (1951): 45-48.
Marcel, Pierre Ch. *The Biblical Doctrine of Infant Baptism*. Trans. Philip Edgcumbe Hughes. London: James Clarke & Co., 1953.
Maring, Norman H. "Is Baptism a Sacrament?" *Foundations* 3, no. 1 (1960): 74-83.
Marsh, H. G. *The Origin and Significance of the New Testament Baptism*. Manchester: Manchester University Press, 1941.
Masters, Victor I., ed. *Re-Thinking Baptist Doctrines*. Louisville: The Western Recorder, n.d.
McCall, Duke K., ed. "Consultation on Believers' Baptism." *Review and Expositor* 77 (1980): 3-108.
McClendon, James W. "Baptism as a Performative Sign." *Theology Today* 23 (1966-1967): 403-416.
_____. *Systematic Theology*. Vol. 1, *Ethics*. Nashville: Abingdon Press, 1986.
_____. *Systematic Theology*. Vol. 2, *Doctrine*. Nashville: Abingdon Press, 1994.
McIntyre, Luther B., Jr. "Baptism and Forgiveness in Acts 2:38." *Bibliotheca Sacra* 153 (January-March 1996): 53-62.
Middleton, Robert G. "Believers' Baptism and the Sacrament of Confirmation." *Foundations* 11, no. 2 (April-June 1968): 136-147.

Moda, Aldo. "Le Bapteme Chretien: Sacrement ou Action Humaine?" *Revue d'Histoire et de Philosophies Religieuses* 54 (1974): 219-247.
Moody, Dale. *Baptism: Foundation for Christian Unity.* Philadelphia: Westminster Press, 1967.
_____. "Baptism in Recent Research." *Review and Expositor* 65 (1968): 13-22.
_____. *The Word of Truth: A Summary of Biblical Doctrine Based on Biblical Revelation.* Grand Rapids: Eerdmans, 1981.
Morrison, Charles Clayton. *The Meaning of Baptism.* Chicago: Disciples Publication Society, 1914.
Mueller, John Theodore. *Christian Dogmatics: A Handbook of Doctrinal Theology for Pastors, Teachers, and Laymen.* St. Louis: Concordia Publishing House, 1934.
Mullins, Edgar Young. *The Christian Religion in Its Doctrinal Expression.* Philadelphia: Judson Press, 1917.
Murphy Center for Liturgical Research. *Made, Not Born: New Perspectives on Christian Initiation and the Catechumenate.* Notre Dame: University of Notre Dame Press, 1976.
Murray, John. *Christian Baptism.* Philadelphia: Committee on Christian Education, Orthodox Presbyterian Church, 1952.
Neighbour, R. E. "The Moral Significance of Baptism." *Review and Expositor* 8 (1911): 420-430.
Nelson, J. Robert. *The Realm of Redemption.* 2nd ed. London: Epworth Press, 1953.
Neunheuser, Burkhard. *Baptism and Confirmation.* Trans. John Jay Hughes. London: Burns & Oates, 1964.
Newport, John P. "The Theology and Experience of Salvation." *The Greek Orthodox Theological Review* 22 (1977): 393-404.
Ott, Ludwig. *Fundamentals of Catholic Dogma.* 2nd ed. Trans. Patrick Lynch. Ed. James Bastible. Cork: Mercier Press, 1957.
Paul, Robert S. *The Atonement and the Sacraments: The Relation of the Atonement to the Sacraments of Baptism and the Lord's Supper.* New York: Abingdon, 1960.
Pieper, Francis. *Christian Dogmatics.* Vol. 3. St. Louis: Concordia Publishing House, 1953.
Pinnock, Clark H. *Flame of Love: A Theology of the Holy Spirit.* Downers Grove: InterVarsity Press, 1996.
Pohle, Joseph. *The Sacraments: A Dogmatic Treatise.* Vol. 1. Trans. Arthur Preuss. St. Louis: B. Herder, 1915.
Polhill, John B. *Acts.* Vol. 26, *The New American Commentary.* Nashville: Broadman Press, 1992.
Poole-Connor, E. J. *Evangelicalism in England.* London: The Fellowship of Independent Evangelical Churches, 1951.
Porter, Stanley E. *The Paul of Acts.* Tübingen: Mohr Siebeck, 1999.
_____ and Anthony R. Cross, eds. *Baptism, the New Testament and the Church: Historical and Contemporary Studies in Honour of R. E. O. White.* Sheffield: Sheffield Academic Press, 1999.
Prenter, Regin. *Creation and Redemption.* Trans. Theodor I. Jensen. Philadelphia: Fortress Press, 1967.
Quick, Oliver Chase. *The Christian Sacraments.* London: Nisbet & Co., 1932.
Reid, J. K. S. "Theological Issues Involved in Baptism." *Expository Times* 61 (1949-1950): 201-204.
Richardson, Alan. *An Introduction to the Theology of the New Testament.* New York: Harper & Row, 1958.
Roark, Dallas M. *The Christian Faith.* Nashville: Broadman Press, 1969.

Robertson, Archibald Thomas. *A Grammar of the Greek New Testament in the Light of Historical Research*. Nashville: Broadman Press, 1934.

_____. *Word Pictures in the New Testament*. 6 vols. Nashville: Broadman Press, 1930-1933.

Robinson, William. *The Biblical Doctrine of the Church*. Revised edition. St. Louis: Bethany Press, 1955.

_____. *The Shattered Cross: The Many Churches and the One Church*. Birmingham: Berean Press, 1955.

_____. *What Churches of Christ Stand For*. Birmingham: Berean Press, 1959.

Rogers, E. R. "Yet Once More--'One Baptism'." *The Reformed Theological Review* 50 (1991): 41-49.

Russell, Horace O. "The Relationship Between the Faith of the Individual and the Faith of the Community in Baptism, the Blessing of Children and Confirmation: A Baptist Perspective." *Review and Expositor* 77 (1980): 83-87.

Saucy, Robert L. *The Church in God's Program*. Chicago: Moody Press, 1972.

Schillebeeckx, Edward. *Christ the Sacrament of the Encounter with God*. Trans. Paul Barrett, Mark Schoof and Laurence Bright. New York: Sheed and Ward, 1963.

Schlink, Edmund. *The Doctrine of Baptism*. Trans. Herbert J. A. Bouman. St. Louis: Concordia Publishing House, 1972.

Schnackenburg, Rudolf. *Baptism in the Thought of St. Paul*. Trans. G. R. Beasley-Murray. New York: Herder & Herder, 1964.

Schneider, Johannes. *Baptism and Church in the New Testament*. Trans. Ernest A. Payne. London: Carey Kingsgate Press, 1957.

_____. *Die Taufe im Neuen Testament*. Stuttgart: W. Kohlhammen, 1952.

Schwarz, Hans. *Divine Communication: Word and Sacrament in Biblical, Historical, and Contemporary Perspective*. Philadelphia: Fortress Press, 1985.

Skoglund, J. E. "Recent Trends in Baptist Thinking about Baptism." *Foundations* 7 (1964): 209-216.

Smith, B. F. *Christian Baptism*. Nashville: Broadman Press, 1970.

Stafford, Thomas Polhill. *A Study of Christian Doctrines*. Kansas City: Western Baptist Publishing Company, 1936.

Stein, Robert H. "Baptism and Becoming a Christian in the New Testament." *Southern Baptist Journal of Theology* 2, no. 1 (Spring 1998): 6-17.

Stookey, Laurence Hull. *Baptism: Christ's Act in the Church*. Nashville: Abingdon, 1982.

_____. "Personal and Community Faith In Relation to Baptism and Other Rites of Christian Initiation." *Review and Expositor* 77 (1980): 71-81.

Stott, John. "The Evangelical Doctrine of Baptism." *Churchman* 112, no. 1 (1998): 47-59.

Strege, Merle D., ed. *Baptism & Church: A Believers' Church Vision*. Grand Rapids: Sagamore Books, 1986.

Synge, F. C. "The Holy Spirit and the Sacraments." *Scottish Journal of Theology* 6 (1953): 65-76.

Thiessen, Henry Clarence. *Introductory Lectures in Systematic Theology*. Grand Rapids: Eerdmans, 1949.

Thurian, Max, ed. *Churches Respond to BEM: Official responses to the "Baptism, Eucharist and Ministry" text*. Vols. I-IV. Geneva: World Council of Churches, 1986-1987.

_____. and Geoffrey Wainwright, eds. *Baptism and Eucharist: Ecumenical Convergence in Celebration*. Geneva: World Council of Churches, 1983.

Tidwell, Josiah Blake. *Christian Teachings*. Grand Rapids: Eerdmans, 1942.

Torbet, Robert G. "The Nature and Communication of Grace: The Baptist Perspective." *Foundations* 12, no. 3 (July-September 1969): 213-222.

Torrance, T. F. *Conflict and Agreement in the Church*. Vol. 2, *The Ministry and the Sacraments of the Gospel*. London: Lutterworth Press, 1960.
_____. *God and Rationality*. London: Oxford University Press, 1971.
_____. *The Mediation of Christ*. Exeter: The Paternoster Press, 1983.
_____. "The One Baptism Common to Christ and His Church." In *Theology in Reconciliation*. London: Geoffrey Chapman, 1975.
_____. *Theology in Reconstruction*. Grand Rapids: Eerdmans, 1965.
Tull, James E. "The Ordinances/Sacraments in Baptist Thought." *American Baptist Quarterly* 1 (1982): 187-196.
Turner, Nigel and James Hope Moulton. *A Grammar of New Testament Greek*. Vol. 3. Edinburgh: T. & T. Clark, 1963.
Vanhetloo, Warren. "Ordinance, not Sacrament." *Calvary Baptist Theological Journal* 1 (Fall 1985): 16-25.
Vogel, Heinrich. "The First Sacrament: Baptism." Trans. G. W. Bromiley. *Scottish Journal of Theology* 7 (1954): 41-58.
Wainwright, Geoffrey. *Christian Initiation*. London: Lutterworth Press, 1969.
_____. "Developpements Baptismaux depuis 1967." *Etudes Theologiques et Religieuses* 49 (1974): 67-93.
_____. *Doxology: The Praise of God in Worship, Doctrine, and Life*. New York: Oxford University Press, 1980.
Wallace, Ronald S. *Calvin's Doctrine of the Word and Sacrament*. Grand Rapids: Eerdmans, 1957.
Walvoord, John F. and Roy B. Zuck, eds. *The Bible Knowledge Commentary: New Testament*. Wheaton: Victor Books, 1983.
Ward, Wayne E. "Baptism in Theological Perspective." *Review and Expositor* 65 (1968): 43-52.
Warns, Johannes. *Baptism: Studies in the Original Christian Baptism*. Trans. G. H. Lang. Grand Rapids: Kregel Publications, 1957.
Watts, Ronald F. *The Ordinances and Ministry of the Church: A Baptist View*. Toronto: Canadian Baptist Federation, 1986.
Weber, Otto. *Foundations of Dogmatics*. Vol. 2. Trans. Darrell L. Guder. Grand Rapids: Eerdmans, 1983.
Whale, John Seldon. *Christian Doctrine*. Cambridge: University Press, 1941.
Wilburn, Ralph G. "A Theology of the Sacraments: The Nature of the Church and Our Salvation." *Encounter* 24, no. 3 (Summer 1963): 280-302.

Historical Background

Armour, Rollin Stely. *Anabaptist Baptism: A Representative Study*. Scottdale, PA: Herald Press, 1966.
Ball, G. H. *Christian Baptism: The Duty, the Act, and the Subjects*. Dover: Freewill Baptist Printing Establishment, 1860.
The Baptist Catechism: Commonly Called Keach's Catechism. Philadelphia: American Baptist Publication Society, 1851.
Beddome, Benjamin. *Baptism: Extract from a Scriptural Exposition of the Baptist Catechism; by way of Question and Answer*. London: Whittingham and Rowland, 1813.

Booth, Abraham. *Paedobaptism Examined*. In *The Baptist Library*. Ed. Charles G. Sommers, William R. Williams, and Levi. L. Hill. 3 vols. New York: Lewis Colby & Co., 1846.

──────────. *A Vindication of the Baptists from the Charge of Bigotry, in Refusing Communion at the Lord's Table to Paedobaptists*. In *The Baptist Library*. Ed. Charles G. Sommers, William R. Williams, and Levi L. Hill. 3 vols. New York: Lewis Colby & Co., 1846.

Breakenridge, Melvin. "The Scottish Connection: John Glas, 1695-1773." In *The Campbell-Stone Movement in Ontario*, ed. Claude E. Cox, 43-59. Lewiston: Edwin Mellon Press, 1995.

Briggs, J. H. Y. *The English Baptists of the Nineteenth Century*. London: The Baptist Historical Society, 1994.

Brine, John. *The Baptists Vindicated from Some Groundless Charges Brought against Them by Mr. Eltringham*. London: John Ward, 1756.

Brown, J. Newton. *The Baptist Church Manual*. Philadelphia: B. R. Loxley, 1853.

Brown, Raymond. *The English Baptists of the Eighteenth Century*. London: The Baptist Historical Society, 1986.

Campbell, Alexander. *Christian Baptism*. Bethany, VA.: by author, 1853.

Carroll, B. H. *Baptists and Their Doctrines*. Nashville: Broadman Press, 1913.

Cathcart, William, ed. *The Baptist Encyclopedia*. Philadelphia: Everts, 1881.

Clarke, William Newton. *An Outline of Christian Theology*. 4th ed. New York: Charles Scribners, 1899.

Coggins, James Robert. *John Smyth's Congregation: English Separatism, Mennonite Influence, and the Elect Nation*. Waterloo: Herald Press, 1991.

Coxe, Benjamin, Hanserd Knollys, and William Kiffin. *A Declaration Concerning the Publike Dispute*. London: 1645.

Cramp, J. M. *A Catechism on Baptism*. Philadelphia: American Baptist Publication Society, 1865.

Danvers, Henry. *A Treatise of Baptism*. London: 1674.

Dargan, Edward Charles. *The Doctrines of Our Faith*. Rev. ed. Nashville: Sunday School Board of the Southern Baptist Convention, 1920.

Davies, Horton. *Worship and Theology in England*. Vol. I, *From Cranmer to Hooker, 1534-1603*. Princeton: Princeton University Press, 1970.

──────────. *Worship and Theology in England*. Vol. II, *From Andrewes to Baxter and Fox, 1603-1690*. Princeton: Princeton University Press, 1975.

Davye, Thomas. *The Baptism of Adult Believers Only, Asserted and Vindicated; and that of Infants Disproved*. London: John Darby, 1719.

Duncan, George. *Baptism and the Baptists*. London: Baptist Tract and Book Society, 1882.

Dutton, Anne. *Brief Hints Concerning Baptism: of the Subject, Mode, and End of this Solemn Ordinance*. London: J. Hart, 1746.

Eltringham, William. *The Baptist Against the Baptist: or a Display of Antipaedo-baptist Self-Inconsistency*. London: J. Waugh and W. Penner, 1755.

Finney, Charles Grandison. *Lectures on Revivals of Religion*. Ed. William G. McLoughlin. Cambridge, MA: Harvard University Press, 1960.

Fuller, Andrew. *The Complete Works of the Rev. Andrew Fuller: with a Memoir of His Life, by Andrew Gunton Fuller*. 3rd ed. 3 vols. Philadelphia: American Baptist Publication Society, 1845.

Gale, John. *Reflections on Mr. Wall's History of Infant-Baptism*. London: John Offor, 1820. Orig. published 1711.

Garner, Robert. *A Treatise of Baptism*. London: no publisher, 1645.
Gates, Errett. *The Early Relation and Separation of Baptists and Disciples*. Chicago: The Christian Century Company, 1904.
Gill, John. *Baptism a Divine Commandment to be Observed*. London: G. Keith, 1765.
_____. *A Body of Doctrinal and Practical Divinity*. Paris, Arkansas: The Baptist Standard Bearer, 1989. Orig. published 1769-1770.
_____. *The Divine Right of Infant Baptism Examined and Disproved*. London: J. Ward, 1749.
_____. *An Essay on Scripture baptism: in Which It Is Shewn That Infant Baptism Is Destitute of Proof Either from The Holy Scriptures or from Ancient Ecclesiastical Writers*. London: J. Barfield, 1815.
_____. *An Exposition of the New Testament*. 3 vols. Philadelphia: William W. Woodward, 1811.
_____. *Infant-baptism, a Part and Pillar of Popery*. London: G. Keith, 1766.
Grafton, Thomas W. *Alexander Campbell*. St. Louis: Christian Board of Education, n.d.
Grantham, Thomas. *Christianismus Primitivus*. London: Francis Smith, 1678.
_____. *A Sigh for Peace: or The Cause of Division Discovered* (London: printed for the author, 1671).
Graves, James Robinson. *The Act of Christian Baptism*. Texarkana: Baptist Sunday School Committee, 1881.
_____. *The Relation of Baptism to Salvation*. Texarkana: Baptist Sunday School Committee, 1881.
Haley, J. J. *Debates That Made History*. St. Louis: Christian Board of Education, 1920.
Hall, Robert. *On Terms of Communion, with a Particular View to the Case of the Baptists and Paedobaptists*. In *The Works of Robert Hall, A.M.*, ed. Olinthus Gregory. 4 vols. London: Henry G. Bohn, 1843.
Hayden, Roger. *English Baptist History and Heritage*. London: The Baptist Union of Great Britain, 1990.
Haykin, Michael A. G. *Kiffin, Knollys, and Keach*. Leeds: Reformation Today Trust, 1996.
_____, ed. *The Life and Thought of John Gill (1697-1771): A Tercentennial Appreciation*. Leiden: Brill, 1997.
Hicks, L. Edward. "Rational Religion in the Ohio Western Reserve (1827-1830): Walter Scott and the Restoration Appeal of Baptism for the Remission of Sins." *Restoration Quarterly* 34 (1992): 207-219.
Hinton, John Howard. *The Theological Works of the Rev. John Howard Hinton, M.A.* London: Houlston & Wright, 1865.
Holifield, E. Brooks. *The Covenant Sealed: The Development of Puritan Sacramental Theology in Old and New England, 1570-1720*. New Haven: Yale University Press, 1974.
Hudson, Winthrop S., ed. *Baptist Concepts of the Church*. Valley Forge: Judson Press, 1959.
Hulse, Erroll. *An Introduction to the Baptists*. 2nd ed. Haywards Heath, Sussex: Carey Publications, 1976.
Humbert, Royal, ed. *A Compend of Alexander Campbell's Theology*. St. Louis: Bethany Press, 1961.
"An Index to Notable Baptists, Whose Careers began within the British Empire before 1850." *Transactions of the Baptist Historical Society* 7 (1920-1921): 182-239.
Ingham, R. *A Hand-Book on Christian Baptism*. Vol. 2, *Christian Baptism: Its Subjects*. London: E. Stock, 1871.

Jeter, Jeremiah B. *Campbellism Examined.* New York: Sheldon, Lamport, & Blakeman, 1855.
Keach, Benjamin. *The Ax Laid to the Root.* London: by the author, 1693.
_____. *Gold Refin'd; or Baptism in its Primitive Purity.* London: Nathaniel Crouch, 1689.
Kiffin, William. *Remarkable Passages in the Life of William Kiffin.* Ed. William Orme. London: Burton & Smith, 1823.
Kinghorn, Joseph. *A Brief Statement of the Sentiments of the Baptists on the Ordinance of Baptism.* Norwich: S. Wilkin, 1824.
Lawrence, Henry. *Of Baptisme.* London: F. Macock, 1659.
Leith, John H., ed. *The Creeds of the Churches.* 3rd ed. Atlanta: John Knox Press, 1982.
Lumpkin, William L. *Baptist Confessions of Faith.* Philadelphia: Judson Press, 1959.
McBeth, H. Leon. *The Baptist Heritage.* Nashville: Broadman Press, 1987.
McClendon, H. R. *The Bible on Baptism.* Louisville: Baptist Book Concern, 1896.
McGlothlin, W. J. *Baptist Confessions of Faith.* Philadelphia: American Baptist Publication Society, 1911.
Moore, Walter Levon. "Baptist Teachings and Practices on Baptism in England, 1600-1689." Unpublished Th.D. thesis, Southern Baptist Seminary, 1950.
Murray, Iain. *The Forgotten Spurgeon.* London: The Banner of Truth Trust, 1966.
Nettles, Thomas J. *By His Grace and for His Glory.* Grand Rapids: Baker Book House, 1986.
Newman, A. H. *A History of Anti-paedobaptism.* Philadelphia: American Baptist Publication Society, 1896.
Noel, Baptist W. *Essay on Christian Baptism.* New York: Harper & Brothers, 1850.
_____. *Sermons on Regeneration, with Especial Reference to the Doctrine of Baptismal Regeneration.* 2nd ed. London: "The Pulpit" Office, n.d.
Novak, Michael James. "Thy Will Be Done: The Theology of the English Particular Baptists, 1638-1660." Ph.D. thesis, Harvard University, 1979.
Old, Hughes Oliphant. *The Shaping of the Reformed Baptismal Rite in the Sixteenth Century.* Grand Rapids: Eerdmans, 1992.
Patterson, W. Morgan. "The Role of Baptism in Baptist History." *Review and Expositor* 65 (1968): 33-41.
Pengilly, Richard. *The Scripture Guide to Baptism.* In *The Baptist Library.* Ed. Charles G. Sommers, William R. Williams, and Levi L. Hill. 3 vols. New York: Lewis Colby & Co., 1846.
Perkin, J. R. C. "Baptism in Nonconformist Theology, 1820-1920, with special reference to the Baptists." D.Phil. thesis, University of Oxford, 1955.
Powell, Vavasor. *The Life and Death of Mr. Vavasor Powell.* No publisher, 1671.
Rainbow, Jonathan H. "Confessor Baptism: The Baptismal Doctrine of the Early Anabaptists." *American Baptist Quarterly* 8 (1989): 276-290.
Roberts-Thomson, E. *Baptists and Disciples of Christ.* London: Carey Kingsgate Press, 1948.
Robinson, Robert. *The History of Baptism.* London, 1790. Reprinted with introduction and notes by J. R. Graves. Nashville: Southwestern Baptist Publishing House, 1860.
Ross, J. M. "The Theology of Baptism in Baptist History." *The Baptist Quarterly* 15 (1953-1954): 100-112.
Ryland, John. *A Candid Statement of the Reasons Which Induce the Baptists to Differ in Opinion and Practice from So Many of Their Christian Brethren.* London: W. Button, 1814.

Smyth, John. *The Works of John Smyth*. 2 vols. Ed. W. T. Whitely. Cambridge: University Press, 1915.
Sommers, Charles G, William R. Williams, and Levi L. Hill, eds. *The Baptist Library: A Republication of Standard Baptist Works*. 3 vols. New York: Lewis Colby & Co., 1846.
Spilsbury, John S. *A Treatise Concerning the Lawfull Subject of Baptisme*. London: n.p., 1643.
Spurgeon, Charles Haddon. "Baptismal Regeneration." Sermon preached June 5, 1864. *Metropolitan Tabernacle Pulpit*, Vol. X (1864). Pasadena, Texas: Pilgrim Publications, 1981.
Starr, Edward C. *A Baptist Bibliography*. 25 vols. Rochester: American Baptist Historical Society, 1947-1976.
Stennett, Joseph. *The Works of the Reverend and Learned Mr. Joseph Stennett*. Vol. IV. London: n.p., 1732.
Stovel, C. *The Baptismal Regeneration Controversy Considered*. London: Houlston & Stoneman, and Dyer & Co., 1843.
Strong, Augustus Hopkins. *Systematic Theology*. Valley Forge: Judson Press, 1967. Orig. published 1907.
Taylor, Dan. *The Christian Religion: An Exposition of Its Leading Principles, Practical Requirements, and Experimental Enjoyments*. London: J. Smith, 1844.
Thompson, Philip E. "A New Question in Baptist History: Seeking A Catholic Spirit Among Early Baptists." *Pro Ecclesia* 8, no. 1 (Winter 1999): 51-72.
_____. "People of the Free God: The Passion of Seventeenth-Century Baptists." *American Baptist Quarterly* 15, no. 3 (September 1996): 223-241.
_____. "Practicing the Freedom of God: Formation in Early Baptist Life." In *Theology and Lived Christianity*, ed. David M. Hammond. Mystic, CT: Twenty-Third Publications, 2000.
Torbet, Robert. *A History of the Baptists*. Rev. ed. Valley Forge: Judson Press, 1965.
Wallace, Ronald S. *Calvin's Doctrine of the Word and Sacrament*. Grand Rapids: Eerdmans, 1957.
Wayland, Francis. *Notes on the Principles and Practices of Baptist Churches*. New York: Sheldon, Blakeman & Co., 1857.
Westlake, Thomas. *A General View of Baptism*. In *The Baptist Library*. Ed. Charles G. Sommers, William R. Williams, and Levi L. Hill. 3 vols. New York: Lewis Colby & Co., 1846.
White, Barrington R. *The English Baptists of the Seventeenth Century*. London: The Baptist Historical Society, 1983.
_____. *The English Separatist Tradition*. London: Oxford University, 1971.
_____. "Frontiers of Fellowship between English Baptists, 1609-1660." *Foundations* 11, no. 3 (July-September 1968): 244-256.
Whitley, W. T. *Church, Ministry, and Sacraments in the New Testament*. London: The Kingsgate Press, 1903.
_____. *A History of British Baptists*. 2nd ed. London: Kingsgate Press, 1932.
_____. *The Witness of History to Baptist Principles*. 1897.
_____, ed.. *The Works of John Smyth*. 2 vols. Cambridge: Cambridge University Press, 1915.
Whittle, Robert. *An Answer to Mr. Francis Cornwell's Positions and Inferences*. Appended portions of Francis Cornwell, *The New Testament Ratified with the Blood of the Lord Jesus*. London: W. H., 1646.

Wilson, Samuel. *A Scripture Manual; or a Plain Representation of the Ordinance of Baptism*. In *The Baptist Library*. Ed. Charles G. Sommers, William R. Williams, and Levi L. Hill. 3 vols. New York: Lewis Colby & Co., 1846.

Wright, David F. "One Baptism or Two? Reflections on the History of Christian Baptism." *Vox Evangelica* 18 (1988): 7-23.

Book Reviews

Aldwinckle, R. F. Review of *The Biblical Doctrine of Initiation*, by R. E. O. White. In *Foundations* 4 (October 1961): 372-374.

Allison, Leon McDill. Review of *The Biblical Doctrine of Initiation*, by R. E. O. White. In *Interpretation* 15 (January 1961): 100-102.

Bailey, John W. Review of *An Approach to the Theology of the Sacraments*, by Neville Clark. In *Journal of Bible and Religion* 25 (April 1957): 168.

Barth, Markus. Review of *An Approach to the Theology of the Sacraments*, by Neville Clark. In *Journal of Religion* 37 (1957): 223-225.

Beasley-Murray, George R. Review of *The Biblical Doctrine of Initiation*, by R. E. O. White. In *The Expository Times* 72 (November 1960): 44.

Cerny, E. A. Review of *An Approach to the Theology of the Sacraments*, by Neville Clark. In *Catholic Biblical Quarterly* 19 (January 1957): 160.

Crabtree, A. B. Review of *Baptism and Christian Unity*, by Alec Gilmore. In *Foundations* 10 (April-June 1967): 179-181.

Davies, J. G. Review of *Baptism in the New Testament*, by G. R. Beasley-Murray. In *Journal of Theological Studies* n.s. 14 (October 1963): 478-479.

Dillistone, F. W. Review of *An Approach to the Theology of the Sacraments*, by Neville Clark. In *Journal of Theological Studies* n.s. 8 (April 1957): 216.

England, Stephen J. Review of *The Biblical Doctrine of Initiation*, by R. E. O. White. In *Encounter* 22 (Autumn 1961): 482-483.

Every, George. Review of *Baptism in the New Testament*, by G. R. Beasley-Murray. In *The Baptist Quarterly* 20 (January 1963): 42-43.

Filson, Floyd V. Review of *The Biblical Doctrine of Initiation*, by R. E. O. White. In *Journal of Biblical Literature* 79 (1960): 388-389.

George, A. Raymond. Review of *Baptism in the New Testament*, by G. R. Beasley-Murray. In *The Expository Times* 74 (January 1963): 106.

Green, H. Review of *An Approach to the Theology of the Sacraments*, by Neville Clark. In *Church Quarterly Review* 157 (October-December 1956): 490-491.

Heron, John. Review of *Christian Baptism*, ed. Alec Gilmore. In *Scottish Journal of Theology* 13 (1960): 102-104.

Higgins, A. J. B. Review of *An Approach to the Theology of the Sacraments*, by Neville Clark. In *Scottish Journal of Theology* 10 (June 1957): 209-211.

Hoekema, Anthony A. Review of *Baptism and Christian Unity*, by Alec Gilmore. In *Calvin Theological Journal* 2 (April 1967): 74-77.

Hull, William E. Review of *The Biblical Doctrine of Initiation*, by R. E. O. White. In *Review and Expositor* 59 (July 1962): 402-403.

Maring, Norman H. Review of *Christian Baptism*, ed. Alec Gilmore. In *Foundations* 3 (January 1960): 90-92.

Marsh, H. G. Review of *Baptism and Christian Unity*, by Alec Gilmore. In *London Quarterly and Holborn Review* 192 (January 1967): 78.

Moody, Dale. Review of *Baptism and Christian Unity*, by Alec Gilmore. In *Review and Expositor* 64 (Spring 1967): 248-249.

_____. Review of *Baptism in the New Testament*, by G. R. Beasley-Murray. In *Review and Expositor* 60 (Spring 1963): 232-234.

Morrison, Clinton. Review of *Baptism in the New Testament*, by G. R. Beasley-Murray. In *Journal of Biblical Literature* 82 (1963): 339-341.

Osterhaven, Eugene. Review of *The Biblical Doctrine of Initiation*, by R. E. O. White. In *Christianity Today* 5 (December 5, 1960): 213-214.

Reid, J. K. S. Review of *The Biblical Doctrine of Initiation*, by R. E. O. White. In *The Baptist Quarterly* 19 (January 1961): 45-47.

Rowley, H. H. Review of *Christian Baptism*, ed. Alec Gilmore. In *The Expository Times* 70 (July 1959): 301-302.

Scaer, David P. Review of *Baptism and Christian Unity*, by Alec Gilmore. In *The Springfielder* 31 (Spring 1967): 75-76.

Schnackenburg, Rudolf. Review of *Baptism in the New Testament*, by G. R. Beasley-Murray. In *Biblische Zeitschrift* n.s. 7 (1963): 305-308.

Story, Cullen I. K. Review of *Baptism in the New Testament*, by G. R. Beasley-Murray. In *Christianity Today* 7 (February 1, 1963): 447-448.

Stuermann, Walter E. Review of *An Approach to the Theology of the Sacraments*, by Neville Clark. In *Interpretation* 11 (April 1957): 238-239.

Titus, Eric L. Review of *Baptism in the New Testament*, by G. R. Beasley-Murray. In *Foundations* 6 (July 1963): 280-281.

Van Roo, W. A. Review of *The Biblical Doctrine of Initiation*, by R. E. O. White. In *Gregorianum* 42 (1961): 150.

_____. Review of *Baptism in the New Testament*, by G. R. Beasley-Murray. In *Gregorianum* 44 (1963): 134.

Wahlstrom, Eric H. Review of *An Approach to the Theology of the Sacraments*, by Neville Clark. In *Lutheran Quarterly* 9 (August 1957): 279-280.

Ward, Marcus. Review of *An Approach to the Theology of the Sacraments*, by Neville Clark. In *The Expository Times* 67 (September 1956): 361-362.

Wilder, Amos N. Review of *An Approach to the Theology of the Sacraments*, by Neville Clark. In *Journal of Biblical Literature* 77 (March 1958): 87-88.

INDEX

Adoption 210
Aland, Kurt 217
Anabaptists 120, 148, 156, 179, 228
Apollinarianism 198
Apostolic succession 221
Argyle, A. W. 120
Arminianism 11, 84, 137
Assensus 201, 237, 240, 243
Aubrey, M. E. 152
Augsburg Confession 11
Aulen, Gustaf 238

Baptism of Jesus 95, 114-115, 135-136, 157-158, 212, 219
Baptism of John 60, 63, 119, 157
Baptismal Commission 158-159
Baptist Catechism 5, 18, 87
Baptist Theological Seminary (Switzerland) 139
Baptist Union of Great Britain 7, 65, 105, 113, 145, 149, 150-152
Barrett, C. K. 138, 198
Barth, Karl 107, 157, 178-195, 212, 249
Barth, Markus 1, 116, 179
Beasley-Murray, G. R. 2, 4, 7, 111, 117-119, 124, 127, 129-132, 133, 139-145, 147, 148, 154, 156, 174-178, 182, 185, 188, 197, 219, 223, 227, 234, 236, 249, 250
Berkouwer, G. C. 208-209, 217
Book of Common Prayer 66, 80, 83
Booth, Abraham 42-46
Brackney, William 1
Briggs, J. H. Y. 58
Brine, John 42
Bristol Baptist College 51
British Council of Churches 233
Brunner, Emil 137, 249
Bunyan, John 226
Buse, S. I. 115-117

Calvin, John 85, 127
Calvinism (Reformed theology) 11, 17, 18, 19, 33, 36, 41, 42, 48, 52, 79, 137, 179, 208, 238-240, 246, 248
Campbell, Alexander 37, 240, 243, 245
Campbell, Thomas 241

Carey, William 48
Carson, Alexander 64-65
Catechism of the Catholic Church 210
Causa salutis 211
Charnock, Stephen 29
Child, R. L. 124, 245
Christ-event 121-123, 135, 187, 207, 208
Church membership 17, 21, 27-28, 36, 57, 90, 103-105, 152, 196, 200, 224-232, 249
Church of England 10, 58, 76, 79, 80-81, 105, 207
Church of Scotland 133
Churches of Christ/Disciples of Christ 128, 240-246
Circumcision 114
Circumcision of Christ 188-189
Clark, Neville 3, 107-113, 121-124, 125, 132, 143, 144, 145, 148, 154, 197, 202, 215, 223
Clarke, Paul 4
Close communion 42, 45-46, 57, 59
Cognitio salutis 178-179, 211
Collins, William 18
Confirmation 216, 221-222
Conner, W. T. 204, 205
Cook, Henry 105-107, 145, 149
Corporate personality 148
Council of Trent 44, 66
Creation 8, 196-199
Covenant of grace 31, 212-213, 217-219, 239
Crosley, David 30
Cross, Anthony 6, 113
Cross as vicarious baptism 206, 212, 216
Cullmann, Oscar 116, 211-212, 215

Dakin, Arthur 102
De Ries, Hans 12
Discipleship 165-166
Dodd, C. H. 120
Dualism 94
Dunn, James D. G. 171, 173
Dutton, Anne 46-48, 53, 55

Ecumenism 4, 7, 8, 105, 128, 154, 242, 248
Ellis, Christopher 8
Eltringham, William 41-42
Evangelical Revival 88
Ex opere operato 66, 99-100, 125, 136, 179, 236
Experience of salvation 3, 5, 6, 19, 21, 24, 27, 28, 32, 36, 47, 52, 65, 70, 72, 73-75, 82-83, 86,87, 92, 93, 99, 114, 138, 139, 154, 243, 244, 245, 251

Faith and baptism 2, 13, 23, 27, 29, 32, 35-36, 41, 49, 52, 62, 64, 76, 80, 81-82, 87, 117-118, 120, 124, 132, 138, 147, 164, 185-186, 191, 196, 199-209, 211-219, 223, 236, 237-238, 243-244, 245, 246, 248
Faith and Order 98, 139, 233
Federal Theology 207
Fiddes, Paul 8
Fiducia 201, 236, 237, 243, 246
Finney, Charles, 251
First London Confession 14, 230
Flemington, W. F. 213-214
Footwashing 6
Forgiveness of sins 6, 10, 12, 16, 19, 23, 24, 25, 27-28, 29, 34, 37, 41, 42, 49-50, 52, 78, 95, 126, 130, 157, 166-170, 181, 200, 210, 217, 218, 221, 239, 242, 245
Free Church Federal Council 150
Friends 231, 233
Fuller, Andrew 48-50

Garner, Robert 20-24
Garrett, James Leo 5
General Baptists 5, 11, 14, 15, 19, 27, 29, 32, 42, 48, 84, 224, 230
Gill, John 33-42, 48, 50, 55, 129, 165
Gilmore, Alec 3, 7, 113, 114, 144, 145-150, 197
Glas, John 240
Gorham, George 76
Grace and baptism 3, 4, 6, 10, 13, 17, 19, 20, 21, 31, 53, 58, 62, 66, 71, 93, 106-107, 131, 136-138, 141, 179, 196, 207-209, 209-219, 223, 235, 242, 246, 248

Grantham, Thomas 27-28
Griffiths, D. R. 119-120, 125

Hall, Robert, Jr. 59-64
Hayden, Roger 58, 105
Helwys, Thomas 11, 128
Henry, Matthew 44
Heron, John 205
High Calvinism 33, 41, 42, 56, 88
Himbury, D. M. 121
Hinton, John Howard 75-79
Historical Jesus 176-177
Hughey, J. D. 124, 126, 128
Hull, William E. 174-178
Hulse, Erroll 4

Inaugurated eschatology 110, 112
Incarnation 96, 101, 102, 123, 138, 196-199
Indiscriminate baptism 217-218
Ingham, Richard 84-85
Initiation 21, 48, 101, 102, 110, 111, 116, 117, 122, 134, 138, 186, 220, 223, 225, 226, 251

Jeremias, Joachim 218
Jewett, Paul 216
Joint Liturgical Group 233
Justification 15, 25, 35, 37, 42, 87, 118, 125, 131, 142, 200, 201, 203-209, 211, 218, 236, 239

Keach, Benjamin 18, 29-30, 57, 129
Kevan, Ernest 124, 127, 128, 129
Kinghorn, Joseph 59

Lambeth Conference 150
Landmarkism 225, 229
Lane, Eric 3
Lawrence, Henry 24-27, 57
Laying on of hands 5, 15-16, 219, 221-222
Longenecker, Richard 161
Lord's Supper (Eucharist) 5, 6, 13, 17, 18, 19, 42, 50, 54, 59, 63, 102, 103, 121, 145, 150-151
Lumpkin, William L. 5
Lutheranism 66, 85, 145, 204, 207, 237-238, 240, 246

Index 275

Mantey, J. R. 167
Maoz, Baruch 4
Marcel, Pierre 212-213
Marshall, Walter 44
Matthews, Isaac G. 98, 100
Mennonites 6, 11, 12
Midland Confession 15
Mitchill, William 30-31
Mode of baptism 1, 2, 3, 12, 14, 15, 17, 18, 30, 33, 40, 43, 53, 57, 87, 121, 161, 248

Necessity of baptism 8, 26-27, 28, 51, 77-78, 132, 141-143, 198, 205, 232-234, 236, 244-246
New Connexion 32
Newman, J. H. 86
Noel, Baptist W. 72-75, 82, 86

Obedience 32, 35, 39, 41, 57, 67, 90, 91, 93, 151, 179, 226, 250
Old Testament 135, 146, 174-176
Oman, John 137
Open communion 59
Open membership 91, 104-105, 111, 123, 144-145, 226-232, 233, 249
Ordinance 2, 4, 5, 6, 14, 16, 17, 18, 19, 21, 25, 29, 31, 46, 53, 54, 55, 87, 105-106, 151
Orthodox Creed 19, 230
Oxford Movement 58

Paedobaptism 12, 19, 30, 51, 54, 66, 67, 68, 87, 103-105, 111-112, 123, 128, 137, 211-219, 227-228, 235, 249
Parousia 110, 112, 125, 187
Particular Baptists 5, 11, 14, 15, 16, 17, 19, 20, 29, 30, 32-33, 41, 42, 46, 48, 52, 88, 225, 231, 248
Payne, Ernest A. 105, 107, 113, 154
Pelagianism 205, 209
Perkin, J. R. C. 59, 121
Philadelphia Confession of Faith 5
Pieper, Francis 237-238
Positive institution 45, 54, 91
Prayer 5, 18, 19, 54
Prayer in baptism 5, 12, 13, 141, 192, 202
Prenter, Regin 238

Prevenient grace 137, 212-219, 238, 246
Prophetic symbolism 96, 136, 148
Propositions and Conclusions Concerning True Christian Religion 13
Puritans 10, 20, 207, 243, 248
Pusey, E. B. 86

Rantism 56
Rawdon College 89, 98
Rebaptism 84, 100, 111-112, 123, 144-145, 148, 227, 231-232, 246
Regeneration 15, 29, 30, 32, 36, 37, 40, 41, 43, 51, 52, 58, 62, 66, 67, 69, 70-72, 73-75, 79, 80-83, 84, 99, 101, 108, 119, 120, 125, 126, 129, 133, 142, 170, 184-185, 235, 237-238, 249
Regent's Park College 89
Revivalism 243, 251
Richardson, Alan 206, 208
Roberts-Thomson, , E. 245
Robertson, A. T. 126, 131, 166-170
Robinson, H. Wheeler 3, 89-97, 103, 108, 129, 135, 136, 148, 196, 198, 199, 202, 219, 227, 245, 249
Robinson, William 241, 243
Roman Catholicism 10, 56, 61-62, 66, 86, 106, 145, 149, 179, 209-210, 235-237, 246
Ross, J. M. 1, 16
Rowley, H. H. 124
Ryland, John, Jr. 51-52, 56
Ryland, John C. 51

Sacerdotalism 198, 106
Salvation Army 128, 233
Sandeman, Robert 240
Savoy Confession 230
Schlink, Edmund 215
Seal 5, 10, 17, 18, 20, 23, 24, 25-27, 28, 41, 44, 47, 50, 53, 55-56, 57, 63, 66, 72-75, 82, 85, 86, 87, 94-95, 98, 114, 198, 204, 211, 227, 231, 239-240, 248-249, 251
Second London Confession 16-18, 31, 229
Service Books 152-154
Shakespeare, J. H. 105, 150

Short Confession of Faith 12
Short Confession of Faith in XX Articles 12
Smyth, John 5, 11, 12, 103, 121, 128, 237
Somerset Confession 15
South Wales Baptist College 108
Southern Baptist Theological Seminary 139
Southern Baptists 250, 252-253
Spirit and baptism 3, 8, 14, 15, 17, 23, 29, 36, 37, 53, 60-61, 78, 89, 90, 92, 95, 96, 101, 109-112, 115, 116, 118-122, 125, 126, 130, 131, 138, 142, 151, 159-161, 163, 170-174, 184-185, 189-190, 196, 200, 210, 217, 219-223, 239, 246
Spurgeon, Charles Haddon 79-83
Spurgeon's College 139
Standard Confession 5, 15-16, 230
Stone, Barton 241
Stovel, Charles 65-72
Strong, Augustus Hopkins 5
Subjects of baptism 1, 2, 15, 17, 18, 31, 53, 122, 248
Symbolism of baptism 2, 4, 14, 15, 18, 21, 34, 38, 43, 58, 85, 128, 140, 161, 170-171

Tertullian 54
Thirty-Nine Articles 10, 66
Thompson, Philip 28, 32
Thurian, Max 7
Torrance, T. F. 206-208
Tractarianism 58, 65, 72, 86, 121
Tradition 113-114, 128-131, 155, 156, 252
The True Gospel-Faith Declared According to the Scriptures 14
Turner, Nigel 167

Unbaptized Christians 127-128, 132, 141-143, 196, 210
Underwood, A. C. 3, 98-100, 151
Union with Christ 4, 18, 24, 38-39, 41, 62, 63, 70, 87, 88, 96, 110-111, 118, 130, 131, 143, 161, 196, 199, 200, 201, 205, 211, 219, 239, 248
Unitarianism 32

Vatican II 209, 249
Visible word 13, 14, 56, 85, 237, 240

Walton, Robert C. 100-105, 106, 108, 129, 143, 144, 145, 148, 197, 198, 223
Wesley, John 46, 88
West, W. M. S. 120-121, 154
Westminster Confession 11, 16, 19, 31, 66, 67, 230, 239
Whale, J. S. 98
White, R. E. O. 3, 114-115, 133-139, 140, 147, 157, 198, 202, 211, 219, 236
Whitefield, George 46, 88
Whitley, W. T. 5
Wikenhauser, A. 147
Winward, Stephen F. 113-114, 153
Word of God 5, 13, 18, 19, 26, 54
Works 201, 202, 203-209, 218
World Council of Churches 151

Zwingli, Ulrich 63, 179

Studies in Baptist History and Thought

David Bebbington (ed.)
The Gospel in the World
International Baptist Studies
This volume of essays deals with a range of subjects spanning Britain, North America, Europe, Asia and the Antipodes. Topics include studies on religious tolerance, the communion controversy and the development of the international Baptist community, and concludes with two important essays on the future of Baptist life that pay special attention to the United States.
2002 / ISBN 1-84227-118-0 / xiii + 361 pp

Geoffrey R. Breed
Strict Communion
*Strict Communion Organisations
amongst the Baptists in Victorian England*
This work, which makes considerable use of contemporary records, identifies the principal strict communion organisations which, whilst working within the framework of the Baptist Union, nevertheless did not compromise what they believed to be scriptural principles of church government.
2002 / ISBN 1-84227-140-7

Anthony R. Cross
Baptism and the Baptists
Theology and Practice in Twentieth-Century Britain
At a time of renewed interest in baptism, Baptism and the Baptists is a detailed study of twentieth-century baptismal theology and practice and the factors which have influenced its development.
2000 / ISBN 0-85364-959-6 / xvii + 530pp

Anthony R. Cross and Philip E. Thompson (eds.)
Baptist Myths
This collection of essays examines some of the 'myths' in Baptist history and theology: these include the idea of development in Baptist thought, studies in the church, community, spirituality, soul competency, women, the civil rights movement and Strict Baptist missions.
2003 / ISBN 1-84227-122-9

Anthony R. Cross and Philip E. Thompson (eds.)
Baptist Sacramentalism
This collection of essays includes historical and theological studies in the sacraments from a Baptist perspective. Subjects explored include the physical side of being spiritual, baptism, the Lord's supper, the church, ordination, preaching, worship, religious freedom and the nature of suffering.
2002 / ISBN 1-84227-119-9

Paul S. Fiddes
Tracks and Traces
Baptist Heritage in Church and Theology
This is a comprehensive, yet unusual, book on the faith and life of Baptist Christians. It explores the understanding of the church, ministry, sacraments and mission from a thoroughly theological perspective. In a series of interlinked essays, the author relates Baptist identity consistently to a theology of covenant and to participation in the triune communion of God.
2002 / ISBN 1-84227-120-2

Stanley K. Fowler
More Than a Symbol
The British Baptist Recovery of Baptismal Sacramentalism
Fowler surveys the entire scope of British Baptist literature from the seventeenth-century pioneers onwards. He shows that in the twentieth century leading British Baptist pastors and theologians recovered an understanding of baptism that connected experience with soteriology and that in doing so they were recovering what many of their forebears had taught.
2002 / ISBN 1-84227-052-4

Brian Haymes, Anthony R. Cross and Ruth Gouldbourne
On Being the Church
Revisioning Baptist Identity
The aim of the book is to re-examine Baptist theology and practice in the light of the contemporary biblical, theological, ecumenical and missiological context drawing on historical and contemporary writings and issues. It is not a study in denominationalism but rather seeks to revision historical insights from the believers' church tradition for the sake of Baptists and other Christians in the context of the modern–postmodern context.
2003 / ISBN 1-84227-121-0

Frank Rinaldi
'The Tribe of Dan'
A Study of the New Connexion of General Baptists 1770–1891
'The Tribe of Dan' is a thematic study which explores the theology, organisational structure, evangelistic strategy, ministry and leadership of the New Connexion of General Baptists as it experienced the process of institutionlisation in the transition from a revival movement to an established denomination.
2002 / ISBN 1-84227-143-1

Peter Shepherd
The Making of a Modern Denomination
John Howard Shakespeare and the English Baptists 1898–1924
John Howard Shakespeare introduced revolutionary change to the Baptist denomination. The Baptist Union was transformed into a strong central institution and Baptist ministers were brought under its control. Further, Shakespeare's pursuit of church unity reveals him as one of the pioneering ecumenists of the twentieth century.
2001 / ISBN 1-84227-046-X / xviii + 220pp

Brian Talbot
The Search for a Common Identity
The Origins of the Baptist Union of Scotland 1800–1870
In the period 1800 to 1827 there were three streams of Baptists in Scotland: Scotch, Haldaneite and 'English' Baptist. A strong commitment to home evangelisation brought these three bodies closer together, leading to a merger of their home missionary societies in 1827. However, the first three attempts to form a union of churches failed, but by the 1860s a common understanding of their corporate identity was attained leading to the establishment of the Baptist Union of Scotland.
2003 / ISBN 1-84227-123-7

Philip E. Thompson
The Freedom of God
Towards Baptist Theology in Pneumatological Perspsective
This study contends that the range of theological commitments of the early Baptists are best understood in relation to their distinctive emphasis on the freedom of God. Thompson traces how this was recast anthropocentrically, leading to emphasis upon human freedom from the nineteenth century onwards. He seeks to recover the dynamism of the early vision via a pneumatologically oriented ecclesiology defining the church in terms of the memory of God.
2004 / ISBN 1-84227-125-3

Linda Wilson
Marianne Farningham
A Study in Victorian Evangelical Piety
Marianne Farningham, of College Street Baptist Chapel, Northampton, was a household name in evangelical circles in the later nineteenth century. For over fifty years she produced comment, poetry, biography and fiction for the popular Christian press. This investigation uses her writings to explore the beliefs and behaviour of evangelical Nonconformists, including Baptists, during these years.
2004 / ISBN –84227-124-5

Other Paternoster titles relating to Baptist history and thought

Keith E. Eitel
Paradigm Wars
The Southern Baptist International Mission Board Faces the Third Millennium
The International Mission Board of the Southern Baptist Convention is the largest denominational mission agency in North America. This volume chronicles the historic and contemporary forces that led to the IMB's recent extensive reorganization, providing the most comprehensive case study to date of a historic mission agency restructuring to continue its mission purpose into the 21st century more effectively.
2000 / ISBN 1-870345-12-6 / x + 139pp

Ian M. Randall
Evangelical Experiences
A Study in the Spirituality of English Evangelicalism 1918–1939
This book makes a detailed historical examination of evangelical spirituality between the First and Second World Wars. It shows how patterns of devotion led to tensions and divisions. In a wide-ranging study, Anglican, Wesleyan, Reformed and Pentecostal–charismatic spiritualities are analysed.
1999 / ISBN 0-85364-919-7 / xii + 309pp

Linda Wilson
Constrained by Zeal
Female Spirituality amongst Nonconformists 1825–1875
Dr Wilson investigates the neglected area of Nonconformist female spirituality. Against the background of separate spheres she analyses the experience of women from four denominations, and argues that the churches provided a 'third sphere' in which they could find opportunities for participation.
2000 / ISBN 0-85364-972-3 / xvi + 293pp

Nigel G. Wright
Disavowing Constantine
Mission, Church and the Social Order in the Theologies of John Howard Yoder and Jürgen Moltmann
This book is a timely restatement of a radical theology of church and state in the Anabaptist and Baptist tradition. Dr Wright constructs his argument in dialogue and debate with Yoder and Moltmann, major contributors to a free church perspective.
2000 / ISBN 0-85364-978-2 /xv + 251pp